THE CHAMBERED CAIRNS
OF SUTHERLAND

FRONTISPIECE. Traligill (SUT 82).

THE CHAMBERED CAIRNS OF SUTHERLAND

AN INVENTORY OF THE STRUCTURES AND THEIR CONTENTS
BY A. S. HENSHALL AND J. N. G. RITCHIE
FOR EDINBURGH
UNIVERSITY
PRESS

© A. S. Henshall and J. N. G. Ritchie 1995

Edinburgh University Press Ltd
22 George Square, Edinburgh

Typeset in Plantin by
Nene Phototypesetters Ltd, Northampton, and
printed and bound in Great Britain

A CIP record for this book is available from
the British Library

ISBN 0 7486 0609 2

Contents

Acknowledgements   vi

Part One

1. Introduction   3
2. Development of the study of the cairns   6
   Early investigations
   An initiative by The Society of Antiquaries of Scotland
   Disappointing progress in the later 19th century
   The work of the Royal Commission on the Ancient and Historical Monuments and Constructions of Scotland
   New information and synthesis
   The survey by Henshall
   Excavations at Embo and The Ord
   Assessment and dating
3. The land, the environment and the location of the cairns   13
   The character of Sutherland
   The evidence for pre-neolithic peoples
   The environment and the neolithic settlement
   The siting of cairns
   Cairns and the ancient landscape
4. The passages and chambers   20
   Terminology and morphology
   The passages
   The structure of the chambers
   Single-compartment chambers
   Bipartite chambers of Caithness type
   Bipartite chambers of Skelpick type
   Unclassified bipartite chambers
   Tripartite chambers
   Unclassified chambers
   Ardvreck
5. The cairns   37
   The structure of the cairns
   Round cairns
   Heel-shaped cairns
   Short horned cairns
   Long cairns
   Forecourts and façades
   Cairns and chambers

6. The use and sealing of the chambers and the history of the cairns   50
   Ritual deposits made during building
   The excavation of burial deposits
   Burial deposits in the two chambers at Embo
   The neolithic deposits in the chamber at The Ord North
   Burial deposits in other chambers
   Interpretation of the burial deposits
   Sealing of the passages and chambers, and external blocking
   Beakers and bronze age burials
   Gradual destruction of the cairns
7. The artefacts   63
   Artefacts from the neolithic deposits
   Beaker sherds
   Artefacts with later burials
8. Orientation, relationships and dating   68
   Orientation
   The distribution and typology of the chambers
   The plans and structure of the cairns
   Chronology and dating
   Chambered cairns and society

Part Two

The Inventory of chambered cairns in Sutherland   79

Appendix 1	Structures previously published as chambered cairns or long cairns, but not included in the Inventory	152
Appendix 2	Human bone recovered from the excavations at Embo (SUT 63)	155
Appendix 3	Note on the location of the finds at The Ord North (SUT 48)	157

References   159
Index   162

ACKNOWLEDGEMENTS

We wish to thank a number of friends and colleagues for help during the preparation of this volume. The archive material held in the National Monuments Record of Scotland within the Royal Commission on the Ancient and Historical Monuments of Scotland, Edinburgh, has been fundamental to the Inventory entries in Part 2. Mr J. L. Davidson did much of the preparation work from the NMRS records before fieldwork was begun. The detailed account of The Ord North has been constructed from the excavation archive of the late Dr J. X. W. P. Corcoran housed in the NMRS. Mr R. J. Mercer has generously allowed publication from a number of manuscript sources now in the NMRS. Colleagues in the Commission have provided assistance throughout, particularly Mrs L. M. Ferguson, Mr I. Fleming and Mr K. McLaren in the NMRS, and Mr J. D. Keggie and Mrs A. Martin in the Photographic Department. Dr A. Sheridan and Mr T. G. Cowie arranged for us to study the finds from Embo and The Ord North housed in the National Museums of Scotland and kindly provided additional information. Dr A. Sheridan kindly arranged for the deposits of tiny bones (otter droppings) from Embo to be examined by Dr A. Jones, and for the provision of new radiocarbon dates for Embo through the good offices of J. Lanting, Groningen University. Dr A. Kitchener advised us on the animal remains. We have greatly benefited from the advice of Mr P. J. Ashmore on radiocarbon dating. We have been helped by Mrs C. Allen and Mr I. Maxwell in the final stages in the preparation of the manuscript.

The costs of fieldwork have been covered by a generous grant from the Binks Trust for which we are most grateful.

Assistance with fieldwork and other matters has been given by Mr I. Forshaw, Mr R. B. Gourlay, Mrs R. A. Meldrum, Mr N. M. Sharples and Mr W. F. Ritchie. Landowners and tenants have, without exception, been helpful in allowing access to the monuments.

Figures 2, 8, 10, 13, 14, 18, 19, 20 and 21 derive from the collections of the NMRS (which include material formerly in the possession of the Society of Antiquaries of Scotland). These illustrations are all Crown Copyright: Royal Commission on the Ancient and Historical Monuments of Scotland. Figure 3 has been redrawn from three maps published in *The Sutherland Book*, by kind permission of Mr D. Omand and *The Northern Times*. The photographs reproduced in plates 4, 6, 9, 14 and 15 were taken by the late Dr Corcoran; plates 1, 7, 12 and 17 were taken by A. S. Henshall; plates 2, 3, 5, 8, 10, 11 and 13 were taken by J. N. G. Ritchie; all are in the NMRS collections and are Crown Copyright: Royal Commission on the Ancient and Historical Monuments of Scotland. Plate 16 is reproduced by kind permission of Dr J. Close-Brooks.

PART ONE

1. Introduction

1.1) The northernmost part of the mainland of Scotland is divided into two regions, reflecting the contrasting character of highland Sutherland and lowland Caithness. The former county of Sutherland is a huge area extending from coast to coast, predominantly mountainous, scenically magnificent, and, until the second half of the 20th century, remote and undeveloped, though with a gentler and more prosperous area along its SE coast. In this landscape there are remains of many prehistoric structures, sometimes surviving as prominent features, but, without close examination, appearing as little more than stony mounds or upright stones. The earliest of these structures, the first stone buildings in the land, are the neolithic chambered cairns built by the first farmers in the 4th millennium BC as tombs to receive the remains of their dead.

1.2) Chambered cairns can truly be regarded as architecture. Although now greatly ruined, or occasionally still largely hidden beneath conspicuous but featureless mounds, their original appearance and the skills used in their construction can be rediscovered. This requires careful observation of the ruins and collation of data from numerous sites both in Sutherland and from similar cairns elsewhere. Most of the Sutherland chambers were designed to a general formula, though no two are identical; a single chamber, or more often two linked chambers, were provided, the largest of a size which would allow several people to move about freely beneath a high domed roof. The roofing of a space of this size by layers of oversailing slabs was a particularly challenging operation. The chambers were approached along narrow low passages and sometimes through a low-roofed ante-chamber. The chamber and passage were enclosed within a cairn, an essential part of the construction, but in many cases this was enlarged and sometimes it was elaborated to give the chambered cairn an even more impressive appearance. In their present state of ruin it is very difficult to appreciate the impact of these monuments, the grandeur of their chambers, the skills of their builders, or the labour investment in their construction by communities who were not equipped with metal tools. It is clear, too, that the cairns had an importance beyond their function as tombs. They were foci for ceremonies and rituals, probably based on ancestor-worship, which were concerned with the welfare of the local communities. While the social and especially the mystical significance of the cairns are largely beyond our understanding, these aspects of the cairns may well have been of supreme importance to their builders.

1.3) This volume is the third in a projected series of four, intended to describe the large number of chambered cairns of passage-grave type found in northern Scotland. The volumes dealing with the chambered cairns of Orkney and Caithness were published by Davidson and Henshall in 1989 and 1991, and it is hoped that the fourth volume, covering the S portion of Highland Region, will follow shortly. The prime purpose of these volumes is to record the cairns in detail as they are visible at the present time, without any disturbance of the remains or excavation. The writers feel that this is an important task for two reasons. Destruction by either natural or human agency, of either minor (but significant) features or on a devastating scale, is in time the lot of all monuments. Comprehensive and consistent recording allows an overview from which policies for future work can be framed, and the essential foundation on which interpretation and speculation alone can be safely built. Certainly future excavations will fully reveal some of the structures and will provide a vast amount of information on their usage, but it is impossible to predict which sites will undergo destruction and/or exploration. Our record of each cairn is presented in an entry in the Inventory which forms the second part of each volume, together with additional information available from earlier sources and from excavations. A catalogue of the finds from excavated cairns has also been included. Synthesis of the structural evidence is provided as a description of the cairns in Part 1 of the volumes.

1.4) Besides the information which derives directly from the study of the structures, chambered cairns can yield invaluable information on the lives of their builders as well as on their mortuary practices. The excavation of the deposits in the chambers, depending on various circumstances, may produce the bones of those buried in them, material for anatomical and demographic studies. The deposits may also contain remains of the animals that were exploited for food and for other uses, and some of the material equipment of the community, all contributing to the understanding of the economy and social structure.

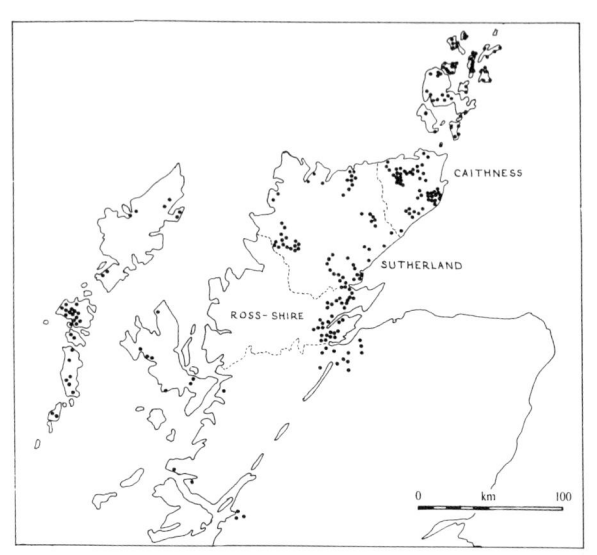

FIGURE 1. The distribution of Scottish passage-graves, excluding Shetland. (After Fraser 1983, 6.)

Material for radiocarbon dating, which will enable construction of a chronological framework for the building and use of the cairns, and by extension for associated artefacts, and for the societies of which they were such an important part, can only come from excavations. Beneath the cairns, and protected by them, are contemporary soils which may hold information on farming practices and the environment. Study of the distribution of the cairns in the landscape, their relationship to the geology and the soil types, and, on a more intimate scale, their actual siting, together with their orientation, can all contribute to an understanding of the organisation and economic bases of these earliest farming communities, and perhaps, with caution, a glimpse of their cosmological beliefs. All these matters are discussed in the first part of each volume.

1.5) To date, little of this kind of information is available from Sutherland cairns, but their resources have hardly been tapped and it is essential to appreciate their potential. As yet, only two cairns have been carefully excavated, at Embo and on The Ord, and both have unfortunate histories. The excavation records survive, and re-examination of them, together with the general advances in understanding chambered cairns, has allowed presentation of a fuller and somewhat different interpretation of these structures and their contents. All but one of the Sutherland cairns belong to the passage-graves of the Orkney-Cromarty group, found widespread in the N mainland, in the Western and the Northern Isles, and less commonly in other parts of the Highlands (figure 1).

1.6) Seventy-two chambered cairns have been included in the present volume. The cairns of Sutherland were recorded briefly in a survey which covered the whole of Scotland, and which was organised according to the county boundaries as they were before 1975 (Henshall 1963, 1972). Following local government reorganisation in that year, the parish of Kincardine and Croick, formerly in the county of Ross and Cromarty, became part of Sutherland District. Thus a small group of cairns in the N tip of the parish may now be considered alongside those in SW Sutherland, from which formerly they were administratively separate. This is very much to the advantage of the present study. The rest of the parish, which comprises the S side of Strath Oykel and Strathcarron, appears to be without comparable monuments. It was not the purpose of our survey to undertake extensive prospective fieldwork, but there is little doubt that gaps in the cairn distribution are real. Comprehensive field survey by officers of the Archaeology Division of the Ordnance Survey was undertaken up to 1981, and all sites which were listed as possible chambered cairns were visited by us. Strath Halladale, another blank area in the distribution, was not only examined in the course of the Ordnance Survey work but was also walked by teams under the direction of R. J. Mercer. Some structures previously regarded as chambered cairns have been re-classified by us (listed in Appendix 1), and a few chambered cairns doubtless remain to be identified, either within intact cairns or ruined and obscured beneath later structures.

1.7) The numbering of Scottish chambered cairns follows the system established for the rest of Britain, using the county code (SUT Sutherland, CAT Caithness, ORK Orkney, ROS Ross-shire, INV Inverness-shire etc.) followed by a number which, when appropriate, tallies with that in Henshall op. cit. (the cairns formerly in Ross-shire have been given new SUT numbers). Throughout this volume 'Ross-shire' refers to the area of the former county, and 'Ross and Cromarty' is used only when referring specifically to the present District of that name.

1.8) In the Inventory the description of each cairn is provided, where possible, with a plan. In order to maintain consistency for the whole of Scotland the plans are at the scale used in Henshall 1963 and 1972, even though this is now inconvenient as it is based on imperial measurements. Cairn material is shown stippled, and unless the present edge is very vague or is obviously distorted by later interference, it is edged by dashes. The chambers are shown without stipple even when filled with displaced cairn material. Details which are no longer visible and have been added from earlier plans or descriptions are shown by lines of dots. It should be noted that the size and shape of chambers where the walls are no longer to be seen are indicated only very approximately. True north is shown on all plans.

1.9) The heading for each entry includes the site number in the National Monuments Record of Scotland (NMRS) to aid identification of the monument. In the heading are short references to publications, with minimal references in the following text to allow identification of the source or a page within a source, full references being listed on pp. 159–61. In the text all upright structural stones (orthostats) are recorded with the major horizontal measurement as 'length' and the transverse measurement as 'thickness'. With paired orthostats the measurement of the left slab is given before that of the right slab as seen looking into the chamber from the entrance. When it is reasonably certain that the tops of orthostats are intact this has been noted; a broken upper edge, unless obviously shattered, is of little significance, as it may be original. In the catalogues of finds the museum registration number is given in brackets after each entry, and in the text our catalogue number is quoted in italics. The plans made by the writers in the field, at the scale of 10 feet to 1 inch, have been deposited in the National Monuments Record of Scotland.

2. Development of the study of the cairns

Early investigations

2.1) Interest in the prehistoric monuments of Sutherland began late and progressed slowly. As far as we are aware, only two chambered cairns were recorded in the 18th century, apart from the Kinbrace cairns (SUT 33–35) which were shown on a wildly inaccurate mid-18th-century plan of a 13th-century battle (NMRS Ms SUD/21/3). Bishop Richard Pococke visited Lothbeg (SUT 45) on his Scottish tour in July 1760. At that time the chamber was evidently roofed and accessible and was described as a Pict's house. Twelve years later the cairn was shown on an estate plan as 'Cairnlea'. Pittentrail (SUT 50) was plotted on an estate map of 1788, titled as 'cairn'. Other chambered cairns may be recorded on the maps made for the Sutherland Estates, titled as cairns or stone circles or druids' temples, but are now difficult to identify. In 1800 Adam de Cardonnel made a brief tour of the north of Scotland gathering pre-Roman and Early Christian material for a companion volume to his 1788 publication of medieval ruins. He included a delightful but imaginative water-colour of Lothbeg and another of the long cairn at Skelpick (SUT 53). In the latter was 'a passage 3 ft (0.9 m) square composed of large hill stones, covered on the outside with smaller ones shelving so as to throw off the rain – both ends of this passage are open! Tradition says that buildings as this were used in the hunting season for sleeping in, and securing women and children from the wolves once numerous in that country' (Cardonnel 1800, plate XIII, 2; his measurements are often inaccurate).

2.2) Information on the archaeological remains in Sutherland was just as scanty through the first half of the 19th century, though there was increasing antiquarian activity in the rest of the country. In 1851 the publication by Daniel Wilson of the first overview of Scottish prehistory must have had considerable impact, though few chambered cairns or long cairns had yet been recognised. However, he did regard them as distinct classes of monuments within the wide variety of 'sepulchral memorials' (1851, 65), and using the newly introduced three-age framework he tentatively assigned them all to the Stone Period, thus acknowledging their great antiquity.

2.3) The first efforts to investigate the archaeology of Sutherland came in the 1860s, largely stimulated by the work of A. H. Rhind and Joseph Anderson in Caithness. Naturally enough, their work had been concentrated on the most obvious prehistoric features in the landscape, the brochs and the cairns. In 1851 a close-knit group of cairns in the Yarrows-Watenan district had been listed by Rhind, and two years later he excavated four of the chambers. His investigations were extended in 1865 and 1866 by Anderson and R. I. Shearer excavating a number of other chambered cairns in the same group. Rhind and Anderson published their results promptly, and Anderson was notable for the detailed and stimulating discussion in his several papers (Davidson and Henshall 1991, 6–8). It had been shown that in a restricted area of Caithness there were stone burial chambers of a distinctive type with several variants, covered by carefully designed cairns which might be round or long, the former occasionally and the latter normally having concave forecourts formed by projecting horns. The contents of the chambers, artefacts and bones of humans and animals, varied greatly and unpredictably in quantity. Simultaneously, investigations in the Orkney Islands were revealing chambered cairns of a different type (Davidson and Henshall 1989, 6). The question now was whether comparable groups of chambered cairns existed in other parts of the north mainland of Scotland.

2.4) In August 1863 the first brief specifically archaeological notes to include chambered cairns were made by the Rev. J. M. Joass on an expedition into Strathnaver (1864 a and b). En route he noted Achany (SUT 3), and in the strath he noted Dun Viden and probably Skail (SUT 27, 52), though they were not recognised as denuded chambered cairns; finally he saw in the distance 'a large heap of stones ... fast being demolished for fence building' which he was told was a chambered cairn, identifiable as Skelpick Round (SUT 54). Joass (1830–1914) became minister of Golspie in 1866, and was active as an antiquary until the end of the century, working almost entirely in Sutherland. Before 1868 he provided Anderson with information and a plan of the chamber in Benbhraggie Wood (SUT 12) for comparison with Caithness chambers, and later he gave practical help and advice to the Society of Antiquaries of Scotland, and to others, during their archaeological investigations. He evidently came to know of more chambered cairns, having for instance acquired several finds from them

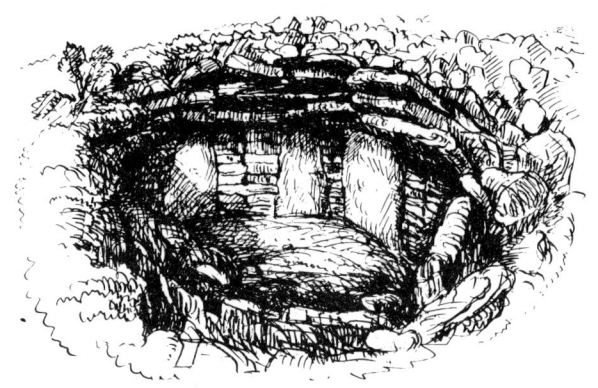

FIGURE 2. Skelpick Long (SUT 53). Drawing of the main chamber taken from the E end of the lintel over the inner portal stones, by J. Horsburgh 1866.

over the years for the Duke of Sutherland's omnivorous museum at Dunrobin Castle, and he opened Kinbrace Burn (SUT 33) and Allt nam Ban (SUT 6) (Curle 1909b, 69), but he did not publish further information.

2.5) In the summer of 1866 James Horsburgh, of Lochmalony, Fife, visited north Sutherland. He was a keen sportsman with a military background, and an amateur artist and antiquary; he was probably related to Robert Horsburgh who lived in Tongue House through the middle of the century and who may be the 'Mr Horsburgh' who had done mapping for the Sutherland estates around Tongue in 1828. In Strathnaver in 1866 James Horsburgh made passing notes of many antiquities, including Grumbeg (thought to be a small cromlech but which we consider not to be prehistoric), probably Skail (SUT 52), Dun Viden (SUT 27, dismissed as not prehistoric), Skelpick Round (SUT 54), Coille na Borgie (SUT 22, 23, recognised as two long cairns, but the orthostatic façade misunderstood), and near the coast he saw the cairns at Fiscary (SUT 29). In the last three cairns the chambers had not yet been exposed. At Skelpick Long (SUT 53) he investigated the highest part of the cairn which appeared to be undisturbed, but he found that the roof of the main chamber had already been removed: as already noted in ¶ 2.1, Cardonnel had seen part of the chamber in 1800. Horsburgh had the chamber emptied of 'stones and rubbish' but 'nothing whatever was found in it' (figure 2). He also visited Tongue, and near to Tongue House 'cleared out' a chamber (SUT 57), but this structure has not been identified satisfactorily by the writers and remains something of a mystery.

An initiative by The Society of Antiquaries of Scotland

2.6) The Society had been responsible for publishing some of the work done in Caithness and Orkney and was aware of the need for similar investigations in Sutherland and Ross-shire. The project appears to have been started by the Secretary, John Stuart. Rhind, who died in 1863, had been persuaded to leave £400 to the Society 'to be expended in practical archaeological excavations in the north-eastern portion of Scotland, where the remains are mostly unknown to the general student, and are often in good preservation, and, from ethnographical reasons, are likely to afford important information ...' (Stuart 1868, 289). A Committee was set up to administer Rhind's fund, and Stuart was requested to make a tour of the northern counties and report on the 'nature and condition' of the prehistoric remains. On his return he very sensibly advised that the Committee should concentrate on the excavation of relatively small monuments, with the assumption that chambered cairns would have priority. He recommended 'that the central chambers and deposits shall only be opened under the eye of competent observers, and with the means of recording, by drawing and otherwise, their appearance before they are disturbed. ... The Committee ought to obtain careful ground-plans and architectural drawings of these chambers, so as to show the construction of their walls and vaulting' (ibid., 304–5). Anderson and Shearer had offered to help the Committee, and it was hoped that George Petrie of Kirkwall would also assist. Stuart was asked to send copies of his report to the northern counties 'in the hope that additional information and local cooperation may thus be secured' (ibid., 307). With this laudable strategy agreed, there should have been systematic and rapid advances in the study of chambered cairns in Sutherland.

2.7) During his tour in September 1866 Stuart visited a wide variety of monuments including the long cairn at Salscraggie (SUT 51) in the Strath of Kildonan, and in Strathnaver he saw the long cairns Coille na Borgie North and South (SUT 22, 23) and four cairns at Skelpick. At Skelpick Long (SUT 53) he appreciated that Horsburgh had exposed only one compartment of a larger chamber; at Skelpick Round (SUT 54) he noted the remains of a large chamber on which Horsburgh had not commented, and at Skelpick South (SUT 55) he recognised that the cairn was of the unusual short horned plan comparable with two which had been excavated in Caithness.

2.8) The following year, 1867, W. McKay (or Mackay) of Skelpick opened the chambers in Coille na Borgie North and South (SUT 22, 23), and the rest of the chamber and the passage at Skelpick Long (SUT 53). He forwarded a report to Stuart, which has been lost, and sketch plans and views, which survive. The latter record the long cairns and their chambers with moderate accuracy, though there is more than a suspicion that some of the details of Coille na Borgie South are due to expectation rather than observation (figure 18; see ¶ 4.31, 5.27). The forecourts at all three cairns, and the orthostatic façades at Coille na Borgie, were overlooked. In an undated letter (NMRS Ms/28) Stuart asked McKay to do further clearance of the chambers to ensure that there were no deposits on the floors as he had evidently reported, and to complete the plans and include the passages, as the passage at Coille na Borgie North had not been exposed (and apparently never was). Stuart undertook to pay his total expenses. (The date of these operations, given in Munro 1884, 229, is confirmed by their having postdated Stuart's visit, and, according to his letter, predated Horsburgh's death in January 1868). Sadly, after so much thought and effort, the Committee achieved no further work on chambered cairns, and Rhind's bequest was used to explore brochs (Anderson 1880, 131).

Disappointing progress in the later 19th century

2.9) At the same time Dr G. L. Tait was exploring the eastern side of Sutherland. In passing he mentioned the chambered cairn at Pittentrail (SUT 50) without giving any particulars, all the more regrettable as it was still recognisable but was soon to be entirely destroyed.

2.10) The Coille na Borgie cairns (SUT 22, 23) were visited in 1883 by the Rev. R. Munro of Old Kilpatrick, who published a description with sketch plans and views. He regarded them, reasonably enough, as three separate cairns, noting some of the façade orthostats and kerb-stones, and he was able to give details of the two chambers which had been opened by McKay. It was evident to Munro that the cairns were comparable to the horned long cairns which Anderson had investigated in Caithness. In 1891 Cathel Kerr, when on holiday in Farr parish where he had been brought up, found that one of the cairns on top of the hill at Fiscary (SUT 29) 'had been broken into, and stones removed from it for building purposes' (1892, 66). He had the chamber opened up, and made sketch-plans and elevations (figure 13), though only his short description was published.

2.11) Anderson, in his Rhind Lectures of 1882 (published 1886), gave the first comprehensive account of chambered cairns in Scotland. Anderson was now Keeper of the National Museum of Antiquities of Scotland, and with these lectures the study of Scottish chambered cairns was put on a professional basis. By now the information available had increased, and he could also draw on the great advances in the study of chambered cairns, and the stone age in general, which had been made in Britain and on the continent. Anderson placed the chambered cairns firmly in the stone age, and saw them as one structural type whatever their architectural differences, designed for a distinct multiple burial rite, in contrast to later burial rites and the structures provided for them. He also noted the equipment and the domestic animals available to the cairn builders. He ended his account: 'with regard to these chambered sepulchres, ... it is apparent that the enormous magnitude of these peculiar structures is fitted to convey an instantaneous impression of energy and power, while the intention, so obvious in their construction as "the houses of the dead", instinctively challenges our respect for their builders' (ibid., 304), an interesting comment at a time when anything pre-Roman in Britain was considered to be crude and barbaric. Nonetheless, Anderson referred to only three cairns in Sutherland, the long cairns SUT 22, 23, 53, and he published McKay's plans (ibid., 260–4).

2.12) Although by no means clear from the inadequate publications, by now two tripartite chambers, three bipartite chambers, and one seemingly single-compartment chamber were known (SUT 23, 29, 12, 53, 54, 22). They had been shown to differ slightly from the chambers which had been recorded in Orkney and Caithness, while the neighbouring chambered cairns of Ross-shire were still virtually unknown. These Sutherland chambers were found to have been built with a combination of orthostats and walling of horizontal slabs, with paired transverse orthostats forming portals and subdivisions; part or all of the chambers evidently had been roofed by oversailing corbel stones forming a vault. Three more cairns (SUT 50, 51, 55) had been recognised as chambered or of the distinctive short horned plan. Additionally, five cairns (SUT 15, 16, 21, 32, 58) had been identified by the officers of the Ordnance Survey and titled 'chambered cairn' or 'long cairn' on the first edition of the 6-inch maps published in 1878–9, though no details were available. More were recorded on the maps as antiquities, but their exact nature was either not revealed or was misunderstood. The maps were to form the basis for the first professional investigation thirty years later. But all considered, by the end of the century disappointingly little had been achieved.

The work of The Royal Commission on the Ancient and Historical Monuments and Constructions of Scotland

2.13) Real progress was made in the summer and autumn of 1909 when A. O. Curle (1866–1955) undertook single-handed a 'survey and examination of the monuments' for the second report of the Commission to produce the Inventory for the county of Sutherland (RCAMS 1911). This provided the first overview of the whole county, and at last a picture of the variety of cairns and chambers, and of their distribution and condition, began to emerge (ibid., xxxiii–xxxvii). An appreciation of Curle's contribution to Scottish archaeology, throughout his long and active life, has been published by Graham (1956). Considering the conditions in 1909 in such a remote and mountainous part of the country, the huge area to be covered, and the paucity of archaeological information, Curle's achievement there was remarkable. Although, over eighty years on, we sometimes disagree with his interpretation of the structures, his observations were generally admirably accurate and indeed often percipient. Some indication of his difficulties, his dedication to the task, and his stamina, can be glimpsed by following one day of fieldwork (Curle 1909b, 68–73: 1st June, 'a most lovely day'). He left Tongue for Strathnaver, with his camera, at 7 a.m. 'It is a fearsome journey in a motor laden with luggage as high as a corn stack behind and down most appalling gradients.' He walked up the strath to Achcheargary, 'a place whose name is different every time it is spoken', and recorded SUT 4, the adjacent cairnfield, four cairns nearby, and another cairnfield. Crossing the River Naver to Skelpick, he noted yet another cairnfield and detoured to photograph a broch on his way to the Coille na Borgie cairns (SUT 22, 23) which he examined in detail. From Invernaver Bridge he took 'the motor', returning to 8 km short of Tongue to explore the moor to the N of the main road where, following directions of an old keeper, he found two hut circles and a cairnfield. He then walked back to Tongue, diverting to see the remains of the broch at Rhitongue. In the evening he and his wife 'wandered down' to Castle Varraich. He had walked at least 23 km.

2.14) Curle was able to record forty-five neolithic cairns in the county, taking together chambered cairns and long cairns without visible chambers, and supplied sketch plans of six (SUT 3, 12, 28, 33, 55, 58) and photographs of two (SUT 34, 35). In addition he noted two cairns which probably contained chambers, a 'megalithic structure', and two destroyed chambered cairns. Out of this total of fifty, we have dropped four from our list. Curle also recorded another eight cairns which are now known to contain chambers. He recognised four categories of cairns, having found three horned long cairns, seven horned round cairns, nine unhorned long cairns and twenty-six round cairns (RCAMS 1911, xlii, though some of his cairns are now classified differently). He suggested that the horned long cairns were probably the earliest, evidently thinking in terms of a sequence with the round cairns last as they most nearly resembled bronze age cairns. Following the archaeological thinking of the time, he assumed that the cairn builders had come from the Mediterranean. Nineteen of the chambers were sufficiently exposed for classification; he found that the majority were bipartite but tripartite and undivided chambers were also present; there was no correlation between cairn form and chamber plan. Curle drew attention to the uneven distribution of the cairns, mainly in the E part of the county and in Strathnaver. Further, he saw that the distribution of long cairns was largely restricted to the lower ends of two major valleys, Strathnaver and the Strath of Kildonan; the distribution of horned round cairns (now called short horned cairns) appeared to be more scattered. He also commented on the frequent occurrence of small cairns and hut circles close to the chambered cairns.

2.15) No comparable Inventory was made at that time for the county of Ross and Cromarty, and the parish of Kincardine and Croick, included in the present volume (see ¶ 1.6), remained unexplored.

New information and synthesis

2.16) Between Curle's survey and that undertaken by Henshall in the 1950s a certain amount of information emerged piecemeal. Curle excavated Achaidh (SUT 2) in 1909. He had noticed that the cairn was short horned in plan, and the partial exposure of a massive lintel indicated the existence of a chamber. He found the roof intact though ready to collapse, and he had enough of it removed to allow him to examine and describe the chamber, but its contents were disappointing. The unusual Ardvreck chamber (SUT 9) was dug out, but not published, by J. E. Cree in 1925. Two cairns with exposed chambers at Allt nam Ban and Badnabay (SUT 6, 10) were fully described, without excavation, respectively by W. D. Simpson in 1928 and A. J. Boyd in 1952. Another partially successful interpretation of the Coille na Borgie cairns (SUT 22, 23) was offered by C. S. T. Calder in 1951.

2.17) In this same period several works of synthesis appeared, dealing with the Scottish tombs as a whole and attempting to set them in a cultural and chronological context. V. G. Childe, the first Professor of Prehistoric Archaeology at the University of Edinburgh, saw that they belonged to two distinct traditions. In one tradition, the gallery-graves, found in the SW of the country, the chambers were rectangular and were entered directly from outside and were usually covered by a long cairn; in the other tradition, the passage-graves, in the NW and N of the country, the chamber plans were variable but were often polygonal and were always approached down a passage and were usually covered by a round cairn. Chambered cairns of the latter type are found widespread in western Europe, though with great variations in their plans and size. Childe had to grapple with the complexity of the typology of the Scottish chambered cairns, especially where the two traditions appeared to coalesce, and with the limited but confusing information regarding their usage, and lastly with the question of their origins which he concluded lay ultimately in France or Iberia or the W Mediterranean (Childe 1935, 22–61; the development in understanding the chambered cairns, and particularly Childe's contribution in a number of papers, is discussed in Daniel 1962). In 1954 S. Piggott, Childe's successor, published his comprehensive work on the British neolithic. As far as the north of Scotland was concerned, he was dealing in greater detail with the same problems as Childe, and came to similar conclusions. He introduced the term 'Orkney-Cromarty group' for the northern passage-graves (including in it the tombs of Maes Howe type which are confined to Orkney and are now regarded as a separate group). He felt that long cairns, inappropriate to passage-graves, were derived from the gallery-grave tradition of the SW, and so the cairns of this form were not early among the northern chambered cairns. He dealt with the material equipment of the tomb-builders in general and discussed their economic basis, but what is so surprising with hindsight, he placed the Orkney-Cromarty cairns in the middle and late neolithic, which, before radiocarbon dates were available, were dated between about 1750 and 1550 BC. By 1960 the first radiocarbon dates for W European chambered cairns were just appearing. It was evident that the tomb chronology had to be extended, but the earliest dates of about 3000 BC (uncalibrated in those days) were not really believed (Henshall 1963, 6).

The survey by Henshall

2.18) A county-wide survey of the cairns was undertaken between 1951 and 1957 as part of a project to record the chambered cairns and long cairns in the whole of Scotland. For Sutherland it was largely a matter of expanding the entries in the RCAMS Inventory and adding three, and providing plans of most of the cairns (Henshall 1963, 304–332, 344–5, 350). Subsequently, during a county revision undertaken by the Archaeology Division of the Ordnance Survey, a few additional cairns were identified, mostly in the W. Henshall did further work between 1963 and 1968 to bring her record up to date, and to provide plans of some long cairns which had been published without plans in the 1963 volume (Henshall 1972, 564, 570, 572–87). Seventy-one cairns had now been recorded, of which we have omitted ten as being wrongly identified.

Excavations at Embo and The Ord

2.19) In 1960 Henshall and Wallace undertook rescue excavation at a greatly damaged cairn at Embo (SUT 63), as part of the former's duties whilst on the staff of The National Museum of Antiquities of Scotland. To their surprise the cairn was found to cover remains of both a single-compartment and of a bipartite chamber. In the better preserved chamber there had been two phases of burials, with animal bones but without artefacts, separated by a deliberately introduced layer of earth and stones. After the second phase the entrance had been deliberately sealed. In the bronze age the cairn had been used for inhumations in cists and for cremations. In 1971 a single radiocarbon date of 1920±100 bc (BM 442) was obtained, which related to the actual building of the bipartite chamber. It was soon to become clear that this date was disconcertingly late for a chamber that was not expected to be amongst the latest of the northern passage-graves.

2.20) In 1967 J. X. W. P. Corcoran, with his students from the University of Glasgow, excavated The Ord North (SUT 48) on behalf of the Inspectorate of Ancient Monuments. This followed his excavation of three large and complex cairns at Loch Calder, Caithness, in 1961 (CAT 58, 69, 70; Corcoran 1966). These huge and complex excavations were a heroic undertaking, and they remain the chief source of information on the structure and usage of chambered cairns in the N mainland of Scotland. At The Ord North Corcoran revealed a large bipartite chamber, well preserved except that it was filled with the collapsed upper part of its vaulted roof. No bone survived from the neolithic period, but sherds of diverse neolithic pots and some flints were recovered from the floor and from a layer of soil above it. As at Embo

(SUT 63), the entrance had been blocked, and the cairn had been used later for bronze age burials. An unusual feature, already noted by Curle in 1909, was a platform which had been added around the cairn. Neolithic studies suffered a great loss when Corcoran, who had spent his whole professional life working on chambered cairns in all parts of Britain, died prematurely in 1975. A report of the excavation was published by N. M. Sharples in 1981, and included discussion of the artefacts and interpretation of the deposits in the chamber. Comparisons were made mainly with the tombs which had been excavated in Orkney in the 1930s. Three radiocarbon dates relating to the use and the filling of the chamber (and incidentally also relating to the pottery) were obtained, lying between about 3600 and 3000 BC in calibrated terms. Later, when dates were available from chambers in Caithness and Orkney, The Ord chamber was seen to be roughly contemporary with the former and somewhat earlier than the latter; on typological grounds the latter chambers are likely to be among the latest to have been built (Sharples 1986, 6).

Assessment and dating

2.21) Meanwhile in 1972 Henshall attempted an assessment of what had emerged from her surveys of Scottish chambered cairns. She was able to take account, rather conservatively, of an increasing number of radiocarbon dates, though only that from Embo came from a northern passage-grave. She proposed that the earliest passage-graves were small single-compartment chambers and might indeed date from about 3000 BC, that larger chambers with two or three compartments had probably been built through the third millennium, and that long cairns were likely to have appeared about 2800 BC. Use of the tombs, and possibly building too, were thought to continue well into the second millennium (Henshall 1972, 278-83). A further advance had come from the realisation that chambered cairns might be complex multi-period constructions. By 1972 it had been demonstrated at several excavations in Scotland, Wales, and England, and it had been deduced at certain other cairns, that major structural additions might be made to tombs (Corcoran 1969a; 1969b, 83-92; Powell 1963; Scott 1969; Ritchie 1970). Most relevant for the N of Scotland was Corcoran's excavation of Tulach an t-Sionnaich in Caithness (CAT 58) which had shown that a small passage-grave had been covered and sealed by a heel-shaped cairn which subsequently had been incorporated into a long cairn (Corcoran 1966, 5-12).

2.22) With these possibilities in mind, excavation of several British cairns continued to produce evidence of multi-period construction, and the theoretical dissection of complex cairns into their component parts was felt to be justified. The problem, of course, is in the application of this approach; with hindsight it is evident that it was over-enthusiastically applied by both Henshall and Corcoran in 1972. The most important investigation relating to the north mainland was undertaken during the 1970s by Corcoran, followed by Masters, at Camster Long (CAT 12). In this monument two passage-graves had almost certainly been incorporated into a later long cairn (the full report not available at the time of writing).

2.23) The implications of multi-period construction, together with the longer time-span for the building of chambered cairns, have been profound. Since about 1970 it has been possible to consider long cairns, or even short horned cairns, or the then newly recognised heel-shaped cairns, independently of the chambers they contain, on the assumption that some at least had been added to existing round passage-graves, and possibly long after these had been built. This new approach has removed some of the typological confusion inherent in treating each cairn as a unitary concept, and it has confirmed what had become increasingly clear, that the design of chambered cairns everywhere was largely due to local developments and short-range influences. This also relieved the expectation that the continental origins of the tomb-builders could be identified, though it pushed the question of their ultimate origins into a more distant and more obscure past. With further evidence, particularly from his work in SW Scotland and at Camster Long (CAT 12), Masters has re-examined the relationship of chambered cairns with long cairns and long barrows, endorsing the view that they had separate origins and, when found together, they are structurally and chronologically distinct (1981).

2.24) In the 1970s afforestation of many large areas of the northern counties was being planned, and later was carried out. In advance of this work R. J. Mercer, with students from the Department of Archaeology in the University of Edinburgh, undertook a programme of intensive survey on behalf of the Inspectorate of Ancient Monuments. The surveys were important in many ways, not least because monuments of all periods were recorded, planned in detail, and mapped at scales that allowed their preservation in areas which were left unplanted. This policy of preservation echoed the call in the Inventory of 1911 that the attention of proprietors should be drawn to the damage caused by planting trees on ancient monuments (RCAMS 1911, vi). As it happened, only two of the surveyed areas in Sutherland included chambered cairns, the Ledmore/Loubcroy area of Assynt (the actual surveying undertaken by J. M. Howell) and the coastal strip E of Tongue. The survey programme led to Mercer's consideration of the structural complexity of long cairns in the N of Scotland and the evidence of neolithic settlement. In the first place he was dealing with the N and SW of Sutherland, but as the survey moved to Caithness he concentrated on the better-preserved cairns of that region (Mercer 1980, 69–70; 1981, 6–10; 1985, 2–32). His interpretation of the chambered cairn phenomenon in Sutherland, Caithness and Orkney was published in 1992.

3. The land, the environment and the location of the cairns

The character of Sutherland

3.1) Sutherland occupies the NW tip of the Scottish mainland with Caithness to the E and Ross and Cromarty to the S. Its coastline looks out to sea in three directions, to the Moray Firth on the SE, the Atlantic Ocean to the N, and across the Minch to Lewis on the W. Sutherland owes its name to its southerly location within the political framework of the Norse earldom of Orkney in the early middle ages, although evidence of Norse settlement is sparse and for the most part is limited to placenames. One of the largest Districts in Scotland, Sutherland occupies over 5,000 sq. km (more than 2,000 sq. miles), but its small and scattered population today gives it one of the lowest densities in Scotland. An authoritative introduction to Sutherland is provided in *The Sutherland Book* (Omand ed. 1982), with particularly relevant chapters on the geology, landscape, soils and climate.

3.2) The geology of Sutherland is very complex, as a glance at even a simplified geological map shows (figure 3, *2*). However, a short account of the rock formations is essential, as the underlying geology has had such an important effect on the topography, the soils, and thus on the early settlement of the area. In western Sutherland the Lewisian Gneiss, which is now dated as the oldest rock in Europe, is the basis of a distinctive landscape. The rock is very hard and has been subjected to severe glaciation. The elevation is generally low and the surface is undulating, though the Foinaven and Arkle ranges provide impressive mountain scenery (figure 3, *1*). For the most part the area consists of rounded rocky ridges bare of soil and vegetation or is covered by peat, and it is speckled with the many lochans which occupy much of its surface. The gneiss was overlaid by Torridonian Sandstone, now largely removed but leaving isolated massifs that are such a spectacular feature of this region; the mountains Suilven, Canisp and Quinag rise sheer from flat moorland, and it is difficult not to suppose that they had a mystical significance in the remote past.

3.3) The major part of Sutherland is formed of the Moine Series of metamorphosed sediments, interrupted by areas of Lewisian gneiss and granitic intrusions. Together these have produced wide expanses of peaty moorland bounded by mountain ranges 700 to 960 m high, with large freshwater lochs grading down in size to the many small lochans. Between these two major geological zones the Moine Thrust runs from N to S; a series of thrust planes has carried rocks from the E to overlie rocks to the W, producing a complex interleaving of rocks of different types and ages which include, most importantly for the present study, the discontinuous narrow band of Cambrian limestones outcropping down its western edge. The elucidation of the most complex part in Assynt, by the eminent geologists B. Peach and J. Horne between 1883 and 1907, was an important landmark in geological studies. In this area, around Inchnadamph-Knockan-Loch Ailsh, there was intensive settlement in neolithic times.

3.4) The coastal plain down the E side of Sutherland and the hills behind it are made up of sedimentary rocks of Old and New Red Sandstone age. The low-lying sandstone areas are the most fertile in Sutherland, a remarkable contrast with the rest of the District, and naturally they have attracted settlement at all periods. This is partly due to the profound effect that the mountains of W Sutherland have on the climate. The prevailing winds are from the SW, coming moisture-laden from the Atlantic. When they encounter the high land prolonged heavy rainfall is caused in the W, and as a result the air is drier and warmer to the E of the mountains. The most sheltered part, and thus climatically the most favoured, is the SE corner. West Sutherland is one of the wettest parts of Scotland with an average annual rainfall from 1,500 to over 3,000 mm mainly according to height, and the rainfall diminishes eastwards to less than 750 mm at Dornoch (the average at Edinburgh is 660 mm, and at Kew is 598 mm).

3.5) The underlying geology is but one of the factors which have shaped the topography of Sutherland, for during the glaciations of the Pleistocene period major changes took place. Massive ice sheets occupied the central part of northern Scotland with the ice flowing to the N, to the SE and to the W. These movements modified the valleys, and thus the drainage pattern, and consequently the communication pattern from the coast into the interior (figure 4). With the retreat of the ice glacial debris was left over much of central and eastern Sutherland. Moraines are common features of the landscape, and deep deposits of fluvial-glacial material in the lower straths have gradually been cut through by the rivers to leave terracing.

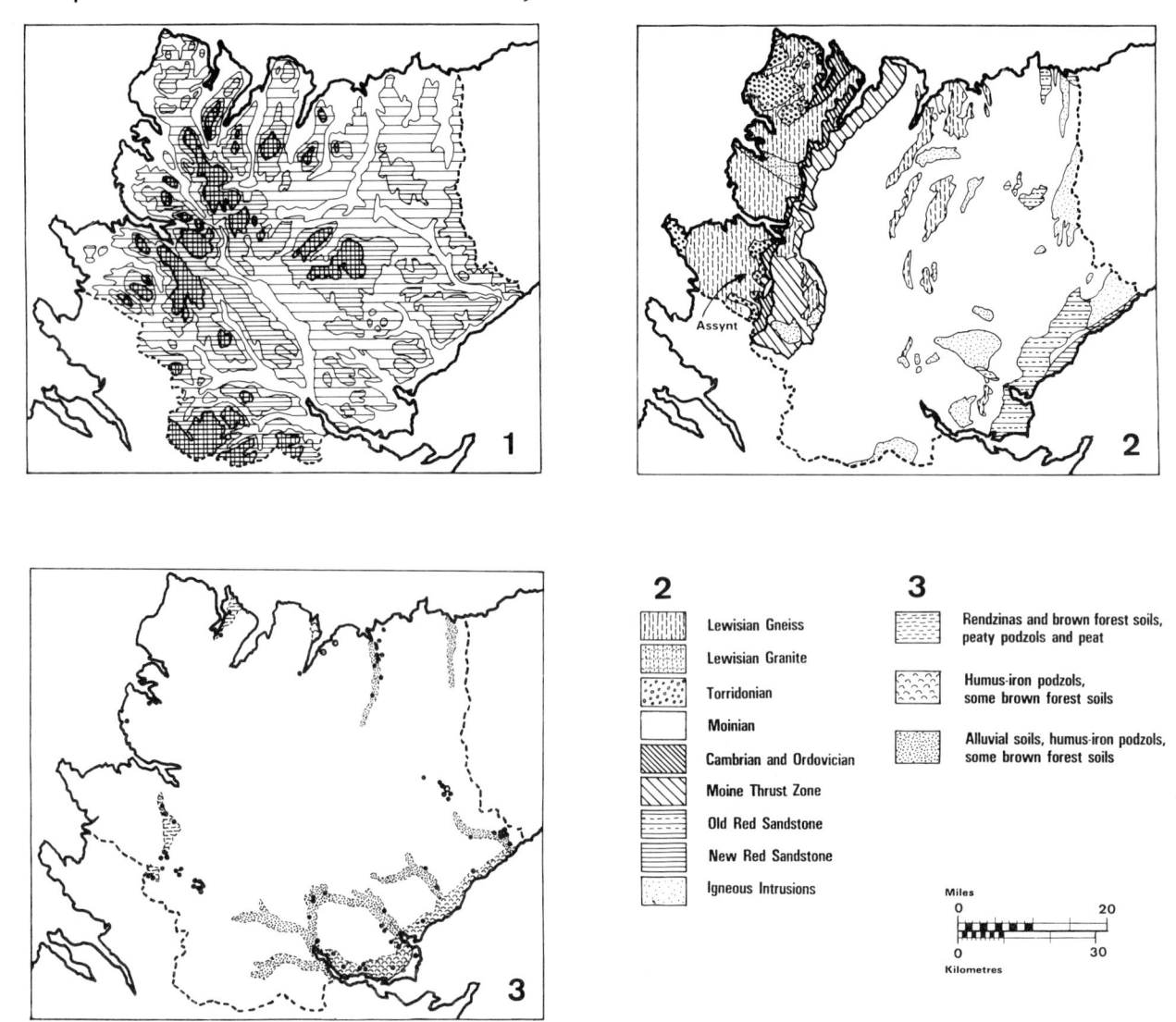

FIGURE 3. Maps of Sutherland. *1* Relief, contours at 122, 244 and 427 m (400, 800 and 1,400 ft); *2* Geology; *3* Selected soil types with the cairn distribution. (Redrawn from Omand ed. 1982, 43, 22, 66.)

3.6) On the E side of Sutherland the rivers run from NW to SE; there are three major valleys, the Strath of Kildonan in which flows the River Helmsdale, and Strath Brora and Strath Fleet with rivers of the same name. Further S the swiftly flowing River Shin drains Loch Shin and joins the River Oykel flowing into the Dornoch Firth. The E coast is edged by long sandy beaches for almost its whole length. The eastern seaboard has been the principal line of communication from S to N, formerly with small ferries across the two coastal firths, now spanned by bridges. In this fertile and nodal area are the present main centres of population, at Dornoch, Golspie and Brora. The N coast is rugged, with high cliffs and sea stacks off shore, but also with sandy bays, and it is deeply penetrated by the sea at the Kyle of Tongue, Loch Eriboll and the Kyle of Durness. The drainage pattern is broadly from S to N with Strath Halladale and Strathnaver providing the major arteries into the interior. The western coast is similarly rugged and is interrupted by several long fjords reaching far inland, but it is varied by many small inlets and beaches; the hinterland is dominated by the mountains already mentioned, creating some of the most beautiful wilderness scenery in Scotland. Along the N coast, and less frequently down the W coast, there are small

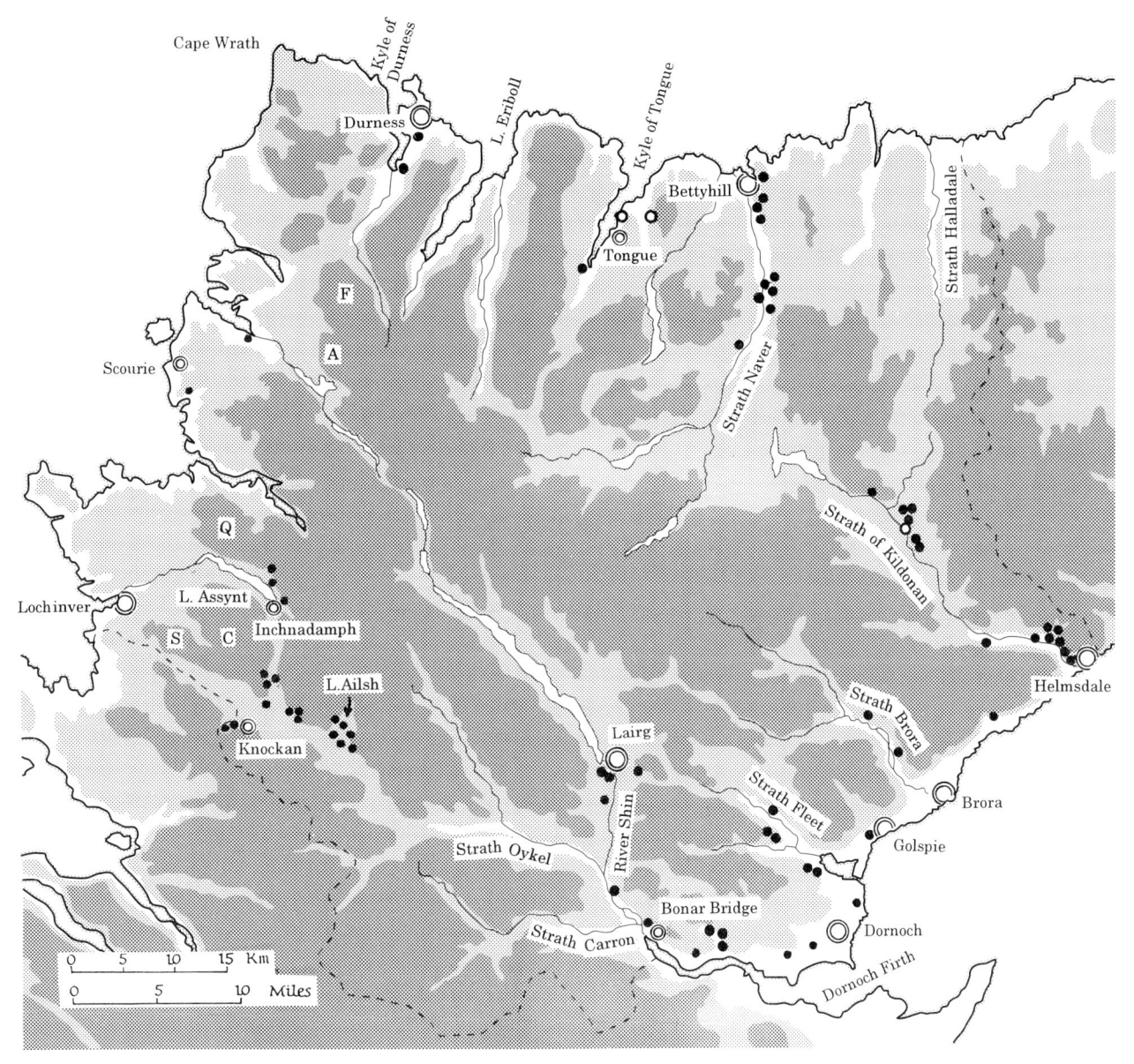

FIGURE 4. Map with the main place-names used in the text (the mountains Foinaven, Arkle, Quinag, Suilven and Canisp are shown as F, A, Q, S and C respectively), and the cairns listed in the Inventory (uncertain sites are shown as small open circles).

scattered communities wherever there is cultivatable land or an anchorage.

The evidence for pre-neolithic peoples

3.7) Scotland appears to have cast off its mantle of ice by 14,000–10,000 years ago to reveal a tundra landscape. With the improvement in environmental conditions birch, hazel, pine and elm were established, and a range of mammals (deer, pigs, wolves, bear) and birds appeared in the new lands. Tantalisingly uncertain evidence of early human activity was found in a cave at Inchnadamph during excavations in 1926 (Callander, Cree and Ritchie, 1927); fragments of at least 900 reindeer antlers were recovered from geological contexts which suggested that the deposit was earlier than the latest glaciation. More recently radiocarbon dates have been obtained from the antlers, and these suggest three different phases of activity, two prior to the latest glaciation and one about 8,000 years ago. Of the various possibilities for the accumulation of the antler deposits human intervention is but one; it cannot be ruled out, but it cannot be proved. The presence of the antlers, however, is important evidence for the environment in pre- and immediately post-glacial times (Lawson and Bonsall 1986 a and b; Dennison 1994; Wickham-Jones 1994, 43–4).

3.8) The earliest certain traces of occupation in Scotland have been found on the Isle of Rhum and date to some 9,000 years ago. There is evidence that from about this time there were groups of people throughout northern Scotland living in a mesolithic economy, dependent on exploiting the natural resources of the lochs and the forests. It has been suggested that a coastal environment stimulated colonisation (Woodman 1989, 20, 24). Artefacts of this date have been found on the W coast only a little to the S of the Sutherland border at Shieldaig and Redpoint in Ross-shire (Wickham-Jones 1994, 62–3); no artefacts of distinctly mesolithic type have yet come from the W coast of Sutherland, which may be merely a reflection of the lack of fieldwork. A flint scatter at Bettyhill at the mouth of Strathnaver suggests that the varied natural resources of the river and its hinterland were appreciated long before the arrival of the farming communities who were responsible for the construction of the many cairns in the strath (Wickham-Jones 1994, 65). On the E coast the occasional flint of mesolithic date has been discovered in the sandy links (Henshall 1982, 135–6), and the range of material from the Moray Firth shores has been put into better context as a result of excavations in Inverness (Wordsworth 1985). The absence of mesolithic material in the extensive archaeological investigations S of Lairg may underline the coastal nature of the initial colonisation of the area (McCullagh 1992).

The environment and the neolithic settlement

3.9) By the earlier centuries of the 4th millennium the climate was perhaps not very different from that of today, though slightly warmer and drier. Most of the peat which is so widespread in Sutherland had not formed, and the natural cover was woodland in the more favoured parts, and scrub elsewhere probably reaching a height of 250 m or so. The mountains and high moorland of the greater part of Sutherland mean that only the straths and coasts offer areas suitable for agriculture and settlement. It is no surprise to find that the chambered cairns and long cairns, as indicators of the neolithic settlement pattern, are clustered in distinct geographical areas with large bare tracts between, but what is perhaps remarkable is the number of cairns within some of the compact clusters. The main clusters of monuments, which presumably indicate long-established neolithic settlement in the locality, are in Strathnaver, the upper and lower reaches of the Strath of Kildonan, and the Inchnadamph-Knockan-Loch Ailsh area, with considerable numbers of cairns more widely scattered along the coast and the lower straths of the SE. However, there are puzzling gaps in the distribution, in Strath Halladale, Strath Oykel and Strathcarron, where neolithic settlement might be expected.

3.10) The distribution of the cairns on figure 3, *3* is plotted in relation to some selected combinations of soil types. This provides a much simplified illustration of neolithic settlement in relation to the most favourable soils; it also shows that what are now peat, peaty podzols and peaty gleys, covering so much of inland Sutherland, were largely avoided. A more detailed study of the relationship of settlement with soil types requires specialist treatment, because the classification and distribution of soil types is very complex, and the changes which have taken place in the soils over five millennia are largely unknown. Even so, a few points may be made. The most fertile part of Sutherland is the SE corner, from Bonar Bridge to Dornoch and Brora, and it is here that there is likely to have been the greatest loss of cairns without record, due to intense cultivation particularly during the last two centuries. The acid soils (humus-iron podzols with some brown forest soils) which have been developed on the drift deposits are fairly free draining. Twelve cairns are situated in this zone, and there are ten more in the straths running inland. These straths contain similar soils, brown forest soils having formed on the lower slopes and alluvial soils on the valley floors. At the lower end of the Strath of Kildonan, which here is narrow and steep-sided so that cultivatable land is very restricted, there are six cairns in a 3-km stretch, a concentration which is difficult to explain. There are nine cairns in Strathnaver, six of them in the short stretch between Bettyhill and Skelpick where brown forest soils have developed. The lower parts of all the straths have small areas under cultivation and were formerly more extensively cultivated, but at the present time they are mainly pasture and often rough pasture.

3.11) Unlike the cairns of E Sutherland which are part of a distribution which extends N and S beyond the boundaries of Sutherland, the cluster of eighteen cairns in the Inchnadamph-Knockan-Loch Ailsh area is isolated as no similar cluster exists in the W Highlands, and there are no neolithic cairns at all in west-

PLATE 1. Carn Richard (SUT 18) from the NE, overlooking the upper Strath of Kildonan, photographed in 1957.

ern Ross-shire. These cairns are surely explained by the outcrops of limestone in this area. Twelve of the cairns (and also two cairns on the Kyle of Durness) can be directly related to the free-draining soils (rendzinas) which develop on these calcareous rocks, and which support a base-rich grassland, today providing moderate quality grazing. The contrast with the surrounding country is remarkable, and in prehistoric times must have been more so with appreciably more fertile areas standing out from the scrub or moorland round about. The location of the six remaining cairns of the cluster, a short distance to the SE, must in neolithic times have shared in the same advantages, though this is not apparent as they are in peat-covered moorland based on moraine, now partly afforested. The solid geology includes limestone, occasionally seen as tiny outcrops, and this presumably affected the nature of the drift deposits and allowed the formation of calcareous soils in the distant past. The reason for the presence of seven cairns in the upper part of the Strath of Kildonan, which here has expanded into a wide shallow valley, is unclear. Today the valley sides are mainly peat-covered moorland, partly afforested, and the valley floor is covered with deep peat (plate 1). It can only be supposed that before the peat formed the area was favoured in some way which has been obscured. Observing the strath today it might have been expected that the middle part would have been as attractive to early settlers as the lower or upper reaches.

3.12) The almost total lack of information on the early neolithic economy in Sutherland reduces comments to inference and speculation. It is probable that in western and northern regions it was more dependent on stock-raising (and therefore pasture) supplemented by hunting than on crop-raising. From Embo (SUT 63) and from the Caithness and Orcadian tombs there is the evidence of the bones of sheep, ox, pig, deer and dog. The work at Lairg, as yet only published in interim form (McCullagh 1992, 6), has provided environmental evidence for a mature farming economy early in the fourth millennium BC, and presumably this evidence is applicable to much of the eastern part of Sutherland. The production of cereal crops contemporary with the use of chambered cairns is testified elsewhere in the north by the rare finds of cereal grains and the presence of querns, either in tombs or at habitation sites, for example Knap of Hower in Orkney (Close-Brooks 1983, 284; Davidson and Henshall 1989, 84; 1991, 14; A. Ritchie 1983, 56, 115).

The siting of cairns

3.13) While the siting of several cairns is visually dramatic, for instance the hilltop position of Fiscary (SUT 29), many cairns are sited in locations the reason for which is not immediately obvious, for instance Badnabay and Allt a' Chaoruinn (SUT 10, 74) (plate 3) are in an unremarkable positions close to the shore. The siting of many cairns, particularly those on the flanks of hills, might be related to their visibility from settlements, or to their position in an uncultivated or

PLATE 2. Loch Awe (SUT 42) from the SW looking over the loch.

uncultivatable patch of land, or for religious reasons that are unfathomable. In such broken country altitude itself is no guarantee of visible dominance. The highest cairns in Sutherland include the pair at Creag nan Caorach (SUT 24 and 25), Loch Awe (SUT 42) and Carn Richard (SUT 18) (plates 8, 2, 1), at between 228 and 200 m; though they may command extensive views, they give the impression today that their site relates to such practical considerations as being at the upper limit of cultivation as much as to their being intended as landmarks. But there is no doubt that several cairns, such as Lothbeg (SUT 45) and Skelpick South (SUT 55), make dramatic statements. The question of the significance or not of intervisibility of monuments was considered at each site, and it was concluded that it was unlikely to be important. Perhaps an underlying rocky boss or the immediate availability of stone were more important reasons for the choice of individual sites.

3.14) The siting and orientation of long cairns may, in some cases, have been imposed by the desire to incorporate a pre-existing structure, but siting and orientation are also likely to have been influenced by the advantage of building on an underlying ridge of rock or on an elongated shelf on a hillside, and by the easy availability of stone. Such topographic considerations probably lie behind the placing of Coille na Borgie North and South (SUT 22 and 23) and Skelpick Long (SUT 53); Salscraggie (SUT 51) runs along the edge of a river terrace, and Carn Laggie (SUT 17) and Caen Burn West (SUT 16) are situated at the edge of cultivatable ground with a steep hillside rising immediately to one side. Less readily explained in topographical terms are Caen Burn East and North (SUT 13 and 14), the former slanting across the grain of the hillside, and the latter across the terrace on which it sits; similarly Kinbrace Long (SUT 34) has the axis lying across the contour.

Cairns and the ancient landscape

3.15) Our method of survey precluded detailed recording of cairns in their landscape setting, but this is such an important consideration in terms of conservation, or of the potential of individual monuments to contribute to any overall research strategy, that it was assessed at each site. For some the immediate surroundings had been so altered by agriculture, by subsequent peat growth, or by afforestation, that little could be seen. In a few cases, however, considerable chronological depth can be detected in the immediate surroundings; the best known example is on The Ord (SUT 48, 49). The potential of the upper Strath of Kildonan as an area for detailed study may be illustrated by the survey of a part of it in 1991, with the discovery of many burnt mounds, hut-circles and

PLATE 3. Allt a' Chaoruinn (SUT 74) from the S.

ancient cultivation remains, in an area where the beginnings of settlement lie in the neolithic period (RCAHMS 1993). Similarly detailed field survey in Strathnaver would doubtless illustrate the chronological depth of settlement and might reveal patterns in which the location of neolithic cairns could be seen in relationship to monuments of other periods. Less well known is the extensive area of prehistoric and early historic settlement to the NW of Creag an Amalaidh (SUT 61), where the cairn is the earliest indication of long occupation of the valley. The hill slopes around several other cairns would certainly repay detailed field walking and survey, as the cairns are but one element in the historic landscape.

4. The passages and chambers

Terminology and morphology

4.1) In considering the architecture of the chambered cairns of Sutherland, it is convenient to describe the passages, and the chambers to which they led, before describing the cairns which will be dealt with in Section 5. Out of the seventy-two cairns recorded in the Inventory, six long cairns (SUT 13, 14, 16, 32, 34, 61) are without any indication that they contain or contained chambers. One large intact round cairn (SUT 35) has been included on the strong presumption that it covers a hidden chamber. Two other round cairns, Tongue House and Blandy (SUT 57, 76), have also been included, though with reservations. There is only a brief and baffling record of the former chamber, and the visible remains in the latter cairn are difficult to interpret. The remaining sixty-three cairns provide information ranging from detailed to minimal, but there is little doubt that they are all chambered.

4.2) The following terminology has been used to describe the passages and chambers. *Chamber:-* the entire structure beyond the passage. *Ante-chamber:-* the outer compartment of a bipartite or tripartite chamber, roofed either by slabs at a low level or by a vault. *Main chamber:-* the largest compartment in a bipartite or tripartite chamber, roofed by a high vault. *Cell:-* a low-roofed area accessible from the main chamber. *Portal stones:-* a pair of upright stones set with their faces more or less at right angles to the axis of the chamber and passage and designed to carry a lintel. Portal stones may be at the outer end of the passage (*entrance portal stones*), between the passage and the chamber (*outer portal stones*), between the ante-chamber and main chamber (*inner portal stones*), or form the entry into a cell (*cell portal stones*). *Divisional stones:-* paired transversely-set stones in chambers where the plan is not known in detail. *Compartment:-* the areas within a chamber between pairs of portal/divisional stones. *Orthostat:-* an upright stone which forms part of the wall of a passage or chamber (or of the edging of a cairn). *Eke-stone:-* a small slab inserted to level up major structural stones.

4.3) The chambers may be classified into four types, all variants of the Orkney-Cromarty passage-grave design (excluding the exceptional chamber at Ardvreck, SUT 9, which is described separately in ¶ 4.33). Single-compartment chambers are roofed by a vault. Bipartite chambers are of two sorts: the Caithness type which has a small ante-chamber roofed at a low level leading to a vaulted main chamber, and the Skelpick type which has an ante-chamber almost as large as the main chamber with each part roofed by a vault. Tripartite chambers may have a low-roofed ante-chamber, a vaulted main chamber, and a low-roofed cell at the rear, but there are several variants of this plan.

The passages

4.4) Passages are the most vulnerable parts of the structures because, being near the edge of the cairn, the lintels were easily exposed and these useful stones could be removed with little trouble. In describing the passages the portal stones at both ends have been included for the sake of consistency (so the lengths given may not tally with those in the Inventory where the portal stones are generally described separately). Some portal stones, in both passages and chambers, still support their lintels, either directly, or with eke-stones which bring a shorter portal stone up to the level of its partner.

4.5) Only two intact passages have been recorded in Sutherland, but between them they exhibit most of the features that can be seen individually elsewhere. At Kinbrace Burn (SUT 33) there is a pair of portal stones at the outer end (one not exposed at the time of the record), set transversely to the axis and projecting slightly from the line of the walls to narrow the entry. The passage is 1.5 m long and 0.9 m wide, with the walling at the inner end butting against and largely masking the portal stones at the entry into the chamber. The roofing is by three lintels, the outer resting on the entrance portal stones, the other two lintels set progressively slightly higher. The roof height is uncertain due to debris on the floor but is unlikely to be less than 0.7 m at the outer end. The entry to the passage at Skelpick Long (SUT 53) is similarly narrowed, to 0.56 m, by a pair of portal stones. The passage is larger than that at Kinbrace Burn, 2.43 m long and increasing from 1.15 to 1.3 m wide. Each wall consists of a large orthostat laid on its long edge, supplemented at each end by short lengths of walling and above by two or three courses of slabs. The walls butt against and almost hide the portal stones at the inner end. The roofing is by four lintels, rising from 0.7 to 1 m above the floor, each just overlapping the upper surface of that in front; they seem to be relatively thin slabs (one broken) mainly supported by the cairn material behind the passage walls. A fifth lintel which rests on the portal stones forming the entry into the chamber is different in character. It is set at a slightly lower level and is very large. These two passages are carefully designed and well built, and represent the normal range of dimensions except that some passages are only 0.6 m or so wide (SUT 2, 23, 58, 63, 74).

4.6) The entrances to passages seem generally to have been between low portal stones, which carried the outermost lintels, an arrangement which would have formed a neat return at the junction of the passage with the edging of the cairn. Ten cairns certainly, and probably eight more, have entrance portal stones, but two do not (SUT 48, 63). The widths of entrances vary between 0.8 m (SUT 10) and 0.55 m (SUT 36), and exceptionally only 0.45 m at one small chamber (SUT 74). Only at Skelpick Long (SUT 53) is the height of an entrance known, a little over 0.7 m, though judging by their portal stones it was sometimes greater (e.g. at SUT 5, 7, 10). At two cairns (SUT 2, 37) the outer lintel is or was visible, one of them almost 2 m long, and the rest of these hidden passages is likely to be intact. The two innermost lintels remain at Allt nam Ban, Torboll and Allt a' Chaoruinn (SUT 6, 58, 74); at the first the lintels lie side by side though the inner has probably been at a slightly higher level; at the other two they are stepped with the inner higher, overlapping the outer. In all three cases the roof height at the inner end of the passage is about 1 m. The passage walls may be built with large orthostats laid on their edges with only a small amount of supplementary walling (besides Skelpick Long SUT 53, at 12, 27, 65, 74), or entirely of walling (besides Kinbrace Burn SUT 33, at 6, 23, 63), or of a mixture of these methods, sometimes using boulders instead of regular slabs (best recorded at The Ord North, SUT 48, also at 58, 63, and possibly at 10).

4.7) The passages are generally short. Kinbrace Burn (SUT 33) at 1.5 m long is not unusual, for several more are about the same length (SUT 60, 70, 73, 74), proven by excavation at the S passage at Embo (SUT 63). The Ord South (SUT 49) appears to have the shortest passage, only 1 m long, which might raise doubts on structural grounds, but a pair of orthostats looks convincingly like entrance portal stones, and the slope of the site makes it difficult to envisage a longer passage. Five passages besides Skelpick Long (SUT 53) are between 2 and 3 m long (SUT 10, 36, 45, 58, 66), and four more (SUT 23, 75, 3, 54 in order of length) are up to about 3.7 m long. Four passages appear to be, and one certainly is, between 4 and 5 m in length. Three of these, Achaidh, Kyleoag and Loch Borralan East (SUT 2, 37, 43) lead to architecturally similar chambers, and the estimated length of the passage rests on the assumption that there is no hidden low-roofed ante-chamber at the inner end. The passage at Evelix (SUT 28) is more problematic (figure 7). The ruined chamber was large and built of massive blocks, and the remains can be interpreted in two ways. The passage may have been 2.4 m long terminating at a missing pair of portal stones, beyond which was an ante-chamber; in this case the passage seems rather short for the size of the chamber. Alternatively the passage may have been about 4.2 m long, and unusually wide at 1.35 m with the two orthostats at the inner end as parts of the passage walls rather than the walls of an ante-chamber. The latter interpretation may seem more appropriate to the scale of the structure, but the former interpretation seems the more likely, with the passage only slightly shorter than that at Skelpick Long. Because of its state of ruin there are similar difficulties in understanding Allt a' Mhuilinn (SUT 5) (figure 12). The two portal stones, each with their partner missing, were probably at either end of the passage which would have been 2 m long, with an unusually tall entrance portal stone over 1 m high. The alternative interpretation, that these stones were at each end of an ante-chamber, would present a chamber of exceptionally, but not impossibly, large size and of unusual proportions (see ¶ 4.29). A lintel over 1.5 m long lies in front of the putative entrance portal stone.

4.8) It is probable that some cairns were enlarged after the chamber and its covering cairn were built, and this is particularly likely to have happened at cairns with forecourts and façades. In some cases such enlargements probably involved extending the passages. Thus some of the longer passages noted above may reflect two periods of construction, and indeed it may be that no passage was more than 3 m long in its original form. The excavated passage at The Ord North (SUT 48) can certainly be interpreted in this way (figure 10). The passage is about 4.5 m long without entrance portal stones, but it is unique in Sutherland, as far as is known, in having a pair of transversely-set stones protruding from the walls and carrying a lintel about midway along. This arrangement of orthostats and lintel is suggestive of an entrance, 0.65 m wide and about 0.9 m high, to a passage which was about 3 m long. The only other surviving lintel was over the portal stones at the entrance to the chamber; this lintel was larger, set 1.3 m above the floor, and, like that at Skelpick Long (SUT 53), it had evidently been lower than the passage roof because part of the passage wall remained to a height of 1.48 m. The absence of the rest of the roofing may indicate that the other lintels had been smaller. The passage was evidently rather roomier than many, up to 1.2 m wide, and built in the same style as the chamber with boulders linked by walling, and corbel stones along the upper part. The outer part of the passage was about 1.6 m long and had been much ruined, but it too had a boulder incorporated into the wall.

4.9) The situation is different at Coille na Borgie South (SUT 23). A passage about 5.7 m long would be required to connect the chamber with the forecourt. The passage is visible for 3 m from the chamber, with traces of a short extension after a vertical joint in the wall, but there is no sign of the outer 2 m or so, and, in spite of a plan and sketch of 1867, it may be doubted that it ever existed (figure 18, and discussed further ¶ 5.27). Two lintels remain midway along the passage, and at this point it is only 0.5 m wide and 0.7 m high, a barely functional size, and at the outer end it is narrower still. When first described Kinbrace Burn and Allt nam Ban (SUT 33, 6) were assumed to have passages as long as 7.3 and 8 m, as each of the existing outer ends were such a great distance from the edge of the cairn, but with the recognition that cairns may have been enlarged, or that forecourts may have been deliberately infilled, the passage at the former may safely be accepted as intact, and the length of the latter may be expected to be within the normal range. At Kinbrace Hill Round (SUT 35), where no passage is visible, a pair of orthostats have the appearance of entrance portal stones, but their height and irregular positioning in relation to each other warns that their appearance may be misleading.

The structure of the chambers

4.10) None of the Sutherland chambers retains its roof, and none has been consolidated and presented for public inspection. One of the most impressive chambers (SUT 48) had to be filled in after excavation because of its unstable condition, and others which are in a reasonably complete state are choked with stone or vegetation and are thus difficult to examine. In spite of these obstacles, by extrapolating from ten or so of the better preserved chambers and from the fuller information available at similar chambers in Caithness, it is possible to build up a picture of the Sutherland chambers.

4.11) The design of the chambers, and their appearance, were influenced by the types of stone available in different parts of the county. A detailed account of the structural considerations and techniques used in building chambers has been provided by Barber (1992), though his observations are largely based on the Orcadian chambers built with a more tractable stone than was available anywhere in Sutherland. Here the lower walls of the chambers were built with a combination of orthostats and dry walling or were occasionally entirely of walling. The orthostats may be quarried slabs, or boulders, or sometimes a mixture of the two. The quarried slabs have evidently been prized from outcrops as the slabs often retain a rounded weathered edge. The boulders were generally selected for a flat surface which could be incorporated into the wall-face, and irregularities of shape were largely hidden in the completed structure. Excavation showed that the boulders used at The Ord North (SUT 48) had rounded bases which had been steadied by chock-stones, but the sandstone slabs at Embo (SUT 63) had merely been placed on the ground and had sunk slightly into the gravel subsoil. The orthostats were sometimes closely set, and especially if they were regular in outline only small panels of walling were needed to link them; or the orthostats might be more widely spaced, or irregular in profile, requiring a greater proportion of walling. The walling was always neatly laid, almost always of split slabs, and typically (if practicable) with only a single horizontal slab in each course.

4.12) All or part of each chamber was covered by a vaulted roof. To construct this the character of the walling changed at between 0.7 to 1 m above the floor, and large flat corbel stones were employed. The lowest ones, if resting on walling between orthostats, sometimes continued the vertical wall-face, but from roughly the level of the tops of the orthostats each layer of corbel stones slightly oversailed that below, and in effect the upper parts of the roofs were formed by corbel stones laid in rings of progressively smaller diameter. The corbel stones were substantial slabs, generally 0.15 to 0.4 m thick, 0.4 to 0.8 wide and 1 to 1.5 m long, and at The Ord North (SUT 48) there were even larger slabs estimated to weigh a ton or more. The corbel stones were set with their axes radially to the chamber wall and sloping slightly down away from the chamber (figure 2, plates 4, 7). The stability of the vault was dependent on the counterbalancing weight of the cairn on the outer parts of the corbel stones, and thus the core of the cairn was an integral part of the construction. The slope of the corbel stones also served to drain water away from the chamber and so

PLATE 4. The Ord North (SUT 48), the chamber from the NW during excavation in 1967 showing the circle of roof corbel stones (scales in feet).

to keep it relatively dry. Only the inner ends of the corbel stones were visible from the chamber, giving the upper part of the wall and roof a rather rough appearance, contrasting with the neat smaller-scale walling below. At some ruined monuments the contrasting types of stone lying around the orthostats may be recognised as either rounded irregular cairn material, or relatively small split slabs from the lower walling, or large slabs (either quarried or boulders of suitable flat shape) from the corbelled upper part, or larger elongated blocks which had been major lintel stones.

4.13) The excavator of Achaidh (SUT 2) began his investigation from the top of the cairn. He found the vault intact but about to collapse due to the deterioration of some of the supporting stonework, so partial dismantling was necessary. The roof, sketched by Curle (figure 5), consisted of the uppermost ring of radiating corbel stones which had almost closed the span leaving a small central hole. This was plugged by a tapering block of stone about 0.2 m in diameter and 0.3 m deep. The stability of the vault was not dependent on this stone so it was not a true key-stone. Its purpose was to close the apex of the vault, though the support it may have given to the upper corbel stones and the absence of a capstone may have helped to delay collapse when the structure weakened. The height of the roof was about 2.2 m, covering an area

FIGURE 5. Achaidh (SUT 2). Drawing of the complete chamber roof seen from above, by A. O. Curle 1909 (from Curle 1910, 107).

of 2.7 by 2.1 m. The corbelling technique is still clearly displayed at this chamber, as four layers of corbel stones round the back of the chamber were exposed in cross section when the front of the chamber was reduced in height. Evidence for closing a vault by what may be termed a false key-stone is only available at intact chambers and so is difficult to find, but a similar arrangement was observed at the north chamber at Camster Long (CAT 12). It is generally assumed that vaults were closed by a capstone, and indeed this may be the usual method, as displaced slabs which were almost certainly capstones can be seen at several cairns (SUT 18, 33, 63, 66), and capstones *in situ* may occasionally be observed at cairns elsewhere (e.g. CAT 13).

4.14) The main chamber at The Ord North (SUT 48) is larger than that at Achaidh (SUT 2), and the corbelled walls remained 3 m high at the time of excavation. As at a number of unexcavated chambers, the interior was found to be filled with dislodged corbel stones, and with these in place the original height of the roof may be estimated as about 4 m, covering an area of 3.4 by 3.2 m. When the main chamber of Skelpick Long (SUT 53) was more complete the roof height was estimated as having been 3 m. There is additional imprecise information from the small main chambers at Kinbrace Burn and Loch Borralan East (SUT 33, 43) where the walls stand 1.82 and 1.75 m high, and thus the roof height is likely to have been over 2 m and probably nearer 3 m; it may be noted that the roof of the small main chamber at Lothbeg (SUT 45) was said to be about 2.3 m high. The upper surfaces of the corbel stones exposed at Skelpick South (SUT 55) are estimated to be about 2.6 above ground level, and the roof must have been somewhat higher over what is evidently a large chamber. At several cairns (SUT 42, 55, 72, 81, 82) only the corbelled upper part of the chamber can be partially seen, and of these Loch Awe (SUT 42) is unusual. The cairn material has been pulled away from one side of the main chamber, and amongst the lithic chaos beside the inner portal stone there are exposed the outer ends of stacked corbel stones. These are long, almost square-sectioned quarried blocks lying radially side by side, in two or three rows vertically, and tilted down from the hidden chamber; they are mostly about 1.5 m long by 0.4 m wide and thick. The use of blocks of this shape, evidently for the lower part of the vault, has not been observed elsewhere. Adjacent to them and mostly at a higher level there are two or three layers of the usual flat corbel stones, used for the higher part of the vault.

4.15) In general portal stones were well paired, though seldom exactly the same height, and either eke-stones, or corbel stones incorporated into the wall, were necessary to bring them to the same level. Eke-stones remain over many portal stones, and sometimes (as at SUT 48 and 58) they were used over both stones to increase the height of the lintel they bore. Portal stones are quite frequently boulders rather than split slabs, and they often survive intact; occasionally long split slabs extending back into the cairn were used, notable examples being 1.34 and over 1.52 m long at SUT 36 and 70. Some portal stones have clearly been chosen for their substantial form and horizontal upper surface, but with others this does not seem to have been a consideration; the contrast between a massive boulder and a thin slab is particularly striking at Strathseasgaich (SUT 73). The outer portal stones usually project from the chamber walls to reduce the widths of the entries into the chambers to between 0.55 and 0.7 m, the extremes being 0.44 m at SUT 58 and 0.8 m at SUT 37 and 53. The widths of the entries from the ante-chambers to main chambers, between the inner portal stones, are similar, though increasing to a maximum of 1.06 m at SUT 53. The heights of entries are seldom known exactly, as either the original floor level is uncertain or no lintel survives, and the portal stones, even if intact, only give a minimum height because eke-stones may have been used. Probably the outer entries were generally about 1 m high, and the inner entries were generally a little more. At Skelpick Long (SUT 53) the heights of the two entries are a little over 0.86 and 1.4 m, and at The Ord North (SUT 48) the heights are 1.3 m and a little more; the outer entries at Achaidh and Allt nam Ban (SUT 2, 6) are 1.2 m high, and portal stones allow the inner entries at Allt nam Ban and Loch Borralan West (SUT 44) to be estimated as at least 1.6 and 1.22 m high. A progression from low portal stones at the entry to the passage to relatively tall portal stones at the entry to the main chamber is well displayed at the denuded chambers of Badnabay and The Ord South (SUT 10, 49), and, though less obvious where roofing survives, a progression can also be noted at Skelpick Long and Torboll (SUT 58).

4.16) The lintels over the outer and inner portal stones, and also those over cell portal stones, were the most important for the stability of the chamber, as they carried the wall and vault over a void. These major lintels at small chambers may be as little as 1 m long, and exceptionally only 0.15 m thick at SUT 58 (where it has cracked), but about 1.7 m long by 0.4 to 0.7 m thick is more usual. Regular-shaped blocks of stone were not always obtainable; the lintel over the outer entry at Skelpick Long presents an impressive triangular face to the chamber. The design of Skelpick-type chambers, with both the ante-chamber and the main chamber vaulted, created particular structural difficulties where the two vaults coalesced above the inner lintel. The two largest known lintels occur in this position: they measure about 3 by 1 by 0.35 m, and formerly 3.35 by 1 by 0.53 m, at Skelpick Long and Cnoc Chaornaidh South-east (SUT 53, 70). The lintels over the inner entries at Lothbeg and Loch Awe (SUT 45, 42) have relatively thin rectangular

THE PASSAGES AND CHAMBERS 25

junction of the vaults was contrived. Certainly corbel stones round the chamber walls formed an open figure-of-eight plan with the lowest courses butting against the vertical faces of the inner lintel. After a number of courses the chamber walls/roofing would reach a point where the two sides met over the lintel. It might then be possible to place an elongated slab along the axis of the chamber to form the base of the short stretch of the vaults which passed over the centre of the lintel.

Single-compartment chambers (figure 6)

4.17) Only two small chambers are certainly of the simple single-compartment type, for it is just possible that other chambers included here may have a hidden ante-chamber, and another chamber (SUT 8) which could have been included is mentioned later in ¶ 4.22. The excavated, but greatly ruined, north chamber at Embo (SUT 63) (figure 8, *8*) was small, roughly 1.1 by 2 m, and irregular in plan. The orthostats were under 1 m high, though the roof was probably higher than the small scale of the structure suggests. The similar small north chamber at Camster Long (CAT 12) was roofed by a corbelled vault with a height of 2 m. The partly exposed small chamber at Allt a' Chaoruinn

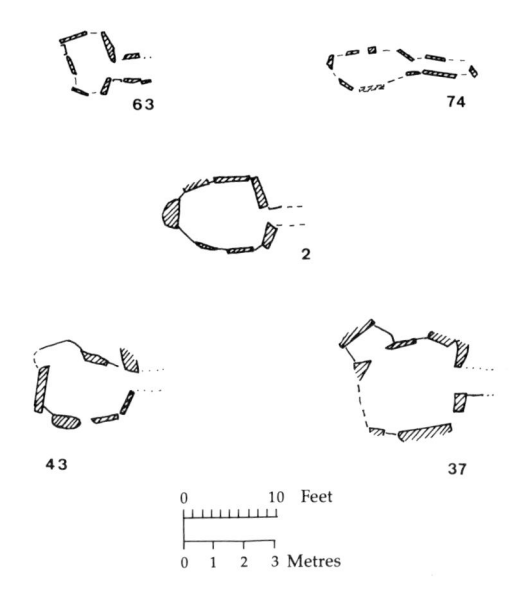

FIGURE 6. Plans of single-compartment chambers.

cross-sections and are set on their long sides so that they are 1.18 and 0.85 m deep by 0.4 and 0.25 thick; two more examples of a lintel placed on the side rather than flat can be partly seen at Creag nan Caorach West and Traligill (SUT 25, 82). Setting lintels in this way increased their strength, and also reduced the vertical height to be provided by corbel stones, but presumably at the expense of stability. As no Skelpick-type chamber roof is intact it is not known how the

PLATE 5. Kyleoag (SUT 37), the cell (metric scale).

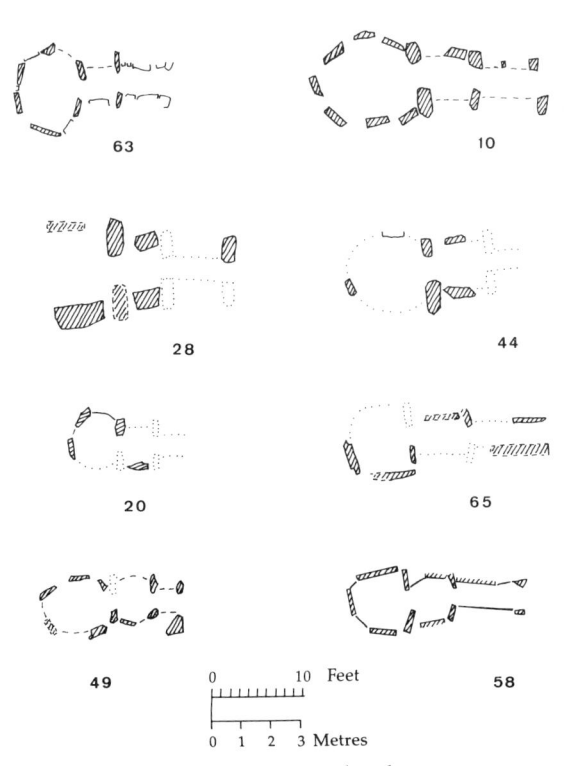

FIGURE 7. Plans of Caithness-type chambers.

26 THE PASSAGES AND CHAMBERS

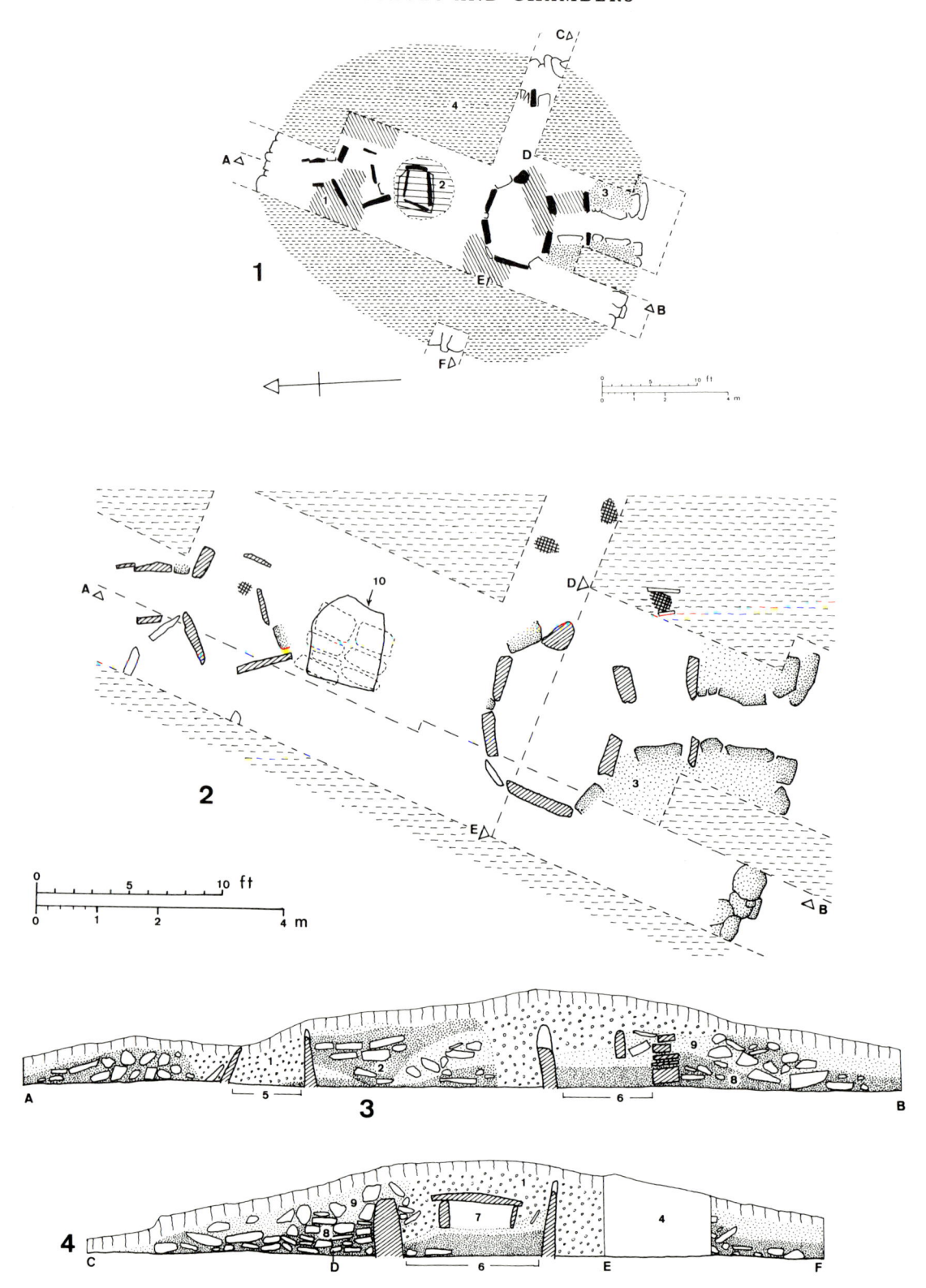

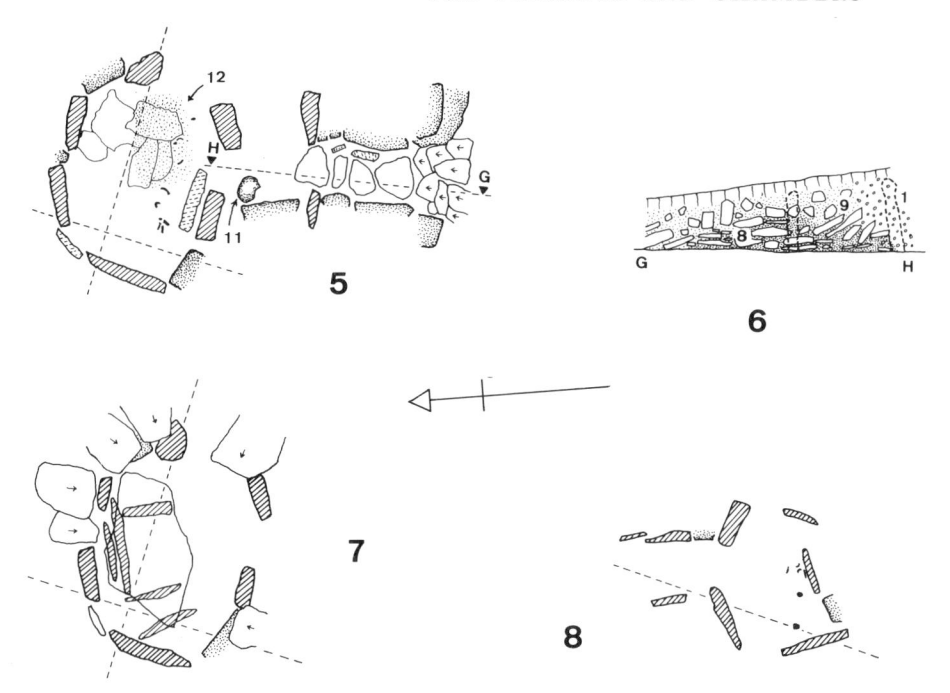

Key:
1 recent disturbance
2 hollow made for the cist
3 area not excavated to ground level
4 unexcavated
5 north chamber
6 south chamber
7 cist in south chamber
8 dark gravelly soil
9 sand
10 cist capstone with slabs over
11 skull
12 charcoal
Bones shown black, cremations cross-hatched.

FIGURE 8. Embo (SUT 63). *1* The cairn, showing the excavated area and the areas of disturbance at ground level; *2* The central area of the excavation; *3* Section A–B; *4* Section C–D–E–F; *5* Plan of the south chamber at floor level, with the passage blocking; *6* Section G–H (the W portal stones projected); *7* Plan of the south chamber and cist at about 0.5 m above ground level, the lowest course of corbel stones superimposed (arrows indicate upward tilt); *8* Plan of the north chamber.

(SUT 74) has a more regular elongated plan with a back-slab 1.6 m high, and this vault also was probably about 2 m high. The entrances to both chambers were between splayed orthostats, not the characteristic paired portal stones.

4.18) At Achaidh (SUT 2) the chamber, but not the passage, was excavated. The inner end of the passage, said to be 0.6 m wide, can be seen from the chamber, with one wall forward of the end of the adjacent portal stone. It thus seems highly probable that the chamber is of the single-compartment plan. The entry is about 1.2 m high, between a pair of portal stones and beneath an impressive lintel. The chamber is regular in plan and larger than those mentioned above, 2.7 by 2.1 m, and the tallest orthostat is the back-slab set across the axis. The vault, already described ¶ 4.13, rose to a height of about 2.2 m. The nearby chamber of Kyleoag (SUT 37) appears to be of one compartment as the walling of the inner end of the passage is just visible, though the possibility has to be considered that the walling belongs to an unusually narrow ante-chamber such as that at the S chamber at Embo (SUT 63). The Kyleoag chamber is large, 3 by 2.7 m, and less regular in plan than Achaidh, and it has a cell entered from the right inner corner. The entry to the cell is between two orthostats, and had it been walled up it would not have been readily detectable. The cell is roughly rectangular, 0.7 from front to back by 1.3 m wide, built with an orthostat at the back and walling along the sides. It is roofed by walling oversailing from above the top of the back-slab to butt against a lintel across the front, at a height somewhat over 1.4 m (plate 5). The Loch Borralan East chamber (SUT 43) is included here as the plan resembles Kyleoag, but the passage is only indicated by displaced lintels, certainly allowing the possibility of a hidden low-roofed ante-chamber. The well-preserved chamber is the same size as Achaidh, with a somewhat larger cell than that at Kyleoag. In this case the cell is built entirely of walling and is roofed by oversailing corbel stones. The entry to the cell was said to have been 'marked off by a double line of flat slabs, partially superimposed', possibly the last remnants of walling which once closed the entrance.

Bipartite chambers of Caithness type (figure 7)

4.19) Bipartite chambers, consisting of an ante-chamber and a vaulted main chamber, are of two types, distinguished by the method of roofing the ante-chamber, which in turn affected the ground plan. In chambers of Caithness type the ante-chambers were little more than slightly enlarged extensions of the passage, approached between the outer portal stones and terminating at the inner portal stones which formed the entry to the main chamber. The ante-chambers were generally roughly rectangular in plan and only slightly wider than the passages; the side walls hid all but the projecting ends of both pairs of portal stones. None of these ante-chambers retains its roof, but there can be little doubt that the passage lintels were continued at a relatively low level up to the inner portal stones. This arrangement can be seen at several bipartite and tripartite chambers in Caithness (Davidson and Henshall 1991, 23,) and at the tripartite chamber at Kinbrace Burn (SUT 33, ¶ 4.27). The contrast between the Caithness-type plan with its small square ante-chamber, as at the south chamber at Embo (SUT 63), and the Skelpick-type plan with its larger oval ante-chamber which is known to have been vaulted, as at Skelpick Long (SUT 53), makes the point that there is a real difference, and that the former type was not vaulted.

4.20) The ante-chamber of the Embo south chamber (SUT 63) is only about 1 m square, with straight sides built of walling (figure 8, *2*). At Badnabay (SUT 10) the ante-chamber is about 1.4 m square, with an orthostat in the surviving wall. In both cases the main chamber is oval and, compared to the ante-chambers, relatively large, 2.3 by 1.9 and 3 by 2.6 m. The main chamber at Embo is unusual in having the long axis at right angles to the axis of the passage. The chamber was built with the inner portal stones forming part of the chamber walls, together with four spaced orthostats. It was tentatively suggested that a puzzling gap in the wall at the inner left corner might have been the entry to a destroyed cell, perhaps similar to that at Kyleoag (SUT 37). The Badnabay main chamber has a regular plan with seven orthostats, and with the walls butting against the portal stones. All the portal stones are boulders contrasting with the taller quarried slabs used in the main chamber; at Embo all but one of the orthostats (a pillar-like boulder) are sandstone slabs. In both chambers the tallest orthostat is somewhat over 1 m high.

4.21) At Evelix the chamber (SUT 28) was built of massive blocks, the largest 1.65 by 0.8 m and 1.2 m high. The preferred interpretation of the remains (already discussed ¶ 4.7) suggests a rectangular ante-chamber about 1.25 m long by 1.35 m wide, with a rectangular main chamber about 2.3 m wide and over 2 m long. If this is accepted, then the chamber must be of Caithness type. The chambers at Cnoc an Daimh, Loch Borralan West and Kinbrace Farm (SUT 20, 44, 65) are also likely to be of this type, but they are only partially visible. Cnoc an Daimh is very small with the main chamber only 1.55 m in diameter; outside it, amongst a mass of loose stones, is a single orthostat which is difficult to explain other than as the side of a rectangular ante-chamber. At Loch Borralan West, too, only a few orthostats can be seen, because the passage and outer portal stones have been removed and the main chamber is largely covered by cairn material. The visible orthostats appear to belong to a rectangular ante-chamber 1.4 m wide and of uncertain length, and the main chamber is almost certainly polygonal. The shattered stumps of a few orthostats at Kinbrace Farm evidently belong to a chamber of unusual proportions. The rectangular ante-chamber is long and narrow, suitable for a lintelled roof; the probably D-shaped main chamber is the same length, 1.8 m, but wider.

4.22) The chamber at Torboll (SUT 58) is more complete. The walls of the ante-chamber stood over 1.1 m high in 1957, and the walls of the main chamber somewhat higher. In overall size the chamber is much the same as those at Embo and Kinbrace Farm (SUT 63, 65), but it differs in the irregular plan of the ante-chamber. Both the outer and inner portal stones are set skew to the axis, and one side of the ante-chamber is concave in plan with walling masking the adjacent inner portal stone; the other side is more nearly rectangular. The main chamber is D-shaped, similar in size and shape to Kinbrace Farm; the walls consist of the inner portal stones and three more orthostats. There is no reason to doubt that the ante-chamber was roofed by lintels as the width is only 1.35 m, and parallels for its non-rectangular plan exist at Kinbrace Burn (SUT 33) and in Caithness. It is probable that the first of the missing lintels overlapped the upper surface of the existing inner passage lintel, and that one more overlapping lintel completed the ante-chamber roof. The ruined chamber at The Ord South (SUT 49) may have been similar with a low-roofed ante-chamber of irregular plan, and an oval main

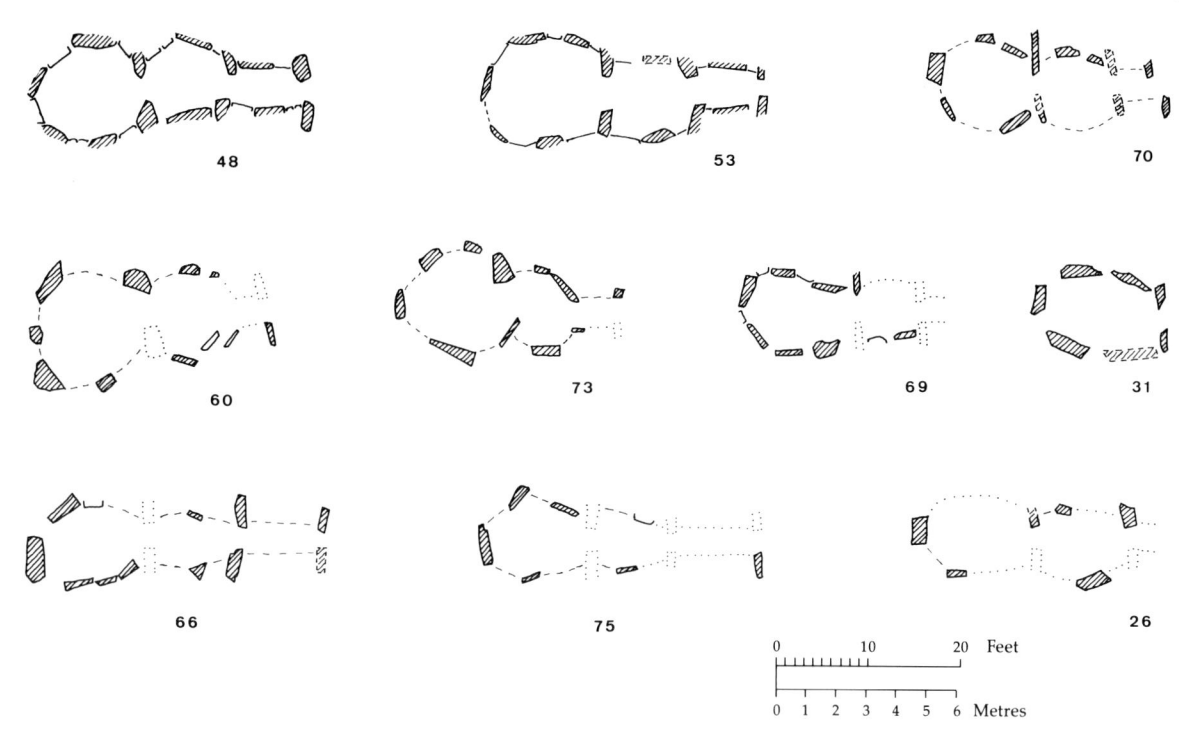

FIGURE 9. Plans of Skelpick-type chambers.

chamber. A small polygonal chamber with remains of a substantial vault at Allt Sgaithaig (SUT 8) is close in size to the main chamber at both The Ord South and Cnoc an Daimh (SUT 20), but it is uncertain whether it is of Caithness type or a single-compartment chamber.

Bipartite chambers of Skelpick type (figure 9)

4.23) The Skelpick-type chambers are distinguished by their relatively large ante-chambers which were vaulted. The chambers are consistently large overall, their lengths varying between 6.7 and 5.6 m (SUT 53, 73) compared with 5 to 3 m among the Caithness-type chambers. Two relatively well-preserved chambers, Skelpick Long and The Ord North (SUT 53, 48), are closely similar in size and proportions (figure 10, plate 6). The entries from the passage are 0.86 and 1.3 m high, beneath large lintels. The ante-chambers are about 2.6 m long by about 2.4 m wide, but somewhat asymmetrical in plan with one side straight and one concave. There is an orthostat in each wall, a little over 1 m high, and above them the oversailing corbelled walls remain to 1.7 m high at Skelpick Long, and to 2.4 m high at The Ord North; at the latter it can be estimated that the vault was closed at a height of not less than 3 m. At Skelpick Long the entry to the main chamber is unusually spacious, 1.06 m wide by about 1.4 m high, spanned by one of the largest lintels recorded; at The Ord North the entry was about the same height and 0.6 m wide, and the lintel was displaced and broken. The main chambers are polygonal and virtually round in plan, at Skelpick Long 3.5 m long by about 3.25 m wide and marginally smaller at The Ord North. Respectively, they are built with four and five orthostats up to 1.22 and to 1.5 m high (with the exception of one orthostat 2 m high at The Ord North), and the walls stand to up to 1.7 m high at Skelpick Long and up to 3 m high at The Ord North; the roof height is likely to have been about 4 m. The exceptionally tall orthostat at the back of the chamber at The Ord North is off centre, but it is the only orthostat which is visible from the passage entrance, and it is a quarried slab with a flat surface contrasting with the boulder orthostats. It is also exceptional in that above ground level the walling linking it to the adjacent orthostats does not butt against the sides, as happens elsewhere in the chamber, but passes behind it. The excavator had no opportunity to investigate behind the tall orthostat, which would have entailed the removal of a huge amount of cairn material. However, he speculated in his notebook that

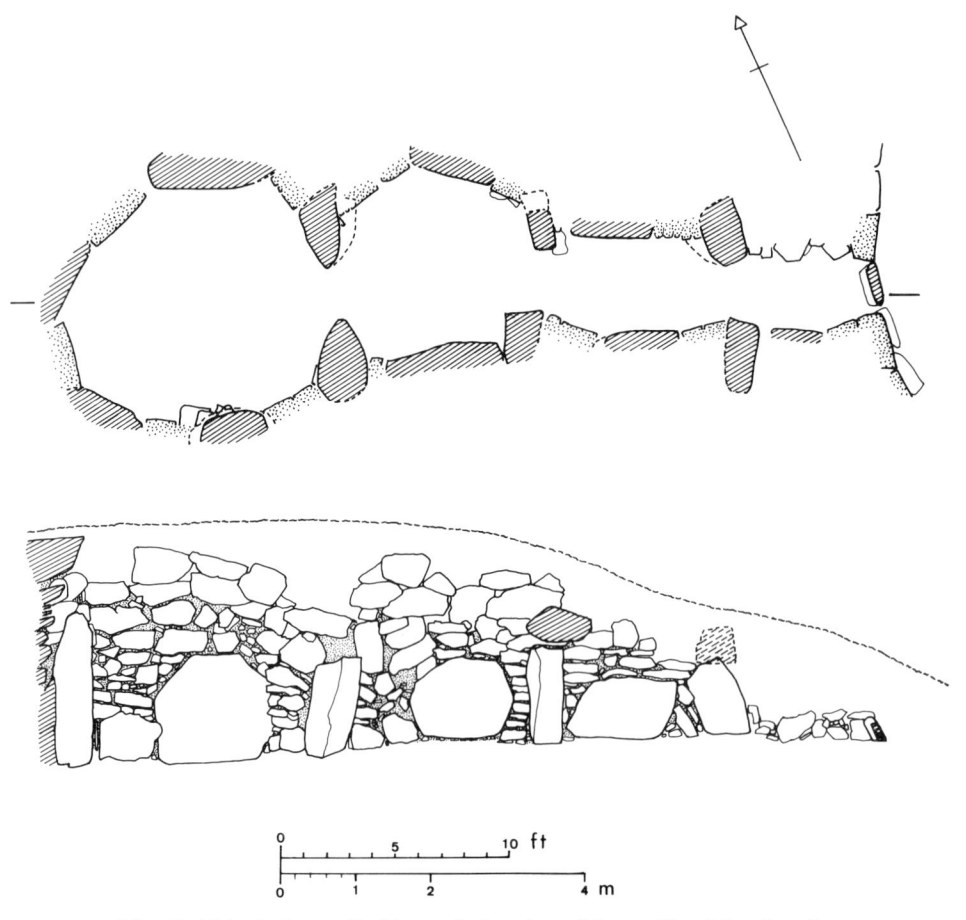

FIGURE 10. The Ord North (SUT 48). Plan and elevation of the N side of the chamber and passage (redrawn from Corcoran 1967a, SUD 115/5, 115/4).

the orthostat might conceal a feature, possibly a cell, but later he felt that this was unlikely (Corcoran 1967a, 29th and 30th August). Nonetheless, this orthostat does seem to have special significance: apart from anything else, it is the tallest recorded among the Sutherland chambers.

4.24) Five more chambers, now reduced to a setting of orthostats projecting from the last remains of their cairns, are clearly of Skelpick type. Cnoc na Moine, Cnoc Chaornaidh South-east and Strathseasgaich (SUT 60, 70, 73) have almost round main chambers, and, as far as can be seen, almost round ante-chambers. At Ledbeg (SUT 66) both the ante-chamber and the main chamber are evidently oval in plan with widths of only 1.66 and 2.5 m, and it is unfortunate that the exact position of the inner portal stones is not known. Cnoc Chaornaidh North-west (SUT 69) similarly has an oval main chamber with some corbel stones surviving, and the ante-chamber has one straight wall but the other wall is not visible.

The tallest orthostats at these last two chambers are about 1.7 m high. Two more chambers, Benmore Forest and Druim Liath (SUT 75, 26), appear to have been of the Skelpick type with relatively narrow proportions, but though a considerable amount of each survives, they are at present mainly obscured. The former is chiefly notable for the very large lintel lying slightly displaced over the hidden inner portal stones. A tenth chamber, Loch Awe (SUT 42), is almost completely concealed within a high cairn, but is probably of Skelpick type. There appears to be an ante-chamber 1.75 m wide and over 2 m long, with (like Benmore Forest) a large lintel over hidden inner portal stones. The indications are that the main chamber is over 3 m in diameter, and its substantially intact corbelling has been mentioned already (¶ 4.14). On the basis of brief descriptions it can be tentatively suggested that the totally ruined chamber at Skelpick Round (SUT 54) was of Skelpick type.

PLATE 6. The Ord North (SUT 48), the chamber from the SE after excavation in 1967 (scales in feet).

Unclassified bipartite chambers (figure 11)

4.25) At Invershin (SUT 31) orthostats define an oval chamber 3.9 m long by 2.27 m wide (figure 9). Regrettably, nothing remains of the passage or of an ante-chamber, so there is the theoretical possibility that this was a single-compartment chamber. But it is the equal for size of the main chambers of Skelpick type and is of almost the same dimensions as that at Cnoc Chaornaidh North-west (SUT 69), and it is nearly 1 m longer than the largest main chamber certainly of Caithness type (SUT 10). It would be reasonable to expect that the design of some chambers was intermediate between the Caithness and Skelpick types if the latter developed from the former. The little that remains of the Kinloch chamber (SUT 36) again suggests the Skelpick-type plan; the main chamber is of virtually the same dimensions as

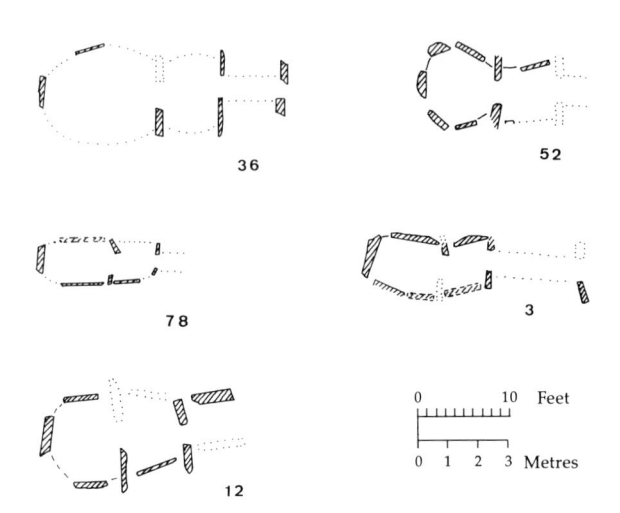

FIGURE 11. Plans of unclassified bipartite chambers.

Skelpick Long (SUT 53) but the ante-chamber is proportionately rather short. It is only half the length of the main chamber, whereas at Skelpick-type chambers where the relative lengths of the ante-chamber and main chamber are known, the former is two-thirds or three-quarters the length of the latter. Skail (SUT 52) consists of a well-built polygonal chamber of moderate size, but the partly destroyed ante-chamber is unexpectedly large and its plan is unclear.

4.26) The plan of the Achany chamber (SUT 3) is fully revealed and can be regarded as a version of the Caithness-type chamber. Achany is unusual in the main chamber being rectangular, and the ante-chamber axis being skew to that of the main chamber. The Craig a' Bhlair chamber (SUT 78), of which less can be seen, is similar in size and in its long narrow proportions, but has a straight axis. While their ante-chambers were probably roofed by lintels, the precise method of roofing the main chambers is uncertain. The seven orthostats which alone remain of the Benbhraggie Wood chamber (SUT 12) give the impression of a huge oval chamber divided in half by transverse slabs, but if the span is considered realistically they have to be interpreted more conventionally as inner portal stones between a large ante-chamber and a D-shaped main chamber. The plan cannot be exactly paralleled, and the roofing of the two parts must have entailed considerable corbelling, but again the precise arrangement is uncertain. From the little that is known of the Lothbeg chamber (SUT 45), it is concluded that it was bipartite and probably of Caithness type, about 4 m long.

Tripartite chambers (figure 12)

4.27) The tripartite chambers are distinguished by having three pairs of transverse slabs, and usually also a back-slab, but the relative lengths of the three compartments of the chamber are variable, reflecting differing roofing patterns, and the overall lengths of the chambers range from 4.26 to 5.17 m. The relatively small chamber at Kinbrace Burn (SUT 33), when seen in 1957, retained much of the roof, but the chamber was subsequently filled in. There is a small ante-chamber 1 m long, with the side walls concave and largely masking the outer and especially the inner portal stones; both pairs of stones are skew to the axis. The five lintels roofing the passage and ante-chamber are laid side by side, not overlapping, and rise gently from the outer to the inner end. The vaulted almost round main chamber has a small orthostat in each wall, but it is mainly built of dry walling (plate 7). The main chamber is 2.28 m wide and would be almost the same length if it were not for the cell portal stones at the rear which are parallel with the inner portal stones and so skew to the axis. The lintels over the entries to the cell and to the main chamber have cracked, but in 1957 both still bore the circular vault which stood to 1.82 m high above debris on the floor. The cell is aligned on the axis and is reached through an entry 0.5 m wide and of uncertain height, but lower than the entry into the main chamber. The cell is 0.76 m from front to back by 1.3 m wide, with walling linking the portal stones to the back-slab. The lintel

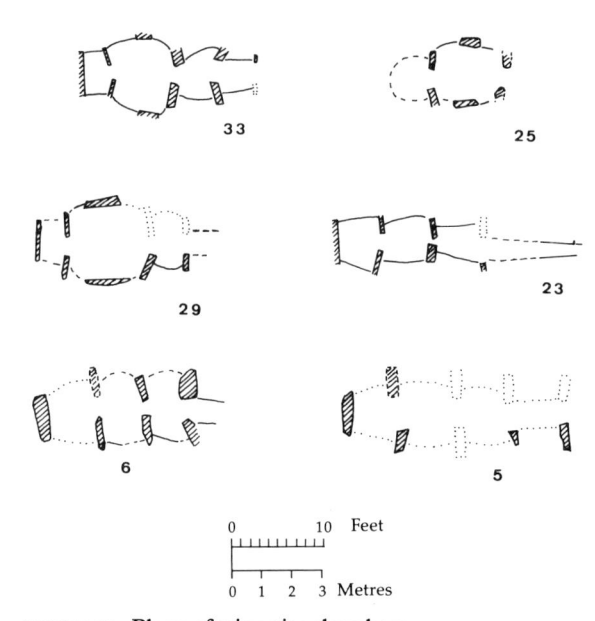

FIGURE 12. Plans of tripartite chambers.

PLATE 7. Kinbrace Burn (SUT 33), the main compartment of the tripartite chamber with the entrance to the ante-chamber on the left, photographed in 1957 (scale in feet).

over the entry forms part of the roof, which is completed by a second lintel partly supported by the back-slab. The chamber resembles the bipartite Caithness-type chambers, particularly that at Torboll (SUT 58), with the addition of a cell like that at Kyleoag (SUT 37) aligned on the axis.

4.28) The chamber which is partly exposed at Creag nan Caorach West (SUT 25) appears to have been similar. The area where an ante-chamber is to be expected is covered with loose stones, but the main chamber is largely visible. The cell is roofed at a low level and can be viewed from above; two contiguous roofing slabs lie parallel to the axis, supported by the lintel spanning the cell entry and by two of the semicircle of corbel stones which belong to the cell wall. The Fiscary chamber (SUT 29) (figure 13), now largely concealed beneath displaced cairn material, is a somewhat larger version of the same plan. One side of the small ante-chamber can be seen, and beyond is the main chamber measuring about 2.36 m long by about 2.3 m wide, with a large orthostat in each side wall. The cell, between the cell portal stones and a low back-slab, is 0.94 m from front to back and 1.5 m or so wide. In 1891, when the chamber was already ruinous, it was said that the cell 'had the appearance of being covered over with slabs'. It is assumed that the chamber roof was in three parts as at Kinbrace Burn (SUT 33), low over the ante-chamber, vaulted over the main chamber, and low over the cell.

4.29) The plan of the chamber at Allt nam Ban (SUT 6) clearly declares a difference in design. The chamber is slightly shorter than, and about the same width as the widest part of, the chamber at Fiscary (SUT 29), but the substantial transverse slabs are evenly spaced down the chamber. The inner compartment is marginally longer than the others, and the side walls, concave between the orthostats, were roughly parallel though probably they converged towards the back, and they were without orthostats. As only parts of the lower walls survive there is no direct evidence as to the roofing arrangements, but they certainly differed from the Kinbrace Burn pattern. It is probable that the outer compartment was an antechamber, a suggestion supported to some extent by the relatively large size of the first pair of transverse slabs, and that the centre and inner compartments were under one roof, the span of which at 3 by 2.5 m would be less than a number of those built at Skelpick-type chambers. In this case the inner pair of transverse slabs would not have reached to roof height, and would have served only to subdivide the main chamber. The alternative, that the whole of the chamber (4.4 m long) was under one roof, an elongated vault which would have to be closed by several lintels rather than by a single stone, seems very unlikely though not impossible. At Allt a' Mhuilinn (SUT 5), not far from Allt nam Ban, there are the last remains of what has evidently been a large chamber.

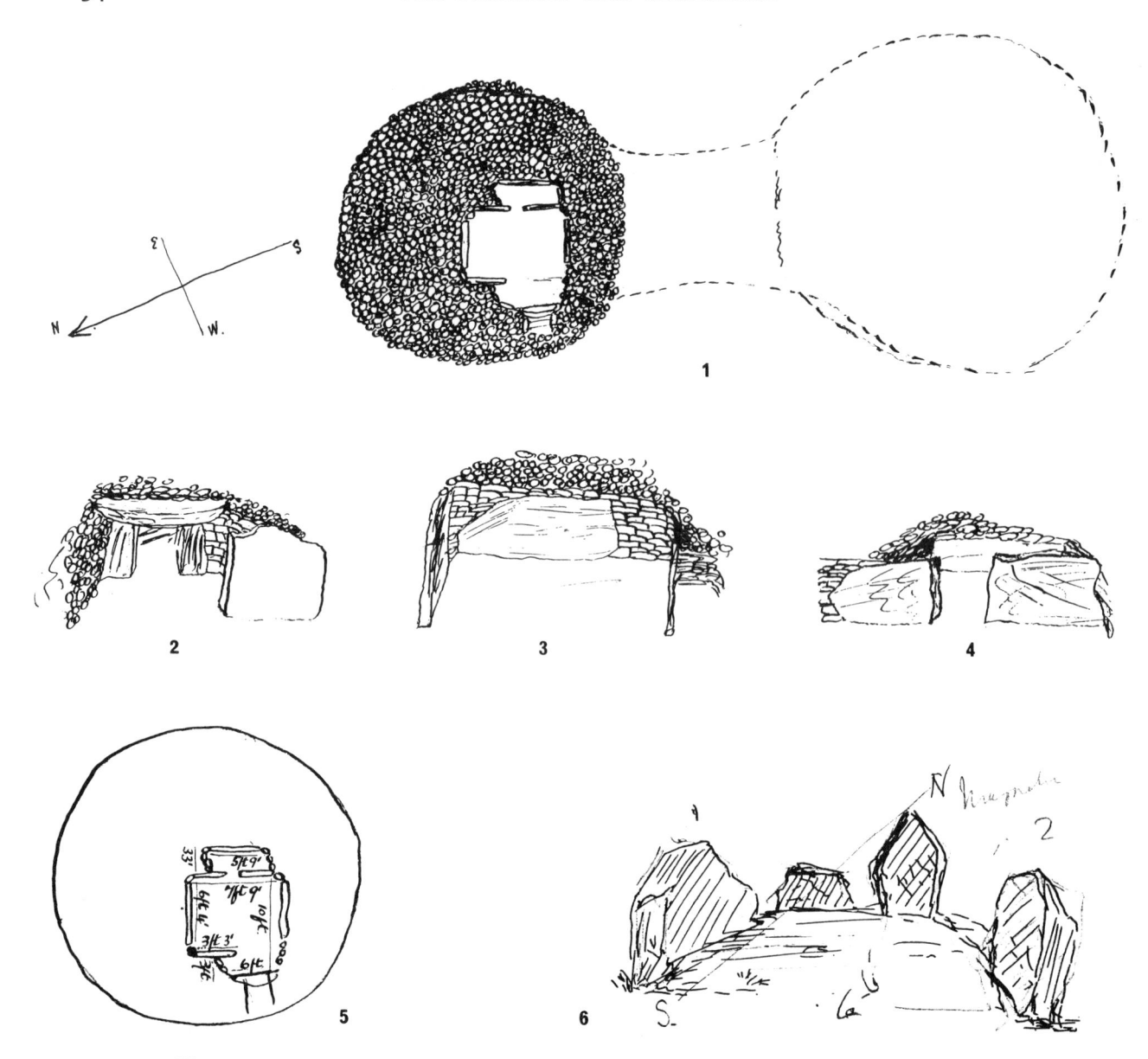

FIGURE 13. *1–5* Fiscary (SUT 29). Sketch plans and views by C. Kerr 1891: *1* plan of the cairn; *2* the entry to the chamber; *3* the N side of the chamber; *4* the back of the chamber; *5* plan of the chamber. *6* Lyne (SUT 46). Sketch of the chamber orthostats by A. O. Curle 1909 (Curle 1909a).

The inner compartment was about the same size as that at Allt nam Ban, and the other two surviving orthostats were probably at the outer end of the passage and at the entry to the chamber (see ¶ 4.7). If so, the chamber was a little over 5 m long, and was probably tripartite with a missing pair of divisional slabs providing compartments of roughly equal length.

4.30) In tripartite chambers the back-slab is an important part of the plan, and at Allt nam Ban and Allt a' Mhuilinn (SUT 6, 5) the back-slabs lean outwards. This might not be considered a deliberate feature were it not for the fact that the back-slabs at three or four polygonal chambers (SUT 22, 31, 43, 73) also lean outwards, and in Caithness and Orkney there are back-slabs and occasionally side-slabs which seem to have been set deliberately at an outward slope (Davidson and Henshall 1989, 19; 1991, 25). In Sutherland a slab set across the axis at the back of a main chamber is a common but not an invariable part of the design, and in most cases it does not seem to have particular significance. It may be the tallest orthostat but is seldom aggressively so (exceptions being SUT 22, 48), and at some chambers it is certainly smaller than adjacent orhostats.

4.31) The chamber at Coille na Borgie South (SUT 23) consists of three compartments all about 1.5 m long, but of varying widths. There is an irregularity in the plan which reflects the treatment of each compartment as a separate unit, but in a different way from at Kinbrace Burn (SUT 33). The Coille na Borgie chamber was well built using shapely quarried orthostats, and it is fairly intact though deterioration of what has been fine walling has led to a certain amount of displacement, and the junction of the passage and chamber is hidden. Only one of the outer pair of transverse slabs is partly visible, and though it carries a lintel it does not project to form a portal. The outer compartment has the appearance of an antechamber, of rather long narrow proportions with walls converging from front to back and almost hiding the transverse slabs at either end. The roofing was by lintels, one of which remains. The axis of this compartment appears to be slightly skew to that of the rest of the chamber. A taller second pair of portal stones, both displaced inwards so that the entry is deceptively narrow, gives access to the middle compartment, also roofed by lintels. It has the appearance of a second rather more spacious ante-chamber. From the entry to the chamber up to the inner end of the second compartment the roof rises from a height of about 0.62 m to about 1.3 m. A third pair of yet taller portal stones form the entry to the inner compartment. This is wider than the others, with the side walls butting against both the portal stones and the back-slab; the walls still stand to 1.63 m high. The two earliest accounts of the chamber, McKay's sketch and reasonably accurate plan of 1867 (figure 18) and Munro's description in 1883, both record an orthostat in each side wall. This is very puzzling as, in spite of the infilling of large stones, it is possible to see the walls to virtually ground level without any sign of orthostats. Munro gave the existing height of the walls as 2.4 m, but his measurements can be unreliable as the height he gave for the middle compartment is certainly an exaggeration. It is unclear whether this compartment was roofed by a continuation of the lintels at a yet higher level, or by a small corbelled vault. The former is certainly possible as long lintels were used, without corbels, for roofing the other compartments, and could have been supplied for this one also.

Unclassified chambers

4.32) Several chambers, reduced to little more than a group of orthostats, are so incomplete that only excavation will reveal their plans. Dun Viden (SUT 27) has been reduced to six orthostats, one of them displaced, which relate to a passage, an ante-chamber, and a large polygonal main chamber 3 m across, but the rear has been removed. The plan suggests a bipartite chamber, but there is the theoretical possibility that there may have been an axial cell. At Coille na Borgie North (SUT 22) there is a polygonal chamber of moderate size and of more conventional plan than the chamber in the adjacent South cairn (SUT 23), but the North chamber is choked with stones and rubbish and it is unknown whether there may be an antechamber. There is the same uncertainty with the polygonal chambers at the more ruined Cnoc Odhar (SUT 21), the almost totally ruined Lyne (SUT 46) (figure 13, 6), and the completely destroyed Pittentrail (SUT 50). All that remains standing at Clashmore (SUT 19) is three orthostats of impressive size, the largest 1.8 by 0.65 m and 1.9 m high, which evidently belong to the back and one side of a chamber at least 5.4 m long. In contrast, the cairns at Skelpick South, Allt Eileag, Loch Borralan South and Traligill (SUT 55, 72, 81, 82) are so little reduced that the plans of the substantially intact chambers which they cover have not been revealed.

Ardvreck

4.33) The chamber at Ardvreck (SUT 9) (figure 14) is unique in Sutherland in that it does not belong to the Orkney-Cromarty group of passage graves but is an outlier of the Clyde group of gallery graves. Chambers of this group were normally entered between portal stones directly from the edge of the cairn, without passages. In general, the rectangular chambers were built with closely fitting slabs forming the lower parts of the walls, and these were given support by transverse slabs which stretched the whole width of the chamber and divided it into two or three compartments. It is characteristic of these chambers that the side slabs were set with their ends overlapping. Roofing was by a row of capstones or lintels resting on corbel stones which increased the wall height. The

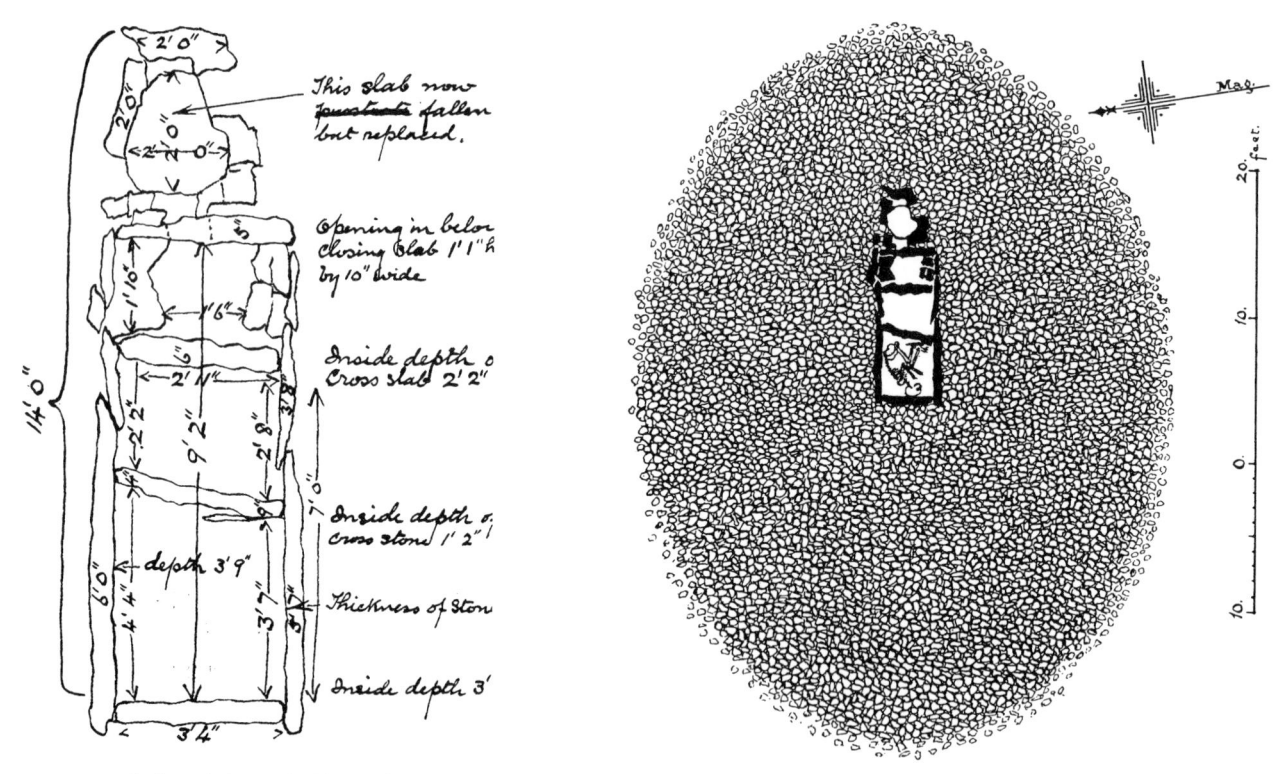

FIGURE 14. Ardvreck (SUT 9). Plans of the chamber and cairn (Cree 1928; Callander and Cree n.d.).

informal report of the hasty excavation of the Ardvreck chamber leaves the arrangement at the entrance to the chamber unclear, but otherwise the chamber can be seen to be typical of its type. The inner part was constructed of three closely fitting slabs of limestone, giving a height of about 1.14 m. The side walls were continued by a pair of less shapely slabs, just overlapping the outer ends of the inner side slabs, and a third pair of small slabs lengthened the chamber to 2.8 m. Two transverse slabs formed two compartments, but the third outer segment of the chamber seems to have suffered interference. The original edge of the cairn and the entrance are to be expected in this area, but instead the excavator found the third segment partially infilled, and outside it a ramshackle collection of stones which he interpreted as a passage. He recorded the cairn as oval, but the present appearance is round with no sign of modern interference, and the outer end of the chamber is roughly 3.3 m within the edge of the cairn. The explanation for this may be deliberate blocking outside the entrance, or that the cairn was enlarged if the inner compartment was indeed used for a later burial as suggested in ¶ 6.17; it is unlikely that the chamber was originally longer.

5. The cairns

The structure of the cairns

5.1) The cairns surrounding the chambers generally seem the least interesting part of the monuments, but their present state disguises the care with which all were built and the complex structural history of some. No cairns in Sutherland have been thoroughly excavated, and at only two, The Ord North and Embo (SUT 48, 63), has there been any considered investigation at all. To understand the Sutherland cairns it is necessary to draw on the information available from the similar cairns in Caithness. A number of these have been partially excavated, and others, because of the more stable building material, can still reflect their former appearance in a way which is lost in Sutherland.

5.2) The cairn material of the Sutherland cairns is the nearest available stone, boulders, cobbles, scree or shattered rock. Very few cairns have entirely escaped interference, often with some resultant distortion of the plans. On the other hand it is not uncommon for the outer margins of cairns, protected by turf or heather, to be left largely undisturbed as rims of cairn material whilst the bare loose stone of the interiors was removed or built into small structures such as bothies or lambing pens. When we recorded the cairns the outermost visible limit of the cairn material was taken (unless it has obviously been spread in relatively modern times), but this is likely to be outside the edge of the cairn as it was designed. Disintegration of the structure of the cairns, and particularly the collapse of confining wall-faces, will have allowed the spread of cairn material until it found its natural angle of rest, generally some 1.5 to 3 m beyond the original limits. Many cairns are in areas of peat-based moorland, and in these situations the gradual growth of peat may cover the outer spread of the cairn material, and sometimes may even have brought the visible edge close to the position of the designed edge. A few cairns were built on quite steep slopes and this sort of situation is likely to cause distortion of the plan, as cairn material tends to spread down the slope on one side, and on the opposite side, due to the damming effect of the cairn, the edge tends to be covered by either a differential growth of peat or by hillwash (plate 8). The heights of cairns have normally been taken from present ground level outside the passage entrances (the passages and chambers being built on a level base, along the contour on sloping sites); these vertical measurements are no more than indications of the remaining amounts of cairn material because the difference between the present and the old ground surfaces is seldom precisely known.

5.3) It may be assumed that all the cairns were edged by a retaining wall-face though these can seldom be seen. Parts of wall-faces have been exposed at the excavated cairns (SUT 48, 63) (plate 9) and their presence can be traced at the two Coille na Borgie cairns (SUT 22, 23), but otherwise there is only a short stretch of rough wall-face visible in the side of the cairn at Loch Awe (SUT 42), and occasional kerbstones (presumably part of the base course) at a few other cairns (SUT 3, 4, 55). At the heart of each cairn (except at some long cairns) was a compact core of carefully-laid stones designed to give stability to the walls of the chamber and particularly to provide the counterbalance on the oversailing corbel stones (see ¶ 4.12). This core, which need be no more than 2 to 3 m in width, was an essential part of the chamber structure and was built progressively with it, as explained in detail by Barber in his study of the corbelled vaults built of sandstone slabs in Orkney and Caithness (1992, 16–25). Whilst the cairn cores have been observed at a number of cairns in these areas, only a small part of one has been seen in Sutherland (at Embo, SUT 63). The rest of the cairn, between the core and the retaining wall-face, was of looser construction and of irregular or rounded stones.

5.4) The cairns, according to their ground plans, are of four types. The greatest number are round, a few are heel-shaped or short horned, and some are long (figures 15, 16). Whilst cairns in the last category are easily recognised, there are sometimes difficulties in distinguishing the cairns of the other three categories.

Round cairns

5.5) The round cairns, in their present state, are mostly featureless except for the chamber placed centrally within them. They vary greatly in size, from those with diameters of 10 or 11 m to nearly three times as large. The smallest cairns tend to contain small chambers, as at Cnoc an Daimh and Allt Sgaithaig (SUT 20, 8), but it is perhaps surprising that

PLATE 8. Creag nan Caorach West (SUT 25) from the E.

a few small cairns contain large chambers. The site of Dun Viden (SUT 27) would have allowed a cairn only about 11.5 m in diameter over a chamber about 3.2 m wide. The cairns at Cnoc Chaornaidh and Strathseasgaich (SUT 70, 73) with diameters of 14 and 15 m, and probably less when built, contain large Skelpick-type chambers. It can be calculated that the width of the cairn around these chambers was less than 4.5 m, over half of which would be cairn core, and the height of the cairn must have been about 4 m to cover the roof. The outer wall-face retaining such a cairn can hardly have been less than 1.6 m high. About thirteen cairns have diameters of 15 m or less. The cairn at Allt nam Ban (SUT 6) is exceptional in being oval, measuring 16 by 14 m, extended along the axis of this long chamber. The short lengths of many passages, some only 1.5 m long, or even 1 m long at one small chamber (SUT 49), confirm that small cairns were quite normal, not much larger than was required to enclose the cairn core with the chamber central to the whole construction. To cover the passage lintels and incorporate the outermost lintel into the bounding wall-face again indicates that the wall-face must have been of considerable height, and the cairn must have risen steeply within it to cover the chamber. About seventeen cairns are somewhat larger with diameters between 16 and 20 m. Only nine cairns extend the size range to 25 m in diameter, and the largest cairns of all, at Skelpick Round and Balcharn (SUT 54, 11), have diameters of 28 to 30 m. It may be suspected that cairns over 20 m in diameter have been enlarged, by excessive natural spread (as at SUT 7, 12, and at 28 where the chamber is not central), or by later structural additions (as at SUT 48 and 3 described below). The most complete cairns, such as SUT 35, 42, and 58, are still 3 to 4 m high.

5.6) The Ord North (SUT 48) is one of the finest steep-sided cairns (plate 16). It is round except for a flattening on the side which contains the entrance, and a slight concavity at the entrance itself (figure 15). The cairn was edged by a wall-face which was never more than 1 m high; larger cairns can be retained by lower walls. The cairn diameters defined by the wall-face were 22 to 26 m, and displaced cairn material extended about 1.5 m outside it. The cairn must have been over 4 m high originally, to cover the chamber roof. It has already been suggested that the outer part of the passage is an extension of the original passage (¶ 4.8), and if so, the outer part of the cairn and the wall-face belong to a second structural phase. Referring to the orthostats which are probably the original entrance portal stones, the excavator wrote in his notebook 'there isn't time to investigate, but I have a suspicion that there may be an inner wall ... extending from [the] orthostats' (Corcoran 1967a, 173). So it may be speculated that the original wall-face bounding the cairn is about 1.6 m behind the recorded wall-face at the entrance, and if the original cairn was truly round, its diameter would be 18 or 19 m.

5.7) At Achany (SUT 3) there is a small forecourt 6.3 m wide, defined by a façade of four orthostats which must once have been linked by walling (figure 15) (¶ 5.31). The forecourt might be compared to the vaguely-defined recessed area at the passage entrance at The Ord North (SUT 48), and the Achany façade

PLATE 9. The Ord North (SUT 48), the cairn wall-face exposed on the SE side of the cairn, the platform partly removed (scales in feet).

too may be part of a secondary enlargement of the cairn. Round cairns which are flattened or slightly inturned at the entrance and lack an orthostatic façade are almost impossible to detect without excavation, especially if, like Achany and The Ord North, there is blocking material outside the entrance (as described in ¶ 6.26–8). Two cairns, Druim Liath and Cnoc na Moine (SUT 26, 60), appear to be flattened on the side with the entrance, but as the first has been much disturbed and the second is greatly reduced, it is no more than a suggestion that they may be similar to The Ord North.

5.8) The cairn at Embo (SUT 63) was exceptional in covering two chambers, built back to back 3.25 m apart, and it was oval, measuring only about 10 by 13 m (figure 8, *1*). Excavation exposed the lower courses of a rough wall-face on each side of the south passage entrance but failed to find any definite edging in restricted investigations elsewhere, possibly due to the greatly reduced state of the cairn. The rewarding part of the excavation was the examination of the cairn around the back of the south chamber. Part of the cairn core was found, consisting of flattish slabs closely laid horizontally in four layers, 0.6 m high, and extending for 2.5 m from the back of the chamber. The interstices of the slabs, and also those between the flat slabs of the chamber walling, were filled with hard dark gravelly soil, which also spread in a thinning layer towards the edge of the cairn. The dark soil, at its maximum reaching 0.7 m high, was a deliberate addition to the structure, presumably intended to consolidate it. According to Johnson (his report in Henshall and Wallace 1963, 26–9) the dark material appeared to have been a surface soil derived largely from sand but in part from gravel, containing plant residues and minute pieces of bone from fish and very small animals (not identified in detail), and it was considered to have come from a marshy place. At the level of the surviving top of the core there were the ritual deposits described in ¶ 6.1. Above this level the character of the core seems to have changed, but for structural reasons the core must have reached almost to roof height. At the time of the excavation the much disturbed cairn above the laid slabs consisted of irregular rounded stones such as were used for the rest of the cairn, and the voids between them had filled with blown sand. Around the north chamber the cairn was too greatly damaged to trace any similar cairn core, nor was there any indication of the chronological relationship of one chamber to the other.

5.9) At The Ord North (SUT 48), after the chamber was no longer in use, a platform was added around the cairn. Stones fallen from the wall-face edging the cairn were covered by the platform, and the blocking outside the passage entrance was incorporated into it. The platform is more likely to have been built at the same time as the blocking than subsequently, as the platform was edged by a kerb of substantial stones with the two largest on the projected axis of the passage; the implication is that the chamber entrance still retained some significance. The kerb is slightly oval, varying in width from about 5 to 7 m and giving overall diameters of 35 to 39 m, with a curious small angular projection to one side. The platform is composed of cobbles and earth and is about 0.5 m high. The cairn of Loch Borralan West (SUT 44) is surrounded by a low platform edged by a kerb with overall diameters of 20.5 to 23 m. The platform is 1.5 to 3 m wide from the present edge of the cairn, but without excavation its true width and its relationship with the cairn are uncertain.

5.10) The cairn at Fiscary (SUT 29) is almost square in plan, and the chamber is considerably off centre. There is no obvious reason for these peculiarities, unlike Clashmore (SUT 19) where the more or less rectangular plan is the result of ploughing parallel to a field fence. Nor is there any indication that the Fiscary cairn was short horned, though cairns of this type can acquire a squarish plan (¶ 5.15). The position of the Fiscary chamber within the cairn strongly suggests that the cairn is not of one period, and that there is likely to be another structure within it to which the chamber may be either primary or secondary. The cairn is only 8.5 m from a larger intact round cairn which may or may not contain a chamber, and which is surrounded by an extensive irregular platform. At

40   THE CAIRNS

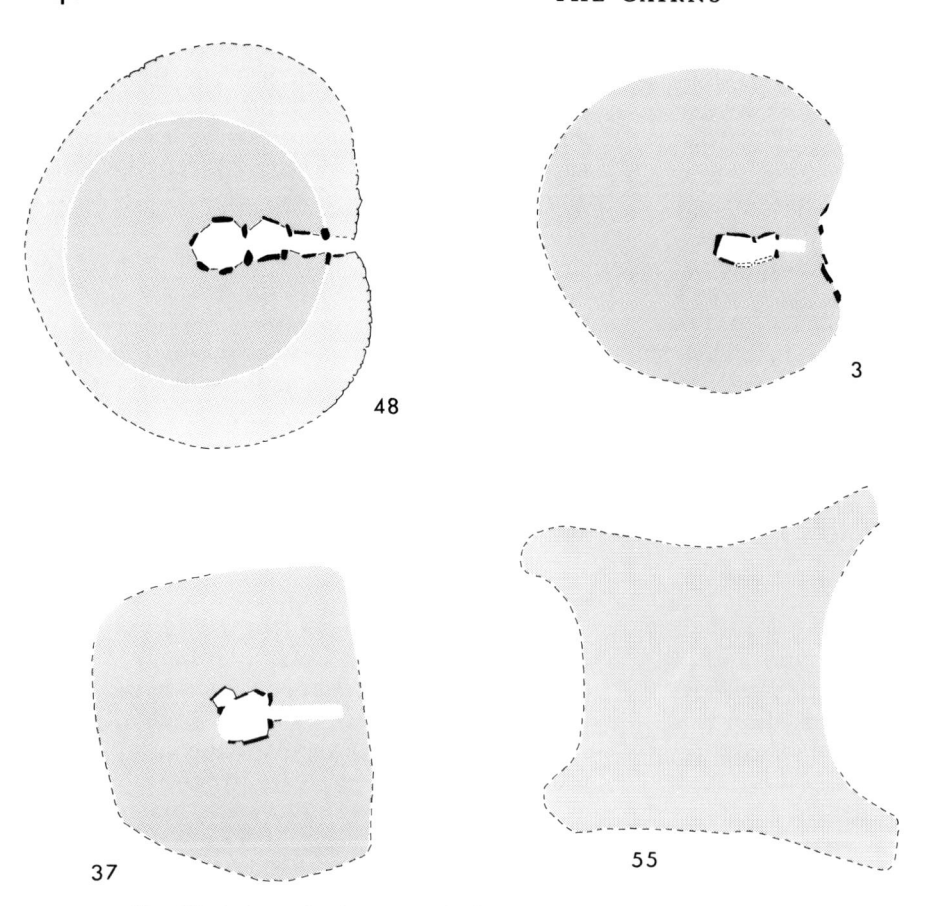

FIGURE 15. Simplified plans of cairns; round cairns with recessed entrances, heel-shaped and short horned cairns.

some time in antiquity the two cairns were linked by a spread of stones. It is obvious that the whole complex has an involved structural history. The cairn at Lothbeg (SUT 45) tends towards a square plan without any hint that the edge has been distorted, and its apparent shape is puzzling.

Heel-shaped cairns (figure 15)

5.11) Heel-shaped cairns are distinguished from round chambered cairns by a wide façade stretching symmetrically from either side of the passage entrance. The façade is either straight or slightly concave in plan, with the ends projecting from the body of the cairn and joining the wall-face around the rest of the cairn at a sharp angle. This plan differs from that of those round cairns with a relatively short façade formed by either flattening the curve of the wall-face around the cairn, or recessing it into the cairn as at The Ord North (SUT 48). In practice the two may be confused when the projecting outer ends of a façade are damaged or covered. The two types of plan are similar in concept, and it is likely that one developed from the other, and that both were embellishments added to simple round cairns. The excavation of Tulach an t-Sionnaich in Caithness (CAT 58) showed that, at this cairn at least, the heel-shaped plan was due to the addition of a relatively low platform to a small round cairn, and that the façade continued unbroken across the passage entrance, effectively sealing it. At other heel-shaped cairns in Caithness the entrance continued to be accessible. The well known cairn Camster Round (CAT 13) is either heel-shaped or round with a flat façade, and the outer end of the accessible passage shows clear signs that it and the façade are additions to the structure. In Caithness it can be seen, too, that heel-shaped cairns were sometimes later incorporated into long cairns (Davidson and Henshall 1991, 40–2, 49–51, 54).

5.12) There are certainly two free-standing heel-shaped cairns in Sutherland. The better preserved, Kyleoag (SUT 37), is about 19 m across the straight front edge, by about 17.5 m from front to back, and is still up to 3 m high; Benmore Forest (SUT 75) is slightly smaller. Cnoc Chaornaidh North-west (SUT 69) may well be heel-shaped, but the cairn has been much reduced, particularly on the side containing the entrance where the edge is difficult to trace; the general shape of the cairn and the slope of the ground suggest that the front edge was either straight or slightly concave. Uniquely in Sutherland, there is a prominent stone 1.6 m wide and high on the edge of the cairn near the back. Four more cairns have formerly been claimed as heel-shaped, but critical re-appraisal in 1993 led to the conclusion that the shape of SUT 18 and 72 is due to interference, the shape of SUT 45 is puzzling (¶ 5.10) and that the supposedly straight or concave edge of SUT 70 simply cannot be traced.

5.13) There are also two heel-shaped cairns which are components of complex long cairns. In each case the heel-shaped cairn is so placed that, although detached from the long cairn, the heel-shaped cairn appears to form the higher wider end of a single monument (see ¶ 5.24). In size and plan these two heel-shaped cairns differ from those just described. At Kinbrace Hill Long (SUT 34) (figure 16) it is very large, 30 m along the axis by over 23 m transversely, and so intact that no chamber structure is visible: the site is sloping and the height at the centre is probably over 4 m. In plan the cairn is almost square with rounded corners. At the slightly wider end, which faces uphill away from the long cairn, there projects a stubby horn 0.5 m high, which evidently defines one side of a forecourt the other side of which is covered by peat. The heel-shaped cairn at Coille na Borgie North (SUT 22) (figure 17) is about 18.5 m along the axis by 17 m wide, and has been considerably disturbed and reduced to under 2 m high. It has had a deep forecourt with orthostats in the façade and also along the straight sides, and the back is rounded in plan. There are reasons for suspecting that the forecourts of both cairns are additions to the heel-shaped plan (see ¶ 5.29).

Short horned cairns (figure 15)

5.14) Cairns of this plan, of which several have been excavated in Caithness, are essentially round cairns with deep forecourts to the front and rear formed by projecting horns. The passage entrance is in the centre of the wider façade. The wall-face of the cairn continues round the square-ended horns which diminish in height towards their tips. Failure to discern horns, as also the tips of façades at heel-shaped cairns, means that more cairns of these plans may await identification. It might be expected that the elaborate exterior of short horned cairns had been added to simple round cairns, but at Tulloch of Assery A (CAT 69), the only example where the cairn has been critically examined, this was not the case and the whole structure appeared to be of unitary design (Corcoran 1966, 22–8).

5.15) Skelpick South (SUT 55) is an impressive example of a short horned cairn, still 3 m high. It is about 15 m along the axis and about 18 m wide, with the clearly visible horns forming forecourts; that at the front is considerably wider than that at the rear. The forecourts are about 19 and 13.5 m across, and both are probably about 3.5 m deep. Achaidh (SUT 2) was probably similar in shape but somewhat smaller. The plan was clearer in 1909 (Curle 1910, 106) when the diameter of the body of the cairn was given as about 15 to 16 m with horns projecting for about 4.8 m. Eighty years later the edges are obscured by heather which particularly affects definition of the horns, and the plan appears to be almost square, though slightly wider across the front than the rear. Dilapidation of short horned cairns tends to produce a square plan by filling the forecourts and concave sides with displaced stone. The greatly ruined cairn at Kinbrace Burn (SUT 33) was clearly short horned in plan, but, owing to peat growth and disturbance, the cairn edge can only be traced along one side with the tip of a horn projecting at each end. The front forecourt was evidently about 6 m deep, but is now completely hidden, in part probably because blocking material was placed outside the passage entrance (see ¶ 4.9, 6.30). Although there is no doubt that the cairn at Creag nan Caorach West (SUT 25) is short horned, the edge is difficult to define precisely due to the encroaching peat.

Long cairns (figure 16)

5.16) All long cairns are wider and, if not robbed, are higher at the front or proximal end than at the rear or distal end. In the N mainland of Scotland there are a few relatively short long cairns which appear to be simple unitary structures, and none of them is known to cover a stone chamber, although as none has been excavated there is no certainty that this is so. In Sutherland the two smallest long cairns, Creag an Amalaidh and Kilournan (SUT 61, 32), are of this type. They are trapezoid in plan, having rounded proximal ends, straight gently converging sides and square or slightly rounded distal ends. The cairns are about 23 and 33 m long, and both are about 13 m wide at the proximal end narrowing to about 9 m wide at

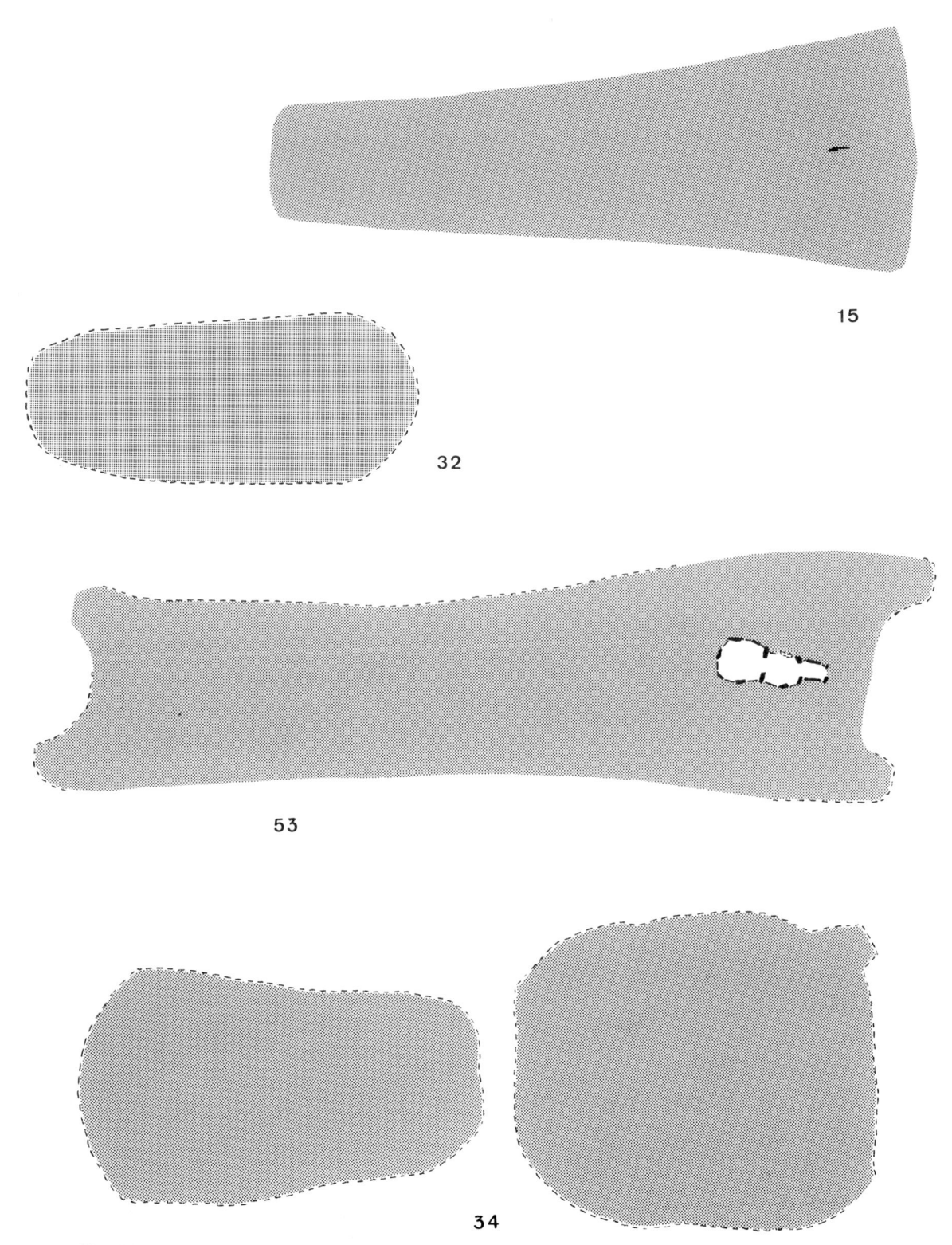

FIGURE 16. Simplified plans of long cairns.

PLATE 10. Caen Burn South (SUT 15) from the NW.

the distal end. Although the cairn material has been disturbed, more so at Creag an Amalaidh, the cairns have not been severely robbed, and Kilournan retains a height of 2.2 m near the proximal end.

5.17) The description and interpretation of the remaining ten long cairns are beset with difficulties. These arise partly from the poor condition of most of the cairns with the consequent obscuring or destruction of diagnostic features, and partly from their composite and almost certainly multi-period character. There is more information available from the comparable long cairns in Caithness, where their external form has been better preserved, and where two (CAT 12, 58) have been well excavated (summarised in Davidson and Henshall 1991, 47–59). Study of the Caithness long cairns has led to appreciation of their complexity and variety rather than to an understanding of the phenomenon of long cairns covering chambers. An example of the multi-period complexity which is likely to be present in seemingly simple ruinous long cairns was revealed by excavation at Tulach an t-Sionnaich (CAT 58) (Corcoran 1966, 5–22). The proximal end consisted of a small round chambered cairn which was later enclosed by a heel-shaped cairn; this was subsequently overlaid by a heel-shaped cairn of slightly different plan; a long low rectangular cairn was added behind the second heel-shaped cairn with a gap left between the two which was partly filled with stones. In its final form this cairn had a 'head-and-tail' shape consisting of a relatively high proximal mound separated from the rest of the long cairn by a transverse hollow. Examination of other long cairns in Caithness has made it clear that most, and possibly all, of the proximal ends contain a chamber, which, with its covering cairn, is likely to be the primary structure; and the primary cairn may have been enlarged and possibly given a façade before being transformed into a long cairn. The 'tails' of the long cairns were a separate element, either rectangular or trapezoid in plan, and were either joined to the proximal mound or extended to encapsulate it. In some cases the long cairn itself may be of more than one period, having been extended or embellished. Long cairns may have horned forecourts, sometimes at both ends, sometimes at the proximal end only, and sometimes (it seems) at the distal end only, and it is uncertain when in the structural sequence these were built. At some long cairns the chambers continued to be accessible, and at some, like Tulach an t-Sionnaich, they were not. A further complication at a few cairns is the presence of a second chamber in the distal end. It is the differing combinations of a selection of these elements, generally largely concealed at unexcavated monuments, which make the north Scottish long cairns so inscrutable. In Sutherland, even though examination of the long cairns has been superficial, some of these elements can be seen, or their presence can be deduced with varying degrees of confidence.

5.18) All six cairns sited close together at the lower

PLATE 11. Skelpick Long (SUT 53) from the W.

end of the Strath of Kildonan (SUT 13–17, 51) have a depressingly, and possibly deceptively, similar appearance because of their state of devastation, particularly at their important proximal ends. In length they range from about 42 m to at least 53 m along the axes, by about 17 to 20 m across the proximal ends. Caen Burn South (SUT 15) (plate 10) is the least damaged of these cairns, though the edges are difficult to trace precisely while they are covered by deep heather. Caen Burn West (SUT 16), a considerably shorter cairn, has one long edge quite well defined. At both cairns there is a hint that while the front half narrows gently from front to back, the rear part is parallel-sided with a square end. Caen Burn North (SUT 14) has lost its proximal end to erosion, but the remaining part is parallel-sided and of the same width as the other two. This suggests that the rear part of all three cairns is a rectangular cairn, without horned forecourts, similar to that added to the proximal mound at Tulach an t-Sionnaich (CAT 58) and discernible at some other Caithness cairns. Nothing can be said about the nature of the proximal parts of these cairns, except to note at the South cairn the two large vertical slabs on the axis which may indicate the presence of a ruined chamber. The edge across the proximal end of this cairn appears to be almost straight but has been severely robbed, and the plan of the ends of the other two cairns is not known. Caen Burn East (SUT 13) provides no useful information in its present condition.

5.19) Salscraggie (SUT 51), which has well defined edges except across the proximal end, is unusual in its very tapering plan, and there are reasons for suspecting that this is the result of the gradual paring away of the original edges. Across the centre of the proximal end there is a wall-face of boulders, apparently the base of a straight façade. There seems to have been a horned forecourt, but the horns are now covered with field-gathered stones. A chamber and passage were totally destroyed last century. Carn Laggie (SUT 17), which has been reduced to no more than a basal layer of stones, differs from the other five cairns in that the plan seems to be slightly waisted, being about 18 m wide near each end and about 15 m wide across the centre part. It might be speculated that each end of the cairn once comprised a separate element linked by the central part of the cairn, a similar arrangement to that which may be present at Skelpick Long (SUT 53) and is known at a few cairns in Caithness (¶ 5.23, 5.17). The length of Carn Laggie is uncertain because one end has been drastically mutilated, and, oddly, the edge at the other end is skew to the axis. A single large slab visible near the axis in the proximal end, together with the record of 'passages', may indicate that the cairn once contained a chamber.

5.20) At Coille na Borgie North and South (SUT 22, 23) there is a unique feature as far as Sutherland is concerned in the incorporation of spaced orthostats in the wall-faces edging the cairns, including the

PLATE 12. Kinbrace Hill Long (SUT 34) from the NW, photographed in 1967 before afforestation.

horns and forecourts. The orthostats projecting through the spread of cairn material indicate the position of these wall-faces which at other cairns can only be discovered by excavation. Along the sides of the Coille na Borgie cairns the orthostats are visible very intermittently, though at the proximal end of the South cairn a run of four are 1.4 m or less apart, and orthostats up to 0.8 m high occur in both cairns. The orthostats in the façades were considerably taller, as appropriate to this important feature.

5.21) Coille na Borgie South and Skelpick Long (SUT 23, 53) (figures 17, 16) are closely similar in plan and in size. Both cairns have a pair of horns forming a forecourt at each end, and the long sides of the cairns narrow gradually from the proximal end to about two-thirds of the distance to the distal end, and then widen again slightly. The length of the cairns from between the tips of the horns is about 71 m. At Coille na Borgie South the cairn defined by the spaced orthostats was 21 m wide at the proximal end, about 9 m wide at the minimum, and 10.6 m wide at the distal end. The width of Skelpick Long, where the bounding wall-face is not visible, is about 20 m at the proximal end, narrowing to 14 m and widening to 16 m at the distal end, a similar size to the spread of cairn material at Coille na Borgie. In passing it may be noted that without the orthostats defining the forecourts and the preservation of the chamber, the ends of this cairn and those of the Caen Burn cairns (SUT 14–16) would appear similar, with a square distal end and an ill-defined squarish proximal end. Similarities between Coille na Borgie South and Skelpick Long also include the positions of the chambers within the cairns. In each the chamber is central in the proximal end, and both chamber axes are skew to the cairn axes by about 13°, and both veer in the same direction. At first sight the passages seem to have been accessible from the forecourts, and this was probably so at Skelpick Long but almost certainly was not at Coille na Borgie South (see ¶ 5.27, 28), an indication, along with the skew chambers, that more than one period of construction is involved.

5.22) Skelpick Long (SUT 53) has been relatively little damaged and remains an impressive monument, enhanced by its siting on an elongated rise (plate 11). For most of its length the cairn has the form of a steep-sided ridge, only seriously disturbed at what would have been the highest part over the chamber and at the distal end. Behind the chamber the cairn is 3.4 m high, and it reduces slightly to about 2.8 m high before it is interrupted by a transverse hollow 12 m from the distal forecourt. The hollow is likely to be an original feature (though confused by modern robbing on one side of the cairn) comparable to the transverse hollows visible at several long cairns in Caithness (CAT 18, 25, 41, 58) and which appear to indicate the junction of separate elements within the cairns.

5.23) Speculation about the form of the distal ends of the Skelpick Long and Coille na Borgie South cairns (SUT 53, 23) can be taken a step further. If the

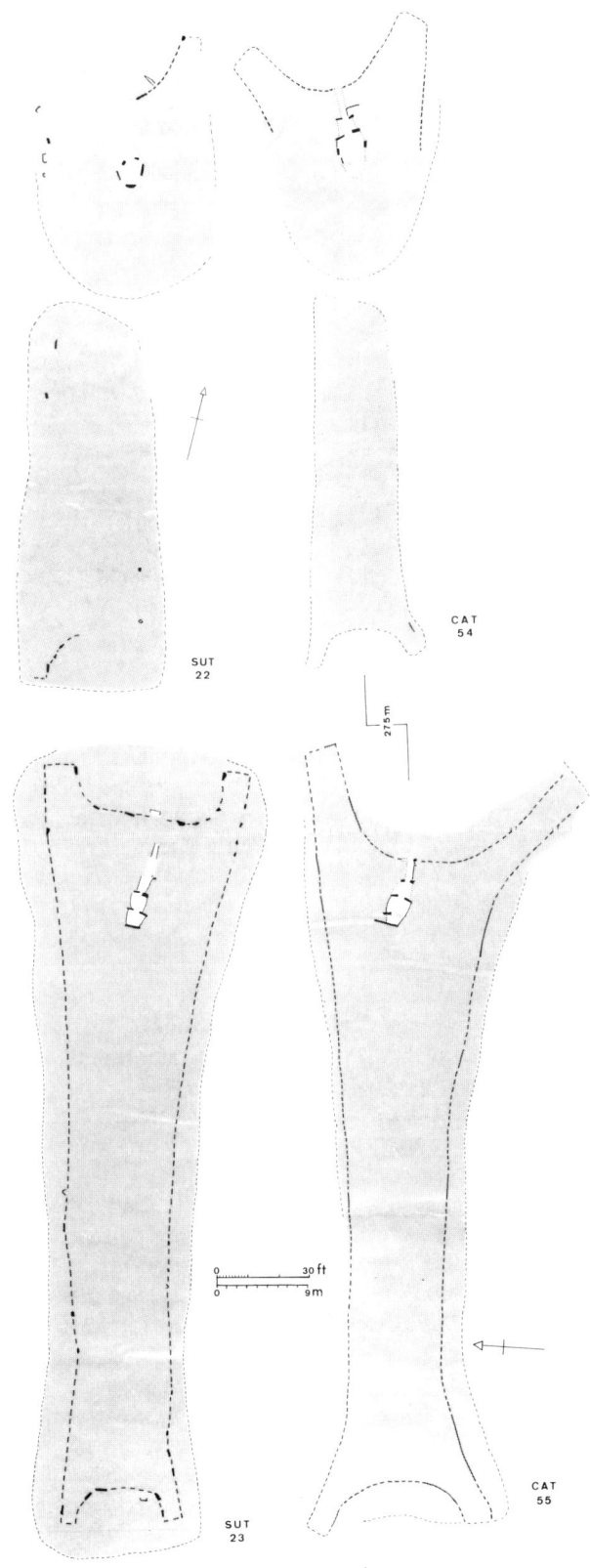

FIGURE 17. Plans of Coille na Borgie (SUT 22, 23) and South Yarrows (CAT 54, 55); the position of the revetting wall-faces is indicated on SUT 23 and CAT 55, and the destroyed proximal façade is indicated on CAT 54.

transverse hollow across the cairn at the former does indeed reflect a division between the components of the cairn, it indicates that there was a mound at the distal end (now largely destroyed as the end of the cairn has been pillaged for 7.6 m from the façade). In its final form, then, the cairn probably comprised a large chamber in the proximal end, a smaller mound at the distal end (perhaps containing a small, and not necessarily stone-built, chamber), and a linking cairn with a smoothly curved edge which merged into the horns forming the forecourts. It has been suggested that perhaps Carn Laggie (SUT 17) similarly had three components, though in this case the two terminals seem to have been about the same size (¶ 5.19). There is no indication that there was a separate mound or chamber in the distal end of the Coille na Borgie South cairn which is about 1 m high. The suggested composition of Skelpick Long and Coille na Borgie South each have good parallels in Caithness though of longer narrower proportions, at Na Tri Shean (CAT 41) where the three parts are signalled in the little-damaged long profile, and at South Yarrows South (CAT 55) which is known not to have a chamber in the distal end.

5.24) Coille na Borgie North (SUT 22) (figure 17) consists of two parts separated by a stone-free gap 2 m wide. The heel-shaped cairn mentioned above (¶ 5.13) forms the proximal end, containing a chamber the plan and axis of which have not been revealed; a trapezoid cairn extends from the heel-shaped cairn and the total length of the monument is about 60 m. The trapezoid cairn is similar in size and proportions to the small long cairn at Kilournan (SUT 32), though it is now only 1 m or so high. It is aligned with its proximal end forming the distal end of the monument. The same arrangement on a larger scale can be seen at Kinbrace Hill Long (SUT 34), a splendid monument 65 m in length which remains virtually untouched (plate 12). The large heel-shaped cairn is separated by a gap of 2.7 m from a trapezoid cairn. Because of the slope of the ground the height of the latter varies from 5 to 2.4 m to produce a horizontal spine. Both parts of the monument are built on the same axis, unlike Coille na Borgie North where the axes of the two parts are parallel but about 4 m apart. At both heel-shaped cairns there is a forecourt edged by projecting horns, though the horns at Coille na Borgie are only inferred from some orthostats belonging to the façade. Projecting orthostats indicate that there is also a forecourt at the distal end of this monument. Additionally there were orthostats in the wall-faces down the sides of the cairn; the few remaining along one side seem to be in line and present a visible link between the two parts of

PLATE 13. Coille na Borgie South (SUT 23) from the N, showing the orthostats of the façade.

the monument, but this is not so along the other side. The provision of a forecourt at each end of the monument and the use of orthostats in the wall-face echo the plan and techniques of the South cairn and suggest again that the heel-shaped and the trapezoid cairns were considered together at least in the final structural phase. The impression given by Kinbrace Hill Long and Coille na Borgie North is that at each the two parts of the monument were intended to be amalgamated into one cairn, which, when completed, would have had the appearance of a 'head-and-tail' long cairn with a prominent proximal mound and an elongated body.

5.25) The two Coille na Borgie cairns (SUT 22, 23) taken together find a close parallel in Caithness at South Yarrows where there are two cairns of almost identical size (figure 17). South Yarrows North (CAT 54) consisted, in its final form, of two detached cairns aligned on a common axis. At the proximal end was a heel-shaped cairn covering a tripartite chamber and fronted by a deep horned forecourt (now destroyed). Behind the heel-shaped cairn is an almost rectangular cairn, of narrow proportions and widening very slightly towards the distal end, with a smaller blind horned forecourt forming the distal end of the monument. According to the 19th-century excavator, a wall linked the two parts of the long cairn. This cairn evidently consists of the same components as Coille na Borgie North. South Yarrows South (CAT 55) is, like Coille na Borgie South, larger than its fellow to the N, and, like it, has a horned forecourt at each end and covers a tripartite chamber on a skew axis. The two pairs of cairns differ in that those at South Yarrows lie almost parallel 260 m apart, and those at Coille na Borgie lie end to end only 5 m apart (shown in their correct relationship in the figure); the former cairns are orientated E to W and the latter N to S.

Forecourts and façades

5.26) The forecourt at the proximal end of Coille na Borgie South (SUT 23) was about 14 m across by about 4.4 m deep, and was rather rectilinear in plan. The façade was evidently a very impressive feature, though now much damaged (plate 13). Eight orthostats survive, quarried blocks set with their wider flat faces outwards. If the spacing of 0.7 to 0.86 m were constant, the total number of orthostats would have been fourteen. The only orthostat to retain its full height of 2.3 m is at the end of the façade, so it is not known whether the orthostats were graded in height, and it certainly cannot be said (as it has been) that the tallest orthostats were at the outer ends. Nor is the height of the intervening walling known, and thus whether the tops of the orthostats projected above it; a broken central orthostat must have been at least 1.4 m high originally and possibly considerably more. The distal forecourt was a small version of the proximal forecourt, about 8 m across. Five orthostats remain and probably three are missing. At the North cairn (SUT 22) only three orthostats of the proximal

FIGURE 18. Coille na Borgie South (SUT 23). View of the chamber looking N; view of the entrance to the passage looking S; and plan of the passage and chamber. Sketched by W. McKay 1867 (note the side slabs in the chamber, referred to in ¶ 4.31, shown on the plan and in the foreground of the upper view).

façade survive, and indicate that the forecourt was narrower and deeper than that at the South cairn. At the distal end another three orthostats belong to one side of a façade; the stones are 0.6 m apart and the tallest is over 1.2 m high.

5.27) The two earliest accounts of Coille na Borgie South (SUT 23) contain no doubts that the passage was accessible through the façade of the long cairn. McKay made a plan and a sketch of the entrance in 1867 (figure 18) showing a passage about 4.8 m long, wholly roofed, without entrance portal stones, ending in an arc of walling which connected it with a façade orthostat on each side. When applied to the modern plan it can be seen that the proposed entrance could not have been symmetrically placed between orthostats, and thus the putative arcs must have been of differing lengths. This arrangement seems most unlikely, and probably McKay's drawings should be regarded as an imaginative reconstruction rather than a record of what he found. Munro, who visited the cairn in 1883, gave the passage length as 5.2 m, but his plan is obviously inaccurate in other respects. The area between the existing end of the passage and the façade is filled with disturbed cairn material without any sign of passage walls. The skew axis of the passage, if extended, would not bring the entrance to the centre of the façade, and the passage would be exceptionally long at about 5.8 m; it may be noted too that the existing outer part of the passage is narrow and low (¶4.9), further suggesting the unlikelihood of a passage of this length. The existence of a blind façade, with the orthostats linked by walling and unbroken by an entrance, need not be surprising, for, as already mentioned ¶ 5.17, blind façades are known in Caithness, though at South Yarrows South (CAT 55), to which the cairn has been compared, the passage was accessible through the façade.

5.28) The forecourts at Skelpick Long (SUT 53) must be much the same size as those at Coille na Borgie South (SUT 23), though the proximal façade is hidden below displaced cairn material. It has been assumed that the passage, which is still roofed, was directly accessible from the centre of the proximal forecourt, and that the blocking in the passage entrance (only visible from the interior) was placed against the façade. It is just possible, though perhaps unlikely, that the façade of the long cairn, like that at Coille na Borgie South, may lie forward of the passage entrance, and if so the façade may be blind. In its present condition the forecourt of Salscraggie (SUT 51) is uninformative.

5.29) The forecourt at Kinbrace Hill Long (SUT 34) is on much the same scale as the proximal forecourts described above, but it raises another question as, like that at Coille na Borgie North (SUT 22), it fronts a heel-shaped cairn detached from the trapezoid cairn behind it. At Coille na Borgie North the orthostatic façade appears to be part of the walling surrounding the whole cairn including the distal façade (though apparently interrupted between the heel-shaped and trapezoid cairns), to produce in the last phase the double horned plan similar to that of the South cairn (SUT 23). The situation seems to be exactly the same at South Yarrows North (CAT 54) where the two parts were linked by walling (exposed during excavation) into a double horned long cairn in the last phase (Davidson and Henshall 1991, 49, 59). From this it follows that the horned forecourts were not part of the design of the heel-shaped cairns.

5.30) The short horned cairns were provided with front and rear forecourts which are similar to those at long cairns. The fuller, but still quite limited, information from Caithness provides no evidence of blind façades, nor that they were secondary to their chambered cairns. At each cairn the passage entrance is in the centre of the wider façade. The front forecourt of the largest and best preserved of the Sutherland short horned cairns, Skelpick South (SUT 55), is larger than any of those at long cairns in Sutherland, being about 19 m wide by probably about 3.5 m deep. The front forecourt at Kinbrace Burn (SUT 33), while not so wide, is probably about 6 m deep.

5.31) One more orthostatic façade, different from those at Coille na Borgie (SUT 22, 23), is to be seen at Achany (SUT 3). This cairn is round and the slightly concave façade, 6.3 m wide, is recessed into it (¶ 5.7). The damaged orthostats are up to 1.5 m in height, and were probably once higher. A fifth much shorter intact orthostat which has the appearance of an entrance portal stone stands in front of and slightly overlapping one of the façade stones. Although it is highly unusual for a passage portal to project in front of a façade, in this case the irregularity of the façade orthostats may have allowed the first passage lintel to be borne by this stone and by its hidden partner.

5.32) An unusual cairn situated on the N side of Cnoc Dair-chair in the Strath of Kildonan (NC 82 NE 17) was visited in the course of the survey. It measures about 14 m in diameter and 1.3 m high. A façade of substantial boulders on its E side form a straight edge some 7.5 m in length. There is, however, no evidence from surface inspection that the cairn is chambered.

Cairns and chambers

5.33) The majority of cairns in Sutherland are round, so it is no surprise to find that all types of chamber may be covered by round cairns. Unfortunately among the cairns of other forms the plans of some chambers are not known. Of the heel-shaped cairns, one (SUT 37) contains a large single-compartment chamber with a side cell, and one and probably another (SUT 75, 69) cover bipartite chambers of Skelpick type. Two short horned cairns (SUT 25, 33) probably cover tripartite chambers and another covers a single-compartment chamber (SUT 2). It is particularly striking that in the three neighbouring long cairns in Strathnaver, SUT 53, 23, 22, the chambers are different, being respectively bipartite of Skelpick type, tripartite of unusual plan, and either single-compartment or bipartite. Viewed the opposite way, the only two single-compartment chambers with side cells are covered by a round and a heel-shaped cairn (SUT 43, 37), and the few tripartite chambers are under round, short horned and long cairns. There seems, then, to be little correlation between cairn type and chamber type. This confusing situation emphasises again the probability that heel-shaped and long cairns are later additions to existing round chambered cairns and, in spite of some evidence to the contrary (¶ 5.14), that the same is true of short horned cairns.

6. The use and sealing of the chambers and the history of the cairns

Ritual deposits made during building

6.1) It is seldom that evidence is available of any ritual activity before or during the construction of chambered cairns. It was chance that small deposits of bones were found beneath the corbel stones outside the south chamber at Embo (SUT 63). The bones had been placed in little heaps on the core of flat slabs which surrounded the chamber, and before the corbel stones had been positioned: there is no doubt that the bones were deposited as the chamber was being built. Three separate deposits were found round the NE side of the chamber, between the E orthostat and the adjacent walling, behind the NE orthostat, and behind the N orthostat; a fourth deposit behind the W inner portal stone was not sealed below a corbel stone but is assumed to belong to the series. Had there been deposits behind the chamber walls on the SE and W sides, these had been removed before the excavation. The first deposit consisted of a strangely random collection of animal remains: the tooth of a dog, one or two bones each from a great auk, guillemot, duck, shag or small cormorant, and fish bones. In the other three deposits there were both human and animal remains. The former comprised three adult teeth, twelve bones from adult hands and feet and a piece of vertebra, part of the humerus of a child about 10 years old, part of the mandible and part of the maxilla and four loose teeth of a child three to four years old, pieces of the skull vault of an infant or foetus. The remains of the second of the children, considered to be from one individual, came from two deposits. The animal remains consisted of one or two bones or parts of bones from dog, sheep, otter, great auk, grebe, gannet, six bones from guillemot, fish bones and amphibian bones. (Detailed lists in Appendix 2, and in Henshall and Wallace 1963, 32, 33, 36).

6.2) The two striking features of these deposits are the small size of the bones or pieces of bone, and the wide range of individuals and species in such a small quantity of material. As will be seen, it reflects the range of human and animal remains recovered from the chamber. This might suggest that the material came from another chamber, perhaps even from the north chamber if this predated the building of the south chamber. The deposits can be interpreted as the physical remains of a ceremony connected with the building of the chamber. The placing of bones round the outside of a chamber has not been otherwise recorded and was observed here because the outside of the chamber was easily available for investigation and the bone was in an excellent state of preservation. These deposits might be compared with the much larger 'foundation deposit' at Isbister, Orkney (ORK 25), which was put below the floor in the first stages of building the chamber. In this case the deposit consisted of bones from fifteen individuals and from animals, both mammals and birds (Hedges 1983, 20, 80, 149). It is possible that there was a pre-construction deposit below the chamber at Tulloch of Assery B, Caithness (CAT 70), as a human femur and a few animal bones were found below paving which ran below the chamber walls (Davidson and Henshall 1991, 62).

The excavation of burial deposits

6.3) While study of the design and construction techniques of the cairns and chambers is relatively straightforward, an understanding of the usage of the chambers largely escapes us. The data can only come from the analysis and interpretation of the deposits in the passages and chambers, but these deposits are likely to be the residue of a series of complex ceremonies and most will have suffered considerable disturbance. Throughout the country information is scarce and its interpretation is difficult and controversial. In Sutherland only four chambers have been excavated, and unfortunately the information from each of them is less helpful than it might have been under happier circumstances. At Achaidh (SUT 2) in 1909 inevitably the work was done without the care and expertise which would be applied in a modern excavation, and the passage was not examined. The two chambers and passages at Embo (SUT 63) were excavated hastily in 1960, and they were found to have been extensively reduced and disturbed in prehistoric and in more recent times. The chamber and passage at The Ord North (SUT 48) were well excavated in 1967 and were found not to have been disturbed since the bronze age. But the death of the excavator before his report was written deprives us of the interpretation of the deposits which only he could have provided. There is also the disappointment that in the acid conditions bone did not survive.

Burial deposits in the two chambers at Embo

6.4) Burials in the south chamber at Embo (SUT 63) were made in two distinct phases separated by a dark earth-and-stone filling nearly 0.3 m thick. The bones of the earlier phase burials lay on the gravel floor or had been incorporated into the lowest part of the filling. Just before the first inspection of the cairn in 1956 a pit had been dug through this filling in the main chamber, between the E inner portal stone and the bronze age cist (figure 8, *1, 7*). At the lowest level two skulls had been found against the N face of the portal stone with other bones nearby, all in a good state of preservation. In 1960, when the cairn was excavated, a mass of bones was found in the cist, evidently having been placed there following further illicit digging after the 1956 visit. This digging had included enlargement of the pit in the main chamber and removal of the E side of the ante-chamber. Some of the bones in the cist were discoloured or had dark earth adhering to them in contrast with the bones recovered from a higher level in the chamber, so it seemed probable that they had come from the first phase of burials. During the 1960 excavation decayed bones were found on the floor of the S part of the main chamber, or pressed into it, some bones being reduced to little more than smears. The bones which were observed *in situ* were not articulated; those which were recognisable were part of a jaw, part of a long bone, a carpal, and ribs. It was particularly disappointing that in the N half, which had remained sealed below the filling layer, there were no bones at all, let alone bones in the condition and quantity that had been dug out of the SE part of the chamber. It is uncertain, of course, whether the absence of bones here may be due to total decay. On the floor a number of large flat slabs gave the appearance of rough paving, and there was a spread of charcoal including some quite large pieces. On the ante-chamber floor there were a complete skull and other bones; the skull was beside the W wall, placed on a small thin slab and protected by other slabs (figure 8, *5*). (The bones are listed in Appendix 2.)

6.5) The minimum number of individuals represented in the first phase of burials is three adults, one over 30 years old, one between 25 and 40 years old, and one of uncertain age, a child 10 to 11 years old (with the possibility that a tooth belongs to another child), and an infant. One of the adults had suffered an abscess in the upper jaw and the loss of a tooth during life. The adult bones were in both parts of the chamber, the bones of the child and infant were all in the ante-chamber. Most of the bones, unless small and solid, were broken and incomplete, though two or possibly three skulls were virtually intact when found. It is clear that only a small part of the skeletons of any of the individuals was present; though the amount of bone lost through decay is unknown, it seems unlikely that this could account for the very considerable amount of skeletal material which was missing. For example, the child, whose skull was intact, was represented otherwise by only loose teeth, a fragment of scapula and a piece of rib.

6.6) The filling which had been introduced to cover the burials was about 0.03 to 0.15 m thick in the ante-chamber increasing to about 0.3 m thick in the main chamber. The filling material was dark gravelly soil (its character already noted in ¶ 5.8) in which were small stones and specks of charcoal, and in the main chamber it included larger slabs lying at varying angles. The filling was very hard except in the ante-chamber and in the main chamber where it had been protected by sloping slabs. It seemed that it had all been deposited at one time, and that in the main chamber it had been compacted by trampling.

6.7) The burials in the second phase were all in the main chamber. At the time they were brought to the chamber it was still intact and empty above the filling. But removal of the roof and building the cist had later caused havoc. Human and animal bones had been pushed aside, a few bones had been pressed into the top of the filling, and a skull was crushed beneath a side slab of the cist. Most of the bones were mixed with the cairn stones and sand which filled the space between the cist and the chamber walls. Subsequently the chamber had been occupied by otters. In 1956 about two-thirds of the deposit was either dug out or turned over.

6.8) Human bones certainly belonging to the second phase were recovered during the excavation in 1960, and other bones had been unearthed before the 1956 visit; also one or two bones which were additional to the skeleton found in the cist in 1956 were evidently derived from the surrounding deposits. Among the bones found dumped in the cist in 1960 those without staining were assumed to have come from the second phase burials. (The bones from these three contexts are listed in item *4* in Appendix 2; in general there is little doubt that the bones from disturbed contexts are correctly attributed as demonstrated by paired pelvic bones of a child, *l*, *k* or *m* in the list, but two pieces of skull *i* and *e* which were attributed to different phases may come from the same individual). Bones gathered from around the upper part of the chamber in 1960 had been thrown out either when the cist was built or in 1956. They are assumed to come mainly from the second phase burials (item 5 in Appendix 2), but in one case at least there is doubt, as a socket in part of a mandible is well matched by a tooth from the first phase.

6.9) A minimum of three adults was represented in the second phase, one over 30 years old, one about 30 years old, and one of uncertain age. Judging by the pieces of femora, one individual was a large male, another was a slighter male, and judging by the pelvis one was female. The minimum number of younger individuals was an adolescent between 15 and 20 years old, three children all about 10 years old distinguished by the varying size of long bones, a child about 5 years old and an infant. Altogether parts of three or four skulls came from this phase. The bones thrown out of the chamber do not increase the estimate of the number of individuals except to add a foetus or newborn infant. The good preservation of the bone indicates that, at this level, none is likely to have been lost through decay. On the whole it seems unlikely that any quantity of bone has been removed from the chamber or immediately around it, nor is it likely that any quantity of bone remained undiscovered as the displaced bone found in the upper levels of the cairn was in the close vicinity of the chamber and well within the area opened during the excavation. Doubtless considerable damage had been done to the bones, both when the cist was built and in 1956, but many of the bones may have been incomplete before then. It seems clear that, as in the first phase, the skeletons themselves were very incomplete, indeed an individual may be represented by only a couple of bones. There was a relatively high number of adult bones from the hands, feet and wrists. With such fragmentary material it is difficult or impossible to distinguish individuals of similar age unless there is duplication of bones. It is thus likely that more individuals are represented in the skeletal remains than the minimum number identified, and if so the skeletons were even more fragmentary than appears.

6.10) In both phases animal remains were mixed with the human bones. A range of species was represented, each by only one to three items (identified and listed by Clarke in Henshall and Wallace 1963, 35, a shortened list in the Inventory p. 140, and discussed ¶ 6.21–3).

6.11) In the north chamber there were relatively few bones. About half the floor area had been dug out and refilled before 1956. Over the rest of the floor there was a layer of dark soil about 0.05 m thick. On it were some bones from the upper part of a skeleton, not articulated but all lying close to the S orthostat (figure 8, 8). Pieces of skull and teeth indicated an individual about 25 years old. One tooth may come from a second individual, and it may be that a solitary piece of skull found near the SW orthostat also came from this individual. At first sight conditions in this chamber seem quite different from those in the south chamber. The dark layer on the floor was thin and without any slabby stones, and there was no sign that there had been skeletal material in the quantity found in the south chamber. But the north chamber had been very greatly destroyed, and local knowledge before 1956 that the cairn was a burial place implies that human bones had been found before then, and most likely whilst digging into this chamber. Nor can it be certain there was not an earlier burial phase, as the area of the floor which remained for excavation may have been just as devoid of bones as the N part of the south chamber.

The neolithic deposits in the chamber at The Ord North

6.12) The chamber at The Ord North (SUT 48) contained no skeletal material in the neolithic levels, but did contain a variety of sherds and some other artefacts. The data from this cairn are thus very different from those from the Embo chambers (SUT 63). The floor of the chamber at The Ord North consisted of a layer of clayey soil. In the main chamber the floor was uneven with a number of hollows dug through it. A considerable amount of charcoal had been scattered on the floor, and some enigmatic organic remains survived in places. The floor of the antechamber consisted of intermittent areas of clayey soil, with scatters of charcoal, but no hollows were recorded in the floor. On the floor of the main chamber, against the wall on the N side, there had been a construction of slabs (figure 19, plate 14). This was found greatly ruined, presumably by the fall of the chamber roof, and its original form and purpose are obscure. At the front edge were two thin pillar-like slabs, the taller 0.6 m high. The centre part of the structure involved a box-like arrangement of slabs with a horizontal 'capstone' 0.3 m above the floor; the interior was filled by a boulder and soil leaving some air spaces. The structure may tentatively be interpreted as remains of a bench similar to those known from several chambers in Orkney. Some of these benches were box-like slab structures built against the chamber walls, and others were built as solid platforms; benches of the latter type were found in Caithness at Tulloch of Assery A, CAT 69. (Davidson and Henshall 1989, 26, 53–5; 1991, 37–8, 62, 63).

6.13) The filling on the floor of the main chamber

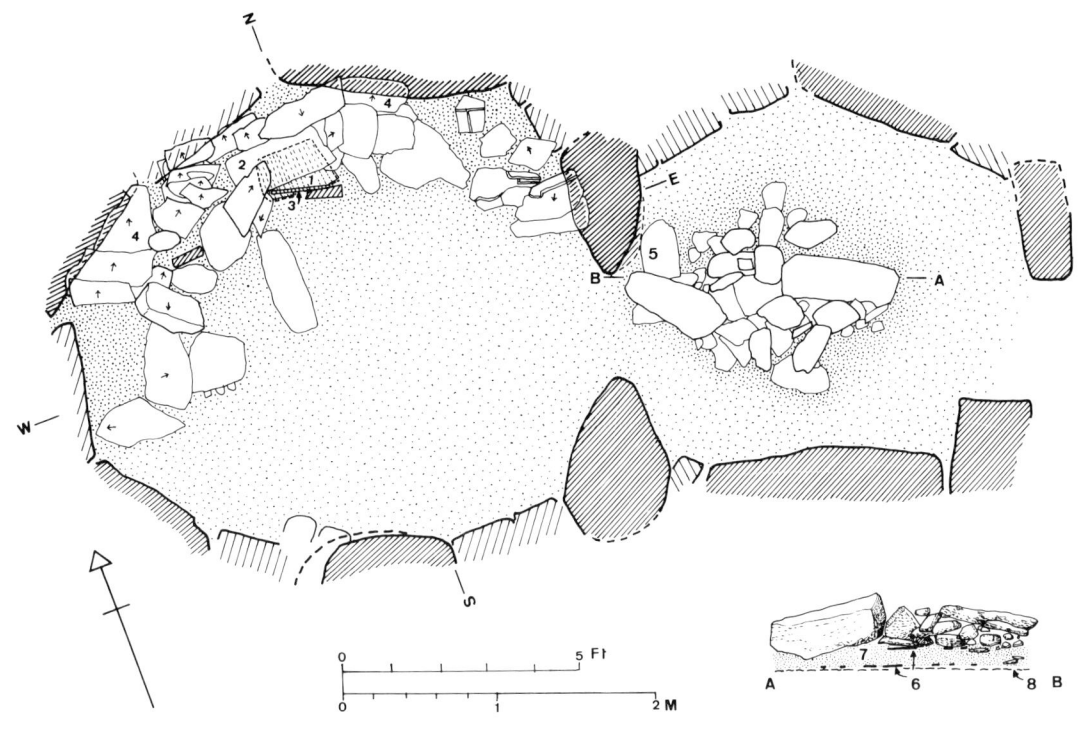

FIGURE 19. The Ord North (SUT 48), plan of the chamber. The main chamber planned at floor level with the slab structure; the ante-chamber planned about 0.15 m above floor level with the pile of stones, and a section through the pile of stones. Annotated by the excavator: *1 floor slab; 2 ?capstone; 3 vertical resting on floor slab; 4 leaning against orthostat. Arrows indicate upward tilt of some slabs; 5 jammed against orthostat (which overhangs); 6 charcoal; 7 moist gravelly soil; 8 intermittent grey clayey soil (turf line?), subsoil below.* (Redrawn from Corcoran 1967a, SUD 115/14–16).

PLATE 14. The Ord North (SUT 48), the slab structure in the main chamber (scales in feet).

covered the slab structure leaving the tops of the pillar-like slabs projecting. The filling was at least 0.38 m deep, indicated by the level of the highest neolithic sherd which can be plotted with certainty, and the depth may have been somewhat greater as the largest corbel stones rested at 0.4 m above the floor and in falling may have slightly penetrated the filling. The lower part of the filling was a light sandy soil with many small fragments of charcoal but few stones; the upper part contained a good deal of small stone, some charcoal and traces of organic material (though the filling is not shown thus on the excavator's only complete section, figure 20, *2*). The filling in the ante-chamber was less fully recorded. It consisted of gravelly soil about 0.46 m deep, in which were intermittent spreads of charcoal, and a pile of stones the base of which was about 0.15 m above the floor (figures 19, 20, *6*).

6.14) The distribution of the artefacts within the chamber filling is crucial to its interpretation (the find-spots are given in Appendix 3). There were sizeable

THE USE AND SEALING OF THE CHAMBERS

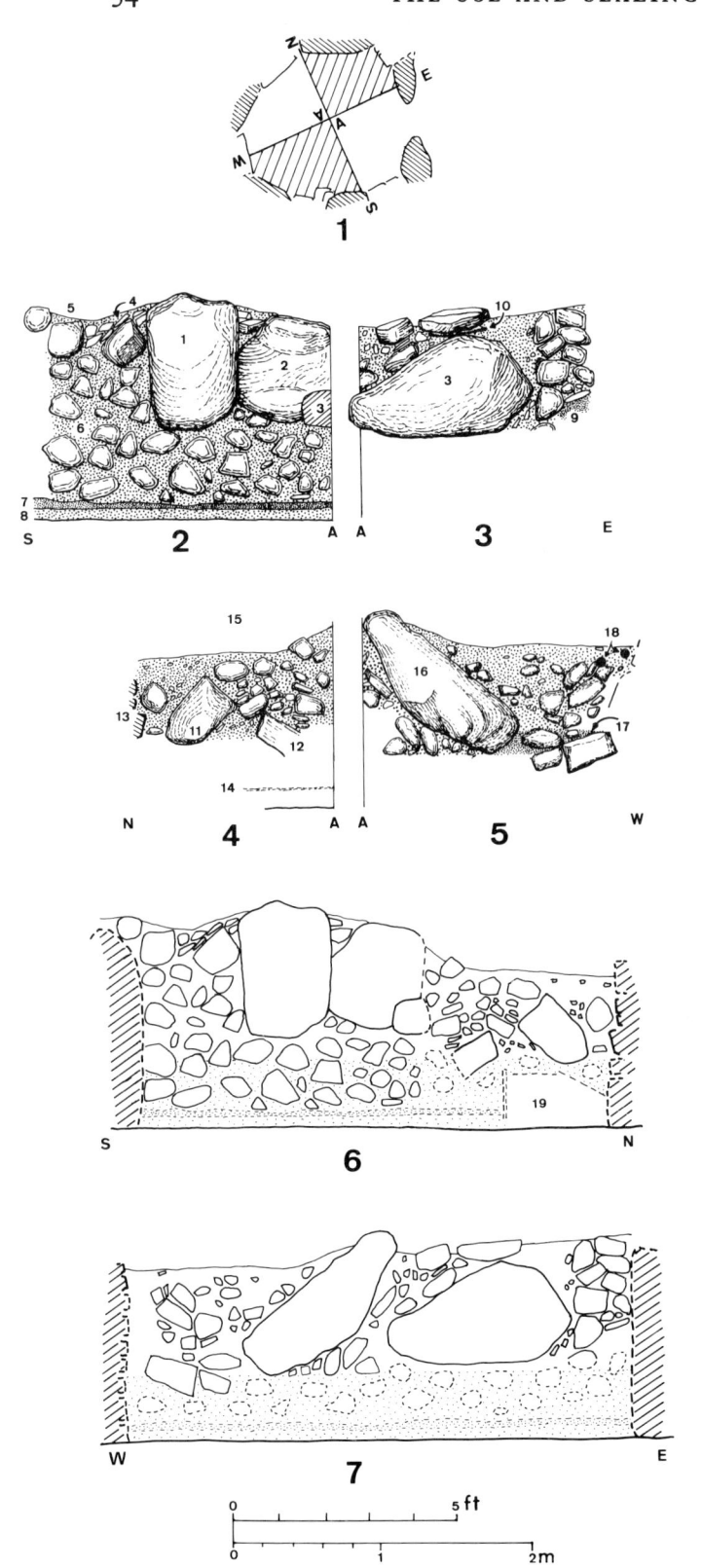

FIGURE 20. The Ord North (SUT 48), sections through the main chamber.

1 Diagram to show the positions of the sections, the NW and SE quadrants having been excavated first.

2–5 the sections copied from the excavator's uncompleted pencil drawings (Corcoran 1967a, SUD 115/10–13) on which are the following annotations: *1* Fallen corbel, triangular in section, lying in vertical position, apex of triangle protruding to W for maximum distance of 1'3" [0.38m] at 3' [0.9m] S. *2* Fallen corbel leaning to E, resting on corbel in E–W section. *3* Fallen corbel, face almost on axis, protrudes uniformly into SE section c.8" [0.2m]. *4* Small tightly wedged stones. *5* Upper limit of fine sandy soil. *6* Light sandy soil with small boulders. *7* Grey clayey soil, ?buried turf-line. *8* Light sandy soil. *9* Damper clay earth. *10* Under flat stone and occupying comparable ? layer of earth with small fragments of charcoal. *11* Fallen corbel, lies athwart N/S axis, projects into NW sector for 1'9" [0.53m] at 2'6" [0.76m] N. *12* Protrudes into NW sector for 8" [0.2m] at 9" [0.23m] N. *13* Walling, schematic only. *14* ?iron pan. *15* Loose disturbed stone [ie. recent refilling of the upper part of the chamber]. *16* Collapsed corbel almost on E–W axis, greatest projection into NW sector c.11" [0.28m] at 2'9" [0.83m] W. *17* Earth below this level more compacted, rather clayey compared with drier earth in upper level. *18* Bone.

6–7 Diagramatic sections based on the excavator's drawings (two reversed) with additional information (*19* slab structure).

parts of only two pots, about half an Unstan bowl, pot *3*, and many sherds (some very small) of an undecorated bowl, pot *4* (figure 22). Unfortunately it cannot be proved that the sherds listed as pot *4* belong to one bowl, but they are so similar that this seems highly probable. The sherds of pot *3* were all in the ante-chamber about 0.15 m above the floor, mainly on the N and NE side, with some sealed below the pile of stones, seemingly a discrete deposit. With them were one sherd of pot *1*, two sherds of pot *2*, and several sherds of pot *4*. But sherds of pot *4* were widely scattered both vertically and horizontally in both parts of the chamber. They were found pressed into or on the floor and at intervening levels up to 0.38 m above the floor in both the ante-chamber and the main chamber. A rim sherd of *4* on the floor closely matches a rim sherd from 0.2 m above the floor, and joining sherds of pot *1* were in the floor and 0.13 m above it; thus it seems that the few sherds found in the floor (and from Corcoran's notes it appears that there were more which are not now identifiable) had been pressed down as the filling material was introduced. The fillings in the two parts of the chamber are also linked by the few sherds of pot *1*, and notably by the joining rim sherds of pot *4* found above the slab structure at the back of the main chamber and close to the S inner portal stone in the ante-chamber. In the main chamber the sherds in or on the floor, with a piece of pumice, were between the inner portal stones and immediately to the W; above them the rest of the pottery and some flints appear to have been scattered fairly centrally and near the SE side. The evidence of the pottery strongly suggests that the filling, though not homogeneous, was introduced in a single act, and that there is no reason to differentiate between the filling in the ante-chamber and that in the main chamber. It might be suggested that the spread of sherds at the level of the pile of stones in the ante-chamber indicates a break in the filling process, but the vertical spread of pot *4* would then have to be explained as due to disturbance. These two interpretations are not compatible if neolithic human activity is postulated as the cause of disturbance, and extensive displacement of material by subsequent animal activity, such as was diagnosed by Barber at Point of Cott (ORK 41) (1988, 59–62), is unlikely to account for the confused distribution of many of the sherds at The Ord. The pile of stones in the filling of the ante-chamber remains unexplained. Whilst it may be assumed that there had been burials on the chamber floor, it is unknown whether there were also burials on the neolithic filling as at Embo (SUT 63).

Burial deposits in other chambers

6.15) The clay floor of the chamber at Achaidh (SUT 2) was largely covered by slabs. On these was a filling which can be estimated as between 0.6 and 0.8 m deep, consisting of two layers. The lower and thinner layer was black stone-free soil with fragments of charcoal; the upper layer was grey sand with particles of quartz and a small amount of charcoal, and contained a little comminuted bone which did not appear to have been burnt. On or in this sand layer, above the floor at the back of the chamber, were human bones, much decayed, thought to be from one adult. Parts of several long bones were recovered, but there were no remains of the skull. The only prehistoric artefact was a flint scraper. Other items, including a sherd of a medieval or later pot and a modern button, were thought to have reached the chamber through interstices in the roof, and remains of a 'rat's larder' is a reminder of the non-human disturbance to which the contents of chambers may be subject.

6.16) Slabs on chamber floors, as at Achaidh and to a lesser extent at Embo (SUT 2, 63), are not uncommon, noted at several chambers in Orkney and Caithness. Sometimes they have the appearance of paving, but generally they seem to be casual and the reason for their presence is unclear. Deposits of charcoal, either on the floor or in the filling, seen at Achaidh, Embo and The Ord North (SUT 48), have been observed in numerous chambers elsewhere.

6.17) A few other chambers have been crudely investigated. The plan of Ardvreck (SUT 9) is unique in Sutherland. Before excavation the innermost compartment, which alone was visible, looked like a large bronze age cist. It contained a crouched burial, and nothing was found in the rest of the chamber. The burial may be neolithic, but equally it may be of later date having been inserted into a seemingly ready-made cist. At Fiscary (SUT 29) the chamber floor was covered by a layer of soil containing numerous pieces of charcoal, but fragments of bone were not thought to be ancient, and this may also be the case with the fragments of animal bone found at Coille na Borgie South (SUT 23).

Interpretation of the burial deposits

6.18) The evidence relating to burial practices is so slight and unsatisfactory that little can be deduced directly. Since the Sutherland cairns are architecturally part of the Orkney-Cromarty passage-grave tradition of northern Scotland, it might have been expected that the excavation of a considerable number of chambers in Orkney and Caithness would have provided insight into the procedures for bringing bodies or skeletal remains to the chambers, and the subsequent treatment of the remains, but this is so only to a limited extent (a summary of the evidence with discussion in Davidson and Henshall 1989, 52–9; 1991, 60–6). In the chambers, and indeed in chambers of other traditions, the number of individuals represented by the skeletal material varies enormously, from nil to several hundred, ten to twenty being about average, but the low numbers are likely to be overemphasised due to insufficiently critical examination of the remains, to the estimates being of minimum numbers, and to unquantifiable loss through decay. It is not unusual to find that the skeletons are very incomplete, and that the bones are damaged and sometimes are fragmentary, conditions which can be shown in some cases not to be due to disturbance in post-neolithic times. The bones may be scattered in the chamber, or heaped together, or gathered into restricted areas. There is evidence from Orkney, and less certainly from Caithness, that there was a special interest in skulls, for they were sometimes collected together or set upright over a group of bones. At Embo (SUT 63) the contrasting quantity of human bone in the two chambers has been noted, and also its disarticulated and its probably incomplete state. The possibly intentional protection of the skull in the ante-chamber of the south chamber, and the very survival of intact skulls in the main chamber, may indicate a concern for skulls.

6.19) The circumstances observed in two relatively recently excavated Orcadian chambers, Isbister and Quanterness (ORK 25, 43; the latter belonging to a different passage-grave tradition), and particularly the detailed study of the large quantity of human bones recovered from them, led to the conclusion that the chambers were used as ossuaries to house the bones only after the bodies had lost the flesh and sinews (Hedges 1983, 216–17; 1984, 133–6; Renfrew 1979, 166–8). This interpretation had already been favoured by Corcoran to explain the conditions found in three Caithness cairns, Tulach an t-Sionnaich and Tulloch of Assery A and B (CAT 58, 69, 70). The excarnation theory involves the de-fleshing of the bodies elsewhere, probably by exposure in a specially-built enclosure or on a platform, and the subsequent incompleteness of the skeletons might be due to parts of them having been lost or removed before they were brought to the chamber. However, it seemed to Davidson and Henshall that, viewing all of the evidence including some from previous excavations which is admittedly less satisfactory, the earlier assumption that complete bodies were brought to the chambers has just as much to commend it. Articulated skeletons, or parts of articulated skeletons, have been found in several Orcadian chambers and in one or more in Caithness. The skeletons were best recorded at Midhowe (ORK 37) where they had been placed on stone benches. The provision of benches, in eight Orcadian chambers and one Caithness chamber, suggests the idea of beds for the newly dead, and, as noted ¶ 6.12, it is possible but by no means certain that there may have been a bench in the main chamber at The Ord North (SUT 48). If the introduction of intact bodies to chambers was the normal rite, then it is clear that extensive disturbance after they were reduced to skeletons was also normal, and that many of the bones were removed. A minor instance of the ritual use of bones probably taken from a chamber has already been noted at Embo (SUT 63) where they were placed round the outside of the south chamber (¶ 6.1). Whichever rite was used, complete clearance of chambers at intervals is highly probable, though undemonstrable. There is no evidence for the cremation of bodies in Orkney, nor (as far as the limited information goes) in Sutherland, but cremation was used extensively but not exclusively in a group of chambers in SE Caithness.

6.20) At Embo (SUT 63) both males and females were present, and individuals ranged in age from over thirty years old through to childhood with a number at the foetal or new-born stage. As with chambered cairns elsewhere, there was no exclusion on the grounds of sex or age. The only unusual point is the number of very young individuals represented, probably due to the exceptional preservation of bone in the upper layer.

6.21) Mixed with the human bones there were animal bones and teeth coming from a wide range of species, but each represented by a small number of items. Such animal remains are a common feature in chamber deposits and have given rise to much discussion in recent years. In particular the study of the large amount of faunal material from three Orcadian chambers, Quanterness, Isbister and Point of Cott (ORK 43, 25, 41), has resulted in differing interpretations and explanations for its presence (Renfrew 1979, 112–56; Hedges 1983, 133–70, 226–42; Barber 1988, 60–2), and the meagre finds at Embo (SUT 63) hardly assist the debate. There are likely to be several explanations for the presence of animal remains even within one chamber as they may have been brought there by human agency, either deliberately or accidentally, or by animal agency. It is generally considered that the bones of food animals (found in quantity in a number of Orcadian chambers) are likely to have been brought to the chambers as food offerings or as the residue of funeral feasting. At Embo there were one to three bones each of sheep, ox, pig, and possibly the few bones of the larger birds, such as duck, great auk, guillemot and fulmar, should be included; the absence of deer bones is rather surprising as deer was usually present in the Orcadian and Caithness chambers. Dog, because of its special relationship with man, may also be expected to have been introduced deliberately; this certainly seems to have been the case in three chambers in Orkney and in one in Caithness (ORK 7, 12, 43, CAT 58) where whole or nearly whole skeletons were found.

6.22) It is the random character of the rest of the animal remains (the smaller mammals, birds, fish, amphibians, and molluscs) which is more puzzling. Activity by predators living in the cairn is likely to have been responsible for some of them, and possibly for most. It is known that there was an otter's holt in the ruined chamber at Embo (SUT 63) because the concentrated mass of tiny fish bones has been identified as from the animal's droppings. So the scattered and uneaten fish bones, and most of the bird bones too, might be explained as the residue of food, being parts of creatures either caught or scavenged and brought into the cairn by a resident otter, or a pole-cat, or a fox. Such bones are presumably post-neolithic and are only relevant to the present study for the disturbance of the chamber deposits that the animals may have caused. The problem, of course, is to isolate this debris from the small miscellaneous remains which appear to have been humanly deposited. The two bones of an otter and the tooth of a pole-cat might even have belonged to animals which had died in the cairn, though if so, it is curious that no more of the skeletons were found. The amphibian bones are likely to be remains of hibernating animals. But two bones of a red squirrel, and one of a capercaillie, both additionally interesting as being woodland species, are unlikely to have been brought to the chamber by animals, and this reintroduces the probability of human activity, either deliberate or accidental. If this is so, then it could be that the bones of the smaller mammals, birds and fish came in the same way, though the reason for, and the means of, their deposition is unclear. In discussing animal debris in some of the Orcadian and Caithness chambers it has been suggested that it was accidentally included in the deliberately introduced filling covering the burials, as this may have included midden material from a settlement (Davidson and Henshall 1989, 78; 1991, 64, 66). At Embo (SUT 63), at least, this is not the case, as the filling over the first phase burials was carefully examined and contained neither bones nor artefacts, and there was no deliberately introduced layer above the second phase burials.

6.23) The animal remains and human bones found round the outside of the south chamber at Embo (SUT 63) were certainly deliberately deposited whilst it was being built (¶ 6.1). The animal remains largely duplicate the species found in the chamber by including sheep, dog, otter, great auk, guillemot, duck, fish bones and amphibian bones, only adding gannet and grebe to the list of species. It can hardly be doubted that these bones came from a neolithic burial deposit, and if so they appear to support the proposal that most of the miscellaneous animal remains arrived in the chamber by human agency. To argue otherwise would mean that animals were living in the chamber whilst it was in use for burials and rituals, and although not impossible, this seems highly unlikely.

6.24) The quantity of artefacts found in chambers in Orkney and Caithness varied greatly, from absence to considerable assemblages, mainly consisting of sherds representing only parts of pots, but also including flints and occasionally other tools of stone or bone. It has generally been assumed that sherds found in chambers came from pots used as containers during the funeral ceremonies, though there is evidence that some were already broken when they were placed in the chambers (Hedges 1983, 245; Davidson and Henshall 1989, 57). Small sherds may simply have been left behind when a chamber was cleared out, but the difficulty in accounting for minor items is essentially the same as that for the smaller animal remains. The artefacts from the Sutherland chambers are few and modest (described in Section 7). At Embo (SUT 63) the only artefact associated with the burial phases was a piece of pumice; the status of a few beaker sherds is equivocal (see ¶ 6.31), and a flint knife is more likely to have been with the cist burial than with the second phase burials. From Achaidh (SUT 2) there is a scraper and from Loch Borralan East (SUT 43) some uncertainly neolithic sherds from a single pot. At The Ord North (SUT 48) the unimpressive collection of sherds, mainly from two pots, and a number of flint and quartz flakes, were in the filling layer, and it is likely that all, with the possible exception of a piece of pumice, arrived together. The circumstances of the finding of a stone axehead at Lothbeg (SUT 45) are unknown.

6.25) The layers of soil and stones which covered the floors of the chambers at both Embo and The Ord North (SUT 63, 48) differed in character, and possibly differed in purpose. At the former the filling was homogeneous and archaeologically sterile, and it separated two phases of burials. It could be regarded as a deliberate sealing of the chamber, which later was re-opened to be used again for more burials by the same rites. Remarkably, the soil component of the filling seems to have come from the same marshy source as the dark soil used in the construction of the cairn (¶ 5.8), and which was to be used again in the blocking of the passage (¶ 6.27). At The Ord North the filling was not homogeneous but we believe it was a single deposit, and it contained artefacts. However, two other possible interpretations may be considered. The filling, with artefacts and perhaps also lost bone, may have accumulated over a considerable time and may have been similar to the deposits found on the floors of chambers in SE Caithness: these fillings contained artefacts and human and animal bone, sometimes in great quantities, and were thought to have built up over a period (summarised by Davidson and Henshall 1991, 60-2, and 64). Alternatively, the filling at The Ord may have been a final sealing layer of the type mentioned below (¶ 6.26), though such fillings in Orkney and Caithness do not (as far as is known) include pottery or flints of the types which are customarily associated with the communal burials, but they may include bones and artefacts of other types.

Sealing of the passages and chambers, and external blocking

6.26) Whilst chambers were in use it would have been desirable to close the entrances, securely but in a way which allowed them to be opened when access was needed. There are numerous and widespread instances of chambered cairns with the outer ends of passages filled by a neat stack of slabs, giving the appearance of walling beneath the outermost lintel. Sometimes there was a similar stack placed at the inner end of the passage. After the last burials had been brought to the chambers and the last ceremonies had been performed, some chambers were subjected to permanent closure by filling or partly filling the passages and/or the chambers with stones and soil. Alternatively, and sometimes additionally, a blocking of slabs or stones was piled against the outside of the entrances. All these practices were widespread in Britain, and in particular have been observed or deduced at a number of cairns in Orkney and Caithness (Davidson and Henshall 1989, 59-61; 1991, 66-7). Indeed the sealing of passages and chambers was probably much commoner than it seems, as, in roofless structures, excavators may have found the deliberately introduced filling material indistinguishable from displaced walling and cairn material.

6.27) The passage into the south chamber at Embo (SUT 63) was deliberately filled with slabs to a depth of at least 0.5 m. They were laid flat, with two small stones set upright against one wall. Just within the entrance two thin slabs carefully placed one over the other, and another two between the portal stones, were suggestive of the neat stacked arrangement mentioned above. The slab filling continued into the antechamber, resting on the dark earthy layer which covered the burial deposit, the slabs slanting up towards the main chamber. The interstices of the sealing slabs were filled with dark gravelly soil, deliberately introduced, and indistinguishable from that used to cover the first phase burials. The burials in the main chamber were not covered by a final sealing layer. Outside the passage entrance was a blocking of several layers of slabs tilted up against the slabs in the passage and against the edge of the cairn. The interstices had been left void and later had filled with sand. Above and around the slabs were rounded stones. The blocking was not fully exposed during the excavations, but it extended at least 2 m from the entrance and was at least 2.7 m wide (figure 8, 5, 6).

6.28) At The Ord North (SUT 48) the stone filling of the badly damaged passage was thought to be collapsed roofing and walling. About a third of the way from the entrance, between the pair of transversely-set orthostats, there was a deliberate rubble blocking but no details were recorded. The passage entrance was partly closed by a slab set on edge, only 0.3 m high. An external blocking of slabs and boulders was piled against it and along the front of the cairn for 3.6 m, and extended 1.3 m outwards (figure 21, plate 15). Below the blocking a thin layer of buried soil covered the bedrock; near the entrance just above bedrock were sherds from two pots (6, 7) and two flakes of quartz (23, 27) which probably had been deposited when the blocking was built. The low platform surrounding the cairn may have been built at the same time as the blocking, or possibly it was added later. As at Embo (SUT 63), the chamber had not been deliberately infilled. Observation at the unexcavated Allt Eileag chamber (SUT 72) suggests that this chamber also remained unfilled.

6.29) Skelpick Long (SUT 53) retains a stack of slabs closing the outer end of the passage, the pile of six slabs almost reaching to the roof. External blocking at round cairns is not generally detectable before excavation, but blocking material is evidently present in several unexcavated horned forecourts. At Skelpick Long the built closure of the entrance is only visible

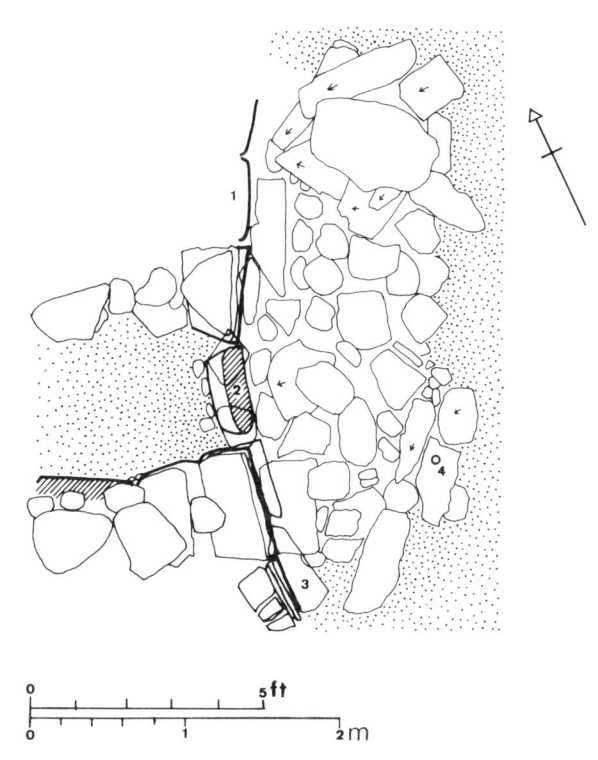

FIGURE 21. The Ord North (SUT 48), plan of the blocking outside the passage entrance (the arrows indicate the upward tilt of some slabs). The excavator's annotations: *1 Wall-face of the cairn; 2 Closing stone leaning to the W; 3 Displaced lower course; 4 Sherds below the blocking* (redrawn from Corcoran 1967a, SUD 115).

PLATE 15. The Ord North (SUT 48), the passage and the outer blocking after excavation in 1967 (scales in feet).

from the roofed passage because of the amount of stone which fills the forecourt. There can be little doubt that some of this is deliberate blocking, but its extent is obscured by cairn material which was thrown over it when the chamber was opened. Robbing at the rear end of the cairn has removed any blocking which may have existed there. The amount of blocking in the forecourts at the proximal ends of the two long cairns at Coille na Borgie (SUT 22, 23) is difficult to assess due to robbing and disturbance, but the smaller blind distal forecourts almost certainly contain a considerable depth of blocking material, reaching to a line between the horns, with the upper parts of the façade orthostats protruding above it. Excavation of the front and rear forecourts at Camster Long, Caithness (CAT 12), both of which were blind at this unusually planned long cairn, exposed blocking of several layers of slabs inclined against the façade, and it may be expected that the blocking at the Sutherland cairns is similar.

6.30) Also in Caithness, the excavation of the two forecourts at the short horned cairn, Tulloch of Assery A (CAT 69), exposed extensive blocking. The appearance of the wider of the two forecourts at the short horned cairns Skelpick South and Kinbrace Burn (SUT 55, 33) suggests that they similarly contain blocking material (see ¶ 5.15). The excavator of Tulloch of Assery A thought it was probable that the extra-revetment material along the concave sides of the cairn had also been deliberately placed, and that this had produced, together with the forecourt blockings, a square plan enclosing the earlier structure of which only the tips of the horns protruded. The squarish plans of two unexcavated Sutherland short horned cairns (SUT 33, 25) may reflect the same treatment, but it is perhaps more likely that the extra-revetment material along the sides is merely the result of the natural disintegration of the stone structure. Achany (SUT 3) is an unusual round cairn with a small forecourt, and there can be little doubt that blocking exists built against the façade. Three substantial stones edge the blocking, but their irregular positioning, and the lack of any parallels for such an edging, makes it likely that they are later additions probably connected with the traces of structures nearby.

Beakers and bronze age burials

6.31) The later history of the Embo and The Ord North cairns (SUT 63, 48) is similar in that both attracted the attention of the makers of beaker pottery, and both were used for burials with food vessels and for unaccompanied cremations. A few sherds from two beakers were found amongst the disturbed second phase burials in the south chamber at Embo. Several small sherds of a third beaker were in the food vessel cist which had been inserted into the centre of the cairn. These sherds had fallen into the cist along with a small amount of silt and were derived from the surrounding cairn which by this time had been greatly disturbed (in the excavation report they were said to be associated with one of the burials in the cist, but reconsideration of the circumstances has led us to the firm opinion that they were redeposited). Theoretically beakers may have been deposited in chambers at any of three stages: as part of the collective burial ritual, though throughout Scotland firm evidence for this is hard to come by; as part of the deliberate sealing process, for which evidence can be found elsewhere; or associated with later burials or as late unexplained deposits (Ritchie 1970, 45–6). At Embo the first is a possibility, the second and third do not apply, and the last seems most likely. A few sherds from the lower part of a beaker came from the chamber at The Ord. They were 0.48 m above the floor, at approximately the level of the top of the neolithic filling, so there is stratigraphic ambiguity in this case also. The status of the few beaker sherds found at cairns in Orkney and Caithness is equally uncertain (Davidson and Henshall 1989, 61, 79; 1991, 76). Sherds of three incomplete beakers were found in a small pit beside a neolithic mound (not a chambered cairn) at Boghead, Moray, and appear to be a ritual deposit (Burl 1984, 52). This gives some support to the suspicion that the beaker sherds in the chambered cairns may be the residue of some ritual activity after the chamber had ceased to be used for communal burials.

6.32) At Embo (SUT 63) there was no sign of blown sand in the cairn until after the second phase burials were placed in the south chamber, the sand presumably reflecting a local environmental change. The chamber contained sand by the time that a short cist was built for the burial of a woman accompanied by a food vessel, a necklace of jet beads, and probably a flint knife. It is perhaps more likely that the chamber roof had already been breached than that the sand had penetrated into the chamber whilst the roof was still intact. Whether the capstone and upper corbel stones were removed by the cist-builders or earlier, the second phase bones and the sand in which by now they were embedded were pushed aside, and the cist was constructed just above the filling over the first phase burials, re-using the capstone and some corbel stones. Following this the hollow above the cist was presumably filled in with cairn material. Ardvreck (SUT 9) may provide another instance of the re-use of a chamber for a single-grave burial (¶ 6.17). The insertion of a second cist into the Embo cairn was a more arduous operation, involving making a hollow through the centre of the cairn, at the bottom of which a pit was dug into the ground to accommodate the cist for almost its full depth. This work must have followed the reduction in height of the south chamber, and the extensive demolition of the north chamber either previously or at this time. In the cist were remains of two babies, a food vessel, and a speck of corroded bronze. The hollow was carefully filled in with horizontal slabs. Secondary cist burials are not uncommon within cairns, and another example where the insertion of a cist had involved considerable effort and skill in manoeuvring large slabs into an unstable hollow has been excavated at Dalineun, Lorn (ARG 3) (Ritchie 1972, 54–5).

6.33) About nine cremations were found in the cairn at Embo (SUT 63), one of them placed in the north chamber after it had been ruined. Two of the cremations were accompanied by bronze razors, indicating that there was continued intermittent use of the cairn for burials till about the middle of the second millennium BC. The collapse of the roof of the main chamber at The Ord (SUT 48) had apparently been caused by the removal of two corbel stones high in the vault in order to insert a cremation. Three or four cremations were found in the rubble, one of them an adult accompanied by a food vessel and an object with a bone mount. Above the blocking in the passage were the cremated remains of a child.

6.34) The grave goods with the female cist burial at Embo (SUT 63) may not rank with the prestige artefacts sometimes found with burials in other parts of Britain and which are indicators of social importance, but her grave goods suggest an elevated status at least in local terms. Insertion of burials into existing monuments, and the amount of effort involved in preparing burial places, also have been seen as reflecting the importance of the deceased (Clarke, Cowie and Foxon 1985, 153). Both the Embo cists required considerable effort to build (strangely, the more difficult operation was for the burial of two infants). Bronze razors appear to have been objects denoting status (op. cit., 158–62), and two of the cremations were accompanied by bronze blades. The bone mount which probably accompanied the cremation with the food vessel at The Ord North (SUT 48) is an exceptional and delicate object. In all, there is cumulative evidence for the veneration of these two chambered

PLATE 16. The chamber orthostats of The Ord South (SUT 49) with The Ord North (SUT 48) in the background.

Gradual destruction of the cairns

6.35) The cairns vary in condition from apparently intact (SUT 32, 34, 35), or structurally intact except for the loss of the chamber capstone and some reduction of the cairn (SUT 55, 82), to total destruction (SUT 50). As mentioned above, at Embo (SUT 63) the cairn had been reduced in height and both chambers had been partly ruined by the early second millennium, and there had been severe disturbance in recent times. After the collapse of the upper part of the vault the large cairn of The Ord North (SUT 48) suffered little interference except for some robbing of the passage area, and it remains an impressive monument. The contrast with the neighbouring South cairn (SUT 49) on the summit of the hill is intriguing; the latter is smaller and likely to be earlier, and has lost almost all the cairn material leaving only some chamber orthostats (plate 16). For most cairns there is no evidence to show when they were ruined, and in most cases the process was probably gradual and intermittent, but without doubt many had suffered long before the first records.

6.36) Destruction was accelerated in the 19th and early 20th centuries mainly due to agricultural improvements and road building. Pittentrail (SUT 50), for example, was evidently a sizeable cairn in 1788, but was gradually removed for 'building purposes' until nothing remained at the beginning of the 20th century. The chamber at Lothbeg (SUT 45), still roofed in the later 18th century, was roofless and greatly ruined by 1909. From the second half of the 19th century the quarrying of cairns for building stone and for road mending is recorded at SUT 54, 12, 29, 51, and 17, and, although undocumented, other cairns were almost certainly reduced for the same purposes (SUT 7, 11, 15, 16, 44, 65, 71). The investigation of several chambers in the 1860s has been described already (¶ 2.4, 2.5, 2.8). They were found roofless but well preserved, and were left open. Deterioration has been due as much to decay of the stone and consequent weakening of the structure as to casual interference, but the chambers are still fairly intact though certainly threatened by the increase of visitors. Tenants of shooting lodges are likely to have opened cairns as a brief diversion, but the only known instance was at Skail (SUT 52) in about 1900.

6.37) Relatively recent destruction at all classes of antiquities was noted in the Report of 1909, and the County Council and landowners were urged to protect monuments; pillaging them for stone, planting trees on or close to them, or unrecorded excavation should cease. 'Vigilance, however, will be required to prevent a repetition of these objectionable practices' (RCAMS 1909, vi). Of the fifty-two cairns recorded in 1909 the great majority remain unaltered or with only slight subsequent interference, though this may have revealed significant features such as parts of passages or chambers as at SUT 42, 72, 78. The chamber at Achaidh (SUT 2) was intact until opened by Curle in 1909, and the well preserved chambers at Kyleoag,

Creag nan Caorach West and Allt a' Chaoruinn (SUT 37, 25, 74) were exposed after his visit but long before the next record in the 1950s or later. Remarkably, only a few cairns are known to have been severely damaged since 1909, the most regrettable being Allt nam Ban (SUT 6) for road metal and Allt a' Mhuilinn (SUT 5) for building a small dam. Two nearly intact chambers which had been left open (SUT 33, 58) have been somewhat reduced in height by stones being tipped from the top of the walls into the cavity, either to prevent sheep from being trapped or as acts of vandalism. The Ardvreck chamber (SUT 9) was left open after excavation in 1925 and has deteriorated badly.

6.38) Extensive afforestation in the 1970s has engulfed eight cairns which remain in small unplanted areas. This has provided protection but has eliminated the landscape, and rank vegetation and deep moss make examination of the cairns more difficult.

7. The artefacts

Artefacts from the neolithic deposits (figures 22 and 23)

7.1) The limited amount of excavation at Sutherland chambered cairns has produced a disappointingly modest number of artefacts. Nothing was found in the chamber at Ardvreck (SUT 9), only a poor flint scraper at Achaidh (SUT 2) (figure 23), sherds of one pot at Loch Borralan East (SUT 43), and only a lump of pumice in the south chamber at Embo (SUT 63). Sherds of at least seven pots, and some flakes of flint and quartz, were found at The Ord North (SUT 48), in the chamber, below the blocking outside the passage entrance, and below or in the platform surrounding the cairn.

7.2) Surprisingly, the small lump of pumice from Embo (SUT 63) is the only object certainly associated with the phase of multiple burials. A larger lump of pumice was found on or just above the floor in the chamber at The Ord South (SUT 48), and may also have been with burials which it is assumed were laid on the floor, though no trace of them survived. Both pieces of pumice had flattened and slightly grooved surfaces, the result of having been used as abrasives. At The Ord North several sherds were found on the chamber floor, or even pressed into it, but reasons have been given in ¶ 6.14 for believing that they (and possibly also the piece of pumice) had arrived in the deliberately introduced material which covered the floor. This layer of soil and stones is assumed to relate to a secondary phase in the use of the chamber, though a chronological distinction may have little significance as the source of the artefacts within it is unknown; and, it may be added, these artefacts may well be strictly or roughly contemporary with the few finds from outside the cairn.

7.3) In the present state of archaeological investigations there is no pottery of earlier neolithic date from domestic or other sites in Sutherland for comparison with the sherds from The Ord North (SUT 48) (apart from a single undecorated rim sherd from Little Ferry in the Dunrobin Castle Museum). There is a complete dearth of neolithic pottery from Ross-shire to the S, and only a small amount is available from the chambered cairns in Caithness to the NE (Davidson and Henshall 1991, 69–75). Consequently the pottery from The Ord North has to be compared with somewhat distant assemblages, chiefly the abundant finds from a few Orcadian chambered cairns and one domestic site at Knap of Howar (Davidson and Henshall 1989, 64–77, their catalogue numbers quoted below; A. Ritchie 1983, 59–72). These assemblages consist mainly of two types of pot. The instantly recognisable Unstan bowls are wide and shallow, with more or less vertical collars defined by a sharp carination and generally decorated by incised lines or impressions. With them is a range of plain bowls with simple rims, varying from quite shallow to deep. The Orcadian pottery is part of a widespread ceramic tradition in northern Scotland. Considerable assemblages including Unstan bowls and plain bowls, but dominated by pots of other forms and decoration, have come from several domestic sites and from a few chambered cairns in the Western Isles; and sporadic minor finds indicate its presence in NE Scotland (the former conveniently summarised by Armit in Crone 1993, 370–5, 378–80; the latter in Henshall 1983, 28–33). All these assemblages show that the pottery found in the cairns was part of the normal domestic range, though there was a disproportionately large number of Unstan bowls in the Orcadian chambers, and perhaps also at The Ord, whilst they are absent from the chambers in the Western Isles, and seem to have been only a minor element in the Caithness chambers.

7.4) At The Ord North (SUT 48) the filling layer in the chamber contained sherds from five vessels (figure 22). Pot 4 was a plain bowl with a thickened rim and a rounded unemphasised shoulder, and the surface is uneven and rather rough. The pot is very incomplete, represented by five rim sherds, a number of wall sherds four of which have a distinct vertical curve from a rounded shoulder, and many crumbs. The important question, bearing on the interpretation of the filling, is whether the sherds all come from one vessel, and the writers feel confident that they do. The rim sherds vary somewhat in profile, the two illustrated being the most dissimilar, but such variation is to be expected in a coarse and irregular pot. The fabric is consistent in all the sherds, except for a few which are laminating and disintegrating and are probably from a rounded base. A single small sherd (4a) from this or a similar pot was found just outside the cairn kerb. There is no reason to view pot 4 as other than a representative of the class of undecorated plain bowls which are a normal component of the assemblages in Orcadian chambers. The thickened rim and

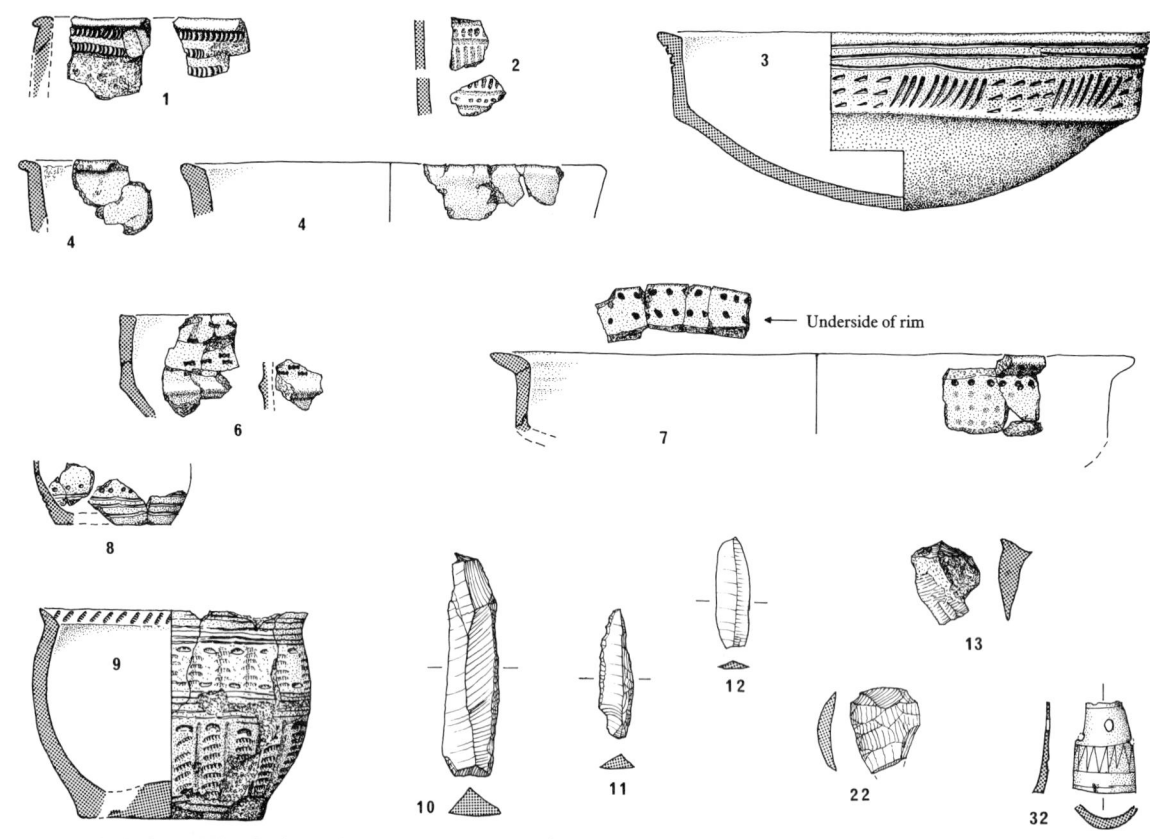

FIGURE 22. Finds from The Ord North (SUT 48). Pottery ¼, other items ½.

slight shoulder may not be typical of these bowls, but both features occur in Caithness as well as Orkney.

7.5) Only three small sherds of pot *1* were found. The rim has a narrow burnished flange, and the grey fabric is notable for its hardness. Decoration is by an unknown number of horizontal rows of deep close-set vertical impressions seemingly made by a round-ended spatula. Immediately below the rim is the scar of a lug which has broken away, presumably one of a pair, or perhaps more. The rim is uneven so the angle of the sherds is uncertain, but the form of the rim suggests that the pot was an unshouldered bowl with the upper part vertical or slightly inturned. No close parallels for this pot can be offered, but there is no need to look for origins outside the earlier neolithic of northern Scotland. The decoration resembles finger-nail impressions, and rustication by this means was recorded on the lost sherds from three Caithness chambers, though the rustication on the surviving sherds and on a few sherds from Orcadian chambers produces a rather different effect. Lugs appear rarely but widespread among earlier neolithic pottery in Orkney, Caithness, and further afield, but they are never combined with heavy decoration. A distinction should be made between lugs placed close to the rim and applied to the vessel, as in this case, and lugs which are formed by pinching out or thickening a carination.

7.6) About half of an Unstan bowl, pot *3*, was recovered. The form and fabric is typical of the larger bowls of this type excavated from chambers in Orkney. The incised decoration, although unusually coarse, is characteristic in design, with horizontal lines below the rim and panels of slanting lines; the alternate panels with rows of stabs is less usual though there are certainly parallels amongst the Orcadian material. Only two tiny sherds of pot *2* survive, almost certainly from the collar of a small and unusually refined Unstan bowl. The black fabric is thin, hard and fine with a burnished outer surface. The decoration is faint, having been partly obliterated by the burnishing; there seem to be two rows of close vertical grooves and a horizontal row of round impressions, separated and bounded by horizontal grooves. Bowls of similar size and quality are not as rare as might at first appear, but in Orkney they are mostly represented by only one or two small sherds. These bowls were present in at least five assemblages, and in particular similar decoration can be seen on Taversoe Tuick sherd *14* and Unstan sherds *13*. The generally very fragmentary condition of the bowls perhaps suggests that they tend to be earlier than the large heavy versions. Pot *5* from The Ord North is represented by a single small sherd, of fine hard dark fabric but distinguished from the rest by the inclusion of white grits.

7.7) Sherds of pots *6* and *7* were found outside the passage entrance. The former pot is fragmentary and much damaged; if the collar is vertical and the diameter is 150 mm or more (as seems probable) it has the proportions of an Unstan bowl, and even if it is of deeper proportions it is clearly closely related to them. The simple impressed decoration can find parallels amongst the Orcadian Unstan bowls, for instance on pots *12–14* at Isbister (ORK 25), pot *11* at Unstan (ORK 51), or pot *1* at Blackhammer (ORK 3). The Ord North pot *7* is, at present, without close parallels. The hard grey fabric, similar to that of pot *3*, and the slight burnishing of the interior (the exterior surface being worn) are characteristic of the best quality earlier neolithic ceramics, but the form is most unusual. The diameter, between 300 and 360 mm, can be matched by several of the largest Unstan bowls from Orkney, but not the exceptional shallowness, and particularly not the shallowness of the lower part relative to the depth of the collar; a large virtually flat piece of the base indicates the proportions of the bowl (the pot is drawn with the minimum diameter in figure 22). Wide flanged rims are not found amongst the pottery from chambered cairns in Orkney and Caithness, though narrow drooping flanges appear occasionally on pots other than Unstan bowls. Decoration by orderly lines of round impressions, and particularly any decoration on the hidden lower side of a projecting rim, is unknown in this area (though, as noted above, other impressed decoration is part of the decorative repertoire). Decoration similar to that on the Sutherland pot appears occasionally in the w, in the chambers at Unival, North Uist, and Beacharra, Argyll (UST 34, ARG 27; Henshall 1972, 309, 533 *16*, 302, 346 *6*), but recalling that The Ord North pottery is in a ceramic lacuna, it would be unwise to put much weight on this apparent connection. In general the pottery from The Ord North appears to be linked with that from Caithness and Orkney.

7.8) The flint blades and the flint and quartz flakes, eighteen in all, came from the chamber filling, from below the blocking, and from the platform at The Ord North (SUT 48). The detailed examination by Wickham-Jones and Bradley (reported in Sharples 1981, 42–7) showed that they were mainly simple cutting and scraping tools. Two blades (*10*, *11*) had been retouched down one side, and the edges of these and of most of the flakes showed evidence of use. An irregular thicker flint flake (*13*) and a flake of quartz carefully retouched across one face (*22*) had been used as scrapers. Only a few flakes and one core trimming appeared to be waste material from knapping. The material of both the flint and quartz tools was local pebbles. A single small blade of pitchstone was of material imported from Arran (its stratigraphic position outside the cairn is unclear). The flint knife from the south chamber at Embo (SUT 63), found before the excavation, is more likely to have been with the cist burial than with the earlier burials (¶ 7.13).

Beaker sherds (figures 22 and 23)

7.9) The origins of beaker pottery lie on the continent but the mechanisms by which it was introduced to Britain are the subject of debate. This pottery was formerly considered to indicate large-scale movements of peoples, but currently this is thought to have been overstressed. There are few beakers from N of the Dornoch Firth and thus even fragmentary examples from the Sutherland chambered cairns are important additions to the overall distribution. In Scotland beakers are generally found either accompanying single inhumation burials in stone cists or as debris on occupation sites. There is no clear explanation for the appearance of beaker sherds at The Ord North and Embo (SUT 48, 63) (see ¶ 6.31).

7.10) At The Ord North (SUT 48) a few sherds from the base of a small vessel, *8*, were found at roughly the level of the top of the deliberate filling of the chamber. The excavator thought that they were from a grooved ware pot, which the incised decoration indeed suggests, and the small size of the pot need be no bar to this interpretation. When Sharples published the excavation he suggested that the vessel was in the beaker tradition (1981, 41–2), though it is incorrect to connect it stratigraphically with either a cremation or with a food vessel, both of which were in the collapsed material above the neolithic filling. The sherds are almost certainly from a small beaker, the vertical curve of the walls being particularly suggestive, but the decoration is unusual with the row of spaced round impressions above the firmly incised lines around the base.

7.11) The abraded sherds, *3*, found redeposited in the central cist at Embo (SUT 63), can be reconstructed as a small all-over-cord beaker (AOC, following

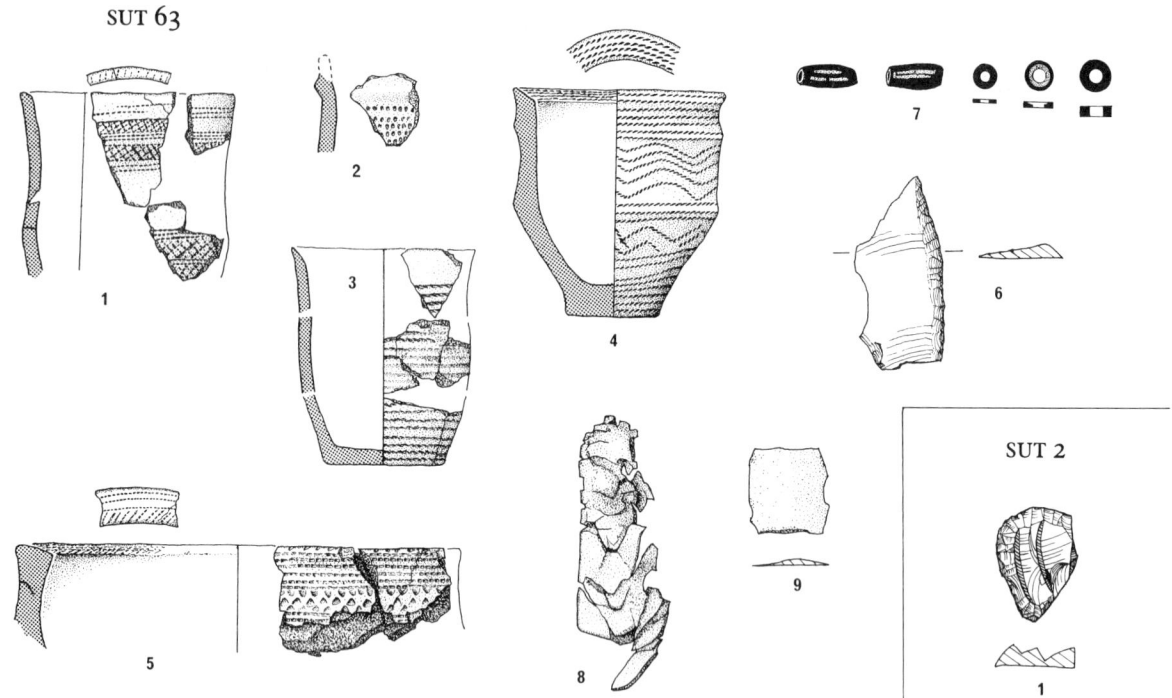

FIGURE 23. Finds from Embo (SUT 63) and Achaidh (SUT 2). Pottery ¼, other items ½.

Clarke's classification, 1970, 38–44). The fabric, though hard, is dark and gritty, and is not of the quality of the best of the beakers of this class. AOC beakers are a widespread European type within the bell beaker group, and they make an early appearance amongst the British beaker series but have a long survival. In N Scotland a few sherds have been found in one or two chambers in Caithness (CAT 38, ?31), and most notably parts of four high-quality beakers were found with sherds of a bell beaker and another of related type at Kilcoy South in Ross-shire (ROS 24) (Davidson and Henshall 1991, 76; Henshall 1963, 255, 349). The sherds at Boghead, Moray (already referred to in ¶ 6.31 in connection with possible ritual deposits at earlier monuments) were also of AOC and bell beakers. At Dornoch Nursery, only 3 km SW of Embo, the presence of makers of AOC beakers is confirmed by a burial according to their normal rite. In 1980 a cist was found which contained an inhumation with unusually rich grave goods, a fine AOC beaker, five arrowheads, a bracer, a flint strike-a-light and an iron ore nodule (and also a probably intrusive cremation) (Ashmore 1989).

7.12) A single sherd, 2, from the S chamber at Embo (SUT 63), was from a relatively large vessel with horizontal lines of coarse comb impressions. Enough survives of another beaker, 1, to show that the decoration by fine comb impressions was certainly in two and possibly in three zones of lattice edged by horizontal lines, with transverse impressions across the rim. This beaker may be compared with a closely similar intact beaker found in a cist at Upper Muirhall, Perthshire, which belongs to the Late Northern group (N 3) according to Clarke's classification (1970, 176–90; Reid, Shepherd and Lunt 1986). These beakers are later in date than the AOC and bell beaker groups. Sherds of beakers belonging to several stages in the development of the Late Northern beakers have come from the chambers at Tulach an t-Sionnaich and Lower Dounreay in Caithness (CAT 58, 38), and from Carn Glas and Kilcoy South in Ross-shire (ROS 12, 24). In two cases (CAT 38, ROS 24) the sherds seem to have been stratified above AOC beaker sherds, and in another case (CAT 58) they arrived in the chamber after it had ceased to be used for collective burials. In Sutherland only three beaker burials in cists are known besides that at Dornoch Nursery, and these beakers belong to Clarke's North/North Rhine group; two were near Skail in Strathnaver (Gourlay 1984) and one in Dunrobin Park near Golspie (Mitchell 1934, 188). This last is of particular interest as the cist also contained over a hundred small shale discs of which six were perforated, linking it with the Embo cist burial mentioned below (¶ 7.13).

Artefacts with later burials (figures 22 and 23)

7.13) The cist burial of a female inserted into the south chamber at Embo (SUT 63) was accompanied by a food vessel, some beads, and probably by a flint knife. Her necklace (7) consisted of fourteen disc beads and two fusiform beads, all of cannel coal except for one fusiform bead of jet (Sheridan and Davis, forthcoming), and possibly more beads of organic materials which did not survive. The signs of wear show that they had been strung and worn for some time prior to deposition. The association of disc beads with food vessel burials is well known, and they are also found with late beaker burials (Ritchie and Shepherd 1973, 31; Shepherd in Watkins 1982, 103–4). The numbers of beads with a burial may vary from two to over two hundred. In the beaker cist burial at Dunrobin Park 8 km N of Embo, mentioned above, most of the beads were unfinished. The closest example of a food vessel associated with disc beads, but not in a cist, is at Achinduich in the Shin valley (McCullagh 1991). A cist burial inserted into the chamber at South Yarrows North in Caithness (CAT 54) invites general comparisons with the Embo burial in that the lost vessel accompanying it sounds similar to the Embo food vessel and was with a disc bead necklace. A second cist in the cairn at Embo contained two babies and the collapsed remains of a large food vessel. Only a speck of corroded bronze remained to indicate that a small object of this metal had been included with the burials.

7.14) At The Ord North (SUT 48) a cremation accompanied by a food vessel (9) had been inserted into the upper filling of the chamber. A delicate mount of bone or antler, part of which survives but is somewhat distorted by scorching (32), probably was with this burial. The mount is 24 mm long, and was cylindrical with a diameter of about 18 mm; the base may have been solid. Parts of a small perforation can be seen in each of the broken side edges, and a third larger perforation is not in alignment with them; presumably these were for securing-pegs. The decoration of horizontal lines and a band of zigzag is by fine incision. The mount is at present without parallel, and there is no indication of the nature of the object of which it was an embellishment, probably on a slender handle or shaft.

7.15) The category of food vessel embraces pots with a considerable diversity of shape and decoration; however, a broad distinction can be made between those of bowl shape and those with more vase-like proportions (Burgess 1974, 182–4). Food vessels are scarce in northern Scotland so those from Embo and The Ord North (SUT 63, 48) are of particular interest. The intact vessel 4 from Embo is small, of tripartite form, decorated with impressed cord in zones of horizontal and chevrony lines. It is clearly in the vase tradition. The small vessel from The Ord North belongs to the bowl tradition, and the thickened convex base links it to the squat globular bowls rather than the more elegant Irish bowl type (op. cit., 185; Simpson 1968, 202–7). Two zones of decoration are defined by groups of incised horizontal lines, and each zone is filled by vertical rows of whipped cord 'maggot' impressions. The rim sherds 5 from Embo are from a large food vessel, probably of the ridged bowl form common in Scotland, with characteristic decoration in zones of comb-impressed lines and rows of triangular impressions made by a spatula. The small number of radiocarbon dates for food vessels in east/central Scotland (listed by Cowie and Ritchie 1991, 107–8) indicate that they were in use during the early second millennium BC.

7.16) At Embo (SUT 63) two of the cremations placed in the cairn were each accompanied by a bronze razor. Such razors fall into two categories: Class I razors have leaf-shaped blades often lacking a midrib, and a tang which may be perforated; Class II razors have bifid blades notched at the tip and perforated just below the notch, with a pronounced midrib, and a tang which is unperforated (Coles, following C. M. Piggott, in Henshall and Wallace 1963, 25–6; Coles 1964, 120). The bronze fragment 9 from Embo had evidently been a small simple oval blade, but the top and the bottom edge with its tang are missing; it evidently belonged to Class I. Almost half of blade 8 was found, but in a fragmentary and distorted condition; the tang and the angular base of the blade survived but it lacks the upper edge. It was identified as being of Class II, although this has been questioned (Burgess 1976, 93). In a re-assessment of all the western European razor-knives the Scottish examples were set in a wider typological framework, and both the Embo fragments were interpreted as early razor-knives (Jöckenhovel 1980, 43, Tafel 5). Most razors have been found in cremation deposits, as was the case in SE Sutherland at Balblair near Bonar Bridge and Learable in the Strath of Kildonan, and probably at Rogart (the blade was with 'mouldered bones') (Coles 1964, 149). Razors appear to be objects of status during the second quarter of the second millennium BC and beyond.

8. Orientation, relationships and dating

Orientation

8.1) The state of preservation of some forty-one chambers and passages allows their orientation to be assessed at least in broad terms. The precise alignment of a passage may be difficult to assess if it is not exactly straight, and there may thus be some leeway in interpretation. There is, however, a clear preference for the chamber entrance to face between the E and S, with a smaller group facing the NE quadrant of the compass (figure 24). The principal exceptions are Fiscary (SUT 29), Allt nam Ban (SUT 6) and Skelpick Long (SUT 53) which look to the WSW, WNW and NNW. The orientation of Coille na Borgie North (SUT 22) is less clear, but it was certainly W of N. The orientation pattern is thus closely comparable to that recorded in Caithness, with a rather larger proportion between E and SE than was the case in Orkney. There is no consistent pattern within the local clusters in Sutherland. The preferences in orientation mean that the entrances of the majority of the tombs surveyed lie in the arc between the major northern and southern moon rises. An interest in lunar cycles can be inferred, but it is much more difficult to interpret this interest in practical terms. The low entrance passages make it unlikely that the light of the moon could penetrate the interior darkness; equally it is unlikely that anyone within the tomb could make meaningful observations. Burl has stressed that orientation of entrances is likely to have been symbolic (1982, 146–7). This is not to deny that deliberate orientation on celestial events could be achieved, as at Maes Howe (ORK 36) which faces the midwinter sunset, but it seems unlikely that any of the tombs in Sutherland was orientated in such a precise way.

8.2) The long cairns also favour an orientation towards the eastern half of the compass with the proximal ends facing in this direction, though Skelpick Long and Coille na Borgie North and South (SUT 53, 22, 23) face towards the N and NW. The choice of orientation for these three cairns, and possibly others, was limited by the orientation of the earlier passage graves which they covered; in other

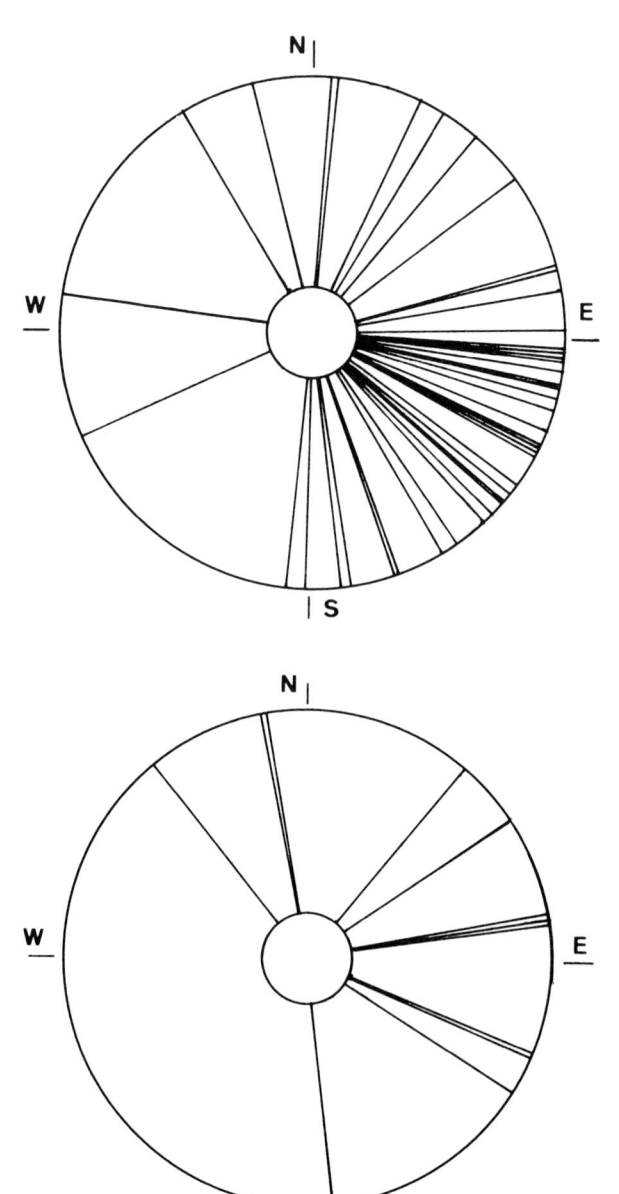

FIGURE 24. Orientations. The axes of chambers in the upper diagram, the axes of long cairns in the lower diagram.

cases considerations of topography and visibility may have imposed the siting which in turn controlled the orientation, for instance when a long cairn was built along a narrow terrace.

The distribution and typology of the chambers

8.3) Passage-graves of Orkney-Cromarty type are found over a large part of northern Scotland (figure

1), and Sutherland has a central position within the province. The design of chambers is in part a response to the local building stone; over much of the province flat stones of any size were difficult to come by, in the sandstone areas extending down the E coast of Sutherland and Ross-shire shapely slabs were generally available, and in Caithness and Orkney the sandstones and flagstones provided first-rate building materials. Variants of the chamber plan were favoured and developed in particular areas, and these developments indicate, in very general terms, a typological and chronological framework within which to consider the structures. Typology, handled with common sense within viable geographical and chronological limits, continues to provide a basis for the study of chambered cairns, as has recently been re-affirmed by Mercer (1992, 56). A firm chronology for the chambers is not available: there are too few radiocarbon dates from Scottish tombs, and these may refer to the use of a chamber (which may be intermittent and prolonged) rather than to its construction (¶ 8.18–22).

8.4) Scattered throughout the province there are a few single-compartment chambers of small size, and there can be little doubt that these are early among the chambered cairns, both for practical reasons if they are to be attributed to the earliest farming communities, and because of their widespread but rare appearance (Henshall 1972, 257–9). There are two small chambers in Sutherland, far apart in the E and NW at Embo and Allt a' Chaoruinn (SUT 63, 74), and there are several in Caithness. A larger chamber at Achaidh (SUT 2), almost certainly of single-compartment plan, is of a size and style comparable with the main chambers of bipartite chambers. Whilst single-compartment chambers of medium and large size became the dominant type in the Hebrides and the SW of the province, chambers with bipartite plans were by far the commonest type built in Sutherland and Ross-shire.

8.5) In its simplest form the bipartite plan merely involved placing a small ante-chamber between the passage and chamber, to produce relatively small chambers designated the 'Caithness type' in this volume; the S chamber at Embo (SUT 63) is a good example. In fact bipartite chambers are not common in Caithness, but the excavation of several well preserved examples has revealed their design. The larger and structurally more challenging Skelpick-type chambers are only found in Sutherland and Ross-shire. They are an impressive development of the bipartite plan, reflecting increased experience and confidence in building large roofed structures in stone. The roofing of the ante-chamber and the main chamber by contiguous vaults which met over the lintel between the two compartments presented a structural difficulty (see ¶ 4.16).

8.6) There are at least twenty-five bipartite chambers in Sutherland, and doubtless there are many more among the same number of unclassified chambers. Beyond noting that the distribution of bipartite chambers is widespread, comment on the distribution of the Caithness-type and Skelpick-type chambers is inhibited by the number of chambers which cannot be classified, and in any case it is probably misleading to distinguish the two types too rigidly (figure 25). The Caithness-type chambers appear to be fairly widely spread but perhaps with an emphasis on the SE. Including probable examples, there are four in SE Sutherland (SUT 49, 28, 63, 58), one in the upper Strath of Kildonan (SUT 65), but none in the N; there are two on the W coast (SUT 10, 20) and one in the SW cluster of cairns around Inchnadamph and Loch Ailsh (SUT 44). The distribution of Skelpick-type chambers is more western and northern; there are only two in the SE (SUT 26, 48) and none in the Strath of Kildonan, two in Strathnaver (SUT 53, 54), one near Durness (SUT 60) and six among the Inchnadamph-Loch Ailsh cluster.

8.7) Two Sutherland chambers have side cells, a feature which appears to have led to the emergence of tripartite chambers, a development probably parallel to that of the Skelpick-type chambers. Kyleoag (SUT 37) almost certainly has a single-compartment chamber of quite large size; the smaller chamber at Loch Borralan East (SUT 43) may be of single-compartment or bipartite plan. Kenny's Cairn (CAT 31), a bipartite chamber, is the only other example with a side cell (as far as is known, but this is a feature which is particularly likely to be hidden or destroyed). These three chambers are distant from each other, in SE Sutherland, W Sutherland and E Caithness. The tripartite chamber plan evidently arose from aligning a cell on the chamber axis. Tripartite chambers were the normal type built in Caithness where the excellent building stone invited refinement and enlargement of the basic design. The typologically earliest of the several variants is the Yarrows form where the inner compartment was roofed at a low level and separately from the vaulted main chamber and thus retained the character of a cell. The chamber at Kinbrace Burn (SUT 33) was certainly of this type, and probably also those at Creag nan Caorach West and Fiscary (SUT 25, 29). Allt a' Mhuilinn and Allt nam Ban (SUT 5, 6) contain large tripartite chambers

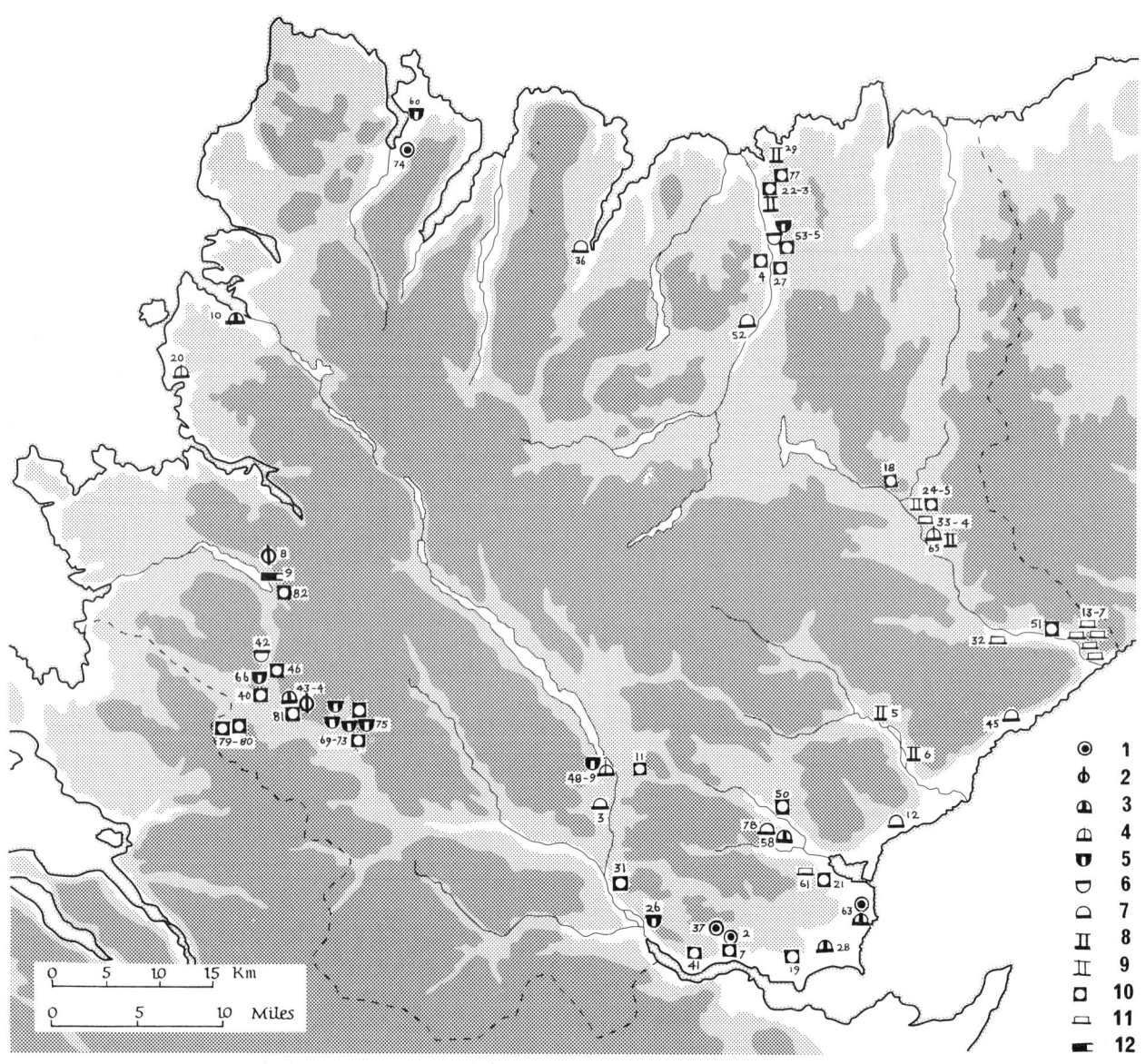

FIGURE 25. Distribution map, the cairns plotted according to the chamber plan.
Key: 1 single-compartment; 2 single-compartment or bipartite; 3 bipartite Caithness type; 4 bipartite probably Caithness type; 5 bipartite Skelpick type; 6 bipartite probably Skelpick type; 7 bipartite unclassified; 8 tripartite; 9 probably tripartite; 10 unclassified; 11 long cairn without recorded chamber; 12 Clyde type. SUT 35, 57 and 76 omitted.

which are thought not to have this roofing pattern, and the latter chamber is particularly notable for its size. On typological grounds it can be suggested that these two chambers, geographically close together in Strath Brora, were built relatively late; their design and the lack of side-slabs in the walls seem to owe more to developments in Caithness than to those in Sutherland. The plan of the sixth tripartite chamber, at Coille na Borgie South (SUT 23), defies useful comment, but its fine walling without side-slabs and the tall slender inner portal stones are in the style of Caithness chambers rather than those of Sutherland. Nearby Fiscary, almost on the N coast, may also derive from Caithness. The distribution of the tripartite chambers, with two each in Strath Brora, upper Strath of Kildonan and lower Strathnaver, is puzzling,

PLATE 17. Embo (SUT 63) from the N during excavation in 1960, the N chamber in the foreground, the S chamber in the background and a later cist between them (scale in feet).

and the more so if the chambers with side cells are also considered.

8.8) Embo (SUT 63) is the only cairn in Sutherland to contain two chambers (plate 17), but this arrangement occurs occasionally in Orkney, Caithness and Ross-shire. Sometimes the chambers were contemporary (ORK 23, 49, CAT 34, 48) and sometimes they were not (ORK 1, 8, CAT 12). The Embo chambers were back-to-back 3.25 m apart on parallel axes, which might suggest that they had been built at the same time and thus are comparable with Langwell (CAT 34), but the differences in their design rather suggests that the N chamber, with a small cairn, was the primary structure on the site.

The plans and structure of the cairns

8.9) The chambers of Orkney-Cromarty passage graves are normally covered by round cairns. In Sutherland thirty-six chambers are, or were, covered by cairns of this form and two oval cairns can be added. A further eleven cairns are unclassifiable but most of them are likely to have been round. It is the relatively few cairns of other shapes which invite attention, and particularly the interest in creating forecourts, presumably as a setting for ceremonies. The lack of correlation between chamber type and cairn form has already been noted (¶ 5.33).

8.10) A small shallow forecourt was built at the passage entrance at two round cairns, The Ord North and Achany (SUT 48, 3), and almost certainly each was part of an enlargement of the original cairn. It seems probable that the heel-shaped plan, with its much wider but still shallow forecourt defined by a façade, was an extension of this requirement. Only two or three independent heel-shaped cairns have been recorded in Sutherland (SUT 37, 69, 75), but identification of cairns of this plan is difficult. One is in the SE and two are in the Inchnadamph-Loch Ailsh cluster of cairns. Two more heel-shaped cairns form the proximal ends of long cairns (SUT 22, 34), and these are in upper Strath of Kildonan and

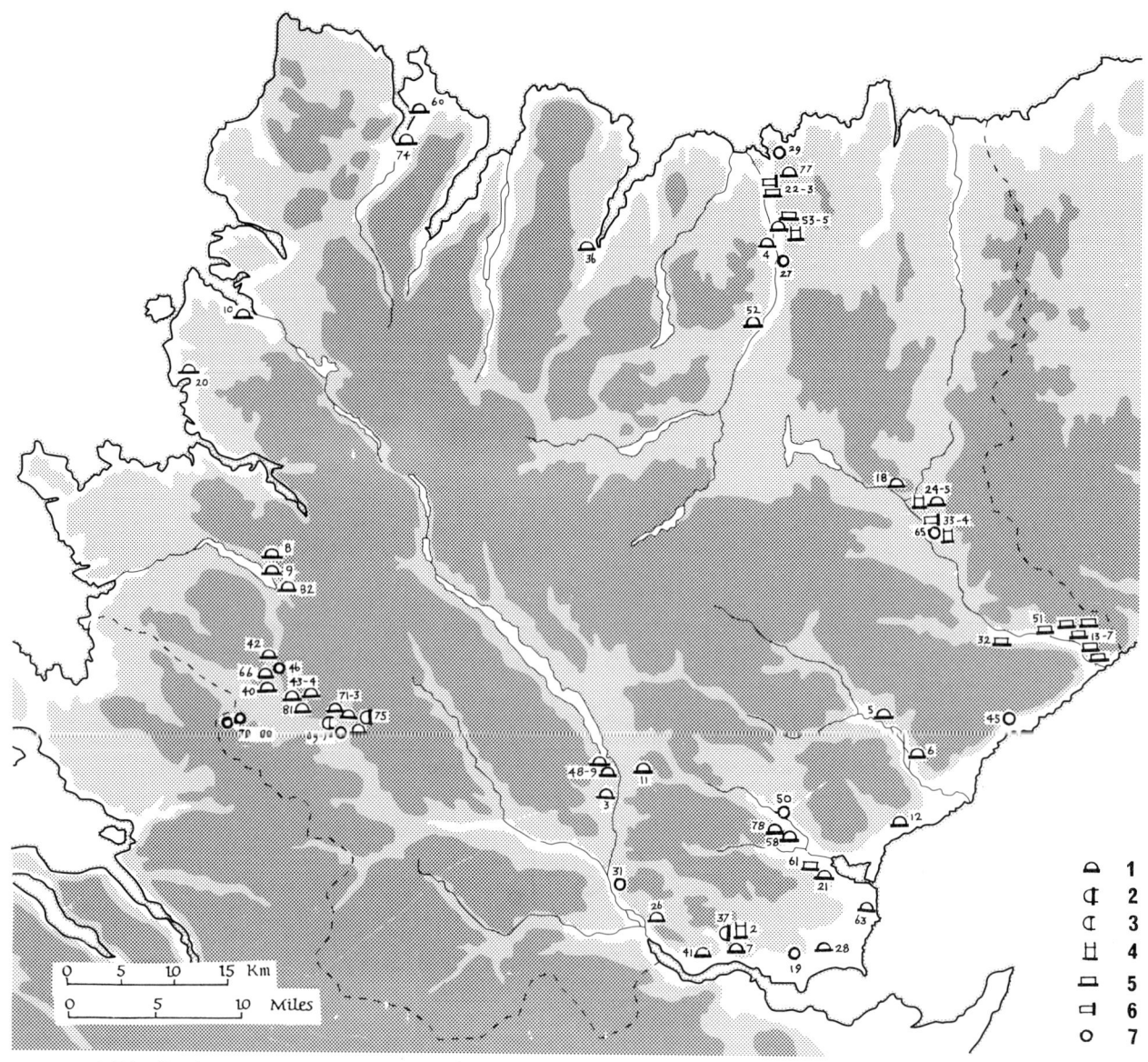

FIGURE 26. Distribution map, the cairns plotted according to shape. Key: 1 round; 2 heel-shaped; 3 probably heel-shaped; 4 short horned; 5 long; 6 heel-shaped and long; 7 unclassified. SUT 35, 57 and 76 omitted.

Strathnaver, so this form of cairn seems to be widely scattered (figure 26). Heel-shaped cairns, either independent or incorporated into long cairns, are almost equally rare in Caithness, and are absent in Orkney, but they are common in Shetland where there are no long cairns. Limited evidence from Caithness shows that, at least in some cases, heel-shaped cairns were later additions to the passage-graves they cover, and in one case a heel-shaped cairn was earlier than a long cairn (¶ 5.11, 17).

8.11) Twelve long cairns are known in Sutherland, and this is likely to be close to the original number because they are easily recognisable unless virtually destroyed. Their distribution seems curious, though it becomes slightly less so when the overall distribution N of the Great Glen is considered. In E Sutherland there is one long cairn at the mouth of Strath Fleet (SUT 61), seven long cairns in the lower part of the Strath of Kildonan (SUT 13–17, 32, 51), and one in the upper part of the strath (SUT 34). These cairns are part of a spread of long cairns through E Ross-shire, Caithness (where they are fairly numerous with a wide distribution) and to Orkney. Yet within Sutherland it should be noted that there is only one small long cairn in the fertile SE contrasted with the concentration in the lower Strath of Kildonan with its very limited agricultural potential. Three long cairns built close together in the lower part of Strathnaver (SUT 22, 23, 53) may be the result of a movement northwards from the Strath of Kildonan or a spread westwards from Caithness.

8.12) The long cairns in the N of Scotland raise a number of problems, most of which will only be solved by excavation. There can be little doubt that the origins of the cairns lie with the non-megalithic long barrows and cairns concentrated in southern and eastern England and scattered through eastern and south-western Scotland, most recently studied by Kinnes (1992a; 1992b, 86–92, 101–3). Excavations have shown that they may cover any of a wide variety of structures of a relatively temporary character built of wood or turf or occasionally of stone; and some long barrows and cairns contain no internal structures at all. The question arises whether any of the long cairns in the north of Scotland may be non-megalithic, and may cover a structure appropriate to that tradition instead of a passage grave. In Sutherland the cairns most likely to be non-megalithic are Creag an Amalaidh and Kilournan (SUT 61, 32); they exhibit no hint of multi-period construction and they are differentiated from the other long cairns by their size (¶ 5.16). The absence of firm evidence of chambers in three of the cairns in the lower Strath of Kildonan (SUT 13, 15, 17) may seem suspicious, but another cairn in this cluster (SUT 51) certainly covered a chamber of which there is now no trace. The presence of non-megalithic long cairns in Sutherland remains a possibility.

8.13) Most of the northern long cairns are complex multi-period monuments, and certainly many contain chambers. In Strathnaver there are three impressive long cairns with chambers (SUT 22, 23, 53); in the Strath of Kildonan there is an intact long cairn of a distinctive form which it is assumed contains a chamber (SUT 34) and also the long cairn just mentioned in which a chamber has been destroyed (SUT 51). The convincing evidence from the first three monuments that the long cairns encapsulated pre-existing passage graves has been presented already (¶ 5.17–29). Two or three structural periods can be detected on surface examination of these and other long cairns, and excavation would probably expose yet more phases of alteration and enlargement. The structural complexities of the northern long cairns, in which two (or more) different mortuary/ceremonial traditions were brought together in one monument, can hardly be exaggerated. Attempts at interpretation can do little more than point to their significance and potential. There are dangers, too, in interpretation at the present level of information, as general application of the very limited hard evidence from a few of the northern cairns (which may be atypical) may both obscure overall trends and lessen appreciation of the structural permutations. Any advance in understanding the long cairns, and thus of the relationships of their builders with the builders of passage graves, can come only from a campaign of large scale excavations.

8.14) Two long cairns, SUT 22 and 34, may represent an early stage in the coupling of long cairns with passage graves. Each monument consists of two physically separate parts, a heel-shaped 'head' and a trapezoid 'tail'. The latter is a small long cairn similar to the possibly non-megalithic cairns SUT 32 and 61, and was built back-to-back with the presumably earlier heel-shaped cairn, a sequence already proven by excavation in Caithness at CAT 58. It is reasonable to expect that the next step was amalgamation of the two parts into one cairn, to produce the usual long narrow plan. The similarity of the three Strathnaver cairns in size and plan (but not in the chambers they contain) with a number of Caithness long cairns is striking, and most especially the near-duplication of the complex features of the paired cairns at Coille na Borgie and South Yarrows (SUT 22, 23, CAT 54, 55) (¶ 5.25; figure 17). Two points of dissimilarity should be noted: it is probable that the façade at Coille na Borgie South was blind (¶ 5.27), an arrangement which can be paralleled at other Caithness cairns; and the Coille na Borgie cairns received façades and side walls which incorporated orthostats as prominent features.

8.15) The external use of spaced orthostats as the final embellishment of the Coille na Borgie cairns (SUT 22, 23) is unique among the cairns of the N mainland of Scotland. The remote origins of this feature almost certainly lie in the massive wooden façades built at non-megalithic barrows and cairns, but its intermediate source is probably the Clyde group of chambered cairns of SW and W Scotland. Impressive façades of orthostats linked by walling are commonly found at the proximal ends of trapezoid Clyde cairns, and some of these cairns were edged by walling with spaced upright stones. The ultimate expansion of the Clyde cairns was to the Western Isles. This is a region with mixed traditions, but predominantly the domain of the builders of passage graves. Façades and edgings enhanced by spaced orthostats commonly appear at round and square cairns as well as at at least one long cairn (UST 10), and all these cairns more often cover chambers of passage-grave than Clyde type (Henshall 1972, 612–19). Thus the use of orthostats at Coille na Borgie is likely to be an innovation from the Western Isles, at the last stage in the structural history of Sutherland cairns. Considering that in Sutherland this treatment appears at two adjacent *long* cairns it might be thought that there was a more direct connexion with Clyde cairns, a suggestion which might be linked with the lone presence of a Clyde cairn in W Sutherland at Ardvreck (SUT 9) (¶ 4.33). But the small size and simple form of the chamber and cairn suggest that this tomb represents an early tentative penetration of the N mainland, pre-dating the appearance of trapezoid Clyde cairns with impressive façades in the Clyde heartland or in the Western Isles. However, an enigma remains in the appearance of an orthostatic façade forming a shallow forecourt at the round cairn at Achany (SUT 3). Its connections may be to the S rather than the N, as two round chambered cairns in the Black Isle (ROS 6, 8) retain parts of orthostatic façades.

8.16) Short horned cairns, though few in number, appear to reflect the distribution of long cairns through the eastern part of the northern highlands (Henshall 1972, 241–4); one is known on the Black Isle in E Ross-shire, four in Sutherland, five in Caithness and one in Orkney. Sutherland short horned cairns are in the SE (SUT 2), in the Strath of Kildonan (SUT 25, 33) and in Strathnaver (SUT 55), in general terms following quite closely the distribution of long cairns. The appearance of square cairns in the Western Isles, Skye and W Inverness-shire, and their ultimate spread to Shetland (without the presence of long cairns), seems to have been a parallel development. The notable group of passage-graves in W Sutherland appears to have remained free of the long cairn and short horned tradition.

8.17) The design of short horned cairns is certainly linked to that of the long cairns with two deep forecourts. The plan of the front and the rear of both types of cairn is the same, even to the front or proximal forecourt being larger than the rear or distal forecourt. The close similarity of the forecourts and façades at the two types of cairns is clear at the excavated examples in Caithness, and there is no reason to suppose that this is not the case in Sutherland. The only evidence as to the relationship of the outer parts of the cairns to the passage-graves they contain comes from the excavation of Tulloch of Assery A (CAT 69) in 1961 where the whole construction appeared to be a unitary design (Corcoran 1966, 26–9; Davidson and Henshall 1991, 44, 56). If correct, this would indicate that the two disparate elements, passage-graves and deep forecourts, were sometimes integrated into a distinctive form of chambered cairn; but the corollary, that the small number of short horned cairns were contemporary with single-compartment, bipartite and tripartite chambers, warns that this is unlikely to be so. Integration of the two traditions may have been achieved in some regions, with passage graves and forecourt cairns designed and built as a unit (evidence has recently come from the long cairn of Point of Cott (ORK 41); Barber 1988, 58, the excavation report forthcoming), but this step is unlikely to have taken place in Sutherland.

Chronology and dating

8.18) The interpretation and presentation of radiocarbon dates is still, after over thirty years of development, a matter of debate. A greater appreciation of the probable accuracy of dates has encouraged the use of a standard deviation of two sigma rather than of one sigma as has been usual until now. The latter gives a probability of only 68% that the date falls within the given bracket; a deviation of two sigmas gives a probability of over 95%.

8.19) In the table (figure 27), the few dates relating to Sutherland chambers have been laid out in a different way from that used in the earlier volumes of this series for dates relating to the Orkney and Caithness chambers. This is because an increasingly cautious approach favours presentation of each determination as a date Before Present (BP, in practice before 1950) with a standard deviation of one sigma, and a calibrated date BC with a two-sigma span. In the table this practice has been adopted and a span is given for the calibrated date within which there is a 95% probability that the event dated actually fell. The determination itself is listed as a date BP with the standard error of one sigma followed by a calibrated span BC to two sigmas.

8.20) From The Ord North (SUT 48) two dates (GU 1168 and 1169) from the ante-chamber filling and a determination from charcoal from the floor of the main chamber (GU 1172) demonstrate that it was in use at some time during the second half of the fourth millennium BC. The date for a layer of hard soil or pan above the W part of the slab structure (GU 1173) must, for reasons of stratigraphy, be chronologically more recent than the date derived from charcoal on the floor but it is not statistically different. The length of time through which the cairn was intermittently used for burials is highlighted by the date from char-

THE ORD NORTH (SUT 48)

Lab no.	Context	Material	Radiocarbon date BP	Calibrated date BC
GU 1167	Cremation lying in collapsed roofing of main chamber.	Betula, Corylus, Alnus, cf. Pinus bark	3435±65	1889–1528
GU 1168	Silty layer above floor of antechamber, associated with Unstan bowl.	Alnus, Corylus, Pinus	4260±60	3614–3106
GU 1169	From ante-chamber in silty soil above floor level and below sherds of Unstan bowl.	Corylus, Pinus	4665±70	3633–3192
GU 1172	Lying on floor of main chamber.	Pinus, Corylus	4510±100	3506–2911
GU 1173	In main chamber, in the layer of 'hard soil' or pan, above the W part of the 'cist structure' about 0.23m above the floor.	Corylus, Pinus	4465±60	3352–2918

EMBO (SUT 63)

Lab no.	Context	Material	Radiocarbon date BP	Calibrated date BC
BM 442	Deposit contemporary with the construction of the S chamber.	Collagen from small animal bones	3870±100	2582–1989
GrA 770	From pocket of clean sand immediately NE of Stone F, under corbel stone of the S chamber.	Infant skull	4010±70	2865–2310
GrA 771	From behind Stone D, under corbel stone of the S chamber.	Part of mandible of infant	4340±70	3305–2700
GrA 772	From behind Stone D, under corbel stone of the S chamber.	Two fragmentary adult vertebrae	3720±70	2320–1900

FIGURE 27. Radiocarbon dates from Sutherland cairns. The calendar dates from The Ord North have been calibrated using the intercept method using CALIB 3.03 (Stuiver and Reimer 1993) to two sigma. The dates from Embo have been calibrated to two sigma using OxCal 2.0 and the same curve. The correction to GU 1173 is based on the Glasgow/SURRC master database.

coal with cremated bone in the collapsed roofing of the main chamber (GU 1167) more than a millennium later. The dates from Embo (SUT 63) give a puzzling span for contexts that should all be contemporary with the construction of the S chamber, and the best that can be said is that they suggest activity in the middle or later part of the third millennium BC. Thus the new dates (GrA 770, 771, 772) have not, as hoped, clarified the interpretation of the earlier, and possibly anomalous, determination (BM 442).

8.21) The shift in emphasis in dealing with radiocarbon dates has led to an increasing insistence that multi-dated sequences offer a much greater degree of internal control than single dates. Also dating based on spans of two sigma is less likely to encourage potentially misleading comparisons of single dates or of sequences. It has also been suggested that some results from the earliest period of research should be treated with caution. It has to be admitted, too, that chambered cairns are not an ideal category of monument for this dating method, for the deposits within the chambers are frequently difficult to interpret (earlier burials may have been cleared out or merely pushed to one side) and material associated with construction phases is difficult to identify or to recover. With these cautions and difficulties in mind, discussion of the dates from northern chambered cairns becomes more generalised, and the close inter-relationship of determinations such as those from Isbister and Quanterness in Orkney (ORK 25, 43) and The Ord North (SUT 48) (Renfrew 1979, 200–9; Hedges 1983, 61–71; Sharples 1981, 53–4, 59; 1986) are less easy to sustain. The dates are, however, comparable to those obtained for cairns in Caithness (CAT 58, 69–70), and there is no reason to doubt Sharples's assertion that Tulloch of Assery B and The Ord North were roughly contemporary, certainly in terms of use (1986, 6).

8.22) It may seem disappointing that a dating method which appears to offer increasing chronological definition should only be used in such a broad-brush way, but what is important is the firm chronological framework within which the use of northern chambered cairns clearly falls in the second half of the fourth millennium BC. The traditional typological approach to chambered cairns indicates that The Ord North is not an early tomb in the Sutherland sequence, and the dates refer to the contents of the chamber and not to the construction, which implies that the building of the earliest tombs is likely to begin considerably earlier. The construction of chambered cairns is not likely to have been undertaken in the initial phase of agricultural activity, but to have begun early in one of subsequent stability. An indication of agriculture at an early date comes from the recent investigations at Lairg where, through pollen analysis, a farming economy can be detected from about 3500 bc, or late fifth/early fourth millennium BC in calibrated terms (McCullagh 1992, 6–7).

Chambered cairns and society

8.23) The interpretation of chambered cairns in social terms has resulted in an extensive literature, and thus a range of postulated roles that go beyond the tidy housing of the dead has to be considered. Topographically the Sutherland cairns are generally sited in places where a relationship with the territory of a local community can be inferred, and it may well be that the monument was thought to confer some degree of 'ownership' based on the evocation of ancestral authority. It is sometimes possible to build up a picture of likely locations for settlements, and the remnants of field walls or small cairns which can be observed around several chambered cairns may indicate early agricultural activity (noted in ¶ 3.15), though not necessarily for cereal growing (Halliday, Hill and Stevenson 1981, 60–1), and whether any of the vestiges are contemporary with the cairns is not known. Landscape surveys of selected areas and in-depth surveys such as that at Lairg are the essential next stage to set the monuments within a broader landscape framework and to locate habitation sites.

8.24) The description and classification of the chambered cairns of Sutherland, taken with the same treatment of the chambered cairns of Caithness, is but a step in the understanding of the neolithic period in northern Scotland for which there is at present so little other evidence. This present study is offered as a building block to which environmental and artefactual evidence must be added. Many of the Sutherland chambered cairns are of comparatively modest size, and their relationship to a local community can be readily envisaged; perhaps that relationship changed in the course of time, possibly from the practical to the symbolic. The effort invested in the construction of large cairns, including several long cairns, may indicate social organisation which involved more than one community; however there is a wide range of estimates for the work force or the time required for the construction of the cairns studied in Orkney (Barber 1992, 29). There is insufficient evidence for useful speculation on social organisation in Sutherland in the way that has been done for Orkney where intensive investigation over the last two decades has provided such a breadth and depth of information (Renfrew 1979, 212–13; Fraser 1983, 409–35; Sharples 1985; 1992, 323–6). Similarly the symbolism involved in their design and use can only be conjectured, but by thinking of the tombs in metaphorical terms Richards evokes something of the religious or cosmological experiences that may have been involved (1992). If the cairns are seen as reflections of neolithic society in Sutherland, the scale and the sophistication of the architecture of many of them bear testimony to a degree of social cohesion and engineering skill that could not otherwise be envisaged.

PART TWO

SUT 2

INVENTORY

1. ABERSCROSS

See p. 152.

2. ACHAIDH (Achu)

Parish Creich
Location 1.4 km NNW of Spinningdale, near the N side of the Dornoch Firth
Map reference NH 671911
NMRS number NH 69 SE 7
References Curle 1909a, 23rd July; 1909b, vol. 1, 241–2, 244–7; 1910, 105–11; RCAMS 1911, 30–1, no. 82; Henshall 1963, 304–5
Plan ASH and JNGR
Excavation Curle 1909
Visited 4.5.57, 17.4.91

Description. The cairn (traditionally known as the Cairn of the Red Dog) is on a moorland hillside scattered with naturally regenerated trees, placed on a wide shelf above the valley of the Spinningdale Burn at 140 m OD. The ground falls steeply to the S, and there is a wide view down the valley and across the Firth to the Ross-shire hills. Kyleoag (SUT 37) is lower on the same hillside 830 m to the W, and Allt nan Eun (SUT 7) is almost on the valley floor 750 m to the S. To the N and E of the Achaidh cairn, on gently rising ground, a number of crofts are now mostly deserted, and beyond them the ground rises to high hills.

The cairn is of irregular bare stones with several birch trees growing on it, and the edge is overgrown with peat and deep heather making it difficult to define precisely. The short horned plan was evidently clearer in 1909 as Curle recorded that 'there were indications of four horns projecting approximately ENE and SE and WSW and NW for a distance of some 16 feet (4.9 m), with a width of about 20 feet (6 m) at their base', and he gave the dimensions of the cairn as 'some 8 feet (2.4 m) in height and about 50 to 53 feet (15 to 16 m) in diameter' (1910, 105). In 1991 the plan appeared almost square though slightly wider on the SE (correctly ESE) side where the horns form projecting corners. The cairn is about 17.7 m along the SE to NW axis and only slightly less transversely, expanding to about 20 m across the SE side, and it still retains a height of 2.4 m on the W side of the chamber. On the NE side a small gravel quarry has approached to the cairn edge, and between it and the chamber the cairn has been reduced in height. Formerly a lintel 1.93 m long and 0.3 m deep was visible in the centre of the SE side of the cairn about 1.5 m within the present edge, 'apparently covering the entrance to the passage' (RCAMS, 30).

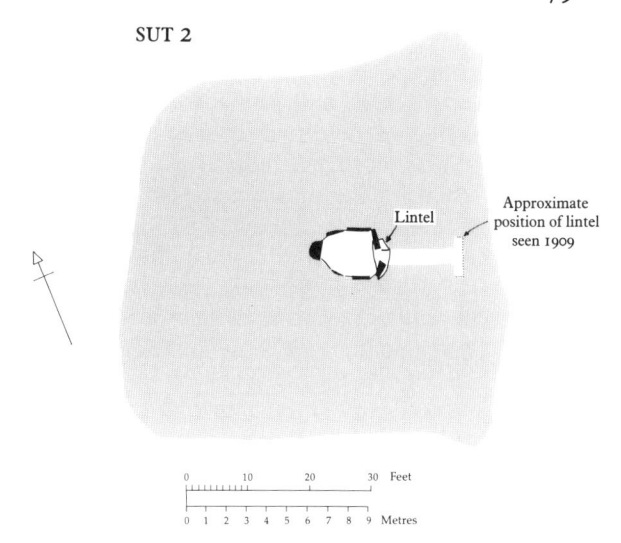

When the cairn was investigated in 1909 the chamber was found to be intact, but in the course of the work part of the roof had to be dismantled. The chamber was left open, and at the back it still survives to near its original height, but the walling round the rest has been reduced and the floor is covered with displaced corbel stones and smaller slabs. The entrance is between a pair of portal stones 0.8 and 1 m long, and 0.35 m and 0.3 m thick. They are set 0.6 m apart, but the NE stone overhangs to reduce the gap to 0.4 m. The portal stones are exposed for 0.6 m, but the true height of the NE stone is about 1.2 m, and the SW stone is 0.33 m shorter. A lintel of impressive size, 1.95 m long, 0.68 m wide and 0.55 m deep, triangular in cross section, covers the inner end of the passage, slightly displaced and tilted to the SE; its lower edge was recorded as 1.2 m above floor level. It rests on the NE portal stone, and on a horizontal slab over the SW portal stone. The next lintel to the SE seems to be missing. In 1909 the passage, 0.6 m wide, was found to be choked with rubble and Curle did not investigate it, and so it remains. There is a clearance of only 0.5 m below the existing lintel, and five courses of the NE wall of the passage can be seen for a length of only 0.4 m. The lintels at either end of the passage were 3.7 m apart, and the length of the passage can thus be estimated as about 4.7 m.

The chamber is 2.7 m long by 2.1 m wide. There is a substantial back-slab, 1 m long, 0.58 m thick, and recorded as 1.37 m high, with two pairs of slabs forming the side walls. On the SW side the slabs are 0.9 and 0.65 m long, and on the NE side they are 1.25 and 0.9 m long (these measurements taken above ground level), and they are between 0.2 and 0.08 m thick as far as can be seen. In height they are a little less than the back-slab but are only exposed for 0.7 to 0.4 m. The first slab on the NE side butts against the adjacent portal stone, and the gaps between the other slabs are only 0.2 or 0.3 m at the narrowest except for a gap of 0.8 m at the W corner. The gaps are filled with horizontal walling, generally with one slab in each course, and at most six courses are visible with the upper two or so oversailing. Above the three inner orthostats and the walling between them there are three or four layers of corbel stones progressively overhanging the chamber. The corbel stones are generally 0.35 to 0.6 m wide, mostly 0.15 to 0.2 m but up to 0.35 m thick, and 0.9 to 1 m from front to back; their long axes run back into the cairn and only their narrow ends are visible in the chamber walls. At the maximum the overhang is as much as 0.6 m in front of the back-slab at a height of 0.6 m above its apex and at a true height of 1.97 m above the floor. It appears that the original amount of overhang has been increased by subsequent settlement probably due to a few slabs cracking; an example of this is visible above the SW shoulder of the back-slab. As the height of the walls has been reduced round the SE half of the chamber leaving only a few of the lowest corbel stones in place, the construction of the vault is exposed in section on each side of the chamber.

The intact chamber was opened from above. 'A number of large flat slabs some 2 to 3 feet (0.6 to 0.9 m) in length lay radiating from a central block of yellow sandstone exposed for a height of 4 or 5 inches (about 0.1 m) and some 8 to 10 inches (about 0.2 m) in diameter. ... This stone, about 1 foot (0.3 m) in depth, tapered downwards and was firmly inserted in the structure, like a keystone. On its removal a view was obtained of the interior of the chamber, the walls of which, built in beehive form, gradually converged upwards' (Curle 1910, 105–6) (figure 5). The height of the centre of the roof was about 2.2 m.

On the chamber floor were deposits about 0.9 m thick. Uppermost was debris which Curle attributed to the partial collapse of walling over the displaced lintel, and dark peaty soil which had probably percolated through the roof. 'Beneath this stratum, which was a few inches in thickness, a layer of grey sand was encountered, throughout which were numerous white particles of quartz and a small amount of comminuted bone, which did not appear, however, to have been burned. A small quantity of charcoal also lay in this deposit. ... Against the back of the chamber lay the remains of an unburnt skeleton, with some portions of bone lying between the building [dry walling] and the back slab. The bones were much decayed, and no part of a skull was found; nor was the position of the body determinable further than that it lay across the chamber with the feet towards the south. ... A few partially burned fragments of bones were found, but it is not certain that these were human. Beneath the sandy deposit was a thinner layer of black soil free from any particles of stone, and which, when dry, resolves itself into a fine black dust. This appears to contain fine fragments of charcoal. It lay on top of flags which for the greater part covered the natural clay surface' (Curle 1910, 110–11).

There is a small cairn 11 m to the SW, about 9 m in diameter.

FINDS
Artefacts. In the Royal Museum of Scotland (figure 23).
1. Scraper of light brown mottled flint, two edges trimmed for use (EO 338).
2. Rim sherd from a small vessel with a vertical neck and high shoulder, hard dark brown fabric, medieval or later though not wheel-turned (EO 339).
3. Modern button.
Found in the sand layer in the chamber.
2 and 3 not illustrated (but 2 illustrated in Curle 1910, 110, figure 5).
Human remains. Lost.
In the sand layer in the chamber were some bones of a much-decayed adult skeleton lying across the chamber with the feet to the S. The bones recovered consisted of one part each of a femur, tibia, fibula and radius. There was also a small amount of comminuted bone, seemingly not burnt, and a few partly burnt fragments of bone not certainly human.
Animal remains. Lost.
A mussel shell and tooth probably from a sheep, probably not ancient, their level in the chamber not recorded.

3. ACHANY
Parish Lairg
Location in the valley of the River Shin, 4.5 km SSW of Lairg
Map reference NC 571020
NMRS number NC 50 SE 26
References RCAMS 1911, 154–6, no. 447; Henshall 1963, 306
Plan ASH and JNGR
Visited 12.7.55, 23.5.91

Description. The cairn is placed where the hills forming the W side of the Shin valley begin to rise from its flat floor. The site, at 67 m OD, is close to the Grudie Burn, a tributary of the Shin, in the corner of

SUT 3

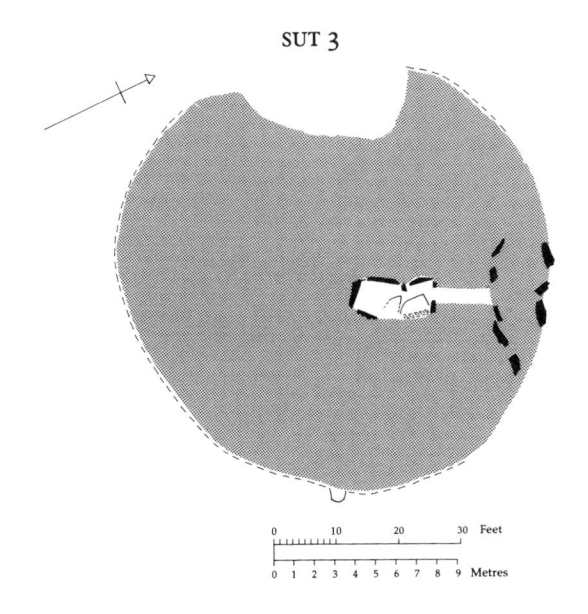

a field of pasture and just E of a road leading up the valley. To the W and N thin natural woodland covers the lower slopes, beyond which there is very extensive conifer afforestation.

The cairn has been severely robbed leaving a very uneven surface, now grass-covered, but it is still 1.4 m high around the chamber and also nearer the SW edge. The cairn occupies a small knoll; the cairn edge can mostly be traced with reasonable confidence though the SE half tends to merge with the natural slope, the W side is interrupted by deeper robbing, and the cairn fades into the ground on the NNE side. The diameter is about 21 m. A large horizontal slab on the ESE edge looks like a fallen kerb-stone, 0.9 m long by 0.4 m thick, and 0.9 m high when vertical; a few other stones which hardly project may be more kerb-stones. The cairn material of rounded stones can be seen in places.

On the NE side of the cairn there are eight orthostats. Five of them form an irregular concave façade within the present limit of the cairn. From NW to E they are 1.02, 0.64, 0.8, 1.45 and 1 m long by 0.2, 0.38, 0.3, 0.4 and 0.35 m thick. The first and second stones at the W end of the façade project 0.4 and 0.3 m, and are 0.58 m apart. The fourth and fifth stones at the E end of the façade project 0.5 and 0.7 m, and are 0.54 m apart. These four stones have irregular tops, the last two obviously shattered. The two inner stones have true heights of at least 1.3 and 1.5 m; the two outer stones are somewhat shorter. The central third stone differs in character as the horizontal upper surface appears to be intact and is flush with the turf, and the stone overlaps the front of the adjacent E stone by 0.12 m. The second and third stones are 1.13 m apart on either side of the extended axis of the chamber and may be portal stones at the outer end of the passage, but it seems more likely that only the third stone is a portal stone and a partner of similar size exists unseen forming a more usual narrower entrance.

In front of the façade a blocking of cairn material remains up to 1 m deep, fading away to the NE. Three orthostats about 2 m in front of the façade, set in an irregular line across the extended axis of the chamber and forming an edging to the blocking, are likely to be later additions. From W to E these stones are 0.7 and 0.23 m apart, 1.1, 0.8 and 1.25 m long by 0.4, 0.35, and 0.55 m thick. The W stone is a prominent pointed block projecting 1.17 m, the E stone is a substantial prone block only projecting 0.4 m, and the smaller third stone set skew between them projects 0.45 m. To the NE of them there has been considerable disturbance, including traces of a curved wall running northwards from the easternmost façade stone to merge with the W side of the cairn and forming an enclosure measuring internally 4.8 m from the W stone of the outer setting by about 7 m transversely.

There has been some deterioration in the condition of the chamber since it was first recorded by Curle in 1909 (RCAMS), and again since it was visited in 1955 (Henshall). The floor level seen by Curle, nearly ground level, was evidently about 0.25 m below the floor level in 1991, thus causing discrepancies in the recorded heights of the structural slabs. The entrance passage may be estimated as 3.15 m long including the portal stones at each end. The portal stones forming the entry to the chamber are 0.56 m apart. They have intact horizontal upper surfaces except for some damage to the E stone. This is 0.6 m long by 0.2 m thick, and its partner is slightly smaller (the W end obscured in 1991). In 1909 these stones were exposed for a height of 0.56 m and bore a lintel 1 m long, 0.6 m wide and 0.23 m thick (in 1991 they were exposed for only 0.3 and 0.15 m; the lintel was removed before 1955). The chamber is 3.55 m long, divided into two compartments. The plan of each compartment is rectangular, and the axis of the outer compartment is skew by about 15° to that of the inner compartment.

The outer compartment is 1.25 m long and was about 1.27 m wide, with a large slab forming each side. The E side slab, now leaning acutely into the chamber but upright in 1955, is 1.5 m long, about 0.3 m thick, and was 1 m high when vertical. The W slab is 1.25 m long, 0.28 m thick, and 0.7 m high, 0.55 m higher than the adjacent portal stone. The E divisional slab was already missing in 1909, and only the stump of the W divisional slab remains. It is 0.5 m long, 0.4 m thick, and was recorded in 1909 as 0.63 m high (projecting 0.1 m in 1991). The inner compartment is 2 m long by 1.7 m wide. The back-slab is 1.45 m long, 0.37 m thick, and was 1.3 m high in 1909 (projecting 1.1 m in 1991), but its true height can be estimated as nearly 1.7 m. Two slabs form the SE wall of the inner compartment, the inner slab 0.95 m long, over 0.2 m thick, and 0.78 m high in 1909 (projecting 0.4 m in 1991); the outer slab had already fallen by 1909 and by 1991 only the tip was visible. In 1955 when more of it could be seen it was suggested that these two slabs had originally been one. The slab on the W side of the compartment is 1.6 m long, 0.3 m thick, and was 1.2 m high in 1909 (projecting 0.95 m in 1991). The chamber orthostats have been rectangular in plan, and their ends have mostly been nearly vertical; the gaps between the orthostats have been small, up to 0.3 m at ground level at the two rear corners, and less elsewhere where observable. Neatly-fitting horizontal slabs were noted filling the gaps in 1909; in 1991 a single slab remained at ground level in the SW corner.

4. ACHCHEARGARY

Parish Farr
Location in Strathnaver, 7 km S of Bettyhill
Map reference NC 719550
NMRS number NC 75 NW 16
References RCAMS 1911, 84, no. 244; Henshall 1963, 306
Plan ASH and JNGR
Visited 26.6.57, 27.10.92

Description. The cairn is in a field of pasture, on the edge of a terrace at about 15 m OD, and only 50 m from and a little above the W bank of the River Naver. There are prehistoric field clearance cairns immediately W of the cairn.

The cairn is a grass-covered uneven mound which has evidently been reduced in height and much disturbed. The cairn edge is clear round most of the circumference, with at least three kerb-stones visible on the E side, the largest 0.75 m long by 0.4 m high. The cairn diameter NW to SE is about 21 m, and NE to SW is 18 m. The maximum height measured from the S side is 1.5 m (the greater N to S diameter and greater height formerly recorded is due to inclusion of sloping ground on the S side which appears to be part of a low knoll on which the cairn was built).

When visited in 1909 three slabs were visible somewhat N of the centre of the cairn as then defined, and seemed to be part of a chamber 'which does not appear to have been cleared out' (RCAMS). The chamber length E to W 'as far as exposed' was 2.1 m and the width was about 1.5 m. At the E end a slab protruded 0.36 m; the other two slabs were on the N and S sides, the N slab being slightly displaced.

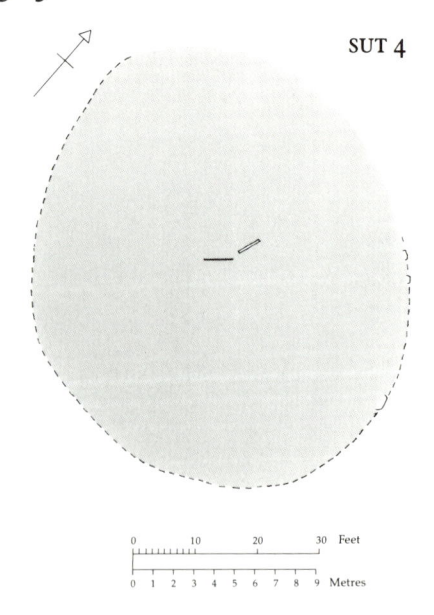

By 1957 only one slab was visible *in situ*, which remains the case. The slab is aligned NE to SW, and is presumably the S slab seen in 1909. It is 1.58 m long by 0.06 m thick, and its N face is exposed for 0.46 m. There has been relatively recent digging on its N side over an area of about 3 by 2 m. To the NNE a second slab, measuring 1.3 by 0.6 m and 0.17 m thick, has been tipped onto its long side and is obviously displaced.

5. ALLT A' MHUILINN

Parish Clyne
Location in Strath Brora, 10.5 km NW of Brora
Map reference NC 827115
NMRS number NC 81 SW 19
References RCAMS 1911, 17, no. 43; Davidson 1946, 33; Henshall 1963, 307
Plan ASH and JNGR
Visited 6.5.57, 26.9.93

Description. The cairn is on a hillside of heather moor in a small side valley of the strath, sited above a tributary of the River Brora at 114 m OD. The cairn looks down the valley and across the flat enclosed pasture on the floor of the strath. There are areas of prehistoric settlement beside the cairn and on unenclosed land in the vicinity.

The cairn occupies an almost level site on the hillside which slopes down fairly steeply from NE to SW. The cairn had been considerably reduced before it was first recorded in 1909, at which time the maxi-

SUT 5

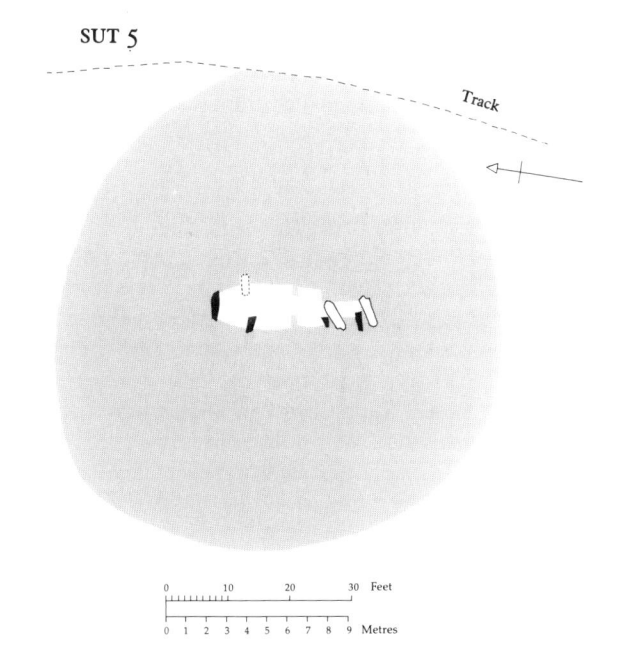

```
0  10  20  30 Feet
0 1 2 3 4 5 6 7 8 9 Metres
```

mum height was 1.8 m (RCAMS). It was further reduced in the 1940s, for the building of a small dam (Davidson). There now remains a rim of cairn material, which on the E and NE side is up to 1 m high, and on the W side, where the ground level is lower, is 1.5 m high. The interior has been robbed to a lower level; the cairn material remains in heaps and hollows, and around the N end of the chamber it has been almost totally removed. The cairn is covered by turf, heather and bracken. A track clips the E side of the cairn, and at the time of the 1993 visit the edges round the rest of the circuit were difficult to trace precisely. The cairn diameter is about 22 m or a little more.

In the centre of the cairn four orthostats, all quarried slabs, are arranged transversely to a S to N axis. They evidently belong to a large chamber, the entrance to which faced slightly E of S. The first three orthostats are on the W side of the structure. From S to N they are 0.93, 0.5, and 0.82 m long, by 0.3, 0.33, and 0.4 m thick. The first stone is 0.86 m high with a jagged broken top, the next stone has been reduced to a stump, but the last stone appears to be intact, 1 m high, with a vertical E side and its upper edge sloping down steeply to the W. About 0.9 m E of the last stone is a rectangular hollow, 1.0 by 0.4 m, probably indicating where its partner has stood. The fourth orthostat at the N end of the group is evidently the backslab. It leans slightly to the N with an irregularly pointed top; it is 0.85 m high measured in a hollow on its N side, and 1.5 m long by 0.3 m thick. The orthostats, except for the stump, are about the same height, and it is unlikely that more than 0.2 m of their bases is hidden. From S to N they are 1.4, 3.3, and 1.47 m apart.

Two elongated blocks, lying respectively to the S of the first stone described and immediately S of the second stone, are almost certainly displaced lintels. The first, its E end broken, is 1.5 m long by about 0.5 m wide and deep. The second is a regularly shaped boulder almost square in cross section, 1.7 m long, 0.56 m wide and 0.45 m deep.

The orthostats can be tentatively interpreted as the remains of a tripartite chamber 5.17 m long. In the order described they are likely to be a portal stone at the outer end of the passage, a portal stone at the entry to the chamber, and a divisional slab at the entry to the inner compartment; if so the divisional slabs separating the outer and central compartments are missing (see ¶ 4.7, 29).

6. ALLT NAM BAN

Parish Clyne
Location on the E side of Loch Brora, 6 km NW of Brora
Map reference NC 856078
NMRS number NC 80 NE 4
References Curle 1909b, vol 2, 68–9; RCAMS 1911, 17–18, no. 44; Simpson 1928; Simpson 1936; Henshall 1963, 307–8
Plan ASH and JNGR
Visited 18.5.55, 27.9.93, 22.4.94

Description. The cairn is 100 m from the E shore of Loch Brora, and close to the S bank of Allt nam Ban, at 37 m OD. The ground rises gently from the loch shore, but a little E of the cairn the hillside rises steeply. In the area around the cairn there are great heaps of stones, probably deposited by the burn, and patches of ground have been cleared long ago for cultivation; indistinct remains of field walls and buildings can be traced, all now overgrown by bracken. The cairn is at the edge of a birch wood, and several trees grow on the cairn itself. The view from the cairn is fairly restricted, across the centre part of the loch.

The cairn has been severely robbed. The W part had been reduced and the chamber had been exposed before the first record in 1909 (RCAMS). Much of the S side of the cairn had been newly removed for road metal shortly before Simpson's visit in 1928. There has been little change in the condition of the cairn since that time, apart from the heavy growth of bracken.

The cairn is oval, measuring about 17 m E to W by about 14 m transversely. A bank of cairn material, composed of bare loose irregular stones, remains on the N side of the chamber rising to its greatest height

SUT 6

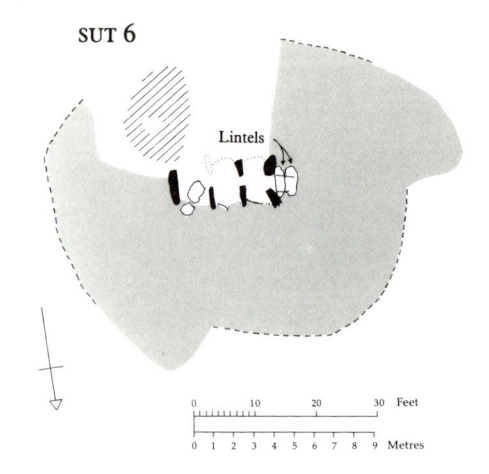

of 2.3 m to the NE of the chamber. A mass of stone has been displaced northwards from the NE side of the cairn. Elsewhere the cairn is greatly reduced, and on the WSW side the edge has been overlaid with field clearance stones. The SE quadrant of the cairn has been virtually removed, and in the cleared area are the foundations of a small structure; an old wall runs southwards from the SE edge of the cairn.

The passage faces W, towards the loch, but only the inner part survives. The original length is unknown, but it is unlikely to have stretched for 8 m as suggested by Simpson (possibly he was misled by the way the cairn had been robbed, see his plan 1928, 487). The S wall of the passage, roughly built of small stones with five irregular courses visible, extends for 1.15 m (1.4 m when seen by Simpson). The N wall is built of larger stones, some set transversely to the wall-face, with four courses visible. The passage is about 0.7 m wide, but displacement of the N wall narrows the W end. Two lintels cover the passage, both tilted down slightly to the W. The clearance at the outer end of the passage, partly choked by debris, is only 0.33 m, but at the inner end the clearance is 0.8 m. The W lintel is a rather irregular block with relatively flat upper and lower surfaces, 1.5 m long by 0.5 m wide and 0.33 m deep. The E lintel is 1.6 m long by 0.5 m wide and deep, being almost square in cross section. The N end rests on a large flat slab which in turn rests on the wall and also covers the top of the N portal stone, the lintel itself only just overlapping the portal stone; otherwise the ends of the lintels rest on the wall-heads. It is probable that a narrow lintel is missing from above the portal stones. The entrance to the chamber is 0.55 m wide. The N portal stone is a rather irregular block set at an angle to the axis; the S stone is a boulder with a flat top and flat faces to the passage and chamber. The stones are over 1.0 and 1.03 m long by 0.45 and 0.63 m thick, and 0.63 and 0.7 m high.

The tripartite chamber was more intact when seen in 1909, though the inner compartment was hidden below debris. The walls of the first two compartments were concave in plan, built of good dry walling. The S wall of the chamber was removed during the subsequent quarrying of the S side of the cairn. All the orthostats, like the portal stones, appear to be intact. The outer compartment or ante-chamber is about 1 m long; Simpson saw a single large stone belonging to the base of the S wall indicating that the compartment was 2.13 m wide. The N wall, 1 m high, is now rather rough in appearance, with some oversailing which is probably due to displacement. A corbel stone remains at the inner end resting against the adjacent orthostat. The entry to the centre compartment is between the inner portal stones, set 0.46 m apart but only 0.3 m apart higher up. The N stone is a regular slab with a rounded top; the S stone is a somewhat irregular block with the straight N edge sloping to the N over the entry, and with an almost horizontal upper surface. The stones are 1.02 and 0.85 m long (the latter expanding to 0.94 m wide at the top), by 0.28 and 0.4 m thick, and 0.9 and 1.22 m high. The centre compartment is about 1.3 m long, and was 2.5 m wide. Simpson recorded that the N wall, then 1.2 m high, consisted of two stones at the base 'set angle-wise, the beehive construction being distinctly in evidence' (1928, 486). In 1993 the W part of the N wall was obscured by rubble, but the E part consisted of quite large horizontal stones, in three courses 0.5 m high. A pair of divisional stones set 0.53 m apart stood between the centre and inner compartments, but the S stone, 0.9 m long, had been removed by 1928. The N stone is 1.04 m long by 0.25 m thick and 0.75 m high with a horizontal upper surface. The inner compartment is 1.5 m long. The N wall is hidden, partly by two large displaced slabs which were probably once one slab. The back-slab, 1.6 m long by 0.5 m thick and 0.6 m high, leans slightly to the E. The total length of the chamber is 4.4 m. The chamber floor is level, and a hollow dug beside the S inner portal stone shows that the original floor level is about 0.4 m lower.

Between the inner portal stones Simpson observed 'a narrow post-like stone set with its axis transversely'; it was 0.38 m long by 0.18 m wide and 0.9 m high. It was no longer in position in 1955, and because the chamber had been much used for shelter by road-menders, it is more likely to have been a modern arrangement than part of the neolithic sealing of the chamber.

7. ALLT NAN EUN

Parish Creich
Location 0.6 km N of Spinningdale, on the N side of the Dornoch Firth
Map reference NH 672904
NMRS number NH 69 SE 8
References Curle 1910, 104–5; RCAMS 1911, 30, no. 80; Henshall 1963, 308
Plan ASH and JNGR
Visited 29.6.52, 17.4.91

Description. The cairn is in a small area of deciduous woodland, on the lower slopes of the valley of the Spinningdale Burn, beside its tributary the Allt nan Eun, at 30m OD. The cairn is 750 m S of, and 110 m lower than, Achaidh (SUT 2). The Allt nan Eun cairn occupies most of a small level shelf at the end of a moraine ridge. The ground drops steeply along the N and W sides, and it is clear that the cairn has spread well beyond its original limits on the W quadrant. The edge is fairly well defined giving diameters of about 24.5 m, but originally the diameter is likely to have been considerably less. The cairn is composed of relatively small rounded stones. A large amount of stone has been removed leaving the centre of the cairn hollowed, with an arc extending from the SE edge robbed down to ground level. A fairly level rim of cairn material remains (except where broken on the SE), 1.9 m high measured from level ground on the S side, but impressively high when viewed from the lower ground on the W and including cairn material which has tumbled down the steep slope.

About 3.5 m within the SSE edge of the cairn a pair of stones is exposed 1.15 m apart. The W stone is a roughly triangular block 0.7 m long by 0.8 m thick, and the E stone, which seems to be somewhat skew to the curve of the cairn edge, is over 0.75 m long by over 0.25 m thick. They are exposed for heights of 0.5 and 0.4 m on their S sides but their true heights are about 1 m. To the SE of the E stone is a prostrate stone sloping slightly down to the N, with the N end covered by cairn material. This slab measures over 1.35 m long by 0.8 m wide (but the SW side appears to have been reduced), and 0.5 m thick with flat upper and lower surfaces. The arrangement of these three stones is suggestive of portal stones at the outer end of a passage facing SSE, though set unusually far apart, and a displaced lintel. Three thin horizontal slabs against the E side of the W upright stone, exposed for a height of 0.25 m, look like a 0.4 m length of dry walling, and they may be the lower part of blocking at the passage entrance.

Two more stones seem to be related to this SSE to NNW axis. The rounded top of an upright granite boulder just protrudes 1.2 m NW of the first stone described. The top measures 0.5 by 0.5 m, and is about 1.2 m above ground level measured from the S. There is a large granite block 4.4 metres to the NNW, near the centre of the cairn. The block is over 1.9 m long (the S end is not visible) by 0.5 m thick and 0.9 m high, but it has been reduced in size as large pieces clearly have been broken off. It is likely to have formed the W side of a chamber the back and E side of which have been destroyed, though more of the structure may well survive to the SSE below the bank of cairn material.

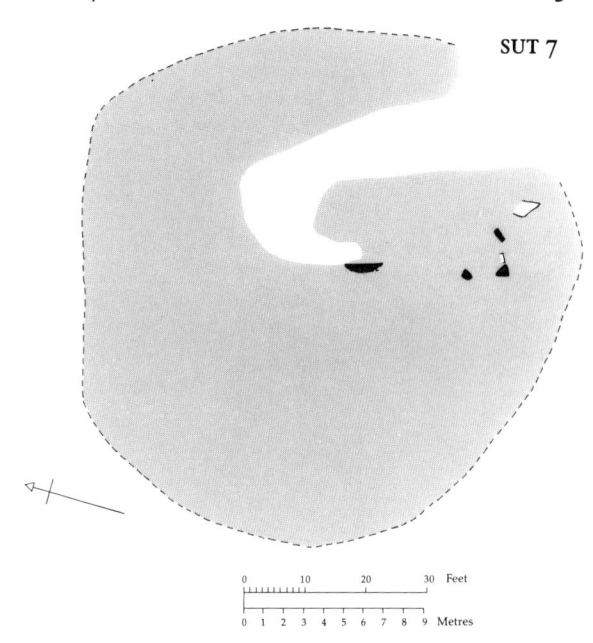

The condition of the cairn has not changed since it was visited in 1952, and probably not since the 1909 record (RCAMS); it had evidently been robbed long before this time. Curle related the legend of its building (1910).

There is a featureless low cairn 40 m to the W.

8. ALLT SGIATHAIG

Parish Assynt
Location 14 km ENE of Lochinver, 4 km NNW of Inchnadamph
Map reference NC 234255
NMRS number NC 22 NW 1
References Henshall 1963, 309; 1972, 572
Plan ASH and JNGR
Visited 24.5.54, 8.10.63, 30.3.93

Description. The cairn is unusually sited on a steep hillside, at 150 m OD, overlooking a small narrow moorland valley draining into Loch Assynt. To the N

SUT 8

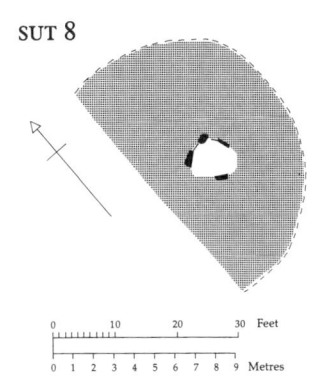

and E the valley is dominated by a range of mountains, and the outlook from the cairn is fairly limited; southwards there is a view down the valley to the loch. The site slopes down steeply from E to W. The main road, the A894, runs immediately W of the cairn but 7 m below it.

When visited in 1954 it was found that the main damage to the cairn had been deep robbing on the NW side, and that the top had been removed long ago (Henshall 1963). The cairn diameter was about 12 m. Since 1954 road works have caused erosion, and about a third of the W side of the cairn has fallen away. Round the rest of the perimeter the cairn rises steeply from a well-defined edge. The greatest height, on the NW side of the chamber, is 1.7 m. The cairn material of rounded irregular stones shows through the thin covering of turf and moss.

A small polygonal chamber, with diameters of about 1.7 to 2.1 m, exists as a deep hollow filled by large flat elongated slabs lying at various angles. Presumably these slabs are displaced corbel stones from the chamber vault, the largest measuring 1.23 by 0.5 by 0.26 m. They obscure most of the walls of the chamber which probably survive fairly complete to a considerable height. Four orthostats can be identified amongst the chaos. The tallest, on the NW side, is a rectangular block with a pointed top, 0.76 m long by 0.36 m thick, and visible for a height of 0.8 m. The orthostat on the NE side is an intact boulder 0.65 m long by 0.45 m thick, its rounded top 0.5 m lower than its neighbour. These two orthostats are linked by a 0.6 m long stretch of walling, of which five courses 0.48 m high can be seen; the E end rests on the W side of the boulder and rises 0.2 m above it. The other two orthostats are rectangular slabs with intact horizontal upper surfaces 0.62 m lower than the first orthostat. The E orthostat is over 0.75 m long (the S end not being visible) by 0.22 m thick; it is 0.5 m from the boulder orthostat and formerly walling could be seen

linking them. The S orthostat is 0.66 m long by over 0.17 m thick. A flat stone partly exposed to the SE of the chamber may be a displaced lintel, but the position of the passage is not evident.

9. ARDVRECK

Parish Assynt
Location 15 km E of Lochinver, 2 km NNW of Inchnadamph
Map reference NC 241237
NMRS number NC 22 SW 1
References Cree 1928, 1–3; Callander and Cree n.d.; Henshall 1963, 309
Plan after Cree, amended by ASH and JNGR (see also figure 14)
Excavation Cree 1925
Visited 24.5.54, 29.3.93

Description. The cairn is in a small area of undulating rough pasture, in a region of predominantly rugged mountainous country. The cairn is 100 m from the E shore of Loch Assynt, on top of the highest knoll in the vicinity, at 76 m OD. The site overlooks two bays which are sheltered by the small promontory on which are the ruins of Ardvreck Castle, and has views up and down the loch.

The turf-covered cairn, though much reduced, remains 1.5 m high around the chamber. The cairn material is rounded stones, exposed where the thin cover is broken. The edge of the cairn is well defined except on the S side, with a diameter of about 13.5 m. The excavator's trench was left open and remains as a deep hollow running from the ESE edge of the cairn to behind the back of the chamber. In 1925 the cairn was recorded as oval, measuring 15.2 m SE to NW by 11 m transversely, but it was not examined by the excavator.

When the cairn was found by Cree the inner compartment of the chamber was exposed, about two-thirds full of peaty soil, and was assumed to be a large bronze age cist. The excavation (recorded in Cree and in Callander and Cree) revealed a chamber entered from the ESE, and said to be approached by a short passage. The chamber was rectangular and was divided into three compartments by two transverse slabs. This plan is unique in the N mainland of Scotland but resembles those of the Clyde group of chambered cairns in SW Scotland (see ¶ 4.33).

The chamber was 2.8 m long. The inner compartment was built of three well-fitting rectangular limestone slabs with notably flat inner surfaces. These, with the inner transverse slab, were still in place and visible in 1954, but by 1993 only the N slab was visible *in situ*, with part of a second slab to the SE. The back-slab, set between the side-slabs, was 1.02 m

SUT 9

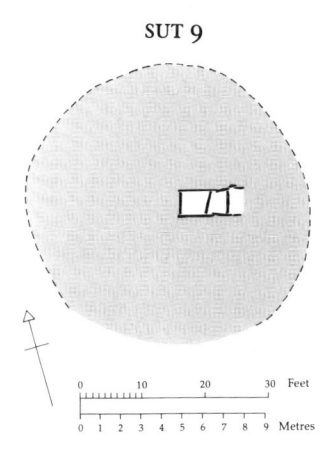

long, establishing the width of the compartment. The side-slabs were 1.7 and 1.8 m long, and all three slabs were 0.15 to 0.23 m thick. The N slab was 1.14 m high, and the S slab and back-slab were very slightly less. The transverse slab forming the E end of the compartment was 0.23 to 0.1 m thick, and 0.36 m high. As it was somewhat skew to the axis, the compartment was 1.1 to 1.32 m long.

The walls of the centre and outer compartments were built of shorter slabs, their heights not recorded. The W ends of the centre pair of side slabs just overlapped the inner faces of the innermost pair. The centre compartment was 0.8 to 0.66 m long and 0.9 m wide, with a transverse slab 0.15 m thick and 0.66 m high across the E end. The outer compartment was 0.56 m long, and probably about 0.9 m wide, with one slab completing the S wall of the chamber and two slabs completing the N wall, all slightly overlapping their neighbours. However, details of this compartment and of the passage are difficult to interpret, possibly because later interference with the structure was not recognised by the excavator. Cree gave the size of the compartment as about 0.6 m square, and on his plan an infilling of stones is shown against each wall reducing the width to 0.46 m. At the E end of the chamber was a transverse slab resting on the infilling and leaving an opening below only 0.25 m wide and 0.33 m high. The 'passage', recorded as 1.2 m long and retaining one lintel, looks unconvincing on the excavator's plan where it is shown bounded by slabs 0.6 m long on the N and E, and by some stones on the S, and roofed by a slab only 0.6 m square 'now fallen in and replaced'. The entrance (to either the chamber or the 'passage') was closed by three quartzite boulders.

In the following account of the deposits in the chamber (Callander and Cree), read 'compartment'

for 'chamber'. 'Although the covering slabs had at some time been removed from all the chambers, I do not think the chambers themselves had been disturbed. In the innermost chamber - that furthest to the west, a skeleton remained in situ. It was lying on its right side in the usual crouching position, the head being at the W end and facing towards the S. The only part out of position was the under jaw, which was found close to the pelvis. ... The skull was dolicocephilic [sic] and all the bones were in a wonderfully good state of preservation. ... No artefact of any description was discovered.'

FINDS
Human remains. Lost.
A crouched skeleton in the inner compartment (see above).

10. BADNABAY

Parish Eddrachillis
Location on the W coast, 6.4 km ENE of Scourie
Map reference NC 218467
NMRS number NC 24 NW 1
References RCAMS 1911, 58, no. 172; Boyd 1952, 206–8, pl. XLIII; Henshall 1963, 310
Plan ASH and JNGR
Visited 30.5.55, 1.5.92

Description. The site of the cairn is in a flat marshy area covered with coarse grass, bog myrtle and heather. It is at under 8 m OD, and only 130 m from the shore of a shallow inlet of Loch Laxford, surrounded by moorland hills.

Fifteen orthostats, the skeleton of a passage and chamber, stand in a slight depression which represents approximately the area from which the surrounding cairn has been removed long ago. The depression is covered by a layer of peat which may be nearly 1 m deep. About 5.5 m NW of the chamber the edge of the cairn is indicated by a slight curved ridge, the very last remains of the cairn. This suggests that the cairn measured at least 14 m NW to SE by a little less transversely. When visited in 1909 the outline of the former cairn was 'distinctly visible' and its area was recorded as 12 m N to S by 11 m E to W; otherwise the condition of the monument has not changed since that time (RCAMS).

The passage, facing the SE, is about 2 m long. The outer end is marked by a pair of portal stones 0.8 m apart. They are over 0.6 and 0.3 m long by 0.4 and 0.3 m thick, their tops just visible. At the inner end a pair of orthostats 0.7 m apart form the portal of the ante-chamber. They are 0.7 and 0.5 m long by 0.36 and 0.5 m thick, and project 0.2 and 0.3 m. Midway between the two pairs of portal stones a small stone projects 0.15 m and probably belongs to the NE wall of the passage.

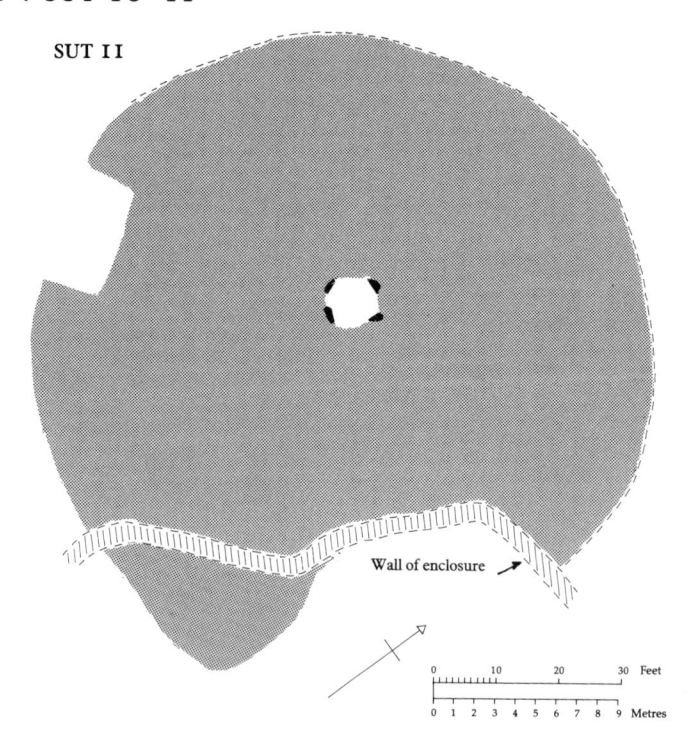

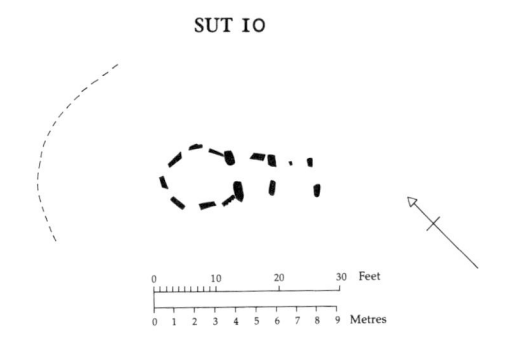

The ante-chamber is about 1.4 m long. On the NE side is an orthostat 0.7 m long, 0.3 m thick and projecting 0.3 m. At the inner end a third pair of portal stones forms an entry 0.75 m wide into the main chamber. These stones are 1.05 and 0.78 m long by 0.55 and 0.5 m thick, and they project 0.55 m. All the portal stones are intact rounded boulders, each pair increasing in height from the entrance. The heights of all the orthostats of the passage and chamber are taken from the same level, the surface of the peat from which they protrude.

The chamber is a regular polygon 3 m long by 2.6 m wide, formed by three orthostats on each side and one at the back. In length they vary between 0.7 and 0.8 m, and in thickness between 0.2 and 0.3 m. The SE pair of orthostats butt against the inner portal stones, and the rest are 0.15 to 0.42 m apart. In contrast with the portal stones, these orthostats are quarried blocks with two parallel faces. The centre stone on the NE side is only a stump, the rear stone has a wide nearly horizontal upper edge which appears to be original, and the rest taper irregularly to pointed tops. Their heights clockwise from the S orthostat are 0.47, 0.9, 1.05, 0.85, 0.86, 0.3, 0.55 m.

11. BALCHARN
Parish Lairg
Location 0.9 km E of Lairg
Map reference NC 596065
NMRS number NC 50 NE 36
References RCAMS 1911, 157, no. 457; Henshall 1963, 310
Plan ASH and JNGR
Visited 5.5.57, 24.5.91

Description. The cairn is in pasture, 100 m W of the farmhouse of Balcharn. It is at 140 m OD on the lower slope of a hillside facing SW, though the actual site is level. Before afforestation the cairn was intervisible with the cairns on The Ord (SUT 48, 49) 2.5 km to the WSW.

The cairn has been severely robbed and disturbed, and the turf-covered surface is very uneven, but cairn material is still up to 1.5 m high around and within the setting of four orthostats in the centre. Around the N half the cairn edge can be traced with confidence, giving a diameter of 30 m. The SE side of the cairn is crossed by a wall forming the W side of an irregular enclosure; the enclosure and the foundations of an adjacent small building are recorded on the OS 25-inch map surveyed in 1873 as respectively a walled garden and a ruin. Another small building has impinged on the W edge of the cairn; and there are also vestiges of a rectangular building, 2.8 m wide internally, extending 5.8 m to the S from the S orthostat.

The orthostats are evidently part of a chamber but its plan is not clear and there is no sign of a passage. The orthostats are granite blocks all of which have been damaged long ago. They are about 1.7 m high, but project 0.75 m or less above the cairn material. The orthostats form two pairs, the stones in each pair set obliquely to each other, enclosing a polygonal compartment about 2.5 m from NE to SW. The stones of the NE pair, 0.9 m apart, are 0.7 and 0.86 m long by 0.44 and 0.35 m thick. The stones of the SW pair are both 0.85 m long by over 0.3 and 0.25 m thick, set 0.7 m apart, and they are 1.7 and 1.66 m from the NE pair.

The condition of the cairn is unchanged since it was first described in 1909, except that the 'foundations of cottages' on the SW side (RCAMS) were evidently more obvious then than in 1991.

12. BENBHRAGGIE WOOD (Rhives)

Parish Golspie
Location on the E coast, 0.5 km N of Golspie
Map reference NC 829006
NMRS number NC 80 SW 4
References Anderson 1868, 494–5; ONB 1873, No. 23, 32; RCAMS 1911, 98–9, no. 289; Henshall 1963, 310
Plan ASH and JNGR
Visited 3.7.51, 13.8.92

Description. The cairn is on the lower slopes of Beinn a' Bhragaidh at 61 m OD. The cairn is in the corner of a deciduous wood with cultivated fields stretching to the N, E and S. It was built on a steep-sided knoll projecting from the hillside, with the entrance facing ESE looking over the fertile land around Golspie, and across the coast.

The orthostats of a large chamber project from the top of a mound. The mound is a combination of the knoll and the last remains of a cairn, which, with the surrounding area, is covered with coarse grass. The limits of the cairn are difficult to define, but an edge can be traced on the less steep NW side, and also on the SE side, giving a diameter of roughly 22 m. The NE side may have been reduced for a field wall which runs about 2 m outside the apparent spread of cairn material. On the SW side the cairn material merges with the slope of the knoll. Although the height of the mound viewed from the ESE is about 2 m, there is probably little depth of cairn material remaining, as the knoll evidently rises below the outer part of the cairn which has spread down the slope.

Eight orthostats of the passage and chamber survive. The easternmost orthostat, parallel with the chamber axis, is 1.35 m long by 0.35 m thick and 1 m high. Immediately to the W is a pair of portal stones. They are set 0.6 m apart, and are 0.95 and 0.8 m long, both are 0.3 m thick, and they are 0.85 and 0.8 m high. The S stone has an intact upper edge, the N half horizontal and the S half sloping down to the S. A little W of this slab is an orthostat, 1.42 m long by 0.14 m thick and 0.55 m high, belonging to the S wall of the chamber. The outer compartment is about 1.8 m long, as a transverse stone to the W is evidently the S member of a pair of inner portal stones forming the entry to the inner compartment. The stone is 1.4 m long by 0.17 m thick and 0.58 m high, and its slightly undulating rounded upper edge appears to be intact. The inner compartment is 2.25 m long by 2.75 m

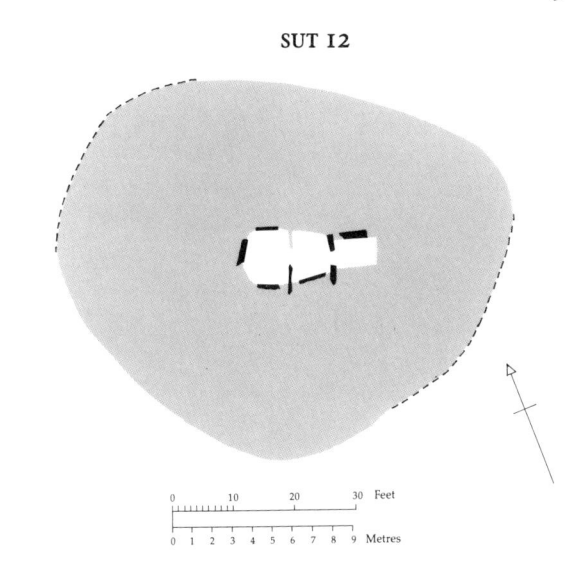

SUT 12

wide, defined by three orthostats and filled by a large tree. The side-slabs are 1.16 and 1.14 m long by 0.3 and 0.15 m thick, and 1.15 and 1 m high. The back-slab is 1.17 m long by 0.28 m thick, and 1.45 m high; the original rounded upper edge remains on the shoulders and only about 0.03 m has been broken from the top. The three side-slabs have shattered upper surfaces and appear originally to have been considerably taller. The heights of all the orthostats have been taken from about the same level. The gaps between the orthostats are only 0.2 to 0.42 m wide except at the W and N corners of the chamber where there are gaps 1.1 and 0.67 m. All the orthostats are regular sandstone slabs except for one which is conglomerate. They have been split from their beds, and some of them retain rounded weathered edges; five have notably flat inner faces.

Three large slabs, presumably displaced orthostats, lie on the cairn. Two are on its SE edge, the larger measuring 1.9 by 0.85 m and at least 0.2 m thick, and one is on the NE slope. Another slab, measuring 1.77 by 1.25 by 0.5 m, is in the field wall beside the cairn.

The orthostats are best interpreted as the remains of a bipartite chamber which was entered by a wide passage. The condition of the monument appears to have been much the same in 1873, as there were then only eight upright stones in the remains of the cairn (ONB). The earliest record is a note and sketch by Joass made in the 1860s (quoted by Anderson). Joass did not state the number of orthostats and the sketch is lost; he wrote 'one large slab is wanting, but I discovered it in a wall near, and think that the many walls all about may have been built from the cairn'. Anderson, who had not seen the cairn, interpreted the orthostats as 'the skeleton of a tricameral cairn' comparable to the tripartite chambers which he had excavated in Caithness except that orthostats (not dry walling) filled the side walls. He gave the number of orthostats as thirteen, but this number and the interpretation as a tripartite chamber is probably his reconstruction rather than a description of the cairn at that time.

13. CAEN BURN EAST

Parish Kildonan
Location in the Strath of Kildonan, 2.5 km NNW of Helmsdale
Map reference ND 014181
NMRS number ND 01 NW 13
References RCAMS 1911, 126, no. 359; Henshall 1963, 310
Plan ASH and JNGR
Visited 19.6.52, 28.9.93

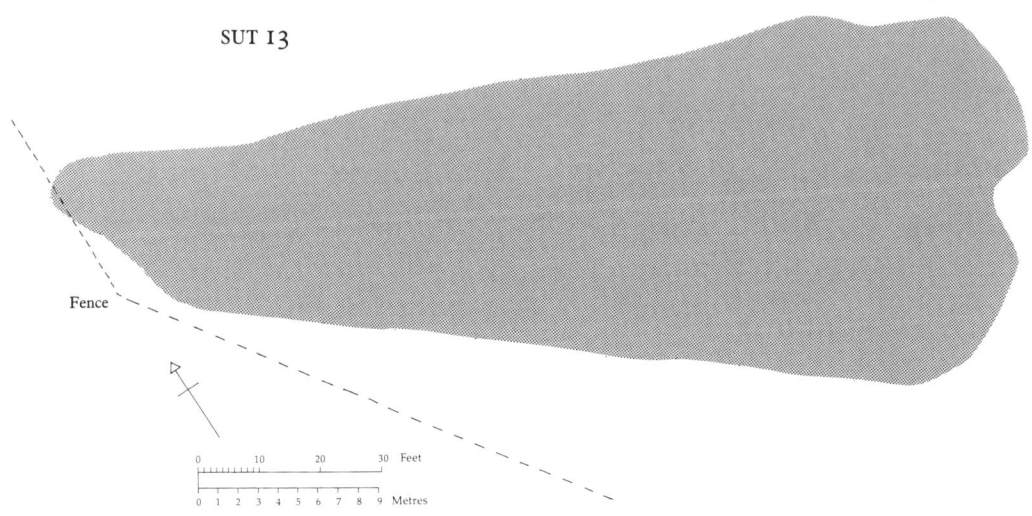

SUT 13

Description. The four cairns near Caen belong to a group of six long cairns (SUT 13–17, 51) in a 3 km stretch at the lower end of the strath. This part of the strath is narrow between steep hillsides of heather moor, with a limited amount of poor pasture on the valley floor. The first three cairns overlook the confluence of the small Caen Burn with the River Helmsdale and the improved grazing around the former croft of Caen. There are remains of extensive prehistoric and more recent settlement up the valley of the burn.

The Caen Burn East cairn is at 70 m OD on a hillside sloping down from NE to SW. The cairn is in rough grazing, above the E side of the burn and immediately above a recently fenced area of improved pasture. The outlook is restricted except for a view to the SE down the strath to the sea. Caen Burn North and South and Carn Laggie (SUT 14, 15, 17) are in sight, 250 m to the WSW, 430 m to the SW, and 1.8 km to the SSE.

The cairn is rather unusually sited with its long axis, running nearly SE to NW, skew to the hill slope. The downhill SE end of the cairn is the wider and appears to be rounded in plan. The edge of the cairn is difficult to trace and in places has been disturbed by robbing. The ground drops away quite steeply at the SE end and along the SW side, and here the bracken-covered edges of the cairn tend to merge into the slope. Along the upper turf-covered NE side the edge is covered by hill-wash, and it is also probably confused by the last remains of an old field wall which can be seen running away eastwards and westwards from this side of the cairn. The NW end of the cairn has been disturbed by recent fencing. Within the overgrown edges the cairn is of bare angular stones. It has been much reduced and disturbed, and is also known to have had several cartloads of stone added to it in recent years. The highest part, a ridge running from 12 to 18 m from the SE end, is only 0.5 m high measured from the NE but is 2.8 m high measured from the SE. The cairn is roughly 48 m long, but in 1911 it was recorded as about 50.5 m long (RCAMS); it is roughly 17 m wide near the SE end, and 7.5 m wide near the NW end.

14. CAEN BURN NORTH

Parish Kildonan
Location in the Strath of Kildonan, 2.5 km NW of Helmsdale
Map reference ND 012180
NMRS number ND 01 NW 5
References RCAMS 1911, 126, no. 358; Henshall 1963, 311
Plan ASH and JNGR
Visited 19.5.52, 28.9.93

Description. The cairn is in heather moorland on the W side of the burn, 250 m WSW of Caen Burn East (SUT 13) which is on the opposite side of a small valley. Carn Laggie (SUT 17) is visible 1.8 km to the SSE, but Caen Burn South (SUT 15) is out of sight only 250 m to the S. The outlook from the North cairn is fairly restricted, up the valley of the burn and down the strath with a glimpse of the sea. The cairn is sited on a terrace at 42 m OD, between a rising hillslope on the W and a steep drop to the valley floor on the E.

The axis of the cairn is ENE to WSW, at right angles to the edge of the terrace. It is clear that an unknown amount of the E end of the cairn has been lost through erosion, which continues slowly to affect the cairn. For about 4 m from the present E edge the cairn has been reduced to the basal layer, and it is crossed by an old track which runs along the edge of the terrace, and by a buried water pipe with an air valve which is accessible beside the track. Westwards of the track the cairn consists of bare irregular stones of varying size, and disturbance has left it with an uneven surface and some deep hollows. The highest part, about 11 m from the E end, is 1.6 m high measured from the S. The long sides and the W end are overgrown with deep heather and appear to have suffered little interference, but the edges are difficult to define precisely except round the W end. The cairn is more or less parallel-sided, 32.5 m long by about 11 to 12 m wide. The remains of an old enclosure wall run SE from the S side of the cairn.

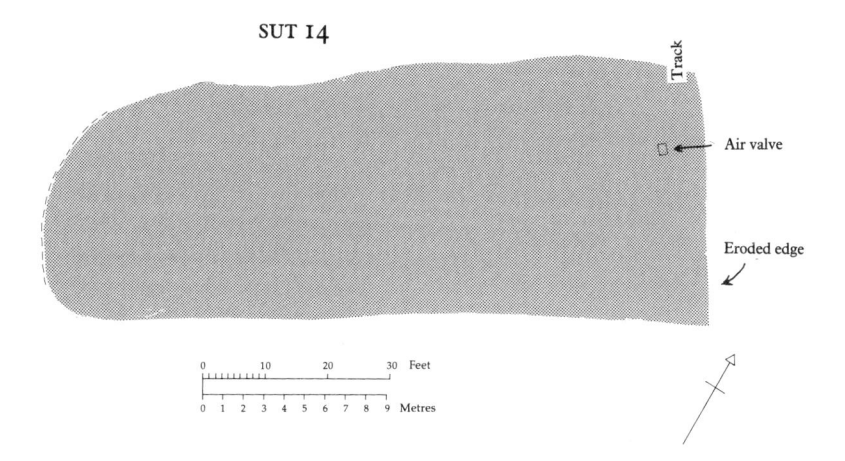

SUT 14

15. CAEN BURN SOUTH

Parish Kildonan
Location in the Strath of Kildonan, 2.5 km NW of Helmsdale
Map reference ND 012177
NMRS number ND 01 NW 3
References RCAMS 1911, 126, no. 356; Henshall 1963, 311; 1972, 572–3
Plan ASH and JNGR
Visited 19.6.52, 17.6.67, 28.9.93

Description. The cairn is on the hillside of heather moorland which forms the N side of the strath. The cairn is aligned E to W along a terrace, at 38 m OD, with the hill rising steeply to the N. The outlook is restricted to a short stretch of the strath and the area of pasture at the foot of the Caen Burn. The Caen Burn North and West cairns (SUT 14, 16) are on the same terrace only 250 and 400 m distant, but are not visible. Caen Burn East (SUT 13) is in sight 430 m to the NE.

The cairn, on a level site, is about 53 m long, by 19.5 m wide at the E end narrowing to 10 m wide at the W end (plate 10). The body of the cairn is bare loose stones and has been greatly robbed and disturbed. In contrast, the edges are overgrown with heather, and except at the E end, they have suffered little interference. The general plan of the cairn is clear, but the exact position of the edge along the sides is difficult to define though it is more easily traced around the square W end. The severe robbing of the E end of the cairn causes difficulty in tracing the E edge which seems to have been nearly straight. The conspicuous but unshapely boulder on the axis near the E end of the cairn (previously thought to be part of a façade) is probably not of special significance; in several places near the median line of the cairn large boulders are visible amongst the cairn material, above ground level. About 5.5 m from the E edge, in a hollow made deep into the cairn, two vertical overlapping slabs have been exposed aligned down the axis. They are 0.03 m apart, and are 1.44 and 0.9 m long by 0.15 and 0.09 m thick. As they are over 0.63 m high their bases are probably at or near ground level, but it is unlikely that both are *in situ*. Westwards of the slabs the cairn rises, reaching its maximum height of 3 m at about 12 m from the E edge, which is likely to be close to the original height of this part of the cairn. Somewhat W of midway along the S side of the cairn a gap through the edge gave access for the quarrying of the centre to almost ground level. Westwards of this the cairn is greatly disturbed and decreases to a negligible height at the W end.

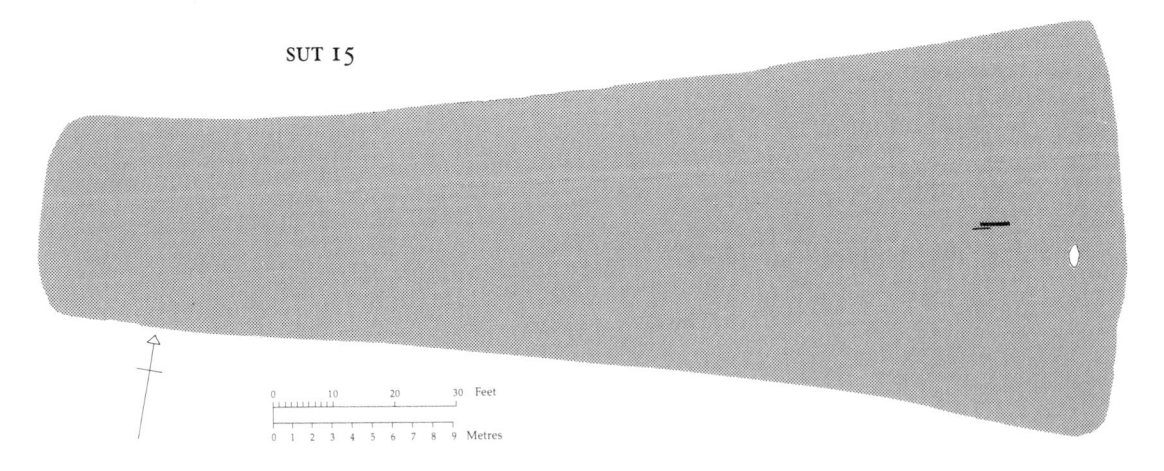

SUT 15

16. CAEN BURN WEST

Parish Kildonan
Location in the Strath of Kildonan, 2.7 km NW of Helmsdale
Map reference ND 007178
NMRS number ND 01 NW 2
References RCAMS 1911, 126, no. 357; Henshall 1963, 311; 1972, 574
Plan ASH and JNGR
Visited 19.6.52, 17.6.67, 15.5.93

Description. The cairn is aligned along a narrow level terrace above the valley floor, at 38 m OD, and immediately below the steeply rising hillside of heather and scree. The cairn is one of the group of six long cairns at the lower end of the strath. It is 400 m W of Caen Burn South (SUT 15) and 620 m ESE of Salscraggie (SUT 51). The outlook from the cairn is restricted because the strath at this point is particularly narrow and is curved, and Salscraggie alone is just visible.

The cairn has been so greatly quarried that it has been reduced to little more than a rim of cairn material generally 1 m high, overgrown with turf and heather. The edge is fairly clear around the NE corner, along the N side, and round the W end. The edge changes direction very slightly about half way along the N side giving a hint that the E half of the cairn narrowed slightly from E to W, and that the W half of

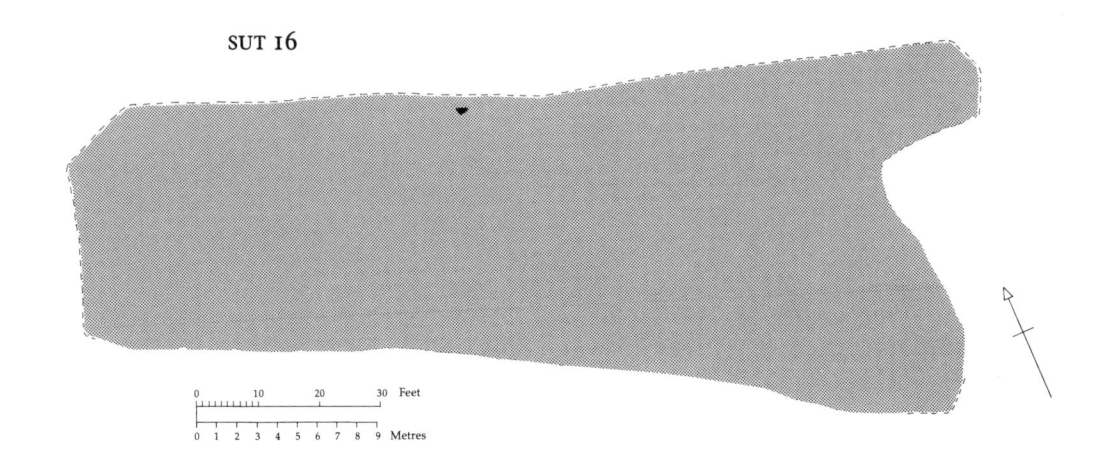

SUT 16

the cairn was parallel-sided. A boulder about midway along this side appears to be part of a kerb. It is 0.6 m long, 0.4 m thick, and 0.5 m high, set with a flat face parallel to the edge of the cairn. Several other boulders may belong to a kerb, but it is difficult to distinguish them from boulders incorporated into the cairn material which is generally of smaller irregular stones. The S edge of the cairn is less easily traced as the cairn merges into the edge of the terrace and cairn material has tended to fall down the slope, but the SE corner of the cairn can be identified with reasonable confidence. The cairn is 44 m long, 17.6 m wide across the E end and about 12 m wide near the square W end.

The cairn was robbed from the E end. A long rectangular hollow stretches about 26 m westwards; it is about 6 m wide and is covered with bracken and heather. A little cairn material remains in the inner part of the hollow but it has been totally removed from the E part and the plan of the E end of the cairn has been lost. To the W of the hollow cairn material is heaped 1.5 m high, measured from the N. Between this higher part and the stony W end of the cairn there is another deep hollow approached through the N side of the cairn.

Just E of the E end of the cairn there are foundations of a wall running N to S, the W side of a small enclosure.

The cairn was evidently in its present condition long before it was first described in 1909 (RCAMS).

17. CARN LAGGIE

Parish Kildonan
Location in the Strath of Kildonan, 1 km NNW of Helmsdale
Map reference ND 023165
NMRS number ND 01 NW 15
References ONB 1871, No. 25, 23; RCAMS 1911, 126, no. 355; Henshall 1963, 312; 1972, 573, 574
Plan ASH and MKM
Visited 6.5.57, 21.6.67, 28.9.93

Description. The cairn is at the lower end of the strath, on a terrace a little above the valley floor at 23 m OD. The site is at the junction of the level lower ground which is mainly divided into fields of pasture (and formerly was extensively cultivated), and the steep hillside of heather and scree; a golf course extends up to the S end of the cairn. The view from the cairn is fairly restricted up and down the strath which in this part is curved, narrow, and steep-sided. Carn Laggie is one of the group of six long cairns (SUT 13–17, 51) located within a 3 km stretch of the strath. Caen Burn East and North (SUT 13, 14) are visible 1.8 km to the NNW.

Carn Laggie is aligned slightly E of S to slightly W of N, closely fitting the narrow terrace on which it was built. The cairn has been very severely quarried, and it remains as a low bare expanse of stone with a surface of uneven humps and hollows. The highest part, on the W side near the N end, is little more than 1 m high. The cairn material is small angular stones (scree from the hillside) and pebbles; it is likely that larger stones have been preferentially removed.

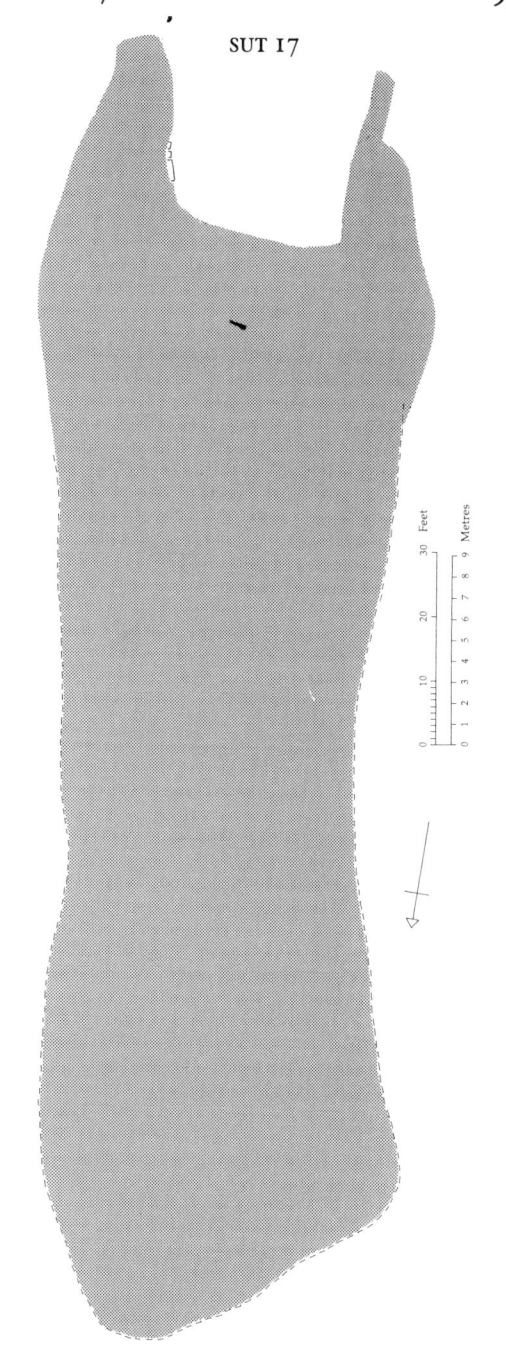

The s end of the cairn has been so badly mutilated that without excavation its original form is quite uncertain. There appears to be a rectangular forecourt (overgrown with turf and bracken) defined by horns 1 m and 0.7 m high; along the w side of the E horn is a short length of the base of a wall-face. It is unclear to what extent the 'forecourt' has been formed by deep robbing, and how far the turf-covered 'horns' are the result of dumping stone, and whether the wall-face is an original or a later feature. When seen in 1911 a bank of broken road metal was observed at the end of the cairn (RCAMS), which supports the suspicion that the 'horns' are largely modern accretions. An undisturbed rim of heather-covered cairn material remains down the sides of the cairn and round the N end. Except towards the s end the edges are fairly well defined, though along the w side the cairn tends to merge with the edge of the terrace, and at the N end the edge is puzzlingly skew to the axis. The present length along the axis is about 52 m, and the overall length including the 'horns' is 62 m. The cairn appears to expand from about 15 m wide in the centre part to about 18 m wide near each end.

The cairn had probably been considerably reduced before 1871, at which time it was described as 'a heap of small stones ..., it is said to be a Pictish Cairn or Barrow, and to have subterranean passages in connection with it' (ONB). This note may indicate that there was a chamber in the cairn, and a vertical slab 0.9 m long, set nearly transversely to the axis near the s end (not visible in 1993), may be part of such a structure.

18. CARN RICHARD
(Carn Tigh nan Coileach)

Parish Kildonan
Location near the head of the Strath of Kildonan, 2.6 km w of Kinbrace
Map reference NC 834321
NMRS number NC 83 SW 1
References RCAMS 1911, 130, no. 373; Henshall 1963, 312
Plan ASH and JNGR
Visited 7.5.57, 14.5.93

Description. The cairn is on the steep N side of the strath, at a little over 200 m OD. Until recently the cairn was in rough pasture which retained visible evidence of prehistoric settlement, but it is now at the top of a field of improved pasture. There are wide views from the cairn to the SE and W, over the wide peat-covered floor of the valley and to the distant mountains beyond (plate 1).

The site slopes down fairly steeply from NNE to SSW. The cairn is round with a diameter of 18 m E to W and a little more transversely across the contour. The maximum height, to the N of the centre, is 2.8 m measured from the E side. The cairn edge is clear except on the NE side where there is a low turf-covered projection which is probably displaced cairn material (in 1957, when heather encroached over the cairn edge, it was misleadingly described as a horn). Turf grows over the edges of the cairn and extends well up the steep N side. There has been considerable interference on the E side, and the centre of the cairn has been totally disturbed and left as a hollow partly filled by a chaotic mass of stones. A shallow hollow runs north-eastwards from the centre; it appears to be a partly infilled trench and may account for the material which distorts the cairn edge on this side. A rough wall has been built on the s side of the central hollow. The cairn material is large rounded irregular stones.

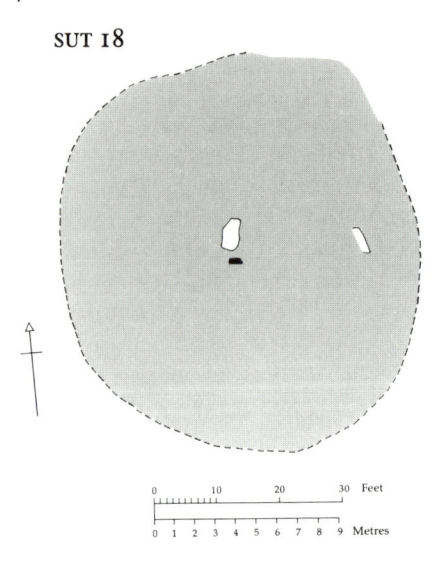

About 2.5 m within the E edge of the cairn is a displaced rectangular block of stone which is probably a passage lintel. It is 1.5 m long, over 0.36 m wide and 0.2 m thick; its W side slopes down into the cairn. Extending WNW from its N end are several smaller flat slabs, all disturbed. Taken together, the stones suggest the presence of a passage running from the E side of the cairn.

In the centre of the central hollow is a large slab, 1.7 by 1 m and 0.25 m thick, lying horizontally on rubble with its upper surface 1.15 m below the highest part of the cairn; it has the appearance of a capstone. S of it, on the s side of the hollow, is a substantial orthostat, the only slab which is certainly *in situ*. Its intact horizontal upper surface is 0.35 m below the 'capstone' at the general level of the infilling of the hollow. The orthostat is over 0.7 m long (the E end not being visible), 0.28 m thick but thicker lower down, and a height of 0.83 m can be measured in a deep hole which has been made against its W end. A number of flat slabs in the central area have the appearance of being corbel stones but it is doubtful whether any of them are undisturbed. Some vertical or nearly vertical slabs can be seen amongst the loose cairn material, but careful observation between the stones shows that none of their bases are at ground level.

19. CLASHMORE

Parish Dornoch
Location on the N side of the Dornoch Firth, 5 km W of Dornoch
Map reference NH 743896
NMRS number NH 78 NW 3
References RCAMS 1911, 49, no. 142; Henshall 1963, 313
Plan ASH and JNGR
Visited 18.7.56, 19.4.91

Description. The cairn is in the low agricultural land which edges the Dornoch Firth. To the N the ground rises gradually into moorland hills, partly afforested. The cairn, at 38 m OD, is on a slight rise, and is crossed by a fence dividing two fields.

Only the base of the cairn remains, covered by grass with some gorse. The cairn was evidently robbed from the E side where it has been removed to virtually ground level as far as the chamber orthostats, and at the maximum it is 1.2 m high to the S and SW of the chamber. The cairn is almost rectangular, about 19 by 15.5 m, with a fairly clear edge except round the NE quadrant, and the chamber is aligned diagonally. The shape is almost certainly due to ploughing during this century as the longer straight sides are parallel to the field fence running almost N to S. The 1st edition OS 6-inch map shows that, when surveyed in 1874, the cairn was in a strip of rough ground between fences running NNE to SSW, and very close to an occupied crofthouse, now demolished. The cairn had already been reduced in height as the monument is shown as three stones and is titled 'Standing Stones'.

The chamber is orientated SE to NW, but only three massive slabs belonging to the SW side and the inner end remain. The SE slab is 1.78 m long by 0.4 m thick, and 1.35 m high, the E face weathered into an uneven surface. The centre slab, 1.4 m to the NW, is a rather irregular block 1.35 m long at the maximum above ground level, 0.6 to 0.7 m thick, and 1.75 m high. It leans to the SSW, and it appears to have pivoted on its NW end so that the SE edge has moved to the E, into the chamber; originally it was probably more or less in line with the first slab. The back-slab, 1.68 to the NW and not quite at right angles to the first slab, is

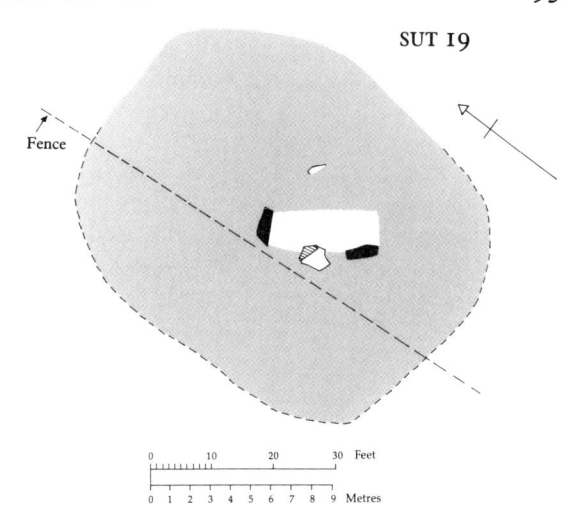

SUT 19

1.8 m long, 0.5 to 0.65 m thick, and 1.9 m high with an intact almost level upper edge. It is a block of granite with a flat face to the SE; in contrast the other two slabs are of sedimentary rock. Part of the top edge of a fourth almost prone slab just projects through the turf 2.6 m to the ESE. The visible part is 0.9 m long by 0.3 m thick but most of the slab extends to the SW below the turf.

20. CNOC AN DAIMH
(Dun Carn Fhamhair)

Parish Eddrachillis
Location on the W coast, 1.6 km SSE of Scourie
Map reference NC 166429
NMRS number NC 14 SE 3
References RCAMS 1911, 57, no. 169; Henshall 1963, 312–13
Plan ASH and JNGR
Visited 17.7.56, 28.4.92

Description. The cairn is in an area of undulating heather moorland with many bare rounded rock outcrops. It is 1 km from the shore, on a rocky knoll at 91 m OD, with wide views except to the N and overlooking inlets of the sea to the SW and W. There are remains of prehistoric settlement on the slope immediately below the cairn and in a small valley about 400 m to the E.

The cairn of irregular and rounded stones is bare except for turf and heather growing over the edges, and it fits closely on the outcrop on which it was built. The cairn has been greatly disturbed and the centre has been hollowed to form a shelter about 2 m across. Because of the steep slope of the knoll much of the loose cairn material has fallen considerably beyond its original limits. On the SW side the rock falls away in a vertical face. Only on the E side can the position of the undisturbed edge be approximately traced. The

SUT 20

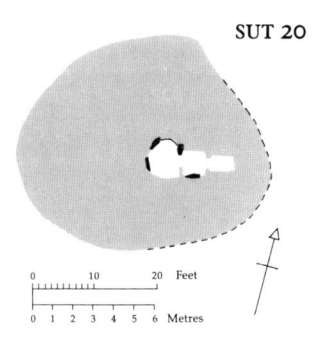

cairn diameters are roughly 10 to 12.5 m, but the original cairn was probably quite small, perhaps about 9 m in diameter. The cairn is nearly 2 m high measured from the NW side, but because the surface of the outcrop rises the remaining depth of cairn material is evidently less. The cairn material forms a level rim about 1 m high around the central hollow, the floor of which is turf and may not be much above the original ground level. A marker cairn has been built to the W of the chamber.

Within the cairn, and lining the central hollow, are three quarried blocks of granite which form part of the NW side of the chamber. From W to E they are 0.75, 0.75 and 0.6 m long by 0.17, 0.25 and 0.3 m thick, and 0.7, 0.9 and 0.84 m high, spaced 0.43 and 0.9 m apart. The last two orthostats are linked by a curved wall-face 0.4 m high consisting of four irregular courses of substantial slabs. It is better built than the other rough walling in the interior of the cairn and is probably original. The chamber is 1.55 m across NE to SW. The last orthostat may be an inner portal stone if a fourth orthostat, 1 m to the SE and almost hidden amongst loose stones, is part of the S wall of an antechamber. If this interpretation is correct, the entrance passage has run from the ENE side of the cairn. The fourth orthostat is over 0.75 m long, 0.17 m thick, and 0.74 m high. Several other vertical slabs can be seen amongst the cairn material but do not appear to be part of the structure.

The condition of the cairn is unchanged since it was recorded in 1909 (RCAMS).

21. CNOC ODHAR

Parish Dornoch
Location on the W side of Loch Fleet, 7.3 km NNW of Dornoch
Map reference NH 767967
NMRS number NH 79 NE 24
References ONB 1873, No. 9, 75; RCAMS 1911, 46–7, no. 132; Henshall 1963, 313–14
Plan ASH and JNGR
Visited 18.8.56, 15.4.91

Description. The cairn is in heather moorland on the eastern slope of Cnoc Odhar, surrounded by vestiges of prehistoric settlement. The cairn overlooks the fertile land of Cambusavie farm and is only 100 m beyond the limit of enclosed pasture. The site, at 76 m OD, slopes down gently from NW to SE.

The cairn of rounded stones and boulders has been severely robbed. The edge can be traced on the N and S sides, but otherwise is difficult to define; on the E side it is further confused by the spread remains of an old wall running downhill to the E. The diameter of the cairn has been about 24 to 25 m. The cairn is mostly about 1 m high, covered with turf and bracken, but on the N and W it has been removed to almost ground level as far as the chamber orthostats leaving an outer rim of cairn material 1 m high and covered with a thin layer of peat. The interior of the chamber is choked with cairn material and is partly obscured by gorse.

In the centre of the cairn is a group of orthostats belonging to a chamber which was evidently entered from the S or a little E of S, and which seems to have been rather irregular in plan. The chamber measures 2 m long by 1.7 m wide. The SW orthostat is set transversely to the chamber axis and appears to have been a portal stone, 0.8 m long, 0.5 m thick, and exposed for almost its full height of 0.7 m at its outer end. No partner for this stone can be seen. About 1.15 m to the E an orthostat is set roughly parallel to the axis, but only the S part is visible; it is over 0.65 m long, 0.55 m thick, and is exposed for a height of only 0.2 m. Immediately to the W a rectangular earthfast stone, 0.4 m long, 0.2 m thick, and exposed for 0.2 m, is skew to the axis and probably is not *in situ*. Two orthostats form the W and NW sides of the chamber. They are 1.4 and 0.85 m long, both are 0.4 m thick, and they are almost fully exposed on their outer sides with heights of 1.25 and 1.3 m. On the NE side of the chamber only the S part of the last orthostat is visible, over 0.6 m long, 0.35 m thick, and exposed for a height of 0.35 m. All the orthostats retain intact upper surfaces except that the tip of the pointed NW stone has been lost. This stone is the tallest; those on either side are 0.3 and 0.4 m lower, and the three stones on the S side of the chamber are 0.85 m lower. To the S of the chamber there lies a boulder, 1.6 by 0.9 m and over 0.35 m thick, sloping down from SE to NW; the two main surfaces are flat and the boulder has the appearance of a displaced lintel.

The condition of the cairn has not changed since it was visited in 1956, and probably not since it was first described in 1909 (RCAMS) though this account

SUT 21

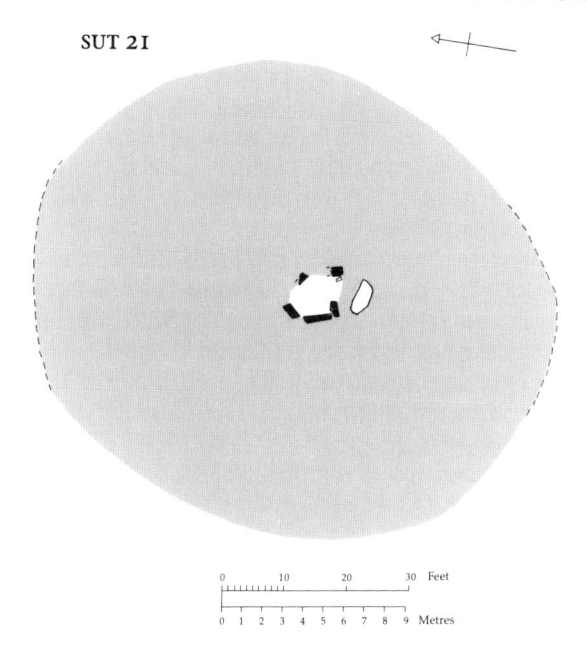

seems to contain some errors. 'Human remains were found here A.D. 1868' (ONB).

Five metres to the NE of the cairn there is a small cairn 10 m in diameter, with a hollowed centre.

22. COILLE NA BORGIE NORTH
(Ach Cill na Borgan, Rhinavie)

Parish Farr
Location in Strathnaver, 2.8 km SSE of Bettyhill
Map reference NC 715590
NMRS number NC 75 NW 3
References McKay 1867; Munro 1884, 228–31; Anderson 1886, 260–3; RCAMS 1911, 83–4, no. 243; Henshall 1963, 314–15; 1972, 574–5, 625
Plan ASH and JNGR
Visited 8.7.51, 19.4.68, 18.5.92

Description. This cairn and the South cairn (SUT 23) lie end to end on a terrace on the E side of the strath, at 15 m OD (figure 17). There are considerable areas of enclosed pasture in this part of the valley, though the cairns are in rough grazing. Along the E side of the terrace the ground rises steeply as bare rock and heather moorland, and along the W side there is a short drop to the road which runs along the E side of the valley. There has been settlement, in prehistoric and in more recent times, in the immediate vicinity of the cairns. Foundations of an old field wall run E to W 2 m from the N end of the North cairn, and traces of older walls, buildings and small cairns can be seen on the terrace to the E. Although the siting of the long cairns along the edge of a terrace exaggerated their height when seen from the W, a more prominent position could have been chosen on the top of a small hill to the SW.

The North cairn consists of two separate parts and has sometimes been described as two cairns, but it is preferable to describe it as a single monument, comprising a heel-shaped cairn to the N (though appearing more or less oval due to additional cairn material on its N side), and a trapezoid cairn to the S (see ¶ 5.13, 24). The total length of the monument is about 60 m. Both parts are made of irregular rounded stones with occasional rectangular slabs. Heather grows up the W sides, but elsewhere only the edges are covered with heather or turf. The ground level is uneven around, and presumably below, the cairns, but in general there is a gentle slope down from N to S.

The heel-shaped cairn has a well-defined edge around the S half; the E and W sides are fairly straight and parallel and the S end is rounded. Northwards, the cairn edge is difficult to trace because the E side has been robbed and on the W side it merges with the edge of the terrace. However, on this side four kerbstones, which are part of the original built edging of the cairn, have been revealed where cairn material has been pulled away; they are well within the ultimate spread of the cairn material. These stones are substantial rectangular blocks; S to N, they are 0.43, 0.78, 0.55 and 0.7 m long spaced 0.9, 1 and 2.6 m apart. All except the third have fallen outwards to a horizontal or almost horizontal position. The upright stone has a true height of 0.8 m, and the others would be 0.63 to 0.5 m high if vertical. The highest part of the cairn is immediately S of the chamber where it is 1.8 m above the ground level to the N, but the height is less when measured from the E.

The cairn evidently had a deep forecourt edged by horns, facing a little W of N, now only indicated by three façade stones belonging to its E half. At the NE corner is an orthostat 0.55 m long by 0.33 m thick, leaning acutely to the E; if vertical its position would be a little to the W and it would be 0.6 m high. The stone evidently tapered to a point before the top was broken off. A little turf-covered cairn material remains between this stone and a prone orthostat 4.6 m to the SW. The latter appears to be intact, its base hidden in cairn material, but it seems to have twisted in falling so that its wider face which would have fronted the forecourt is now vertical on the SW side. When in place the stone was over 0.6 m long by 0.36 m thick, and over 1.3 m high with a thin horizontal top edge. The third orthostat, 0.9 m to the SW, is 1.2 m long by 0.2 m thick and 0.6 m high, and its top is obviously broken. The inner part of the forecourt is filled with tumbled stone continuous with the main

SUT 22

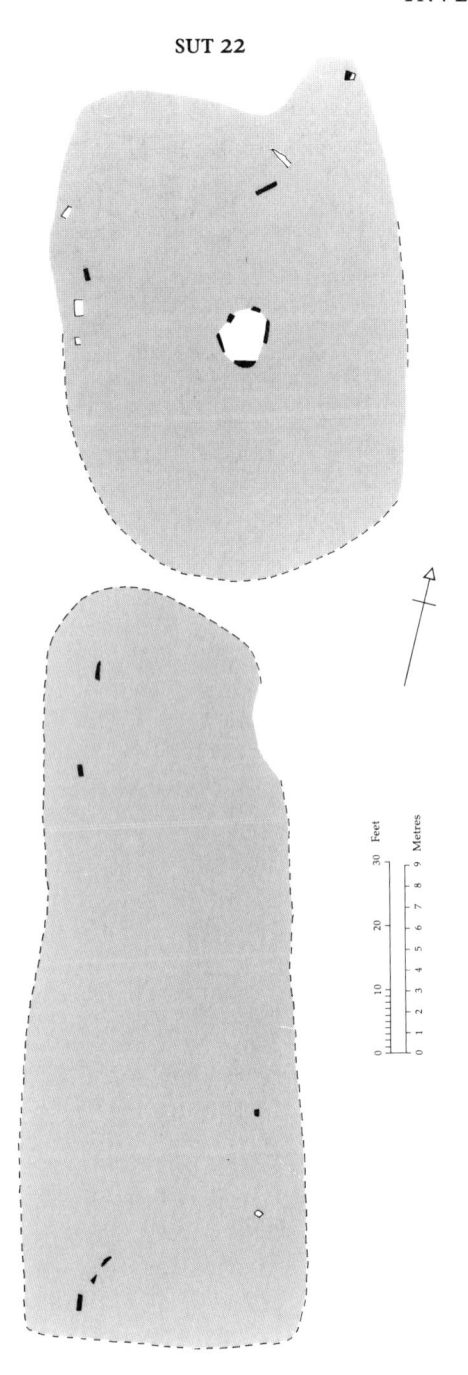

part of the cairn and diminishing in height northwards until it is covered by turf and merges imperceptibly into the ground; the whole forecourt area is very disturbed. The cairn was about 24 m long including the horns, or about 18.5 m long from the centre of the façade, by 17 m wide.

In a hollow in the cairn the tops of five orthostats belonging to the walls of the chamber just protrude above the infilling of domestic rubbish which is probably about 1 m deep. The chamber is 2.5 m long from N to S, by 2.3 m wide, its N end 5.8 m from the W façade stone. The orthostats are 0.53 to 0.9 m apart, and clockwise from the N (as far as can be seen) they are 0.42, 1.23, 1.03, over 0.95 and 0.37 m long, by 0.17, 0.15, 0.28, 0.17 and 0.33 m thick. The first two and the last have flat and probably intact tops, and project 0.3, 0.8 and 0.16 m. The third orthostat is the largest and appears to be the back-slab, deliberately set sloping slightly outwards from the chamber; its estimated true height is nearly 2 m, and it is 0.8 m higher than the NE orthostat. The SW orthostat projects 0.35 m.

The chamber was emptied in 1867, but the area between it and the façade does not seem to have been investigated (McKay). Munro, in 1884, recorded 'the walls of [the chamber] are composed of five rough granitic slabs set on end, the spaces between these being built up with uncemented masonry. The average height is 5 feet (1.5 m); but as the chamber is at present filled with rubbish, it must have originally been about 8 ft (2.4 m). One of the slabs is 7 feet 3 inches (2.2 m) above ground. The others vary from 3 feet 6 inches (1 m) to 6 feet (1.8 m). The diameter is 7 feet (2.1 m) at the top, where there is a slight divergence in the walls, and along the floor the measurement is about a foot (0.3 m) less. The entrance to this chamber is not clearly defined, but there are indistinct traces of its having a passage on the N side.' The estimated height he gives for the chamber walls is almost certainly exaggerated.

The trapezoid cairn is separated from the heel-shaped cairn by a gap 2 m wide. The S cairn is 36 m long by 10.5 m wide at the N end increasing to 14 m wide at the S end, its axis parallel to, but about 4 m W of, the axis of the N cairn. The edges are clearly defined except for a small area of robbing near the NE corner. Two upright kerb-stones near the N end of the W side, and one kerb-stone with a second recorded in 1968 towards the S end of the E side, indicate the position of the original edging of the cairn, 1.6 m or more within the limits of the cairn material. The kerb-stones on the W side are 0.85 and 0.65 m long, both are 0.3 m thick, and they are 0.8 and 0.23 m high, 4.15 m apart; that on the E side is 0.36 m long, 0.26 m thick and 0.4 m high. Three upright stones near the SW corner of the cairn evidently belong to the W side of a forecourt façade. The stones, SW to NE, are 0.65 and 0.6 m apart. They are 0.8, 0.45 and 0.7 m long by 0.25, 0.18 and 0.2 m thick. The SW stone is 0.43 m high and has clearly been reduced in height; the NE stone is 0.8 m taller, and the stone between them is a stump which hardly protrudes. The forecourt is filled with stone. The cairn has been considerably disturbed by hollows which have been made into it. In long profile, from about 8 m from the S end, the cairn is more or less level, about 1 m high when measured from the E side but appearing considerably higher when viewed from the W where cairn material has fallen down the slope.

23. COILLE NA BORGIE SOUTH
(Ach Cill na Borgan, Rhinavie)

Parish Farr
Location in Strathnaver, 2.8 km SSE of Bettyhill
Map reference NC 715590
NMRS number NC 75 NW 3
References McKay 1867; Stuart 1868, 296; Munro 1884, 228–33; Anderson 1886, 260–3; RCAMS 1911, 83–4, no. 243; Calder 1951; Henshall 1963, 315–16; 1972, 574–6
Plan ASH and MM (1968), N façade and chamber ASH and JNGR
Visited 8.7.51, 19.4.68, 19.5.92

Description. The cairn is on the same terrace as the North cairn (SUT 22), separated from it by a shallow natural transverse hollow. The two cairns are end to end, only about 5 m apart. The axis of the South cairn is in line with that of the N part of the North cairn, and is parallel to, but about 4 m E of, that of its S part (figure 17). The actual site of the South cairn is fairly level from N to S though with a slight slope down below its S end, but there is a considerable downward slope from E to W. The cairn is 75 m long overall; across the N end it is 24 m wide, gradually narrowing to about 13 m wide near the S end before the width increases to about 16 m. The cairn of bare stones is still 3 m high around the chamber which is exposed in an elongated hollow near the N end (the height measured from the floor at the S end of the chamber), but from ground level on the E and W sides the cairn height is under 2 m and 3.6 m respectively. Southwards from about 6 m S of the chamber the height of the cairn is generally about 1 m less, but it has been greatly disturbed and left with deep irregular hollows, mainly the result of investigations last century (Munro, 232). All down the long sides and round the S end the cairn edge is well defined though bearing turf, bracken and heather.

At the N end of the cairn a pair of horns has formed a rather rectilinear forecourt 14 m across and roughly 4.4 m deep. There are eight orthostats of an impressive but incomplete forecourt façade (plate 13). The orthostats are quarried blocks, rectangular or triangular in plan with their wider faces fronting the forecourt. Mostly they have pointed jagged tops but

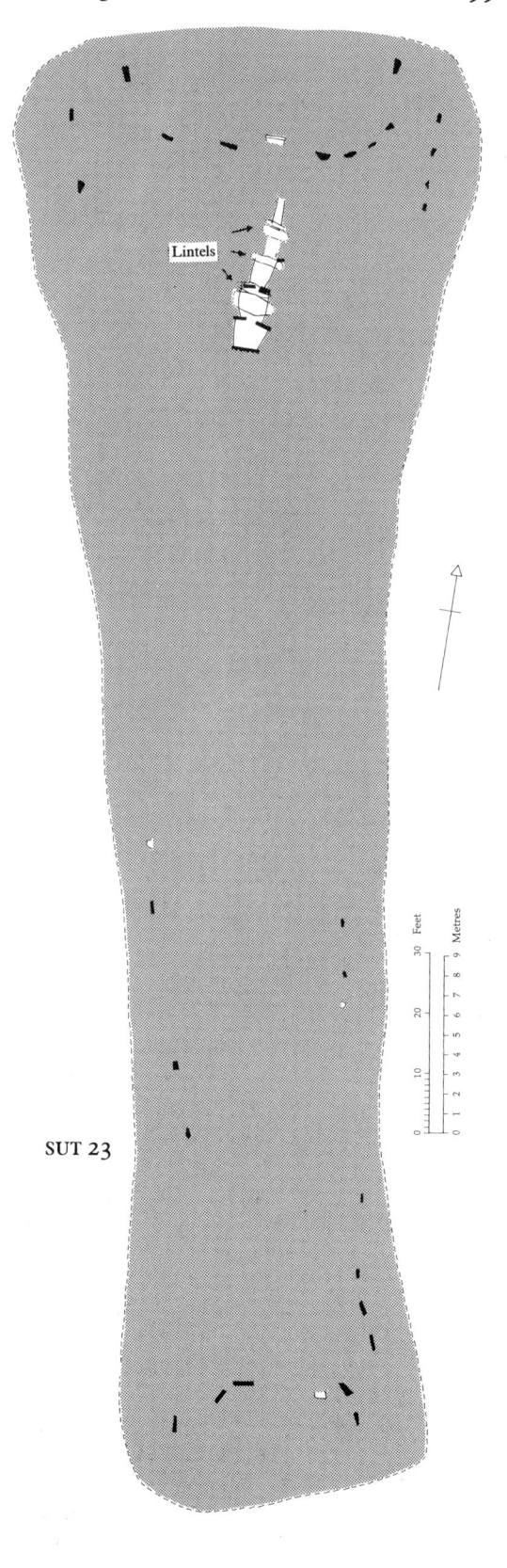

SUT 23

some have been reduced to stumps, and only the westernmost appears to be intact. This stone leans to the W and would be 2.3 m high if vertical. The NE stone is 1.42 m high, leaning slightly to the E, and the other stones are 1.33 to 0.54 m high. The stones are 0.92 to 0.43 m long by 0.35 to 0.2 m thick. The spacing of the second to the fifth stones on the E side is 0.86, 0.7 and 0.7 m. It is likely that the façade was designed with all the stones (some of which are missing) at approximately this spacing as the gap between the NE stone and the adjacent stone is 2.35 m, and the gaps between the three stones on the W side are 2.4 and 3.1 m. The gap between the stones in the centre of the façade is 4.05 m. On the cairn axis in front of the projected line of the façade there is an almost prone slab sloping down to the S, 1.12 m long by over 0.37 m wide and 0.25 m thick. It may be part of a broken ninth orthostat, or it may be a displaced lintel. The forecourt is covered by a fairly shallow spread of disturbed cairn stones, fading away about 1.5 m beyond the ends of the horns.

At the S end of the cairn five orthostats indicate the presence of a smaller forecourt façade, probably about 8 m across. On the E side there are three stones, the western of which has fallen forwards. They are 0.64, 0.8 and 0.6 m long, and 0.37 to 0.15 m thick. The upright stones are 0.4 and 0.5 m high, and if vertical the third stone would be over 0.36 m high and would stand nearly 1 m N of its S edge. The stones are 0.95 and 0.9 m apart. The W stones are 1.1 and 0.85 m long by 0.27 and 0.15 m thick, protruding 0.5 and 0.4 m, set 0.55 m apart. The gap between the two groups of stones is 3.35 m. There is a considerable amount of cairn material in the forecourt, rising steeply from the S edge.

A number of upright kerb-stones can be seen down the sides of the cairn, generally 1.5 m or more within the cairn edge. At the N end of the E side and partly edging the NE horn four rectangular blocks with pointed tops are set 1.4 to 0.8 m apart. The largest at the N end is 0.55 m long, 0.2 m thick, protruding 0.5 m. Down the E side six more kerb-stones can be seen amongst the loose cairn material, similar in appearance except that the penultimate stone is unusually large, 0.7 m long by 0.3 m thick and 0.8 m high. Seven kerb-stones can be seen down the W side of the cairn, the southernmost a large block of similar size edging the SW horn.

The passage and chamber were cleared out in 1867 (McKay), since when they have been left open with some of the roofing in place. Much of the structure can still be seen though it is difficult to examine. The walling of small slabs is in poor condition with many of the slabs shattered, and there has been considerable inward displacement of the walling especially in the upper parts. One lintel is broken through though both pieces are still in place. The chamber floor is covered with a variable depth of fallen cairn material, with less in the passage and in the inner compartment where the lowest level just observable beneath the rubble is likely to be close to the original floor level.

The area between the centre of the façade and the present N end of the passage is filled with disturbed cairn material. The original arrangement at the entrance to the passage is uncertain (see further ¶ 5.27).

The passage as visible in 1992 is about 3 m long, 0.35 m wide at the N end increasing to 0.5 m wide below the first lintel. The upper courses of the E wall overhang probably due to displacement, but the W wall is better preserved. At the N end of the W wall only three courses remain ending at a vertical joint, and northwards a single substantial stone seems to indicate the continuation of the wall for at least a further 0.3 m. On the E side the N end of the wall is broken away. At 1.06 m from the outer end of the passage a narrow lintel, 0.25 m wide and 0.11 m thick, spans the passage at a height of 0.7 m. Behind it a second lintel, 0.47 m wide, is set at the same height. The lintels rest on the W wall here consisting of seven or eight courses, but the E wall has partly collapsed and the E ends of the lintels rest on cairn material farther to the E. The next lintel (or possibly two lintels) to the S seems to be missing and the inner part of the passage is hidden by rubble. A short stretch of the S end of the E wall can be seen from the chamber. The width and height of the passage given by Munro in 1883 (p. 232) agree well with the present dimensions below the first lintel.

The axis of the passage and chamber is skew by about 13° to the axis of the cairn. The chamber consists of three compartments, each entered between a pair of portal stones. The side walls butt against the portal stones except where one stone is displaced (noted below). The orthostats and the thin slabs used for the walling are quarried stones.

At the junction of the passage and outer compartment the W portal stone is hidden by rubble, but the E stone is visible; it is about 0.37 m long by 0.17 m thick and 0.62 m high. The outer compartment is 1.5 m long, and narrows from about 1.08 m wide at the N end to only 0.85 m wide at the S end. The walling remains 0.85 m high on the E side, but less on the W side, and on both sides the upper courses have been displaced inwards. A lintel covers the N part of the compartment with its NE corner resting on the E portal stone. The lintel is 0.43 m wide at maximum (but the N edge which is hardly visible is irregular and seems to have been broken) by 0.24 m thick and over 1.74 m long. The S part of the compartment was presumably covered by a large lintel, or more likely by two narrow lintels, now missing.

A second pair of portal stones form the entry to the middle compartment. They are only 0.25 m apart at the base and 0.1 m apart at the top. Both stones have evidently been displaced inwards and the W stone has also slewed to the S; it has left a recess in the W wall which had accommodated its W end. The E stone has a straight upper surface slanting down to the E; the other stone has a rough upper surface suggesting that it has crumbled though it still supports a lintel. The stones are both 0.55 m long, 0.32 and 0.22 m thick, and 1 and 1.1 m high. The compartment is 1.5 m long by 1.46 in maximum width. The side walls stand to their original height. The E wall overhangs by 0.4 m with the upper part probably slightly displaced inwards. The W wall is in better condition though the upper part at the S end is collapsing. Two lintels cover most of the compartment. The N lintel is 0.56 m wide by 0.2 m thick. It rests on the W portal stone, and on two slabs over the lower E portal stone and on walling; it has cracked right through near its W end. This lintel is about 0.3 m higher than that over the outer compartment. The adjacent lintel to the S is 0.86 m wide by 0.3 m thick, resting on the side walls. As it just overlaps its neighbour it is at a slightly higher level, but it has tilted down to the SW due to failing support. The height of the roof was recorded by Munro as just over 2 m which must be an error as there is no sign that the lintels have been moved, and their true height above the floor can be calculated as hardly more than 1.3 m.

The third pair of portal stones give access to the inner compartment. They are regular rectangular slabs set 0.5 m apart with almost horizontal upper surfaces. They are over 0.74 and 0.7 m long by 0.2 and 0.17 m thick, and 1.58 and 1.1 m high. The compartment is 1.36 m long by 1.7 to 1.2 m wide. The E wall stands to 1.63 m above the floor and oversails by 0.3 m; the W wall is about 0.4 m lower. The back-slab, against which the walls butt, is over 1.4 m long, 0.94 m high, with the top edge slightly rounded. It carries three courses of walling and the total height at the back of the chamber is 1.3 m. The compartment was roofless in 1883, and the walls were recorded as 2.4 m high with an orthostat on each side. The last statement, supported by the McKay plan and sketch (figure 18), is puzzling as the orthostats are not visible even though it is possible to see nearly to the base of the wall.

The only finds made by Munro (p. 231) were 'some pieces of charred wood and fragments of animal bones', but Anderson wrote 'the floors still afford indications of the presence of charcoal and burnt bones' (p. 263).

24. CREAG NAN CAORACH EAST
Parish Kildonan
Location in the Strath of Kildonan, 1 km SE of Kinbrace
Map reference NC 870309
NMRS number NC 83 SE IB
References RCAMS 1911, 128, no. 367; Henshall 1963, 316–17
Plan ASH and JNGR
Visited 7.5.57, 16.5.93

Description. The cairn is on the E side of the strath near its head, on a moorland hillside at 228 m OD. Creag nan Caorach West (SUT 25) is in sight 180 m to the W and 22 m below. There are widespread remains of prehistoric settlement around and below the cairns. Both cairns have a wide view over the open strath and to far mountains to the N and W.

The site of the East cairn slopes down from NE to SW. The cairn has been greatly reduced and disturbed, at most remaining 1.5 m high. It consists of irregular rounded stones partly overgrown with turf and heather. The edge is fairly clear except round the N side where it is obscured by encroaching peat. The diameter is about 15 m.

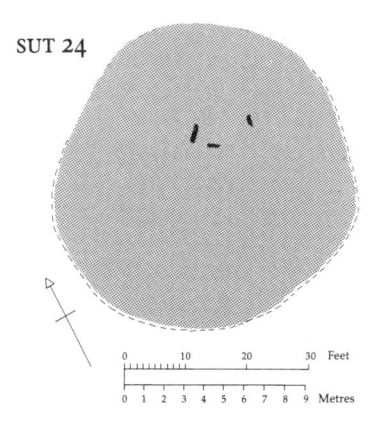

Three orthostats indicate the presence of a small chamber, its axis either ESE to WNW or E to W, placed to the NE of the centre of the cairn as it presently (though probably misleadingly) appears. The orthostats are intact boulders, rectangular in plan. The most obvious is the pointed back-slab, 0.9 m long by 0.2 m thick, and exposed in a hollow for about its full height of 0.93 m. An orthostat 2.45 m to the E is likely to be a portal stone. It is over 0.5 m long, its S end hidden, by 0.2 m thick, and projects 0.4 m. The third orthostat, on the SW side of the chamber 0.73 m from the back-slab, leans slightly to the N. It is 0.6 m long by 0.17 m thick, exposed for 0.35 m but its true height is about 0.57 m. The last two orthostats have horizontal upper surfaces. A slab lying 0.4 m SW of the side-slab was probably a corbel stone; it measures 1.15 by 0.6 m and 0.25 m thick.

25. CREAG NAN CAORACH WEST

Parish Kildonan
Location in the Strath of Kildonan, 1 km SE of Kinbrace
Map reference NC 868309
NMRS number NC 83 SE 1A
References RCAMS 1911, 128, no. 367; Henshall 1963, 316-17
Plan ASH and JNGR
Visited 7.5.57, 16.5.93, 21.4.94

Description. The cairn is in view of Creag nan Caorach East (SUT 24) which is 180 m away at a higher level on the moorland hillside. A small featureless cairn lies 50 m to the NW. The West cairn, at 206 m OD, is on a site sloping down from NE to SW, with the axis of the chamber skew to the slope (plate 8).

The centre of the cairn is bare rounded stones and has been greatly disturbed, but the turf-covered outer parts have not been seriously affected. As presently visible the plan is almost square, about 13.5 m E to W by about 15 m transversely. The edge of the cairn is fairly clear except at the NE corner, but this edge reflects only roughly the plan of a considerably larger cairn the periphery of which is covered by natural deposits. It is clear that a very considerable amount of hillwash has accumulated against the uphill side of the cairn, and around it peat has reached a depth of 0.3 m or more. There can be little doubt that the hidden plan is short horned. When the cairn was seen in 1909 it was about 1.4 m high, and a few flat slabs lying near the centre indicated the probable presence of a chamber (RCAMS). Between that date and 1957 cairn material was removed from the centre in order to expose the chamber and also the outside of the chamber on the W and SW side, and was piled around the central area as a rim of loose stones. The height of the cairn, including this displaced material, when measured from the E and S is 1.15 or 2 m.

The passage evidently faced roughly E, but nothing can be seen of it, nor of an ante-chamber, as displaced cairn material is piled high in this area. The entrance into the main chamber, 0.7 m wide, is between a pair of portal stones which are only partly visible below a lintel. They are over 0.4 and 0.3 m long by over 0.15 and 0.23 m thick; the N stone is exposed for 0.35 m and only the tip of its partner can be seen. Like all the chamber orthostats, they are boulders with flat faces. They support the lower E edge of a lintel which leans

SUT 25

to the W at an angle of 45°; it can only be viewed from the W and from below as its upper surface is hidden beneath cairn material. Originally the lintel almost certainly rested on its long side and its present position is probably the result of partial collapse towards the main chamber. The lintel is 1.8 m long by 0.3 m thick by 0.7 m wide (originally the vertical height).

The main chamber is about 2.2 m long by 1.65 m wide, and is filled to a varying depth with fallen blocks of stone, though all the vertical measurements have been taken from about the same level. Side-slabs, 0.75 and 0.7 m wide, both 0.3 m thick, and projecting 0.75 and 1 m, form part of each wall. At the W end of the main chamber a pair of portal stones set 0.7 m apart gives access to a cell. They are over 0.5 and 0.7 0.7 m long by 0.3 m thick, and both project about 0.3 m. They carry a lintel which was cracked when seen in 1957, and which by 1993 had broken through the centre with the S half tipped down into the entry (shown intact on the plan). The lintel was 1.65 m long when intact, and is 0.5 m wide by 0.4 m thick. On the N side of the main chamber some of the rather rough walling which linked the orthostats may be seen; it is built of quite small flat round-edged slabs. To the E of the side-slab three courses 0.5 m high are exposed; on the W side similar walling is set back from the face of the side-slab with the upper courses resting on the N end of the adjacent cell portal stone. Above the walling there remain two layers of slightly oversailing corbel stones which are supplemented and pinned with smaller stones, and at the E end two slabs on edge fill a gap between the lowest corbel stone and the N portal stone. The upper corbel stones extend over the side-slab. A single corbel stone resting on the cell roof is all that remains of the upper part of the W wall of the main chamber. On the S side only a small stretch of walling can be seen running E from the side-slab and set back from its face; all the corbel stones have been removed. The N side-slab is the tallest orthostat; the N portal stone is 0.4 m lower and the cell portal stones are slightly lower still.

The cell is choked with stone debris, but its roofing by two slabs remains *in situ*. The slabs (shown on a separate detail on the plan) are contiguous; their long axes lie E to W, their E ends rest on the broken lintel, and their W ends are supported by corbel stones at the back of the cell. The roofing slabs are 1.15 and 1.25 m long by 0.68 and 0.75 m wide by 0.3 and 0.25 m thick. Corbel stones lie radially in a semicircle round the cell. The outer parts of six or seven are exposed where the cairn has been removed from outside the back of the chamber. Their inner ends, which form the upper wall-face of the cell, can be glimpsed through small gaps between and around the roofing slabs. The cell is 1 m long from inside the portal stones, and about 1.3 m wide. Its roof is about the same height as the lintel at the entry to the main chamber.

26. DRUIM LIATH (Carn Liath)

Parish Creich
Location 1 km N of Bonar Bridge
Map reference NH 609930
NMRS number NH 69 SW 25
References RCAMS 1911, 32, no. 86; Henshall 1963, 317
Plan ASH and JNGR
Visited 12.7.55, 22.5.91

Description. The cairn is on a moorland hillside which slopes down gently from NE to SW, on which is a natural scattering of Scots pines. At 84 m OD the cairn is close to the upper limit of agricultural land, and there are prehistoric field clearance cairns in the vicinity of the cairn.

The cairn of irregular stones is bare except for a large juniper growing over the centre, and gorse and juniper encroaching on the edges, though the actual edge of the cairn can still be easily traced. The cairn is round except for a flattening of the ESE side. The diameters ESE to WNW and transversely are 21 m; the maximum height is 2.5 m, to the N of the back of the chamber. A deep hollow has been made from the ESE edge to beyond the centre of the cairn in order to expose the passage and chamber which have been aligned along the contour. However, the structure is largely concealed, firstly by infilling the hollow as far as the centre of the chamber with domestic rubbish, then by the juniper already mentioned which totally obscures the next part and only allows observation of the very end of the chamber.

Nothing can be seen of the passage. The ante-chamber, 2.75 m long by about 2.0 m wide, is defined by four orthostats which only just project above the rubbish. The N portal stone at the entry to the chamber is about 5.5 m from the ESE edge of the cairn; the stone is 0.8 m long by 0.45 m thick. On the S side of the ante-chamber there is a slab 1.15 m long by 0.4 m thick; on the opposite side, 1.65 m from the portal stone, is a slab 0.55 m long by 0.32 m thick. The N member of a pair of inner portal stones is 0.65 m W of the N side-slab; the portal stone is over 0.4 m long (its N end not visible) by 0.3 m thick, with an undamaged upper surface. Gaps in the rubbish beside each of these four orthostats allow them to be seen for depths of between 0.3 to 0.45 m; the outer portal stone is the shortest and the inner portal stone is the tallest, and their true heights are considerably more.

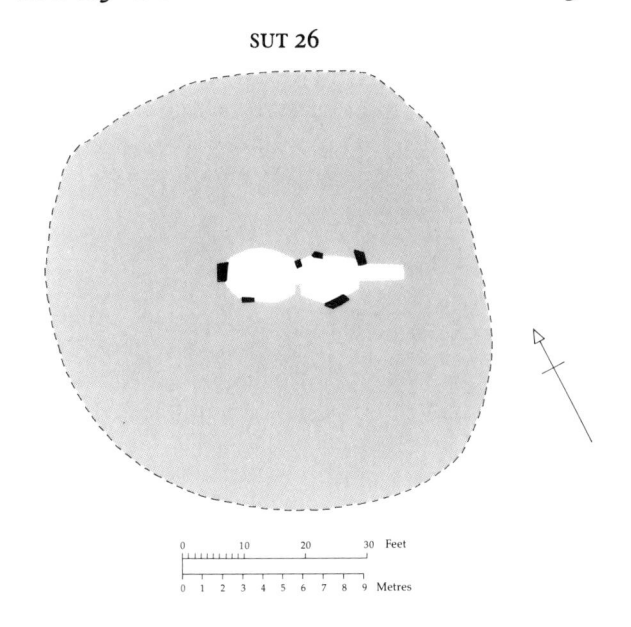

The main chamber, only slightly longer than the large ante-chamber, is 3.45 m long, but only the back-slab and a slab on the S side can be seen, both exposed in a deep hollow. The back-slab is a split boulder set with the split face to the outside and the smooth original surface to the chamber, and the irregular pointed top is undamaged. The slab leans outwards by about 0.3 m; it is over 0.9 m long, 0.45 m thick, and is exposed for 1.3 m, nearly its full height. The side-slab is 1.17 m to the SE; it is 0.6 m long, 0.33 m thick, and exposed for 0.6 m though its intact horizontal upper edge is only 0.3 m lower than that of the back-slab. The chamber is about 6.3 m long.

When visited in 1909 the cairn was in much the same condition, but only the easternmost and westernmost orthostats of the chamber were observed (RCAMS).

27. DUN VIDEN

Parish Farr
Location in Strathnaver, 10 km S of Bettyhill
Map reference NC 727518
NMRS number NC 75 SW 12
References Joass 1864a; 1864b, 360, pl. 24; RCAMS 1911, 89, no. 261; Henshall 1963, 317, 319
Plan ASH and JCW
Visited 8.7.55, 19.5.92

Description. The remains of the cairn are situated at the junction of rolling heather-covered moorland to the E and enclosed pasture of the valley floor to the W and S. The actual site, at 31 m OD, is unusual, on a narrow ridge projecting into the valley. Dun Viden broch is on the higher and wider end of the ridge 70 m to the W. There are foundations of houses and enclosures immediately below the site.

Seven orthostats, the remains of a passage and chamber, are prominent features on the crest of the ridge. All that survives of the cairn which once covered them is a little cairn material in and around the chamber, at most 0.5 m deep. The cairn must have been quite small, not more than 11.5 m from NNW to SSE, as the ground drops away steeply on these sides, though less steeply to the W.

The passage entrance has evidently faced ESE. A pair of slabs, 1.1 to 1.3 m apart, formed part of each wall. The slabs are 1.45 and 1.5 m long by 0.35 and 0.4 m thick. Immediately W of the S stone is a transverse S portal stone, but its partner is missing; the stone is 0.56 m long by 0.23 m thick. These three stones are roughly the same height, exposed for 0.35 to 0.4 m, and have fairly flat and seemingly intact upper surfaces. The portal presumably led to an antechamber about 1.8 m long. The main chamber is represented by four orthostats. The SE stone is intact, 1.25 m long by 0.3 m thick, and 0.95 m high measured from almost ground level at the SW end; the upper surface is flat, sloping down gently to the SW. On the NW face there are eight hollows, 40 to 60 mm in diameter and up to 20 mm deep, which may be cup-marks, but discoloration suggests rather that they are natural and due to differential weathering. The SW and N stones are 0.94 and 0.8 m long by 0.3 and 0.45 m thick, and they are 0.7 and 0.45 m high with broken tops. The width of the main chamber between them is 3.2 m. The E stone leans to the NE and it appears to have slewed round from a position facing nearly W. Its displacement was probably due to a hollow which has been dug against its S face. The stone has a relatively narrow base but is 1 m wide above ground level; it is 0.35 m thick, and would be 1.35 m high if vertical.

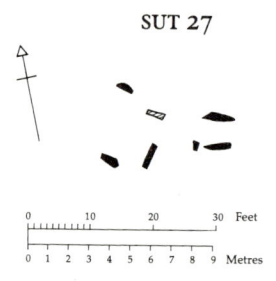

SUT 27

The first brief mention of the monument in 1864 indicates that it was in much the same condition at that time though the positions of orthostats which had been removed were visible (Joass). On his sketch plan Joass shows seven stones and the former positions of three more, but the plan is difficult to interpret. The 1909 description is also somewhat misleading (RCAMS).

28. EVELIX

Parish Dornoch
Location on the N side of the Dornoch Firth, 3 km W of Dornoch
Map reference NH 763899
NMRS number NH 78 NE 12
References RCAMS 1911, 49–50, no. 143; Henshall 1963, 318, 319
Plan ASH and JNGR
Visited 29.6.57, 18.4.91

Description. The cairn is in a level field, at 25 m OD. Agricultural land stretches to the E and N, but immediately to the W there is extensive conifer afforestation and mixed land usage to the S.

The last remains of the cairn, no more than 0.9 m high and grass-covered, are in a small unploughed area at the side of the field. An edge can be traced round most of the cairn giving diameters of about 22.5 to 25.5 m, with the chamber somewhat NE of the centre.

The passage has run from the ESE. About 3 m from the E edge of the cairn is an intact granite boulder set transversely to the axis, probably the N portal stone at the entrance to the passage. It is 0.9 m long by 0.55 m thick and projects 0.55 m, nearly its true height. The chamber orthostats are substantial blocks of stone which are nearly fully exposed. A pair of stones, 2 m to the W of the portal stone, are 0.9 and 0.8 m long; both are 0.6 m thick, and they are 0.8 and 1.0 m high, and the S stone is intact. They are 1.35 m apart, and they are more likely to belong to the walls of an antechamber than of the passage. If so, the passage was about 2.4 m long including a missing pair of portal stones at its inner end (see ¶ 4.7).

SUT 28

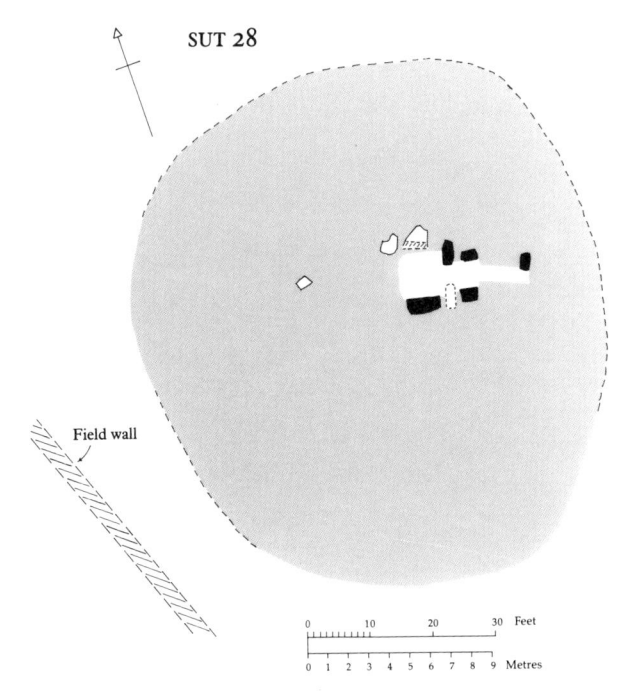

The N portal stone at the entry to the main chamber is 1.2 m long, 0.5 m or so thick, and 0.85 m high with a damaged upper edge. The hollow where its partner had stood could be seen at the time of the 1957 visit. The S side of the main chamber consists of a large block, 1.65 m long though less at the base, 0.65 to 0.8 m thick, and 1.2 m high. Opposite it a slightly smaller block leans acutely to the N. It is 1.2 m long, 0.45 m thick, and would be about 1.2 m high when vertical; the top edge is damaged and the base is almost exposed. The width of the main chamber, now 2.4 m, would probably have been slightly less before the N block collapsed. Just W of this block there is a prone block, irregular in shape and probably reduced in size long ago, now 0.85 by 1.05 m and 0.35 m thick. On the chamber axis, 4.7 m W of the S side of the chamber, a broken stone measuring about 0.8 by 0.5 m and 0.5 m thick appears to be a displaced part of another orthostat. Other stones recorded in 1909 and 1957, to the W of the chamber and on the S side of the passage entrance, are boulders which are not earthfast.

The condition of the cairn has not changed since it was recorded in 1909 except for the addition of some field-gathered stones.

29. FISCARY (Carn Chaoile)

Parish Farr
Location near the N coast, 2.4 km ENE of Bettyhill
Map reference NC 731626
NMRS number NC 76 SW 5

References Kerr 1891; Kerr 1892; RCAMS 1911, 81, no. 236; Henshall 1963, 318, 319; Mercer 1981, 6, 7, 115, fig. 2
Plan ASH and JNGR, additional chamber detail from Henshall
Visited 2.7.55, 25.10.92

Description. A pair of cairns occupies the highest point of a ridge of rough grazing which separates the enclosed land of the small communities of Swordly and Farr. Although the elevation of the cairns at 128 m OD is quite modest, there are spectacular views in all directions, out to sea to the N, to distant mountains to the W, and over rocky moorland to the S and E. There are two more cairns nearby, 180 and 250 m to the SE and W respectively.

The paired cairns appear to be independent structures 8.5 m apart, though a platform extending beyond the base of the S cairn, which has no internal features exposed, spreads to the base of the N cairn, which contains a ruined chamber. The S cairn is at a slightly higher level than the N cairn; the ground slopes away from the bases of the cairns, most gently to the N and most steeply to the SW.

The N cairn is of bare angular stones with turf and heather only encroaching over the edges. Its limits are well defined and give a roughly square plan with short diameters of about 16.5 m. When visited by Kerr in 1891 he found that recently the cairn 'had been broken into, and stones removed from it for building purposes. It had been opened from the top, and there was abundant evidence around the cairn that large slabs of stone had been removed from the interior' (1892, 66). The greatly disturbed cairn has been left with several deep hollows, the largest towards the S side containing remains of the chamber. The cairn is highest near the centre, to the N of the chamber, where it is still about 2 m high measured from the SW.

Kerr exposed the roofless tripartite chamber (figure 13), and most of the structure which he recorded was visible in 1955 (Henshall). Less could be seen in 1992 as the chamber has been largely filled by loose stones, though vertical measurements could be taken from approximately the old floor level. Kerr found that the passage, which ran from the WSW side, was between 0.9 and 1.2 m long and nearly 0.9 m wide. At the inner end the entry to the chamber is 0.55 m wide between portal stones. The N stone, set transversely to the chamber axis, is over 0.6 m long by 0.2 m thick, and 0.65 m high. It appears to be intact, with the upper edge sloping down steeply to the N. The smaller S portal stone, set parallel to the passage, is 0.42 m long by 0.2 m thick, and 0.65 m high. In 1891 the portal stones bore a lintel at a height of 0.9 m. The positioning of the S stone is unusual,

SUT 29

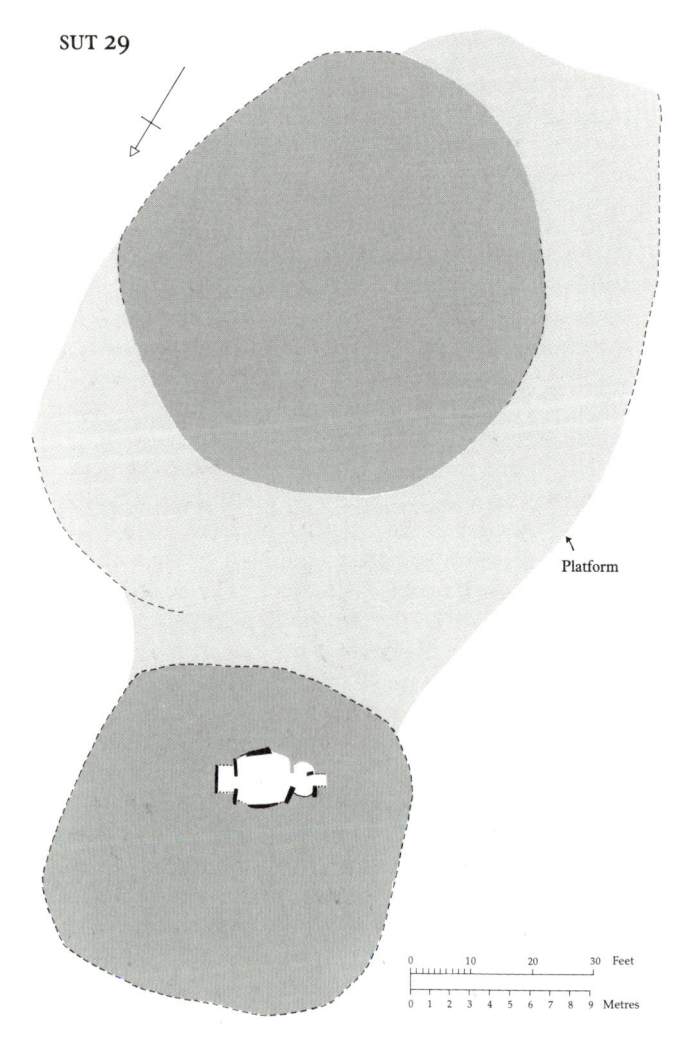

Platform

0 10 20 30 Feet
0 1 2 3 4 5 6 7 8 9 Metres

and it may be suspected that this is not the original arrangement, and consequently that the lintel may have been a replacement.

The total length of the chamber is 4.6 m. The orthostats and walling are all quarried blocks of stone. The ante-chamber is small, at the maximum 0.9 m long. The N inner portal stone, set skew to the axis, is 0.85 m long by 0.3 m thick, and 0.8 m high, with a probably intact horizontal upper surface. This stone is linked to the N outer portal stone by walling 0.55 m high in six courses, with the upper two stones at the W end set skew across the corner to rest on the shoulder of the outer portal stone. The walling butts against the centres of the portal stones, and so indicates that the ante-chamber was quite narrow. The S side of the ante-chamber and the S inner portal stone were already missing in 1891, which lends support to the suspicion that the N outer portal stone is not original.

The main chamber is about 2.36 m long by about 2.3 m wide. Each side is built with a long orthostat supplemented by walling. In 1891 the walls stood to a maximum height of 1.5 m with some oversailing of the upper courses. In 1992 the N wall was entirely hidden, and only a small part of the upper edge of the S orthostat was visible bearing two courses of rough curved walling which extended beyond it to the E. The inner end of the main chamber is formed by a pair of cell portal stones set 0.6 m apart. The S stone is over 1 m long by 0.2 m thick and 0.64 m high; its upper surface slopes down to the N. The N stone was hidden in 1992.

The cell is 0.94 m from front to back by about 1.75 m wide. The back-slab is 1.5 m long by 0.1 m thick and 0.56 m high, and is probably intact. The cell 'had the appearance of being covered over with slabs, some of which stood on edge inside' (Kerr 1892, 67).

It seems likely that the chamber had been thoroughly disturbed before Kerr's investigation. Beneath a filling of stones and earth he found 'what seemed a mixture of ashes and earth, with numerous pieces of charred wood, but no charred bones. ... Underneath that layer was ordinary gravel' (1892, 67). Some fragments of bones were found in the centre and inner compartments, but were not thought to be of great antiquity. There was a small vitrified mass in the floor.

The larger S cairn is bare, steep-sided, and has been little disturbed. The diameters are between 19.5 to 21.5 m, and the height is 5.5 m measured from the NW. The edge is clear for about half of the circuit. The surrounding platform is quite low, and is partly covered with peat and deep heather which in places obscure the edge. The platform varies in width from 4.8 to 7.3 m. On the SE side the cairn edge is clear and there is no sign of the platform. It appears on the NE side where it is largely free of heather, and the cairn material merges into its stones. This part of the platform is edged by a rough kerb which fades away westwards into the spread of stones which links the two cairns. In the area between the cairns the stones are mainly covered by peat on which grow turf and heather. The spread of stones appears to be thin, but on the NW side of the cairn, where there is evidently a drop in ground level, breaks in the peat cover show that here the stone spread has considerable depth. Round the W side the platform is heather-covered, and along the SW part, where the hill drops away steeply, there is a rough kerb at a lower level than elsewhere, within which the surface of the platform rises to the base of the cairn. The S end of the platform, which here is of bare stones, seems to turn sharply towards the S edge of the cairn though the actual edge of the platform is indefinite.

There is no indication that the platform extended round the N cairn, and the line of the platform kerb continuing into the spread of stones which connects the two cairns suggests that the platform and the N cairn were not linked until a later, but ancient, spread of stones filled the gap. The ground level beneath the cairns evidently varies more than is apparent and adds to the difficulties of recording and interpreting the monument. It is clear that the cairns have a complex structural history and the off-centre position of the chamber within the N cairn is particularly notable.

30. GRUMBEG
See p.152.

31. INVERSHIN
Parish Creich
Location 5 km NW of Bonar Bridge
Map reference NH 579958
NMRS number NH 59 NE 4
References RCAMS 1911, 33, no. 90; Henshall 1963, 319
Plan ASH and MJS
Visited 29.5.54, 23.5.91

Description. The ruined chamber is in a small area of deciduous woodland at the foot of a hillside sloping down from E to W, and is only 0.2 km from the shore of the Kyle of Sutherland. The actual site is a slight rise, at a little less than 50 m OD, in a narrow strip of land between the main road and the railway.

The chamber walls were constructed of seven closely-set orthostats, six of which remain in position. The interior of the chamber is filled with stone and an oak tree is growing in the centre, but little cairn material remains on the outside. The entrance has been from the SSE, between a pair of portal stones set 0.77 m apart; they are 0.75 and 0.83 m long and 0.35 and 0.4 m thick. The two orthostats on the E side of the chamber are 1.5 and 1.35 m long by 0.38 and 0.45 m thick, set 0.28 m apart and with the S slab butting against the E portal stone. On the W side of the chamber the S slab was observed fallen in 1909 (RCAMS) and is no longer to be seen; the N slab is 1.58 m long by 0.6 m thick. There are gaps of 0.85 and 0.65 m between the inner side-slabs and the back-slab. The latter is 1 m long by 0.43 m thick, and is exposed for a height of 0.9 m. It leans outwards and is 0.3 m or so taller than the other orthostats, and has an irregular and probably damaged upper edge. All the other orthostats retain their original horizontal upper surfaces and are roughly the same height; they project between 0.35 and 0.7 m above the last remains of the cairn, and their true heights are probably not much over 1 m. The chamber is 3.9 m long by 2.27 m wide.

The cairn has been removed on the N and E sides of the chamber, but a little cairn material extends for about 5 m to the S and perhaps as much to the W. Because the cairn fades into the ground and the whole area is covered by trees and vegetation, no estimate can be made of its original shape and size.

32. KILOURNAN (Kilearnan)
Parish Kildonan
Location in the Strath of Kildonan, 10.5 km WNW of Helmsdale
Map reference NC 924185
NMRS number NC 91 NW 3
References RCAMS 1911, 127, no. 361; Henshall 1963, 319; 1972, 577–8
Plan ASH and ERM
Visited 19.6.52, 7.10.67

Description. The cairn is on the S side of the strath, at 145 m OD, on a spur of the hillside over 100 m above the valley floor. The hillside was formerly all heather moor; about 1970 the cairn was surrounded by a large forestry plantation, but the cairn itself was left unplanted.

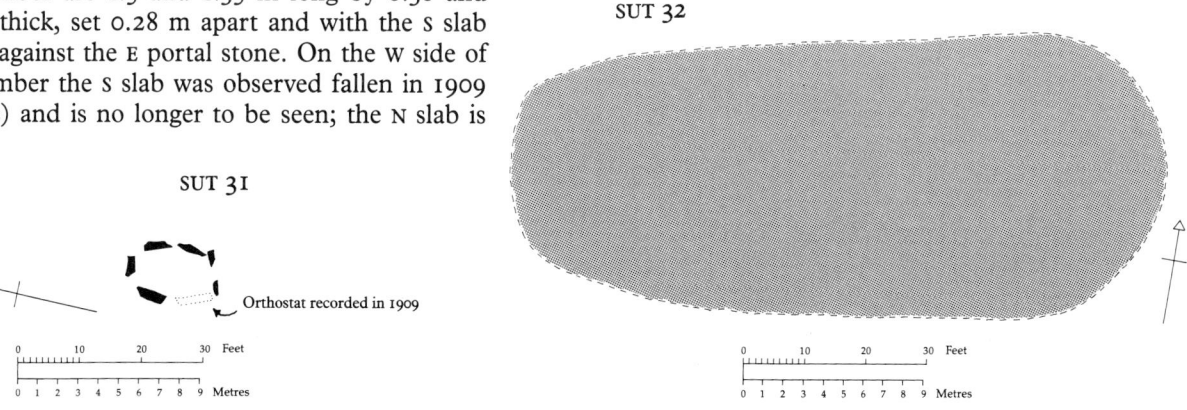

The long cairn has straight sides and rounded ends, with the axis lying E to W. The cairn is 33 m long, 13 m wide across the E end, narrowing to about 9 m wide at the W end. The height at the E end is 2.2 m, but the cairn diminishes to a negligible height at the W end. Various hollows have been made into the cairn but no internal structure has been exposed.

33. KINBRACE BURN
Parish Kildonan
Location in the Strath of Kildonan, 3.5 km SSE of Kinbrace
Map reference NC 875283
NMRS number NC 82 NE 4
References Curle 1909a, 2nd September; 1909b, vol. 2, 93–5; RCAMS 1911, 129–30, no. 372; Henshall 1963, 320–1
Plan CAG and ASH
Visited 8.5.57, 21.6.67, 17.5.93

Description. The cairn is on the lower slope of the E side of the strath, at 130 m OD. The site is 150 m S of the Kinbrace Burn and a little E of its confluence with the River Helmsdale. The hillside is rough grazing, though with small areas of enclosed pasture a short distance to the N and to the W. The Kinbrace Farm cairn (SUT 65) is visible 400 m to the N.

The cairn of loose rounded stones has been greatly robbed and disturbed. Round the N and W sides the outer part has been reduced to a low platform, but to the E and W of the main chamber cairn material remains about 2 m high. The cairn edge is obscured round the S half of the cairn, partly by the growth of peat and partly by dumped stones which spread beyond its original limits. The N edge of the cairn is clear and almost straight between the NW and NE horns; the latter horn is 0.5 m high and well defined. The cairn seems to have been roughly 20 m square. In 1909 the cairn was somewhat higher, and foundations of a building were visible against its W side (RCAMS).

When visited in 1909 and 1957 it was possible to see the chamber and passage which had been excavated by Joass (Curle, RCAMS, Henshall), but in the 1960s the chamber was filled with displaced corbel stones and cairn material. Only the rim of the upper part of the wall of the main chamber is now visible, with two layers of relatively small corbel stones on the SE side, overhanging and tilted down into the chamber. Most of the chamber and passage probably survive, for only the uppermost level of the main chamber has been removed. A large slab which lies to the N of the main chamber was probably its capstone; the slab measures 1.7 by 1 m, by 0.15 m thick, and was once wider as the N side is broken.

The following description of the passage and chamber is based on RCAMS, Henshall, and her field notebook for 1957. The passage faced E with the entrance about 6 m within the cairn edge. It is unlikely that the passage extended further to the E as was assumed by Curle (RCAMS); probably there was a concave forecourt filled with blocking (see ¶ 6.30). On the N side of the entrance was a small transversely-set portal stone projecting slightly from the line of the passage wall and exposed for a height of 0.3 m. Its partner was not visible. The passage was 1.2 m long and 0.9 m wide, and the walls (with six courses exposed) butted against a pair of portal stones at the inner end. The passage was roofed by three lintels, the outer of which rested on the portal stone at the entrance.

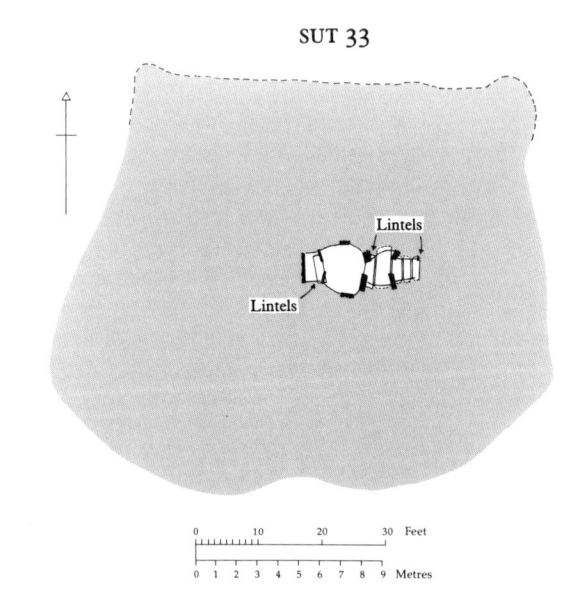

The portal stones forming the entry into the chamber were set skew to the chamber axis, 0.7 m apart and exposed for 0.3 m. The ante-chamber was about 1 m long, and was 1.6 m wide at the E end but the walls converged, almost masking a pair of inner portal stones at the W end. The walls were well built of horizontal slabs and the upper courses oversailed slightly. The ante-chamber was roofed by two lintels. The inner, which rested on the inner portal stones, was over 1.4 m long by 0.56 m wide and 0.2 m thick, and had cracked. The intact roof from the outer end of the passage to the entry to the main chamber rose gradually to give a clearance at the inner end of 0.8 m above the debris on the chamber floor.

The main chamber was 1.98 m long by 2.28 m wide. At the E end the inner portal stones, 0.56 m apart, were set skew to the axis in the opposite direction to the outer portal stones. At the W end a pair of cell portal stones, 0.5 m apart, supported a cracked lintel 1.52 m long, to form the entry to a cell aligned on the axis. The S stone was exposed for a height of 0.4 m; its partner was a little lower and was supplemented by a horizontal slab. The cell portal stones were parallel to the inner portal stones and thus were set at an awkward angle to the almost circular plan of the main chamber. In each side wall was an orthostat, 0.7 and 0.56 m long and a little lower than the inner portal stones. The rest of the vertical lower part of the wall was neatly built of thin slabs. From about the level of the lower surfaces of the cracked lintels, and passing over them, the wall began to oversail. It was built of irregular stones, and the upper part was of corbel slabs. On the S side the wall stood 1.82 m high above the floor debris with an overhang of 0.56 m; the upper part of the N wall had been removed to allow access to the chamber (plate 7).

The cell was rectangular in plan, 0.76 m long by 1.3 m wide, with built sides and a back-slab. Behind the cracked lintel the cell was covered by a second lintel resting on the back-slab. The cell roof was at a lower level than that of the ante-chamber.

FINDS
Artefact.
'When the cairn was excavated there was found in the passage a pierced heart-shaped amulet of polished serpentine, with a diameter of some ¾ in., now in Dunrobin Museum' (RCAMS, but it was not found in the museum in 1957). Not illustrated.

34. KINBRACE HILL LONG

Parish Kildonan
Location in the Strath of Kildonan, 2.5 km SSE of Kinbrace
Map reference NC 871291
NMRS number NC 82 NE 3
References RCAMS 1911, 128–9, no. 369, 370; Henshall 1963, 320–1; 1972, 577, 578
Plan ASH and MKM
Visited 7.5.57, 5.10.67, 17.5.93

Description. Two cairns less than 3 m apart and aligned on a common axis, are regarded by the writers as a single complex monument (plate 12). It is on the E side of the strath, on a gentle hillslope which was formerly rough grazing. The hillside was afforrested in the 1970s, though the area immediately around the cairns was left unplanted. The long axis of the monument lies NE to SW across the contour, at about 150 m OD. Kinbrace Hill Round (SUT 35) was formerly visible 350 m to the NW, and Kinbrace Farm (SUT 65) is 550 m to the SE.

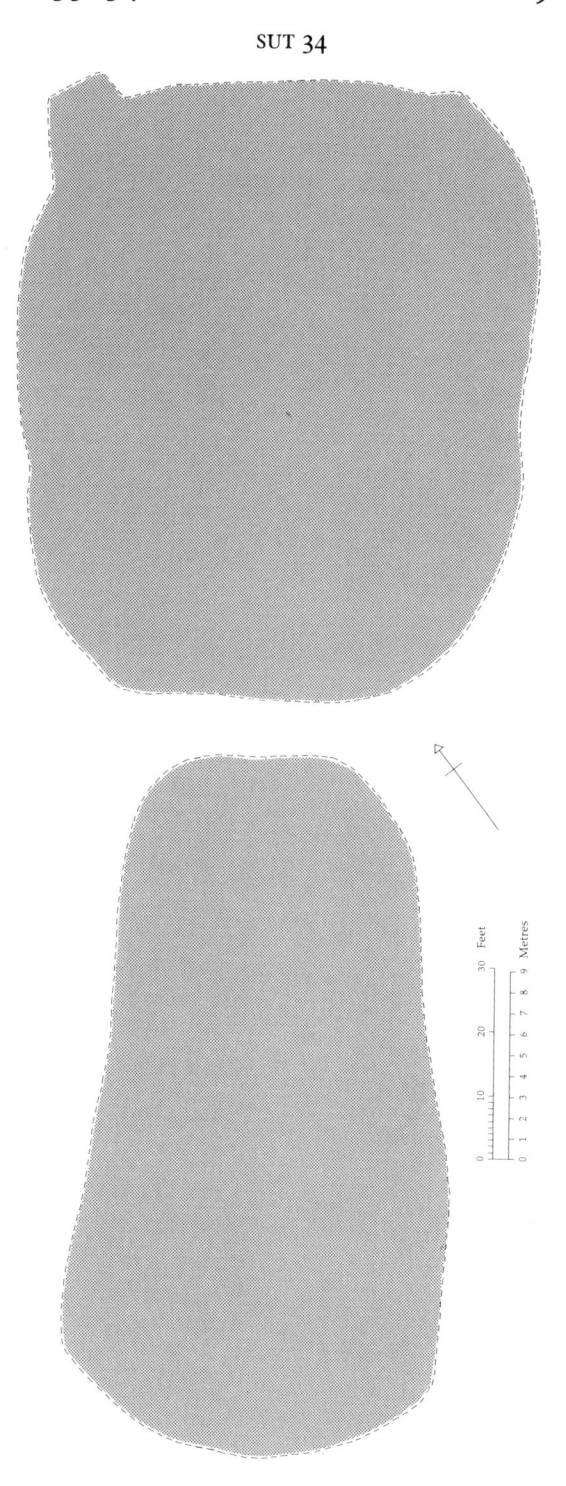

The impressive cairns of loose irregular stones are intact with only occasional signs of superficial disturbance, but they are partly covered by moss now that they are protected by the surrounding trees. The cairns are steep-sided and the edges are generally well defined, with the surrounding coarse grass hardly encroaching. The total length of the monument is 65.5 m.

The NE cairn is almost square in plan with rounded corners, 30 m NE to SW by 25.3 m transversely. The profile viewed from the end or the side is rounded, with a marker cairn on the top. The height measured from the NE and SW is respectively 3.3 or 5.5 m. A horn, partly of bare stone but only 0.5 m high, projects about 3.5 m from the N corner. A corresponding horn at the E corner is not visible, but the growth of peat in this area has covered the lowest level of the cairn.

The two cairns are separated by a gap 2.7 m wide, free of stones. The SW cairn is trapezoid in plan with rounded corners. The wider and higher end is to the SW, though the slope of the ground makes the increased height and width hardly noticeable, and the spine of the cairn slopes down slightly from NE to SW. The cairn is 33 m long by 18.3 m wide at the SW end and 14.3 m wide at the NE end. At the SW end it rises to a height of 5 m at 12.7 m from the SW edge, and extends almost level to 6.8 m from the NE end. From this point, which is 2.4 m high measured from ground level on the NE, the cairn drops fairly steeply to the NE edge. In cross section the cairn is rounded. Foundations of a wall run N from the N corner, probably part of the enclosure built against the cairns which was traceable in 1909 (RCAMS).

35. KINBRACE HILL ROUND
Parish Kildonan
Location in the Strath of Kildonan, 2.3 km SSE of Kinbrace
Map reference NC 868293
NMRS number NC 82 NE 2
References RCAMS 1911, 128, no. 368; Henshall 1963, 321
Visited 7.5.57, 16.5.93, 17.2.94

Description. The cairn is 350 m NW of Kinbrace Hill Long (SUT 34), and a little lower on the same hillside at 130 m OD. The cairn is just within a conifer forest, beside the main road A897. The area immediately around the cairn has been left unplanted and is covered with rank grass. Before afforestation this cairn and the long cairn were prominent intervisible features on the moorland hillside.

Kinbrace Hill Round is an impressive steep-sided cairn 22 m in diameter, built of loose rounded stones and boulders. The site slopes down gently from ENE to WSW, and the height of the cairn taken from the upper and lower sides is 3.3 and 5 m respectively. About 2 m within the ESE edge of the cairn two orthostats are exposed, 0.35 m apart. The larger NE orthostat is aligned roughly NNE to SSW, parallel with the edge of the cairn. The stone is 0.65 m long by 0.3 m thick, and stands about 1.2 m above ground level with a rounded upper edge. The SW orthostat is set slightly further into the cairn at an oblique angle to its partner, aligned roughly NE to SW. It is over 0.45 m long by 0.3 m thick, with a vertical NE edge but its SW side is hidden. It is 0.3 m shorter than the NE orthostat. Cairn material has been removed from in front of these stones (evidently after 1909 when they were not visible, RCAMS), and this is probably the source of the stones spreading for 5 m NE of the NE orthostat. The two orthostats, though not quite in line with each other, are suggestive of the portal stones at the entrance to a chambered cairn, except that no instance of portal stones of this size at the outer end of a passage is known among north Scottish passage graves.

When seen clear of trees in 1957 the cairn was surrounded by turf for about 6.7 m from its base, contrasting with the heather of the hillside, and below the turf there seemed to be a spread of stones. It was suggested that the cairn was surrounded by a platform. This interpretation cannot now be supported. The cairn was re-visited in winter conditions when the vegetation was low and there was no evidence for such a feature; only the slight remains of a building on the S side could be detected.

36. KINLOCH
Parish Tongue
Location at the inner end of the Kyle of Tongue
Map reference NC 549526
NMRS number NC 55 SW 1
References RCAMS 1911, 186, no. 539; Henshall 1963, 321
Plan ASH and JNGR
Visited 7.7.55, 26.10.92

Description. The cairn is in an impressively rugged landscape, surrounded by a huge expanse of moorland and dominated on the S by Ben Loyal and other mountains. The site is on the spine of a ridge at about 65 m OD, but below the summit which is crowned by a broch. The cairn overlooks a small isolated area of pasture and birch woodland at the head of the Kyle, otherwise there is enclosed land on either side of the mouth of the Kyle 6 km or more distant. Neither this land nor the Kyle is visible from the cairn.

The cairn is covered with bracken and turf. The edge can be traced except on the SE quadrant; the cairn diameters are 16 m NE to SW and about 13.5 m NW to SE. The cairn is 1.4 m high measured from the NE side, and about 1.8 m high measured from the SE side; the highest part is on the NW side of the chamber. The surface of the cairn is fairly level though rather uneven, the area of the main chamber is gently hol-

SUT 36

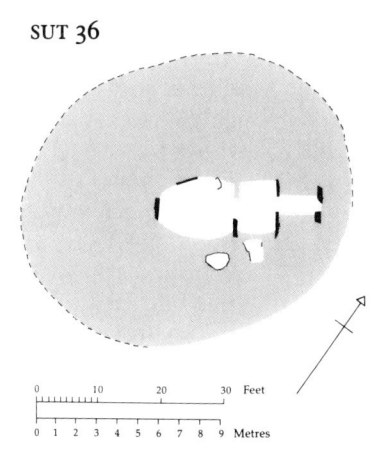

lowed, and small deeper hollows have been made beside some of the chamber orthostats.

The entrance faced NE. About 1.5 m from the edge of the cairn on this side a pair of well-matched intact rectangular stones 0.55 m apart evidently mark the outer end of the passage. The stones are 0.5 and 0.78 m long, both are 0.25 m thick, and they project 0.3 and 0.35 m from hollows in the cairn. The passage has been about 2.2 m long.

The chamber orthostats are thin slabs. A well-matched pair of portal stones, of which the NW slab retains its original upper surface, forms the entry into the ante-chamber. The stones are 0.7 m apart, 1.34 and 0.82 m long by 0.15 and 0.12 m thick, and project 0.3 and 0.2 m. The four portal stones all have fairly level upper edges. The ante-chamber is 1.82 m long. The SE inner portal stone, at the entrance to the main chamber, is 0.9 m long by 0.24 m thick and projects from a hollow for 0.5 m; its upper surface is intact sloping down to the NW. Its partner to the NW is not visible. A partly exposed prone slab, measuring over 0.8 by 0.8 m, is likely to be an orthostat fallen outwards from the SE side of the ante-chamber

The main chamber is 3.6 m long. The back-slab is 1.12 m long by 0.22 m thick, and projects 0.25 m. On the NW side of the chamber, 1 m away, is an orthostat 1.2 m long by 0.1 m thick, projecting 0.65 m. Both these slabs have shattered tops; the latter is the tallest in the chamber and is 0.8 m higher than the SE stone at the passage entrance. On the N side of the main chamber the rounded top of a displaced slab barely projects. The slab is 0.55 m long by 0.2 m thick, and leans to the N. On the SE side of the chamber a prone slab, 1.3 by 1 m and over 0.35 m thick, may be an orthostat which has been displaced from this side of the main chamber. Several other slabs lie about the cairn.

The condition of the cairn is unchanged since 1955, and probably since 1909 (RCAMS).

37. KYLEOAG

Parish Creich
Location near the N side of the Dornoch Firth, 1.8 km NW of Spinningdale
Map reference NH 662911
NMRS number NH 69 SE 3
References RCAMS 1911, 31, no. 83; Henshall 1963, 322, 323; 1972, 578, 579
Plan ASH and JNGR
Visited 30.6.52, 7.10.67, 16.4.91

Description. The cairn is on the N side of the valley of the Spinningdale Burn, at 83 m OD. The hillside is covered by thin natural woodland which has spread over remains of small fields, though recently the area immediately W and S of the cairn has been cleared. Achaidh (SUT 2) is only 830 m to the E, higher on the same hillside.

The site of the cairn slopes down from NE to SW, and the chamber and passage have been aligned along the contour. The bare cairn is heel-shaped with the straight SE edge along the rim of a gully in which flows a small burn. The cairn measures 17.5 m from SE to NW, and probably measured about 19 m across the SE side. The cairn material is irregular rounded stones. Around the S half the cairn rises steeply from a well-defined edge to a height of 3 m and forms a rim around the exposed chamber (measured from the SE side, but the height is 3.5 m from the SW and 1.7 m from the NE sides). On the N side of the cairn the building of a field wall has caused disturbance, and the E corner of the cairn is obscured by the foundations of a small building.

In the centre of the SE side, 1.7 m from the cairn edge, the outermost lintel of the passage is partly exposed in the slope of the cairn. The lintel is 0.9 m long, over 0.35 m wide, and 0.45 m thick, and its lower surface is about 0.6 m above ground level. The passage is about 5 m long but is not visible except for the inner end which can be seen from the chamber. The impressive innermost lintel is 3.2 m long, 0.6 m wide, and 0.7 m thick, with a clearance below it of 0.55 m. A pair of portal stones 0.8 m apart forms the entry into the chamber. They are 0.6 and 0.85 m long, 0.25 and 0.15 to 0.4 m wide, and are exposed 0.4 m high though in a hollow the SW stone can be seen to be over 0.9 m high. The lintel rests on this stone, and on the passage wall to the SE which is just visible for 0.7 m with four somewhat displaced courses exposed; beyond this, the passage is choked with stones. The NE end of the lintel passes above the shorter NE

SUT 37

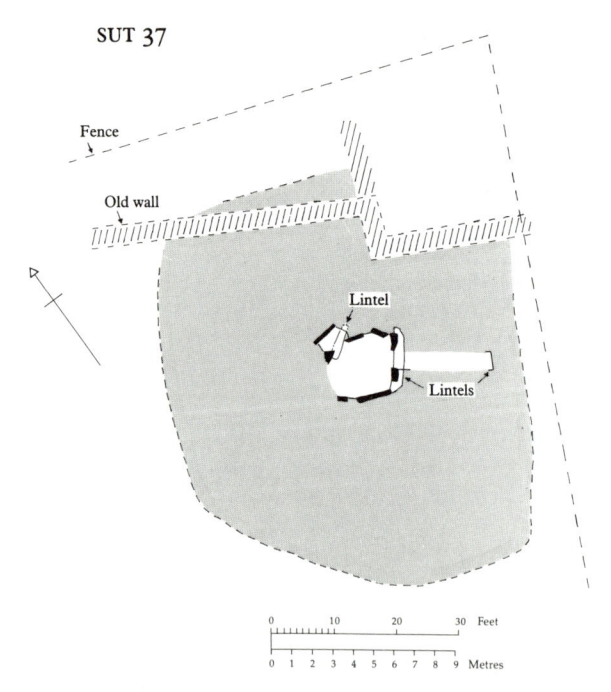

portal stone and rests on the cairn material behind it.

The chamber is rather irregular in plan, 3.0 m long by 2.7 m wide, with a cell entered from the N corner. The chamber walls consist of five orthostats in addition to the portal stones, and probably there is a sixth orthostat at the back obscured by tree roots and tumbled stone. The orthostats are flat slabs, generally 0.3 m or a little more thick. The two on the SW side of the chamber are 1.7 and 0.5 m long. A gap of 0.5 m between them is filled with neat walling which reaches to the level of the tops of the adjacent orthostats. Seven courses are visible, built of slabs 0.04 to 0.2 m thick which run back 0.3 m into the cairn. Two orthostats on the NE side of the chamber are 0.7 and 0.9 m long, and the 0.53 m gap between them is filled with walling (visible in 1952 but obscured by 1991); the E orthostat butts against the NE portal stone. The orthostat at the NW corner of the chamber is over 0.7 m long. The difference in height between the tallest orthostats, the inner on the NE and SW sides, and the shortest, the NE portal stone, is only about 0.45 m, but due to the variable but considerable amount of stone debris on the chamber floor they are exposed for heights of between 1.3 to 0.4 m.

The entry to the cell, between two orthostats, is 0.6 m wide increasing to 0.8 m wide at the top. The cell is roofed by a rather irregular slab, over 1.4 m long, about 0.4 m wide and up to 0.2 m thick, with a clearance below it of 1.05 m (or 1.4 m inside the cell where the floor debris is less). The lintel rests on a corbel stone laid on the top of the W orthostat and on walling behind the taller E orthostat. The back-slab is over 1.35 m long, over 0.15 m thick, and is exposed for a height of 0.7 m. Walling, exposed for seven courses with the upper courses oversailing, links the back-slab with the chamber orthostats and gives the cell a nearly rectangular plan, 1.3 m wide by 0.5 m from back to front at the W end and 0.74 m at the E end. Rough walling of larger slabs oversails above the back-slab and merges with the side walls, and at the top butts against the rear of the lintel (plate 5).

The corbel stone below the cell lintel is the only one *in situ*, but on the chamber floor there are some slabs which are probably corbel stones displaced from the upper parts of the walls; other slabs which appear to have been corbel stones pulled back from the walls lie around the outside of the chamber.

When the cairn was visited in 1909 nothing could be seen of the internal structure except for the lintel at the inner end of the passage (RCAMS). The chamber had been emptied long before the 1952 visit. By 1991 there had been little change in the condition of the monument except that clearance of the small trees which formerly grew on the cairn and in the chamber has made observation easier.

38. LAIRG MOOR NORTH
See p. 152.

39. LAIRG MOOR SOUTH
See p. 152.

40. LEDMORE
Parish Assynt
Location 17 km SE of Lochinver, 2 km E of Elphin
Map reference NC 238121
NMRS number NC 21 SW 3
References RCAMS 1911, 4–5, no.12; Henshall 1963, 323; Mercer 1980, 156, no. 45
Plan ASH and JNGR
Visited 25.6.54, 1.4.93

Description. The cairn, at 130 m OD, is in an area of flat heather moorland a little above the Ledmore River. Extensive deep peat has formed in the ill-drained valley, and peat cutting has reached to the edge of the cairn.

The cairn has been greatly reduced and disturbed, and remains as an untidy mound of irregular stones with turf growing over the outer part. The edge is well defined, giving diameters of about 17 m. As the site slopes down from N to S, the height of the cairn measured from the E side is 1.7 m while from the S side it is 2.5 m.

The central part of the cairn is level, and amongst the loose stone it is possible to identify four orthostats belonging to a chamber. Only their tops can be seen, all at about the same level, but the orthostats must be well over 1 m high. The NW slab is 1.3 m long by 0.25 m thick, and its probably intact flat upper surface slopes down slightly from NE to SW; the slab is tending to shatter vertically. A second orthostat, 0.88 m to the E, is 0.46 m long by 0.18 m thick, with a shattered top. On the S side of the chamber is a rounded intact boulder measuring 0.25 by 0.25 m. The fourth orthostat, 0.75 m to the E and set radially to the chamber, has a shattered top measuring 0.45 by 0.37 m. The chamber is about 2.4 m wide from N to S. Three corbel stones appear to be more or less *in situ*, sloping down to the outside of the chamber. One rests on the NE end of the NW orthostat, another is on the S side of the chamber, and the third is partly over the SE orthostat. At least five more flat corbel stones lie about the cairn displaced outwards from the chamber area. An average corbel stone is 1 m long by 0.8 m wide, and 0.4 m thick. A narrow slab formerly recorded as a passage lintel, 4.3 m from the ENE edge of the cairn, and a flat slab beside it, are also likely to be displaced corbel stones. They rest where deeper robbing of the cairn material deceptively suggests the presence of a passage.

The condition of the cairn probably has not changed since it was visited in 1909 (RCAMS), and the orthostat recorded then is presumably the NW orthostat described above. Although the cairn evidently contains a chamber, its plan remains obscure.

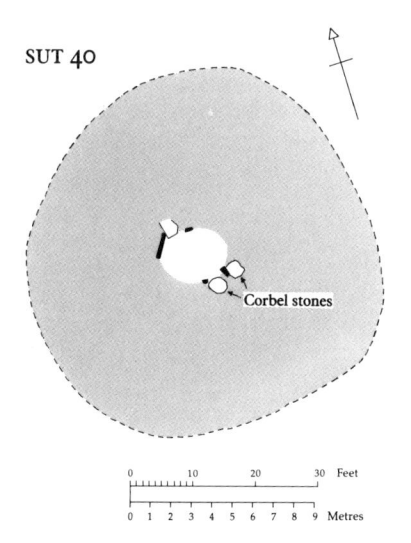

41. LEDMORE WOOD

Parish Creich
Location above the S shore of the Dornoch Firth, 4 km ESE of Bonar Bridge
Map reference NH 653894
NMRS number NH 68 NE 2
References RCAMS 1911, 31–2, no. 84; Henshall 1963, 323
Plan ASH and JNGR
Visited 4.5.57, 22.5.91

Description. The cairn is high on the S side of the ridge which separates the Firth from Loch Migdale. At 137 m OD, the cairn was placed at the break of slope where the steep hillside covered with thick gorse or natural deciduous wood gives way to a gentler rise to the top of the moorland ridge. From the cairn there are wide views across the Firth to the hills of Ross-shire. The actual site, at the edge of the heather moor, is fairly level with a gentle slope down on the E side.

The cairn of large irregular stones is 1.5 m high (if recently-piled cairn material is ignored), with a diameter of 18 to 19 m. The upper part is bare, and the edges are covered by turf and heather except on the W side where the cairn edge is largely obscured by gorse. The 'horn' noted by Curle projecting to the NW (RCAMS) cannot be fully observed at present, but it is unlikely to be an original feature. The last traces of the rectangular structure he noted against the NE edge of the cairn can still be seen. The cairn has been greatly disturbed, most obviously by a hollow reaching to virtually ground level 1.8 m W of the first orthostat mentioned below.

Near the centre of the cairn, and almost hidden in the cairn material, there are a number of orthostats belonging to a greatly ruined chamber which was evidently entered from the N or NNW. The back-slab is 1.08 m long by 0.44 m thick with a horizontal (but probably broken) upper surface which hardly projects. At right angles to it and almost touching is a prominent slab forming part of the E wall of the chamber. The slab is 1.36 m long by 0.5 m thick, and its irregular upper surface rises 0.5 higher than the back-slab; its true height is about 1.5 m. About 0.5 m to the NW a second side-slab is set skew to the apparent axis of the chamber. The slab is 0.6 m long by 0.33 m thick, and its detached upper part lies beside it on the SW; before breakage the slab was about 0.2 m lower than the inner side-slab. These three orthostats are rectangular in plan. To the NW three more slabs, rather irregular in shape, appear to belong to the outer part of the chamber though the plan is unclear. One slab is 2.74 m to the N of the back-slab and nearly at right angles to the assumed axis of the chamber; it may be the W member of a pair of divisional stones.

SUT 41

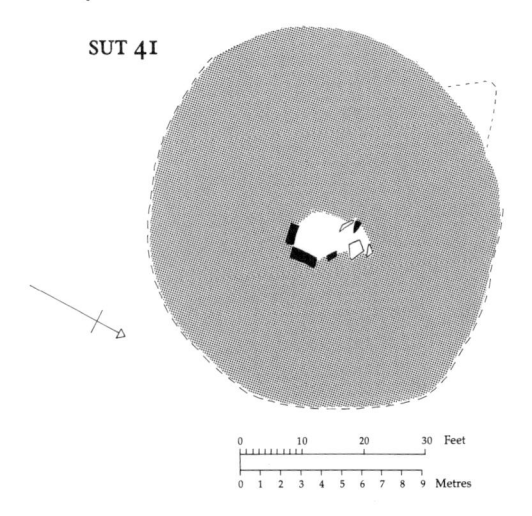

It is 0.65 m long, 0.4 m thick, and projects 0.3 m, but in a cavity in the cairn it can be seen to be over 0.7 m high. Immediately S of it is a skew slab just projecting, 0.9 m long by up to 0.3 m thick. To the NE is a slab 0.9 m long by 0.4 m thick, but as the lower edge descends obliquely only the W part seems to be earth-fast and the slab is likely to have been displaced; it is exposed for a height of 0.45 m. A displaced horizontal slab, 0.95 by 0.8 m and 0.2 m thick, lies S of this last slab, its upper surface well below the tops of the surrounding orthostats. Several other slabs which may derive from the chamber structure lie about on the surface of the cairn.

42. LOCH AWE
Parish Assynt
Location 16 km SE of Lochinver, 7 km S of Inchnadamph
Map reference NC 240146
NMRS number NC 21 SW 1
References RCAMS 1911, 4, no.10; Henshall 1963, 324
Plan ASH and JNGR
Visited 25.6.54, 30.3.93

Description. The cairn is at 198 m OD on a steep moorland hillside, at the upper edge of a small area which was once enclosed pasture (plate 2). The cairn overlooks Loch Awe and an ill-drained valley; the only enclosed land in sight is on the opposite hillside around the croft at Lyne with the cairn SUT 46.

The site slopes steeply down from SW to NE. The cairn of bare irregular stones is 18.5 m in diameter with a clearly defined edge, though it is distorted on the ESE side where there are traces of a bothy having been built into the side of the cairn. A rough wall-face 2.5 m within the E edge can be traced for 2.5 m. The height of the cairn measured from the SE side is 3.4 m, but it is considerably higher if measured from the NE side. A hollow has been made from the NW side into the centre of the cairn. It is evident that the main chamber has been hidden by completely filling it with large slabs and boulders which are looser than the more compact cairn material surrounding the chamber area. This disturbance long pre-dated a visit in 1909 (RCAMS). However, some slight recent interference has revealed a lintel *in situ*, and this has allowed some of the slabs which have long been visible on the surface of the cairn to be recognised as corbel stones. Some of them are still *in situ* and belong to the upper parts of the chamber walls. The centre and SE side of the cairn give an impression of total chaos, but it is probable that much of the chamber remains intact.

The axis of the chamber has been from SE to NW along the contour of the hill. Amongst the cairn material sloping up from the SE edge of the cairn there are a number of large blocks of stone, in most cases only partly exposed; presumably they derive from the passage or an ante-chamber, but none of them is certainly *in situ*. North-west of them, about 5 m from the cairn edge, a pair of orthostats appear to belong to the SW and NE sides of an ante-chamber. They are 1.75 m apart, over 0.55 and 0.9 m long, 0.3 m thick, and project 0.8 and 0.7 m. A metre NW of the NE orthostat is the lintel already mentioned. It is a roughly rectangular elongated boulder set on edge, over 1.75 m long, 0.25 m thick, and 0.85 m deep, with its lower surface about 1.4 m above ground level. The NE orthostat has a shattered top, and both orthostats rise well above the lower surface of the lintel; their true height is at least 1.7 m. Between the NE orthostat and the lintel are two corbel stones, and below them two more can just be seen; all evidently have slipped a little outwards and downwards from their original positions. A fifth corbel stone, displaced further outwards, lies over the junction of the upper two with its inner end level with the top of the lintel.

A number of corbel stones can be seen around the presumed position of the main chamber. Immediately N of the lintel is a row of four massive elongated square-section quarried blocks placed radially to the chamber and sloping down to the NE. The southernmost rests against the end of the lintel, and it and its neighbour may well be *in situ*, with a second row of similar blocks just visible below, probably slightly overhanging the position of the chamber wall at ground level. Others have slipped outwards and downwards from the chamber wall. The first corbel is 1.15 m long by 0.4 m wide and thick, an average size for one of these elongated blocks. Two smaller but similar blocks at a higher level to the NW are likely to belong to a third upper row of the same series.

SUT 42

Description. The cairn is on a steep hillside of heather and coarse grass rising from the E side of the loch. The site, at 175 m OD, is a small platform with the ground dropping from the SW side of the cairn. Loch Borralan West (SUT 44) can just be seen beside the loch 200 m to the WSW.

The cairn, covered in grass, heather and bracken, rises steeply to the top of the chamber walls. The cairn edge is well defined, except on the SW side where the cairn merges into the downward slope of the hill and the edge is less easily traced. The diameters of the cairn are 13.5 to 14.5 m, and the height is 1.8 m measured from the E side, but is about 2.4 m measured from the SW side. The chamber appears to be slightly N of the centre of the cairn, probably because a greater depth of peat against its upper N side overlies its original edge.

The entrance faced slightly S of E. At the edge of the cairn on this side a rounded stone probably marks the S side of the outer end of the passage. The stone is 0.65 m long, over 0.22 m thick, and projects 0.3 m, with a probably intact horizontal upper surface. The passage has evidently been investigated and refilled, as the area between the stone and the top of a lintel at the entrance to the chamber remains as a shallow hollow filled with a jumble of stones amongst which are two displaced lintels. The upper displaced lintel is 1.63 m long by 0.6 m wide by 0.43 m thick, tipped down to the W, and below it is another of similar size. The entrance to the chamber is 4.95 m from the stone at the cairn edge; viewed from the chamber the space below the lintel at the entrance is filled with rubble.

The chamber entrance is 0.53 m wide between portal stones 0.7 and 0.9 m high. The lintel is an elongated rather irregular stone about 1.73 m long, 0.53 m wide and about 0.3 m thick, tilted down slightly to the W, about 0.8 m above the floor. It rests directly on the S end of the N portal stone (which is lower at its S end) and on an eke-stone over the S portal stone. The portal stones are unusual in that the N stone, over 0.68 m long by 0.42 m thick, was set transversely to the chamber wall so that only its S end is visible, whereas the S stone forms part of the chamber wall. The chamber is 2.6 m long by 1.88 m wide. The present level of the floor is probably only a little above the original level, but the chamber (empty in 1909) is partly filled with large fallen stones; it is still possible to take all the vertical heights from floor level. The chamber has an irregular plan, with three close-set orthostats on the S side (including the portal stone), one orthostat on the N side, a back-slab, and a cell in the NW corner. The back-slab is somewhat larger than the other orthostats, 1.23 m long by over 0.2 m thick;

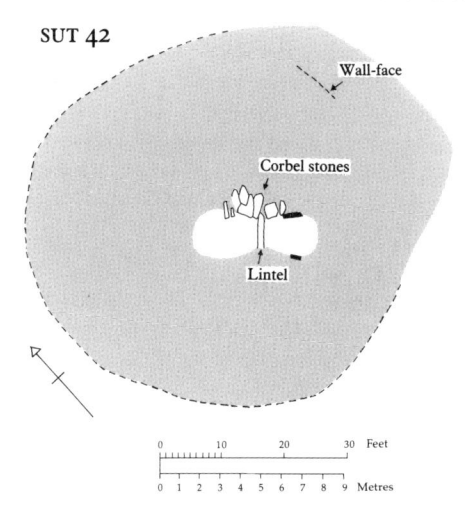

Immediately to the NW of them a stack of three corbel stones, tipped at an angle into the chamber, can be glimpsed beneath displaced cairn material. Many substantial flat slabs, some measuring about 0.85 by 0.5 by 0.2 m, lie about the centre of the cairn, mostly at the same level or slightly higher than the elongated blocks, and some of them may be undisturbed corbel stones. Cairn material remains to a somewhat higher level on the SW side of the main chamber, and no elongated blocks are to be seen there. The NW corner of the chamber may lie about 3.2 m NW of the SW end of the lintel, below two corbel stones which are partly exposed one over the other and which may be undisturbed. Deep below them in a narrow cavity, not accessible for planning, there can just be seen what may be a short stretch of walling running N to S for 0.5 m with the top of an orthostat at the S end aligned roughly NW to SE.

The three types of stone in the cairn, the elongated blocks, the flat slabs, and the cairn material, are markedly different in character, and the relative levels of the first two suggest that the elongated blocks were used for the lower part of the roof vault with the flat slabs used for the upper part below the capstone.

43. LOCH BORRALAN EAST
Parish Assynt
Location 19.5 km SE of Lochinver, 10.5 km S of Inchnadamph
Map reference NC 262111
NMRS number NC 21 SE 2
References Curle 1909a, 11th June; 1909b, vol. I, 110; RCAMS 1911, xxxv, 5, no. 14; Henshall 1963, 324, 325; Mercer 1980, 43, 128, no. 36
Plan ASH and JNGR
Visited 25.6.54, 2.4.93, 22.7.93

SUT 43

Lintels

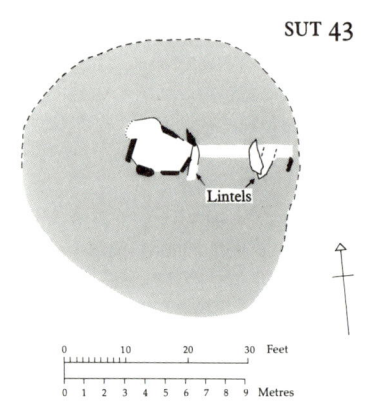

0 10 20 30 Feet
0 1 2 3 4 5 6 7 8 9 Metres

it is 0.86 m high, but it has slumped from a vertical or nearly vertical position to lean steeply to the W, and its height would be 1.05 m if upright. The other four orthostats vary little in size, 0.82 to 0.94 m long by 0.18 to 0.39 m thick, and about 0.96 high except for the portal stone which is 0.7 m high. The S portal stone and the adjacent orthostat fit closely together, the walling formerly visible in the small gap between the latter and SW orthostat is hidden, but between this orthostat and the back-slab, and between the N orthostat and the N portal stone there is walling consisting respectively of three and four courses of split slabs. The top of the walling is 0.25 and 0.3 m below the tops of the adjacent orthostats, and above this level the chamber walls consist of four layers of corbel stones above the walling or two layers above the orthostats. The movement of the back-slab has caused some displacement of the corbel stones above it; the upper corbel stone is a particularly large slab 1.3 m from front to back by 0.75 m wide and 0.3 m thick. The top of the chamber walls is about 1.75 m above the floor except over the lintel where the corbel stones have been removed.

A gap of 1.5 m between the back-slab and the N orthostat gives access to the cell. An arc of rough walling forms the wall, running from the rear of the orthostat and formerly extending to the rear of the back-slab, but the W part of this wall has been pulled away. The cell is 0.8 m from front to back and was about 1.5 m in maximum width. It is roofed by three layers of oversailing corbel stones, with the three stones of the upper layer giving a roof height of 1.5 m. The W stone of this layer is now only supported along its E side so that collapse is likely. In 1909 it was recorded that the outer edge of the cell 'is marked off by a double line of flat stones, partially superimposed, about 6″ or 8″ (0.15 or 0.2 m) in breadth. There are no signs of paving behind it' (RCAMS).

FINDS
Artefacts.
'Several small fragments of unornamented pottery, parts of a single vessel with walls about ¼″ (6 mm) in thickness, were recovered on excavation. They are coarse in quality, the clay being immixed with numerous small pieces of quartz and stone. The interior surface is blackened and smooth. They are preserved in the Museum at Dunrobin' (RCAMS, 5). They were 'of a quality more frequently associated with Bronze Age than with Neolithic interments' (ibid. xxxv). The sherds were not identified in the museum in 1957, nor have they been subsequently located.

44. LOCH BORRALAN WEST

Parish Assynt
Location 19.5 km SE of Lochinver, 10.5 km S of Inchnadamph
Map reference NC 260111
NMRS number NC 21 SE 1
References Curle 1909a, 11th June; 1909b, vol. 1, 110–11; RCAMS 1911, 5, no. 13; Henshall 1963, 324–5
Plan ASH and JNGR
Visited 25.6.54, 11.5.93

Description. The cairn is on a small promontory on the E side of the loch, 30 m from the shore and only a little above it, at 140 m OD. The cairn is close to the main road, A837, which runs on the narrow strip of level rough grazing between the loch and the steep heather-covered hillside rising along its E side. Loch Borralan East (SUT 43) is just visible on the hillside 200 m to the ENE and about 37 m higher. The West cairn is sited partly on a slight rise dropping to the SE, giving the impression that the N side of the cairn is at a higher level than the chamber and the SE side.

The cairn material of rounded stones shows through a thin layer of turf. Except on the SE side, the cairn rises quite steeply from a well defined edge. The SE part of the cairn had been deeply quarried before it was first recorded in 1909 (Curle, RCAMS). In this area the edge has been totally removed, and within this only a thin layer of turf-covered cairn material remains. The maximum height of the cairn, to the N of the chamber, is 3 m measured from ground level on the E side. The cairn is 17.5 to 16.5 m in diameter.

The cairn is surrounded by an intermittent ring of boulders just showing through the turf, though not traceable on the SE side. The boulders appear to be the kerb of a low platform. They are generally 0.15 to 0.6 m long and protrude about 0.1 m or a little more, but there are several bigger boulders on the N side; the largest measures 0.7 by 0.6 m and protrudes 0.5 m. The kerb is 1.5 to 3 m outside the edge of the cairn, and has diameters of 20.5 to 23 m. There is little stone within the kerb, apart from loose displaced

SUT 44

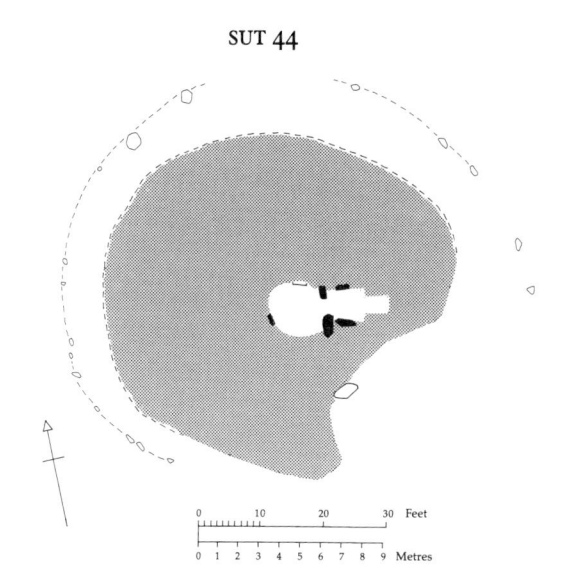

cairn material on the SW side. The surface of the platform is hardly higher than the ground outside, and on the N side the surface between the large kerb-stones and the cairn is slightly dished.

The passage evidently faced slightly S of E, but it has been destroyed. Some 5 m within the probable position of the E edge of the cairn, at the inner edge of the deep quarrying, there are two orthostats belonging to the S and N walls of an ante-chamber, 1.4 m apart. They are 1.07 and 0.73 m long by 0.3 and 0.28 m thick and are exposed for 0.5 and 0.3 m. Portal stones to the W of them form the entry, 0.7 m wide, to the main chamber. They are 1.1 and over 0.7 m long, 0.6 and 0.3 m thick, and project 0.55 and 0.33 m. All four orthostats are intact boulders, except that the rising E end of the first has been broken. The top of the S portal stone is 1.2 m above ground level and is about 0.15 m higher than the other orthostats.

West of the portal stones the level of the cairn material rises and little can be seen of the main chamber. On its N side, amongst the rubble, 0.6 m from the N portal stone and about 0.45 m above it, the S edge of a slab over 0.7 m long (its W end hidden) by 0.25 m thick, sloping down slightly from W to E, with a small stone above it, may be part of the chamber wall. On the W side of the main chamber the top of an orthostat set skew to the chamber axis can be glimpsed 2.26 m from the S portal stone, almost hidden below two corbel stones one above the other. The orthostat is an intact boulder over 0.6 m long, over 0.23 m thick, and projecting 0.28 m; the NW end and SW face are not visible. The lower corbel stone rests on the top of the orthostat, and both corbel stones slope down steeply to the outside of the chamber with their outer ends covered by cairn material. Immediately to the E the upper part of a large displaced corbel stone projects from the rubble filling the main chamber; the stone leans steeply to the W with its top level with the top of the orthostat. Two metres to the N of the orthostat and 1.1 m W of the wall slab the upper part of a large almost vertical slab protrudes for 0.55 m. As the top is 2.3 m above ground level it is unlikely to be a chamber orthostat and it is probably an up-ended displaced corbel stone. It is 0.55 m long by 0.3 m thick, leaning slightly to the NW. The chamber was in the same condition when seen by Curle in 1909, but uncharacteristically his two records (Curle, RCAMS) do not tally and both contain errors.

A large trapezoidal block lies 2.5 m S of the ante-chamber.

45. LOTHBEG (Cairnlea)

Parish Loth
Location on the E coast, midway between Brora and Helmsdale
Map reference NC 946104
NMRS number NC 91 SW 6
References Kirk 1772, no. 3; Pococke 1887, 164–5; RCAMS 1911, 163, no. 472; Henshall 1963, 325; 1972, 578
Plan ASH and JNGR
Visited 17.5.55, 17.6.67, 27.9.93, 22.4.94

Description. The cairn is in a prominent position on a spur of the steep moorland hillside which rises from the narrow strip of cultivated land along the coast. The site is at 53 m OD, in rough pasture, at the mouth of Glen Loth, and has an extensive view along the coast and across the Moray Firth.

The cairn was well known as an antiquity in the 18th century. There can be little doubt that it was the 'Pict's house' visited by Pococke in 1760. He evidently entered a roofed chamber through a passage, but his description is confusing (quoted in full below). The cairn was shown as oval and titled 'Cairnlea' on Kirk's estate plan. The next record, by Curle in 1909 (RCAMS), indicates that the chamber had by then been greatly ruined, but there was still more to be seen than when it was visited in 1955. Since then there has been little change in the condition of the monument.

The cairn is an impressive pile of loose boulders which rise steeply from the edge, and only the outermost part is overgrown with turf and bracken. The ground is level round the N half of the cairn, it drops gently on the SE side and more steeply on the SW side. The plan of the cairn is irregular, between round and square, measuring about 25 m NW to SE by about 22 m transversely. There is no indication that the plan

SUT 45

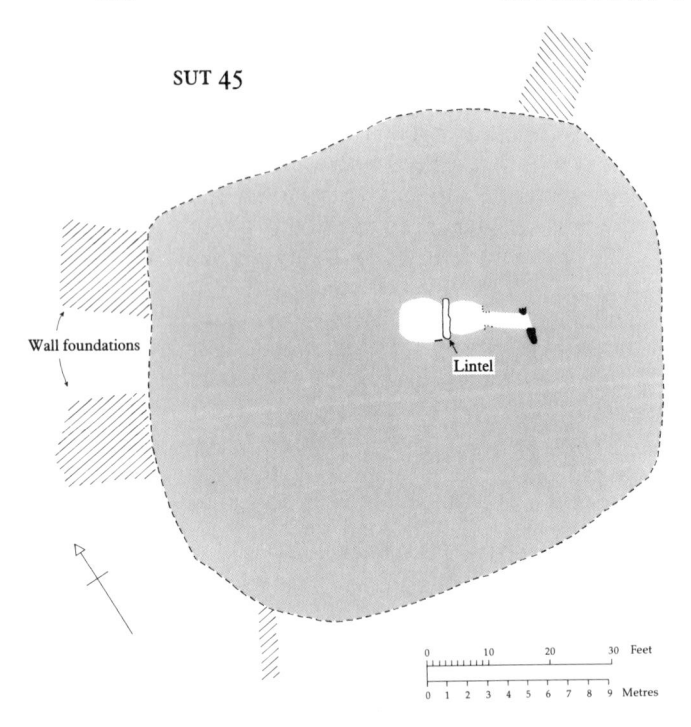

of the cairn is the result of disturbance, even though tumbled walls of an enclosure butt against the NW side (which misled Curle into describing the monument as a ruined long cairn), while other old walls run from the E and SW sides. The height of the cairn measured from the N side is 2.5 m, but from the SW side it is 4 m. Several deep hollows have been made into the body of the cairn.

A hollow filled with rubble and displaced slabs rises from the SE side into the centre of the cairn, indicating the position of the passage and chamber. The top of a pair of granite boulders, presumably portal stones at the outer end of the passage, can just be seen in the hollow about 6.5 m within cairn edge. The stones are 0.66 m apart and not quite opposite each other. Both are the same height, with flat upper surfaces sloping down slightly towards their outer ends. They are over 0.8 and over 0.35 m long, and 0.4 and 0.35 m thick. The passage seems to have been a little over 2 m long and 0.6 m wide, as Curle saw its inner end 1.5 m SE of the lintel described below.

The chamber was evidently bipartite, with an ante-chamber about 1.5 m long and a main chamber about 2 m long. An impressive lintel (3.5 m from the entrance portal stones) spans the entry between the two parts of the chamber. The lintel is the most obvious feature in the cairn. Its top edge is only a little below the highest part of the cairn and 1.2 m above the entrance portal stones. The lintel is set on its side with the flatter face to the NW. It is 1.9 m long by 0.4 m thick, and 1.18 m deep; the lower edge is just visible in a deep hollow which has been neatly made against its NW side. In 1909 it could be seen that the lintel rested on a pair of inner portal stones 0.7 m apart, but in 1994 only the end of the NE stone, 0.3 m wide, could be glimpsed. In 1909 the back wall of the chamber was just visible 2 m NW of the lintel, 'partly formed of a large slab, and partly built' (presumably there was walling rising above the top of a back-slab). By 1955 the back of the chamber was hidden behind displaced slabs. Only a short length of the SW wall of the main chamber could be seen in 1994, consisting of two stones butting against the lintel with the top of the upper 0.5 m below the top of the lintel.

Pococke's account is dated July 1760. 'We here ascended to a Pict's house covered with stones. In two or three parts of which are stones set up on end to denote the entrances, which might be closed on some occasions. One cell is open. We went about nine feet (2.7 m) in the passage. Then one passage is about eighteen inches (0.45 m) lower, and nine feet (2.7 m) more brought us into the oval apartment, seven feet and a half (2.3 m) long and high, and six feet (1.8 m) broad. We saw the light through the top, and where some stones had probably been taken away, and at the end is a little hole as for a convenient recess. There is a great stone over the inner entrance, and another at the end. To the north of the entrance of this cell is a broad stone set up on end, and just before it a small circle of stones set close together, and in the middle of it the mouth as of an entrance made with flat stones, and to the north of it a small square sort of a foundation'.

It is likely that it was the main chamber, then roofed, which Pococke described in 1760 as oval, about 2.3 m long by about 1.8 m wide, and 2.3 m high. The 'great stone over the inner entrance' would be the lintel, and the other great stone he noted 'at the end' would be the back-slab. The broad stone to the N of the entrance may have been the NE inner portal stone, and possibly 'the small circle of stones set close together' in front of it was the wall of the ante-chamber.

FINDS
Artefact. In Dunrobin Castle Museum, Golspie.
A stone axe about 180 mm long, oval in cross-section, with a square butt and rounded cutting edge. Not illustrated.

46. LYNE

Parish Assynt
Location 17.5 km ESE of Lochinver, 7.5 km S of Inchnadamph
Map reference NC 248141

NMRS number NC 21 SW 2
References Curle 1909a, 11th June; 1909b, vol. 1, 109; RCAMS 1911, 4, no. 11; Henshall 1963, 326; Mercer 1980, 43, 126, no. 5
Plan ASH and JNGR
Visited 25.6.54, 31.3.93

Description. The last turf-covered remains of the cairn are on the S bank of the Ledbeg River, and immediately E of the main road A837. The site is on the E side of a moorland valley, a little above its boggy floor at 152 m OD. On the opposite side of the valley the Loch Awe cairn (SUT 42) can be seen 1 km to the NW, and Ledbeg (SUT 66) lies out of sight 1.6 km to the SW. Across the river from the Lyne cairn is the croft of Lyne with its small area of improved pasture.

The cairn was built on a limestone knoll which has been reduced in size leaving the rock exposed in places. On the NW side the knoll has been damaged by the drainage ditch of the road, on the NE side by erosion, and on the S side by quarrying. The cairn material has been almost entirely removed with less than 1 m depth remaining on the top of the knoll; some large boulders lie about the site. When visited in 1909, though 'much dilapidated, and in great part removed', the cairn was evidently somewhat less damaged, and the diameter was recorded as about 11 m (RCAMS). By 1954 it was not possible to assess the original size of the cairn (Henshall).

Two orthostats stand conspicuously on the top of the knoll, both 1.1 m high, set 0.55 m apart. The E orthostat is 1 m long by 0.45 m thick, and appears to be intact. The W orthostat is 0.48 m long at the base increasing to 0.75 m above ground level, by 0.3 m thick; it has been larger, but the sides and upper part of the N face have shattered. From the 1909 description these stones can be identified as the E side-slab and the back-slab of a chamber, four orthostats of which were *in situ* at that time. 'Three of the large upright blocks which have formed the sides and end of the chamber remain *in situ*, and a small stone protrudes between two of the larger ones at the NW. ...

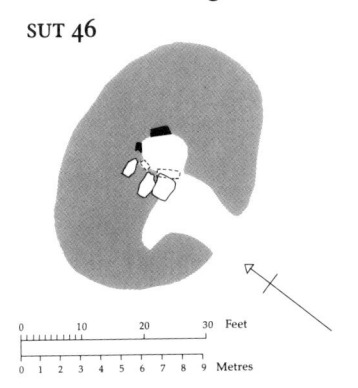

SUT 46

The end stone of the chamber is 23 ft (7 m) from the S edge. The side stones, which are slightly divergent, are 6 ft (1.82 m) apart' (RCAMS). A sketch of the stones (figure 13, 6) shows that the 'small stone' was somewhat longer than the back-slab but much lower; probably it had broken. The two large side-slabs were 1.2 m long by 0.38 m thick, and 0.9 to 1.2 m high (Curle 1909a). The W side-slab is probably the largest of the three prone blocks now lying to the W of the standing stones. It is tilted down to the S into the deeply quarried side of the knoll, and measures 1.16 by 1.03 m, by 0.5 m thick.

47. MELVICH

See p. 152.

48. THE ORD NORTH

Parish Lairg
Location 1 km SW of Lairg
Map reference NC 573056
NMRS number NC 50 NE 16
References RCAMS 1911, 153–4, no. 443; Henshall 1963, 326, 327; Corcoran 1967a; 1967b; Henshall 1972, 578–9; Sharples 1981
Plan after Corcoran (see also our figures 10, 19)
Excavation Corcoran 1967
Visited 28.4.92

Description. The cairn is on a spur just below the summit of The Ord, at 152 m OD, and is 40 m NW of the South cairn, SUT 49, which occupies the actual summit (plate 16). The hill, now largely heather moor used for rough grazing, is covered with remains of prehistoric settlement and more recent rig-and-furrow cultivation.

The impressive cairn of bare stones rose steeply to a height of 4 m and was surrounded by a low turf-covered platform. Before excavation the cairn appeared to be substantially intact and nothing of the internal structure was visible, though numerous shallow hollows had been made into it. Unauthorised investigations in 1965 exposed the highest part of the chamber, and it could be seen that the capstone(s) had long been missing and the interior was choked with fallen stones. These activities led to excavation two years later, when parts of the cairn and platform were examined, and the chamber and passage were fully excavated. The excavations were filled in and the cairn was restored to its pre-excavation appearance though slightly reduced in height. By 1992 interference had exposed a small part of the passage and two lintels. Due to the death of the excavator before an excavation report had been prepared, only brief descriptions of the structure have appeared

SUT 48

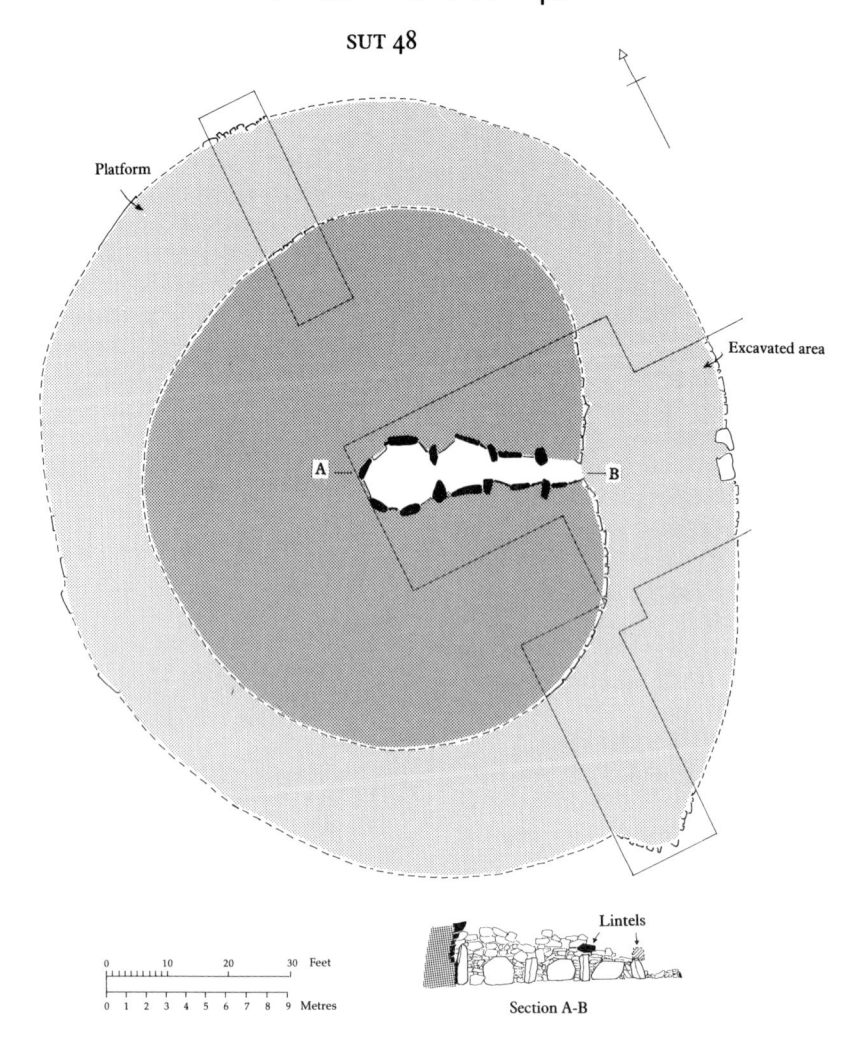

(Corcoran 1967b, Sharples 1981). The following account has been compiled from the excavator's Notebook, photographs, and annotated plans and drawings (Corcoran 1967a), supplemented by limited personal observation.

The cairn is composed of rounded boulders and is edged by a wall-face (not visible at present). The cairn is round except that it is slightly recessed on the SE side to form a shallow forecourt with the passage entrance in the centre. During the excavations the wall-face was exposed round the SE quadrant where it follows a regular curve (plate 9), and for a 4.5 m stretch in a cutting on the N side. The diameter N to S is 26 m, and along the chamber axis the diameter may be estimated as 22 m (the wall-face was not exposed at the rear of the cairn). The total spread of the cairn is considerably more as cairn material has tumbled outside the wall-face; the overall diameter is about 29 by 25 m. The lowest course of the wall-face consists of large rather irregular blocks above which there had been a few courses of thin slabs. On the S side of the entrance a total of five courses survives but elsewhere there are fewer; from 2 m N of the entrance northwards, for a stretch on the S side, and in the N cutting, only the basal course remains *in situ*. Where this is the case a quantity of flat slabs fallen from the wall-face was observed lying on the old ground surface or sometimes vertically against the basal course; the collapse obviously had occurred before the platform was added. At the maximum the wall-face stands to a height of 0.6 m and there is no indication that it was ever much higher, probably under 1 m. The cairn itself was not investigated, except that the upper part around the chamber and passage had to be removed to allow their excavation in safety. It was noticed that at the lower level in this area there was soil amongst the stone, probably derived from disintegrating stones of the cairn.

The turf-covered platform surrounding the base of the cairn is edged by a kerb of substantial stones which can be traced for the whole circuit with only minor breaks. On the projected axis of the passage there are two particularly large slabs, the larger of which measures 1.4 by 0.9 m. The kerb is slightly oval with diameters of 39 by 35 m. In 1967 the platform was examined in three areas, in front of the entrance and in cuttings extending to the N and S. On the N side the platform is 5.8 m wide, and this width appears to be maintained round most of the cairn, but the platform is wider in front of the entrance, and on the S side the platform projects in a point from its expected line. This last was observed as early as 1909 (RCAMS), and when investigated it was found to be a deliberate but unexplained feature with a good edge. The platform originally had a level upper surface, and consists of a layer of cobbles averaging 0.3 to 0.38 m in diameter, and earth. The depth of the platform was not recorded, but, as some kerb-stones rise 0.4 m above the present level of the surrounding turf, it is probably somewhat over 0.5 m. deep. Where not disturbed by excavation, the surface of the platform rises gently from the kerb to merge with the displaced material forming the outer part of the cairn giving the monument a bell-shaped profile.

The entrance to the passage is 0.6 m wide, without portal stones. The passage is about 4.2 m long up to the portal stones at the entry to the chamber, with a maximum width of about 1.2 m. The passage is divided into two segments by a pair of orthostats set transversely to the walls and slightly protruding to reduce the width to 0.65 m. A lintel 1 m long, 0.45 m wide and 0.47 m thick, which was found fallen forwards, was replaced on the transverse stones at a height of about 0.9 m. The outer segment of the passage, about 1.6 m long, is greatly ruined. On the S side a low orthostat butts against the S transverse stone, and a short length of rough walling links it with the wall-face of the cairn; on the N side there was only 'collapsed walling'. The inner segment, 1.74 m long between the transverse and portal stones on the N side, is built with an orthostat on each side supplemented by walling. The N wall is the better preserved with an orthostat 0.67 m high and walling mainly of thin slabs at either end, and also in two courses above it, over which are a few corbel stones set with their long axes at right angles to the wall-face. The wall was found standing to a maximum height of 1.48 m. The portal stones forming the entry to the chamber are 0.65 m apart and not quite opposite each other. A second larger lintel, 1.76 m long, 1.1 m wide, and up to 0.5 m thick but of rather irregular shape, rests on a substantial horizontal slab on the S portal stone, and a slighter stone on the taller N portal stone, with a clearance of about 1.3 m. The roofing of the passage between the two lintels was found collapsed and disturbed in 1967, but presumably the gap between the upper corbel stones had been spanned by a row of lintels; the innermost lintel (that surviving on the portal stones) was at a slightly lower level than the rest.

The method of construction, already described in the ruined passage, is clearer in the better preserved chamber. The lower walls are built with orthostats linked by walling which butts against their sides, above which are courses of oversailing corbel stones. The orthostats, with one exception, are boulders, mostly rounded in shape and often with rounded bases which are steadied by chock-stones. The walling is mainly of rectangular slabs, thinner and more neatly built in the lower courses. The corbel stones are massive rather irregularly-shaped elongated stones set with their long axes radially to the chamber walls, their inner ends progressively overhanging (Sharples, figure 4). To allow excavation no less than thirty-five corbel stones had to be removed by crane; the largest weighed a ton or more and measured up to 1.5 by 1 by 0.5 m. The several types of stone used for the structure, even when displaced, are easily distinguishable from the rounded cairn material. Some of the stone was found to be crumbling or cracking, causing displacement in the walls and collapse of the uppermost courses. There had also been interference with the roof in prehistoric times, and the chamber was found choked with fallen corbel stones.

The large chamber is divided by a pair of inner portal stones into an ante-chamber and main chamber, each of which had been roofed by a corbelled vault (plates 4 and 6). The ante-chamber is 2.6 m long by a maximum of 2.3 wide, and is rather irregular in plan; the S wall is straight and only slightly set back from the line of the passage wall, and the N wall is concave. There is an orthostat on each side supplemented by walling which rises above them; the orthostat on the N side is 1.04 m high. Corbel stones remained to a height of 2.4 m, and the centre of the roof had evidently been considerably higher. The inner portal stones are about 1.3 m high, set about 0.6 m apart. The lintel which they had borne had broken and was found displaced in the main chamber just W of the entrance (the W side of this stone is shown below a long narrow stone aligned along the chamber axis on the plan prepared for publication by Corcoran (Sharples, figure 4), but only on a pencilled plan is it annotated 'smashed lintel'; it may also be referred to in a notebook (Corcoran 1967a under 3.8.67), but it is not otherwise recorded).

The main chamber is polygonal in plan, about 3.4 m long by about 3.2 m wide. It is built with four spaced orthostats linked by walling, three of them 1.3 to 1.5 m high and the last an impressive 2 m high. They are not arranged to provide a back-slab placed transversely to the axis though the tallest and innermost orthostat, skew to the axis and not quite central to it, alone is visible from the entrance to the passage. This orthostat is not only exceptional for its height, but it also differs in character having a smooth face and jagged upper edge, and above floor level the walling on each side passes behind it rather than butting against it (see ¶ 4.23 for further comment). The base of the wall between the tall orthostat and that to the NE is formed by a slab set on edge, 0.63 m high. The upper parts of the walls consist of corbel stones laid radially; a nearly complete circle of these stones remains at a height of 3 m (in 1992 their upper surfaces were visible amongst the cairn material on the top of the cairn). It was evident that the roof had been closed considerably higher, probably at a height of about 4 m. On the S side two of the lower corbel stones had been displaced, one inwards and one outwards, seemingly deliberately, probably to enable access to the chamber during the bronze age (see below).

In the main chamber the floor consisted of a thin layer of grey clayey soil, which the excavator thought was either an old turf line or the result of water action, covering a layer of sandy soil. The floor was very irregular with some shallow pits which seem to have penetrated into the subsoil. One hollow contained some charcoal and another some quartz pebbles. Charcoal, including some quite large pieces, had been scattered on the floor, and in two places where the floor was protected by flat slabs there were enigmatic organic remains. A puzzling and much ruined slab structure had been built on the floor, and had presumably been damaged by the collapse of the roof though the excavator also considered that deliberate destruction was possible. The structure spread in an arc in front of and partly leaning against the N wall, stretching from the N inner portal stone to the walling at the inner end of the compartment (figure 19, plate 14). Two slabs set on end, 0.48 and 0.6 m high, were 0.5 and 0.6 m from the wall. The central feature was a cist-like arrangement of slabs. Its S side was formed by a thin slab on edge set against the N face of the taller of the upright slabs and resting on a floor slab, its N side was the chamber wall, and collapsed stacked slabs may have formed its E and W ends; a 'capstone' was 0.3 m above the chamber floor. The 'cist' was filled by a boulder and soil with some air spaces. The spread of flat stones and a few boulders on each side appeared to be the result of collapse.

The deposit in the main chamber containing neolithic material was at least 0.38 m deep, and so just covered the slab structure with only the tall vertical slabs protruding (figure 20). The deposit consisted of light sandy soil with many fragments of charcoal. In the lower part there were relatively few stones and only a few sherds, but the upper part was noticeably stonier and contained most of the widely scattered neolithic artefacts and some quartz pebbles. Above the W part of the 'cist structure' there was a layer of hard soil up to 0.07 m thick, but because it did not occur below overhanging corbel stones it was thought by the excavator to be possibly a form of iron pan. With it were traces of organic material, charcoal, and a good deal of small stone. A natural origin may also be the explanation of a patch of greyish clayey soil (in which were a number of flints) near the centre of the main chamber at the slightly higher level of 0.25 m above the floor.

Above these neolithic deposits the main chamber was filled with collapsed roofing and cairn material between 0.6 and 1 m deep. A number of large displaced corbel stones were surrounded by small boulders and light sandy soil; probably the soil was derived from decayed stone. Evidently there was no recognisable change in the sandy soil and smaller stones at the junction of the lower deposits and the collapsed roofing, but the lowest fallen corbel stones rested at 0.4 and 0.5 m above the floor, only slightly above the level of most of the neolithic artefacts. It is likely that the deliberate displacement of two corbel stones (mentioned above), possibly to enable the introduction of a cremation burial, had caused the roof to collapse. It is also likely that there was subsequent settlement of the filling due to deterioration of stones in the chamber walls. Clearly the collapse had taken place before the cremated bones of an adult, a bone mount and a food vessel were inserted in the W and SW part of the chamber. The deposits of cremated bone were widely dispersed, and at varying depths but mainly near the top of the filling though extending to 0.33 m below. Some bone and food vessel sherds lay on top of displaced corbel stones. Signs of burning were observed on the upper surface of one corbel stone, and there was a considerable amount of charcoal in the filling. Fragments of at least one other cremation, of an adolescent, were found near the centre of the main chamber at 0.5 m above the floor, and further fragments of unidentifiable cremated bone were found further to the E. Almost at the top of the filling was a deposit up to 0.05 m thick, consisting of soil, disintegrated granite and fragments of charcoal covered by flat slabs. On the NE side there was what appeared to be an old turf line, perhaps 'formed at some time after the chamber had been robbed to this level'. Above the collapsed roofing was the recent infill of stones free of soil.

In the ante-chamber a thin intermittent layer of grey clayey soil, interpreted as possibly a turf-line, presumably equates with the similar floor layer in the main chamber. Above this was gravelly soil (alternatively described as 'silty layers'), over which there were displaced corbel stones, and finally recently disturbed stone. The depths of these layers were not recorded, but the depth of the filling containing neolithic artefacts can be estimated as about 0.46 m. In this layer was a pile of stones, its base 0.15 m above the floor and covering deposits of charcoal. The stone pile occupied much of the ante-chamber, spreading for 1.75 by 1.3 m, and it was about 0.3 m high (figure 19). Most of the stones were quite small, some rounded and some slabby, but there was also a large block 0.8 m long. The sherds were mainly in the E half of the ante-chamber, and were mainly at the level of the base of the stone pile.

The inner segment of the passage was filled with stones assumed to be collapsed roofing and there were no finds. Between the transverse stones there was a deliberate rubble blocking, above which were the cremated remains of a child. The passage entrance was partly closed by a neatly fitting slab 0.3 m high, set on edge but leaning inwards. Blocking composed of slabs and boulders had been piled outside this, extending 1.3 m in front of the entrance and for a total width of 3.6 m (figure 21, plate 15). Below the blocking and the closing stone in the entrance, and immediately above bedrock, there was a thin layer of buried soil with areas of burnt material. Sherds of two pots had been deposited below the blocking just outside the entrance.

FINDS
Artefacts. In the Royal Museum of Scotland (figure 22).
(See Sharples, 32–8, 42–8, for a more detailed catalogue of the sherds by Sharples, and of the stone artefacts by Wickham-Jones and Bradley. After each entry below, Corcoran's numbers are prefixed by ON; Sharples' numbers are prefixed by S. A stroke between ON numbers indicates joining sherds.)
1a. Two rim sherds; three (and possibly originally more) horizontal rows of slightly curved deep close-set vertical impressions, on one sherd a scar with an undecorated space beside it almost certainly due to a lug having broken away; very hard grey fabric with sparse white grits, breaking along the building rings, lacking the inner surface and some of the outer surface, the rim burnished; rim diameter about 150 mm but not regular and the angle uncertain (ON 56/94; S 1,2).
1b. Tiny undecorated wall sherd probably from this pot (ON 92: S 28).
2. Two wall sherds; faint spaced horizontal grooves between which are close-set vertical grooves or round impressions, the decoration almost obliterated by burnishing; hard black fabric with fine grits, smooth inner surface, burnished outer surface (ON 65, 91; S 3,4).
3. About half of an Unstan bowl with a rather irregular profile, reconstructed but lacking some sherds from the collar and part of the body and base, also small loose sherds from the lower part; three rough, irregular, deep grooves below the rim, the rest of the collar filled with bold panels of slanting grooves alternating with panels of nearly horizontal jabs; hard grey fabric, the black-grey-buff surface retains a fine finish in places, some sherds evidently scorched after breakage (ON 35, 63, 64, 66, 68, 81, 82, 88, 89, 90; S 6).
4. Five rim sherds (ON 16/62, 70, 80, 93, 96) and numerous wall sherds, also many crumbs, probably all from one undecorated bowl with a rather irregular profile, four small damaged sherds (ON 16, 31, 38, 64) having a vertical curve either from a gentle shoulder or from near the (presumably rounded) base; black fabric varying from quite hard to very friable, with quartzite and other grits, the grey-buff surfaces uneven and rather rough textured; diameter about 200 mm (ON 16/62, 18, 31, 36, 38, 43, 46, 52, 55, 57, 59, 61, 64, 67, 70, 76, 80, 84, 86, 87, 93, 96, 97, 98; S 8–25, 27, 29).
4a. Small damaged wall sherd, the fabric similar to sherd ON 98 which has been attributed to *4*, both sherds having larger angular grits, both being 8 mm thick; possibly both are from the base of bowl *4* (*4a* listed separately as it was found outside the cairn) (ON 101; S 26).
5. Small undecorated wall sherd; fine hard dark brown fabric with some white grits, 5 mm thick (ON 84; S 5).
6. Sherds from the rim and wall of a greatly damaged carinated bowl of rather irregular profile, the emphasis of the carination being particularly variable; random horizontal rectangular impressions on the collar; dark brown fabric with mainly fine grits, the surface of the collar was slightly striated during manufacture, elsewhere the fine black surface is mainly lost; rim diameter about 140–160 mm (ON 102, 103; S 32).
7. Sherds from the rim and body of a large shallow bowl, one sherd preserving the complete profile of the upper part as the lowest point of the inner surface turns inwards; two rows of deep round impressions on the under side of the rim flange and another row on the body with faint similar impressions below; rim diameter about 300–360 mm. One body sherd measuring 70 by 60 mm and 7 mm thick is almost flat indicating that the lower part of the bowl was only slightly dished. Hard grey fabric with fine pale grits; the buff surface is worn on the outside and on the edge of the rim flange, the inner surface is smooth and slightly burnished (ON 102; S 32).
8. Sherds from the flat base and lower walls of a beaker; a row of round impressions above three firm but rather irregular grooves immediately above the base; rather

friable, heavily gritted, dark grey fabric with many fine white grits, the outer surface brown-grey (ON 33; S 30).
9. The greater part of a food vessel bowl, reconstructed, also a number of small sherds; whipped cord impressions across the rim bevel, fine incised lines below the rim, half way down the body and just above the base, a row of deep curved impressions edging the zones between, the zones filled with vertical rows of short horizontal whipped cord impressions, and in the lower zone each row separated by a wide light groove; the surface much damaged, coarse dark brown fabric with pale grits (ON 30; S 31).
10. Blade of mottled mid-brown flint, retouched down one side, the other side scarred by use (ON 51; S 44).
11. Blade of ginger-brown flint, one edge retouched (ON 51; S 43).
12. Blade of mottled ginger-brown flint (ON 51; S 42).
13. Irregular flake of similar flint, some pebble crust remaining, the steep distal end scarred by use as a scraper (ON 71; S 37).
14–20. Seven flakes of flint 12 to 30 mm long, no retouch but five used for cutting or scraping (ON 100, 51, 69, 60, 45, 22, 40; S 34–6, 38–41).
21. Flake of pitchstone 17 mm long (ON 41; S 45).
22. Flake of quartz, retouched across one face and around the edges (ON 74; S 54).
23–28. Six flakes of quartz 48 to 11 mm long, no retouch but four used for cutting or scraping (ON 102, 23, 58, 58, 102, 69; S 47–52).
29–30. Two lumps of quartz 18 and 21 mm long, one flaked (ON 54, 58; S 46, 53).
31. Lump of black pumice 60 by 50 by 45 mm, with flattened and slightly grooved surfaces (ON 72; S 56).
32. Part of a bone or antler mount, scorched and warped, the diameter about 18 mm; a perforation and parts of two more at different levels presumably for attachment pegs, shallow horizontal grooves inside, the lower edge (as drawn) possibly originally solid as the spongy centre may have decayed; fine incised decoration, a band of zigzag between horizontal lines, a line just inside each edge, and some disorganised lines beside the perforation (ON 27; S 57).

Detailed information on the location of the artefacts is given in Appendix 3. The neolithic deposit in the chamber was at least 0.38 m deep. In the main chamber it contained: sherd *1a*, 0.13 m above the floor; about half the sherds of *4*, varying from on the floor to 0.38 m above; sherd *5*, level uncertain but probably low; flints *10–13, 15, 16–18*, between 0.1 and 0.33 m above the floor. The neolithic deposit in the ante-chamber contained: sherds of *1b, 2, 3*, a few of *4*, quartz *22*, all about 0.15 m above the floor and some sealed below the pile of stones; sherds of *4* varied from floor level to about 0.46 m above; quartz *25, 26, 30* were 0.38 m above floor level; pumice *31* on or just above floor level. In the main chamber, sherds of *8* were about 0.48 m above floor level, so either on or in the top of the neolithic deposit, and pot *9*, flint *19*, quartz *24* and bone mount *32* were amongst the collapsed roofing. Sherds *6, 7* and quartz flakes *23, 27* were below the blocking outside the passage entrance. Sherd *4a*, flint *20* and pitchstone *21* were outside the cairn kerb.

1a, 4a, 5, 14–21, 23–31, not illustrated.

Human remains. Some in The Royal Museum of Scotland.

All the bone recovered had been cremated. Four deposits (*A–D* in Sharples) from amongst the collapsed roofing of the main chamber appeared to be from one adult individual, probably female. Three other small deposits from the collapsed roofing were from an individual about 12 years old (*G*), from another possibly not adult (*E*), the last indeterminable (*F*). A deposit from above the blocking in the passage (*I*) consisted of thirty-three very small pieces, possibly from a child no older than six years (see p. 158 for a note on the location of this deposit). (See Sharples, 48–52, for a detailed report by Denston).

Radiocarbon dates.
See p. 75.

49. THE ORD SOUTH

Parish Lairg
Location 1 km SW of Lairg
Map reference NC 574055
NMRS number NC 50 NE 17
References RCAMS 1911, 154, no. 444; Henshall 1963, 326, 327
Plan ASH and JNGR
Visited 24.6.51, 28.4.92

Description. The cairn was built on a rocky knoll on the summit of The Ord, at 162 m OD. From it there are very extensive views in all directions, in particular down the length of Loch Shin. The much larger North cairn, SUT 48, is only 40 m to the NW (plate 16).

In contrast with the neighbouring cairn, very little cairn material remains at The Ord South, and this is turf-covered with a level though rather uneven surface. The cairn edge can be traced round the N third of the perimeter from a boulder kerb-stone on the E to a flat slab kerb-stone on the NW, but the rest of the cairn edge is indistinct. The diameter NE to SW seems to have been about 15 m, and transversely probably a little less. The stump of a wooden television mast, put up in the 1960s, can be seen a little E of the NW kerb-stone.

Most of the orthostats which formed the skeleton of the chamber and passage survive. All are granitic, and all are rounded erratics except for three quarried slabs. The entrance passage has run from the SE side of the cairn. About 2.3 m from the probable position of the cairn edge on this side there is a pair of stones which look like portal stones forming the entrance, but they are only 0.6 m from a second pair of stones which are clearly the portal stones at the entrance to the chamber, an arrangement which provides a passage little more than 1 m long including both pairs of

SUT 49

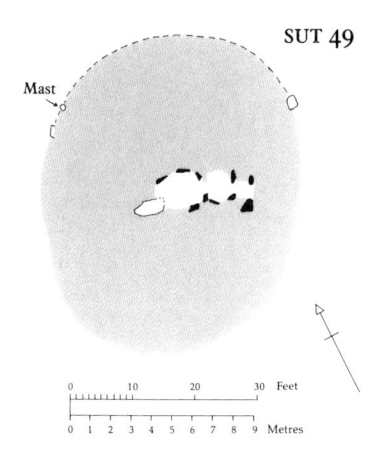

stones. The stones of the outer pair are 0.7 m apart, 0.6 and 0.45 m long by 0.55 and 0.25 m thick, and project 0.45 and 0.3 m. In front of these stones the ground drops quite steeply making it unlikely that the passage was longer (though the steepness is exaggerated by a small amount of quarrying into the knoll just outside the edge of the cairn).

The portal stones forming the entry to the ante-chamber are 0.53 m apart, 0.3 and 0.7 m long by 0.3 and 0.2 m thick, and project 0.3 and 0.33 m. The ante-chamber is about 1.1 m long. On the SW side an orthostat, 0.57 m long by 0.15 m thick and projecting 0.2 m, butts against the SW inner portal stone at the entry to the main chamber. This portal stone is 0.43 m long by 0.22 m thick, and projects 0.3 m. The NE side of the ante-chamber and the NE portal stone are missing. The main chamber was oval, about 2.2 m long by 1.6 m wide, with six orthostats in the wall. Three remain on the NE side set 0.26 and 0.35 m apart; from SE to NW they are 0.56 to 0.78 m long by 0.2 to 0.3 m thick, and project 0.25 to 0.55. The first of these stones has an intact upper surface and thus has always been nearer in height to the portal stones than to the other orthostats in the main chamber, which led to its identification as the NE inner portal stone in former descriptions of the chamber. On the SW side of the chamber only the E orthostat is standing, 0.55 m long above ground level by 0.35 m thick, and projecting 0.85 m. It is followed by a gap with a slight hollow in the ground where the next orthostat is evidently missing, and just to the SW two prone slabs are partly exposed (not shown on the plan), and are either a portion of the missing orthostat and a corbel stone, or two corbel stones. The last orthostat, 1.55 m long by 0.74 m wide and 0.36 m thick, lies intact where it has fallen outwards from the chamber wall, almost horizontal with its W end slightly raised and free of the turf.

Except for some disturbance of the cairn when the mast with its steel guy ropes was erected, the monument is in the same condition as when recorded in 1909 (RCAMS).

50. PITTENTRAIL (Corrie)

Parish Rogart
Location 10 km WNW of Golspie, on the NE side of Strath Fleet
Map reference NC 726020
NMRS number NC 70 SW 2
References Aitken 1788, sheet 19; NSA 1845, 50; Tait 1868, 528; ONB 1871–4, No. 33, 44; RCAMS 1911, 182, no. 524; Henshall 1963, 328
Visited 20.5.91

Description. The site of this totally destroyed cairn is a slight rise in a field of pasture, a little above the valley floor at 23 m OD. It was marked as 'Cairn' on an estate plan of 1788 (Aitken). In 1834 it was recorded as already partly ruined, for 'at a place called Corrie ... imperfect remains of a Druidical circle are to be seen. The inhabitants, quite unconscious of the sacrilege, finding the stones composing it suitable, carried them away for the purposes of building, so that but few of them are now to be seen' (NSA). The next reference over thirty years later states 'at Pittentrail, on a commanding hillock, stand the remains of a large chambered cairn, with its entrance turned to the north-east' (Tait). In 1873 it consisted of 'six stones, three of which are standing the remainder lying, they are placed in a circle about eleven feet (3.3 m) in diameter, and on a small mound situate in an arable field adjacent to Pittentrail Inn' (ONB). The monument was titled 'Stone Circle (Remains of)' on the OS 6-inch map surveyed in 1873, but this was revised to 'Stone Circle (Site of)' in 1904. The last remains had certainly been removed by 1909 when the site was mistakenly said to have been built over (RCAMS). There can be little doubt that the structure was a chambered cairn and the site is titled as such on the 1971 edition of the OS 1:10,000 map.

51. SALSCRAGGIE

Parish Kildonan
Location in the Strath of Kildonan, 3.5 km NW of Helmsdale
Map reference ND 001180
NMRS number ND 01 NW 1
References Stuart 1868, 291; ONB 1871, No. 25, 5; RCAMS 1911, 127, no. 360; Henshall 1963, 328; 1972, 580–1
Plan ASH and JNGR
Visited 7.5.57, 18.6.67, 30.9.93

Description. The stretch of the strath where the cairn was built is particularly narrow between steep

SUT 51

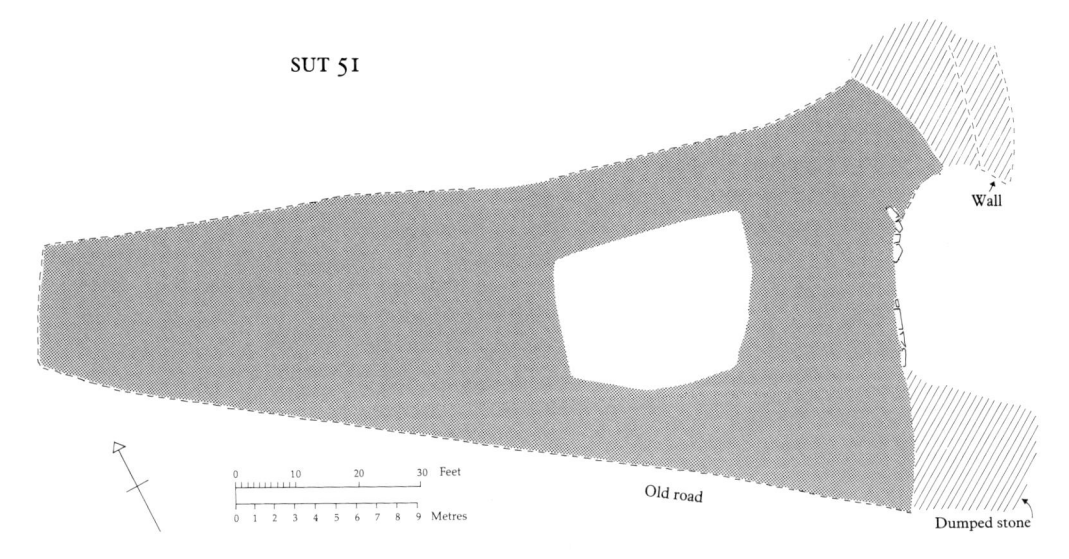

hillsides of heather moor and scree. The restricted amount of flat land along the River Helmsdale is neglected pasture. The cairn has a level site along the edge of a terrace a little above the river, at 23 m OD. There are foundations of enclosures and buildings beside and abutting the cairn.

The long cairn has been badly mutilated, and there are some uncertainties regarding the original plan. In 1909 Curle found the cairn had been 'so recently demolished that the tracks made by the carts which took away the stones from the interior are not yet obliterated. It is said to have had two chambers, but no trace remains of them' (RCAMS; 'two chambers' may mean a chamber of two compartments as in the early description of SUT 54). Forty-three years earlier, when seen in a more intact state, Stuart recorded 'at the east end an opening has been made, which discloses a gallery of upwards two feet (0.6 m) square, formed of flags, leading towards the centre of the cairn, where doubtless one or more chambers are placed. These, however, await examination'.

The axis of the cairn is ESE to WNW, but for ease of description it is described as being E to W. Across the E end is an almost straight line of boulders which appears to be the base of a built façade. It stretches for 7.7 m with a gap of 1.8 m in the centre. The S half consists of four almost contiguous boulders; the largest boulder is 0.6 m long widening to 1.03 m long above ground level, with the boulder to the N neatly fitted below its shoulder, and a well-fitting stone wedged above ground level between it and the adjacent boulder to the S. The N half of the façade is represented by four slightly smaller boulders, two of them somewhat displaced. Beyond them the edge of the cairn can be traced curving to the NE for about 1.8 m, indicating that the forecourt was probably concave between projecting horns. These are now completely obscured. About 4.4 m NE of the façade the foundations of an old wall can be traced running northwards, and the area between it and the much reduced NE part of the cairn is filled with loose stones. The area of the SE horn is covered by a bank of field-gathered stones.

Round the rest of the cairn the edge is sharply defined, rising unnaturally steeply for a metre or less, and covered by turf and bracken. How far the edge reflects the original outline of the cairn is uncertain. Along the N side and across the W end the edge has been formed by the limit of cultivation. A track defines the S edge of the cairn which is now only 2 m from the S edge of the terrace on which the cairn is built. The track was once the road up the strath (shown on the 1964 6-inch OS map, but the road had been re-routed N of the cairn long before the first OS survey in 1871). The terrace has doubtless suffered erosion by the river, and this is likely to have caused the road to impinge on the cairn. If this surmise is correct, it is possible that the unusually tapering plan of the cairn developed because of the gradually shifting alignment of the old road, and the original axis of the cairn may have been more nearly NE to SW. The cairn is 42 m long from the centre of the façade, 20.5 m wide across the façade, and 5.7 m wide across the W end.

Behind the façade the cairn rises in piles of disturbed loose rounded stones, at most 2 m high to the S of the axis, a little less to the N of the axis, and under 1 m high on the axis. The depression in the centre of the E end and the wide gap in the façade may be due to the removal of the large slabs which formed the passage and chamber referred to by Stuart and Curle. About 7 m W of the façade the cairn material has been completely removed to form a cultivation plot 9 m E to W by 8 m transversely, on the N and S sides bounded by the cairn edge left as a low wall-like rim. Access was evidently to the NW corner through the N side of the cairn. Westwards from the plot the cairn remains as untidy low heaps of bare stone, partly covered by turf near the W end where it is 1 m high.

52. SKAIL
Parish Farr
Location in Strathnaver, 15 km S of Bettyhill
Map reference NC 712469
NMRS number NC 74 NW 4
References RCAMS 1911, 80, no. 233; Henshall 1963, 328–9, 330
Plan ASH and JNGR
Visited 27.6.57, 29.9.93

Description. The cairn is on the floor of the strath at 38 m OD, in an area of rough grazing and small birch woods. Immediately to the S this gives way to improved pasture and cultivated fields extending in a narrow strip up the strath. The cairn is on a level site, at the edge of a birch wood, and just E of the main road.

The cairn has been largely removed, though a low rim of cairn material has been left undisturbed round most of the circuit, which allows the edge to be traced fairly easily. The diameters are 18.5 to 20.5 m. More cairn material remains around the chamber with the greatest amount piled against the SE side where it is 1.4 m high above the floor level in the chamber. The whole area of the cairn is covered with grass and bracken, and several trees are growing on it.

In the centre of the cairn a group of orthostats define a bipartite chamber. The orthostats are quarried slabs, with flat surfaces facing the chamber. They were linked by neat walling fragments of which survive, generally with one slab in each course. The chamber has been dug out, and the present floor is only a little above the original floor level. The entrance has evidently been from the NE, but there is nothing to be seen of the passage. The outer portal stones, which it may be assumed once stood between it and the ante-chamber, have evidently been removed; a neatly excavated rectangular area extending 2.6 m to the NE of a pair of inner portal stones would have been expected to have revealed them. The NW wall of the ante-chamber consists of an orthostat 1.05 m long by 0.15 m thick and 0.94 m high, with a jagged broken upper surface. It is linked to the NW inner portal stone by three courses of walling stretching 0.5 m. All that remains of the SE side of the ante-chamber is a single flat slab at the inner end, the last fragment of walling, more of which existed in 1957. An orthostat fallen from the wall was seen in 1909 (RCAMS). The width of the ante-chamber at the inner end was 1.7 m. The inner portal stones, set 0.6 m apart, are intact with flat upper surfaces sloping up slightly to the outside of the chamber. The stones are over 0.9 and over 1 m long, both are 0.25 m thick and up to 0.75 and 0.6 m high.

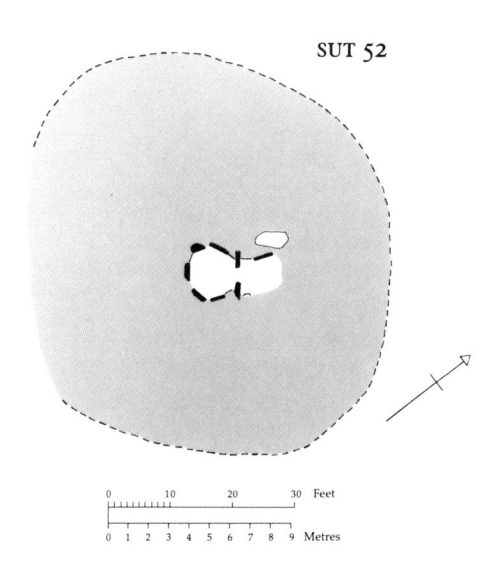

The polygonal main chamber is 2.2 m long and slightly more transversely. It consists of five orthostats set 0.12 to 0.5 m apart. They are 0.76 to 1.2 m long (in three cases the maximum length is above ground level) by 0.15 to 0.4 m thick. Clockwise from the E, the orthostats are 1, 1.66, 1.2, 1.3 and 1.1 m high. The first and second orthostats are intact, the third is obviously broken, the fourth has a rounded top only slightly damaged, and the last may be intact. Between the SE inner portal stone and the first orthostat there remains walling 0.9 m high in eight courses, though slightly displaced. Between the third and fourth orthostats, and between the fifth orthostat and the NW inner portal stone respectively, three and two courses of walling can be seen. The total length of the chamber may be estimated as about 4.5 m.

A large flat slab lies to the N of the ante-chamber.

The cairn was in the same condition when recorded by Curle in 1909 (RCAMS), except that some walling remained between all the orthostats of the main chamber, mostly still surviving in 1957. The chamber had been dug out some years before his visit.

FINDS
Artefact. In Dunrobin Castle Museum, Golspie.
'A steatite cup with a side handle is said to have been found' in the cairn (RCAMS, but not identified in the museum in 1957). Not illustrated.

53. SKELPICK LONG

Parish Farr
Location in Strathnaver, 5.3 km SSE of Bettyhill
Map reference NC 722567
NMRS number NC 75 NW 7
References Cardonnel 1800, plate XIII, 2; McKay 1867; Horsburgh, 1867, 2; Horsburgh 1868, 273–4; Stuart 1868, 296; Anderson 1886, 263–4; RCAMS 1911, 82–3, no. 241; Henshall, 1963 329, 331
Plan ASH and JNGR
Visited 5.7.55, 20.5.92

Description. The cairn is in a small valley, on the E side of the Skelpick Burn, a tributary of the River Naver (plate 11). To the E of the burn is heather moorland, and to the W is rough pasture. The site is on a terrace a little above the burn, at 31 m OD, with the hillside rising steeply on the E side. The outlook from the cairn is restricted except for the view NW down the valley with a glimpse of the sea. On the ridge which separates the burn from the river the two other Skelpick cairns, SUT 54 and 55, are visible 450 and 700 m to the SSW and SSE respectively.

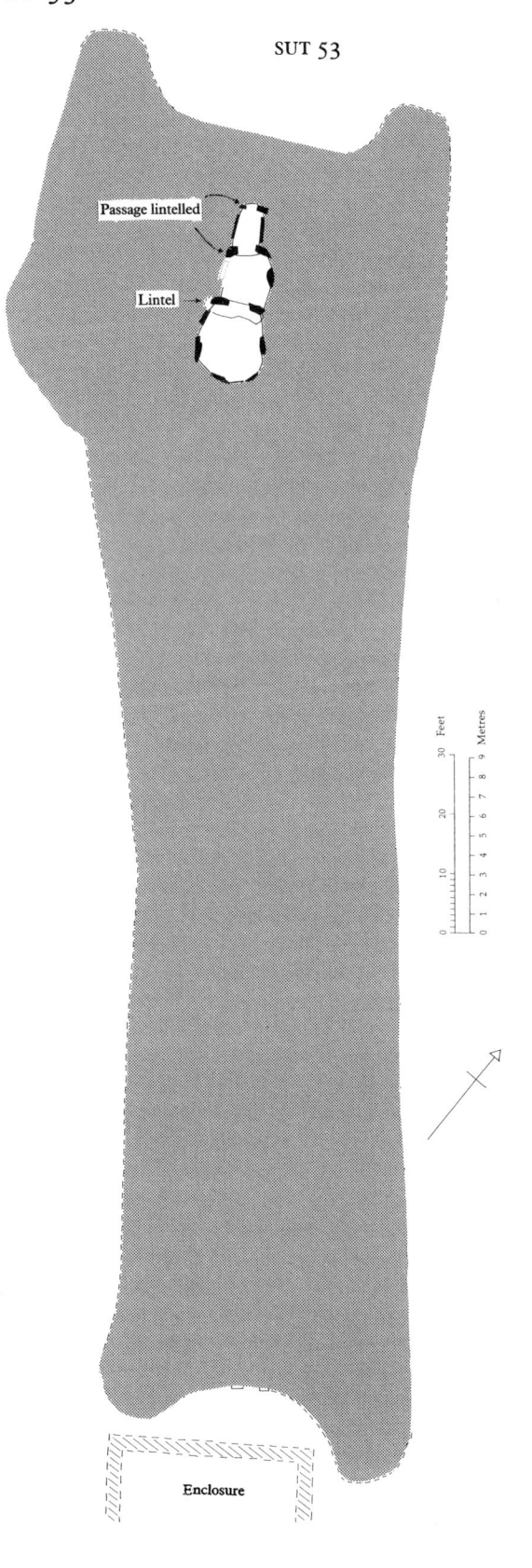

The long cairn occupies a small ridge which serves to emphasize its impressive size. It is aligned NW to SE, but for ease of description it will be treated as being N to S. The cairn is 72 m long overall, including the horns which define a forecourt at each end (due to an error in the 1955 plan the length was given incorrectly in Henshall). The cairn is about 20 m wide across the chamber, narrowing gradually to about 14 m wide at a little S of the centre, and expanding slightly to about 16 m wide at the S end. At the N end the forecourt is difficult to define though the ends of the horns are clear. Between them there is loose rubble which rises steeply to merge with the cairn material covering the passage, and which northwards merges into the downward slope of the ground. The passage entrance is hidden beneath this stony material; presumably there is deliberate blocking immediately in front of the entrance (see below), but this has been covered by cairn material removed from the chamber area when it was investigated. The forecourt is about 13.5 m wide by about 7 m deep. The chamber is exposed in a deep hollow in the cairn, but S of it the cairn remains to a height of 3.4 m (measured from the chamber floor), and from here to near the S end it continues as a ridge of bare irregular stones. Except for a few superficial hollows it appears to be undisturbed, neither robbed nor substantially distorted, and it retains the steep pitch of its long sides. The cairn gradually diminishes in height southwards to about 2.8 m high at about 12 m N of the S forecourt. At this point there is a transverse hollow across the cairn, 2.7 m wide and about 0.7 m deep, which may be an original feature (though in this area a relatively recent deep hollow has been made into the cairn from the E side reaching almost to the median line). The cairn has clearly been robbed from the S end to within 1.7 m of the transverse hollow, presumably to build the square enclosure just to the S. The SE horn is clear, and the SW horn can just be traced though it has probably been truncated. Between them the edge of the forecourt is rather vague except for two laid slabs near the centre which appear to be part of an edging wall-face. The S forecourt has been about 10 m wide and probably about 3.5 m deep. The W edge of the cairn is clear though overgrown with heather, except for 20 m at the N end where it is overlaid with bare stones evidently thrown down when the chamber was opened, and N of this the cairn merges into the natural slope. All along the E side the cairn merges with the slope of the ridge and has deep heather growing almost to the crest, so that the cairn edge is difficult to trace.

The axis of the passage and chamber is nearly NNW to SSE, skew by about 13° from the axis of the cairn. The entrance can only be seen from the roofed passage. A pair of transverse stones set 0.56 m apart forms the portal at the outer end of the passage. They are over 0.7 and over 0.4 m long, 0.25 and 0.18 m thick, and 0.7 and 0.65 m high. The original blocking, a neat stack of six horizontal slabs reaching to within 0.2 m of the roof, is in place between them, with the S edges of the slabs flush with the S faces of the portal stones. To the N of the slabs there can just be seen loose stones, smaller than those of the cairn material.

The passage is 1.8 m long, and 1.15 m wide at the outer end increasing to 1.3 m wide at the inner end. A slab forms most of each wall. The slabs are 1.36 and 1.31 m long by 0.5 and 0.45 m high, with two or three courses of walling above them, though this is displaced inwards and in a precarious state. Walling fills the short gaps at the ends of the stones, though missing from the NE corner. At the inner end of the passage a pair of portal stones forms the entry into the ante-chamber. They are 0.94 and over 0.78 m long by 0.26 and 0.44 m thick, and 0.86 and 0.77 m high, set 0.8 m apart. At the outer end of the passage a lintel rests on the E portal stone and passes a little above the W portal stone, and the N edge of the lintel projects a little N of their outer faces. The lintel is 0.8 m wide by 0.3 m thick, 0.7 m above the floor, tilted slightly down to the S. The next two lintels rise in inverted steps, each overlapping the upper surface of that to the N with the third lintel 1 m above floor level. The fourth lintel is missing and a gap of 0.5 m is spanned by rubble; it is likely that a substantial stone at the top of each side wall is an end portion of this lintel the centre part of which has broken away. The innermost lintel is lower, 0.86 m above the floor, resting directly on the E portal stone and on a corbel stone over the shorter W portal stone at the chamber entrance. The lintel is over 2 m long, 0.65 m wide and 0.75 m thick in the centre, and the face to the chamber is triangular.

The chamber walls are constructed of spaced orthostats linked by panels of walling. All the orthostats are intact. The walling is of quite large rectangular quarried slabs, in general 0.07 to 0.02 m thick, and where well preserved can be seen to have been carefully built. At a height of about 0.7 m the walling changes to courses of large corbel stones, often 0.23 to 0.4 m thick, up to 0.9 m wide, and 1 m or so long. They are laid with their long axes running back into the cairn and their inner ends generally slightly oversailing; their appearance is rougher and heavier than the walling below. There is a considerable amount of displaced stone on the chamber floor, but all vertical measurements are taken from approximately floor level.

The ante-chamber is about 2.5 m long by 2.5 m wide at the S end. The E wall consists of a orthostat 1.3 m long by 0.36 m thick, and 1.1 m high, with a horizontal upper surface. The spaces between it and the outer and inner E portal stones of the chamber are filled with walling about 1.15 m high, and above this and the orthostat are two courses of corbel stones giving a total height of 1.7 m with a considerable overhang, at the SE corner as much as 0.5 m though possibly there has been some displacement. Only a short length at the S end of the W wall is visible. An orthostat set close to the W outer portal stone was visible in the 19th century (Anderson, 264), but this is hidden by rubble.

The entry between the ante-chamber and main chamber has been spacious, 1.06 m wide and probably about 1.4 m high. The portal stones are 0.85 and over 1.06 m long, 0.42 and 0.25 to 0.4 m wide, and 1.1 and 0.9 m high, and their upper edges slope down into the cairn. The lintel above them is somewhat displaced with its wider face tilted down from S to N. Its E end rests on a corbel stone supported by displaced walling to the SE of the portal stone, and its W end rests on displaced walling on the shoulder of the W portal stone and on the panel of walling to the SW. The lintel is about 3 m long by 1 m wide and 0.35 m thick.

The main chamber is 3.5m long by about 3.25 m wide. There are five orthostats in the wall. That on the axis has a horizontal upper surface, and the others are rounded and rather irregular in shape. From the NE clockwise they are 0.7, 0.77, 0.84 (at maximum 1.14), over 1.3 and 0.86 m long, and, as far as can be seen, they vary from 0.1 to 0.4 m thick. They are all of similar height, between 1 and 1.22 m; the tallest is the NW orthostat. Most of the linking walling remains. Between the E portal stone and the E orthostat only the upper courses are visible; between the E and SE orthostats there are six neat courses of walling and above them three courses of corbel stones oversailing by 0.3 m at a height of 1.7 m (though the lowest courses of walling at the N end have been pulled away and the upper part of the wall is in danger of collapse). The walling between the SE and the S orthostats has fallen away, but it was intact in 1955 (Henshall). Between the S and SW orthostats walling remains almost level with their tops and butts against the face of the latter, the S end of which is hidden. The last two panels of walling on the W side of the chamber survive to half the height of the adjacent orthostats.

Part of the chamber was evidently visible in 1800 (Cardonnel; see ¶ 2.1), and subsequently it must have been filled in. Horsburgh investigated the main chamber in 1866 (figure 2). His description and measurements are fairly accurate except that he gave the height of the orthostats as 6 ft and one as 7 ft (1.8 and 2.1 m); this seems to be an exaggeration as the present floor level, also extending down the passage, appears to be at approximately the original level. He estimated that the roof height of the main chamber had been 10 ft (3 m). 'The chamber had been opened from the top, and the whole inside was filled with stones and rubbish, so that I only cleared it out. Before I commenced operations, however, there was no appearance of it having been meddled with, and I dug it by chance, where the cairn appeared to be highest. Nothing whatever was found in it' (Horsburgh 1867, or 1868). In September 1866 Stuart noted that 'a passage leading to another chamber or gallery is blocked up. The walls of the chamber begin to converge at a height of 6 feet (1.8 m)'. Further investigations the following year exposed the ante-chamber and passage (McKay, the plans redrawn and published by Anderson).

54. SKELPICK ROUND
Parish Farr
Location in Strathnaver, 5.5 km SSE of Bettyhill
Map reference NC 721563
NMRS number NC 75 NW 9
References Joass 1864a; 1864b, 360; Stuart 1868, 296; Curle 1909a, 27th May; 1909b, vol. 1, 54; RCAMS 1911, 82, no. 239; Henshall 1963, 329
Plan ASH and JNGR
Visited 5.7.55, 21.5.92

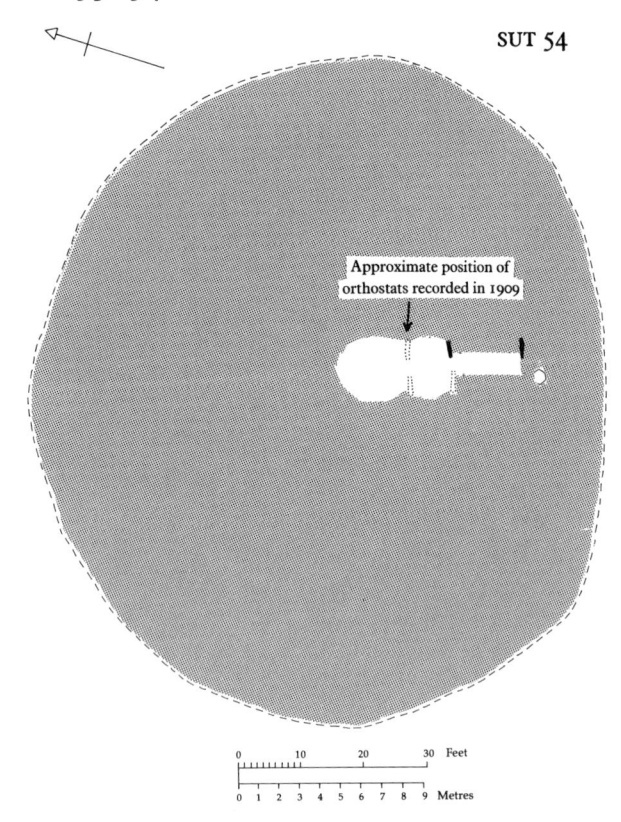

Description. The cairn is in a gently undulating area of rough grazing, a little to the E of the fields of Skelpick which were formed only towards the end of the 19th century. The site of the cairn is a slight rise at 53 m OD. Skelpick Long and Skelpick South (SUT 53, 55) are visible 350 and 450 m to the NNE and SE respectively.

The cairn was 'fast being demolished' in 1863 (Joass). In 1866 Stuart briefly described the 'enormous cairn, which has been opened and partly removed'; it was evidently much more impressive than Skelpick South (SUT 55). In 1909, after further damage, Curle gave the height as up to 2 m (RCAMS). Since then the cairn has been further robbed and left in untidy heaps and hollows; the greatest height a little N of the centre is 1.7 m. The cairn material is mainly small rounded stones but some larger stones are present. The surface is partly turf-covered, and gorse grows on the S and SW sides. The cairn edge is clear, and where the rim is best preserved on the N side it is 1.4 m high. The diameter N to S is 28 m, and transversely it is 32 m.

The 1866 account recorded that the cairn 'contained three chambers. Two of them were large and almost octagonal, formed of great slabs, with good masonry in the intervening spaces. They were 9 or 10 feet (2.7 or 3 m) across, and the covering gone, but the floor had not been dug into. The third adjoined the others on the S, and measured about 6 feet (1.8 m) across' (Stuart). Much less of the chamber could be seen in 1909. From the published description augmented from his notebook and diary (RCAMS, Curle), it is evident that Curle saw a portal stone marking the entrance to the chamber at 7 m from the S edge of the cairn. At about 1.9 m further N there was a pair of inner portal stones, both stones being about 0.9 m long by 0.76 m high. The inner end of the chamber, 'judging by the excavated hollow and remains of one upright stone on E side', was thought to be about 4.5 m to the N of them (probably an overestimate).

Only three orthostats are now visible in the cairn. On the S side a pair of stones set 0.75 m apart have the appearance of portal stones at the entry into the passage. The E stone, about 4 m from the cairn edge, is 0.93 m long by 0.23 m thick near the E end, and 0.36 m high; the upper edge is horizontal but rough, possibly broken. Its partner, leaning steeply to the S, is 0.6 m long by 0.33 m thick, and would be over 0.55 m high if vertical. A disintegrating stone 3.45 m N of the first stone is the E stone of the portal at the inner end of the passage which was seen by Curle. The stone is 0.86 m long by 0.2 m thick and 0.5 m high. The axis of the passage and chamber has evidently been from a little E of S to a little W of N.

Collating these three accounts, there can be little doubt that the chamber was bipartite with orthostats in the side walls, the third 'chamber' mentioned by Stuart being the passage. The plan was perhaps similar to the chamber and passage in Skelpick Long (SUT 53). The total length of the Skelpick Round chamber was between 5 and 6.4 m.

55. SKELPICK SOUTH

Parish Farr
Location in Strathnaver, 6 km SSE of Bettyhill
Map reference NC 724560
NMRS number NC 75 NW 10
References Stuart 1868, 297; RCAMS 1911, 82, no. 238; Henshall 1963, 330, 331
Plan ASH and JNGR
Visited 5.7.55, 21.5.92

Description. The cairn is situated on a ridge in undulating enclosed pasture, on the E side of the strath, at 76 m OD. The ridge and the area to the E of it was unenclosed rough pasture until quite recently; indeed the 6-inch OS map surveyed in 1873 shows that the buildings and fields at Skelpick were constructed after that date. The actual site of the cairn is level, on a slight rise, and the cairn is a prominent feature though more commanding sites are available nearby on the ridge. The cairn is intervisible with Skelpick Long and Skelpick Round (SUT 53, 54) 700 and 450 m to the NNW and NW respectively.

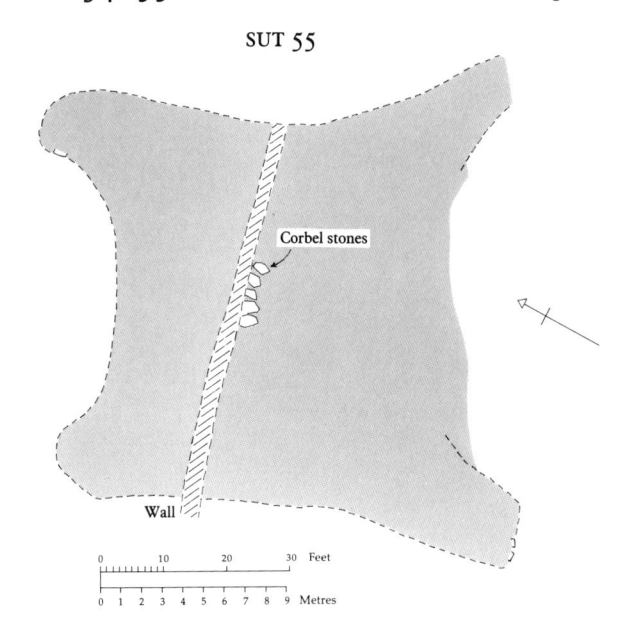

The short horned plan of the cairn is perfectly clear. The cairn is composed of loose irregular stones, and it is still 3 m high to the SW of the assumed position of the chamber. Turf has formed along the edges and over the low horns. One vertical kerb-stone just projects on the W side of the N horn, and two flat kerb-stones are visible at the end of the S horn. Only on the SE side where cairn material has fallen forwards, and at the end of the E horn, are the cairn edges not well defined. Along the SE to NW axis the cairn probably measured about 15 m, and transversely it is 18 m wide. The forecourts facing SE and NW are about 19 and 13.5 m wide, and the NW forecourt is about 3.5 m deep. The horns are about 3 m wide, giving the structure overall a maximum width of 24.5 m at the SE side, and a maximum length of 23 m. The cairn is crossed by a field wall, stones for which have been taken from the top of the cairn; the wall is extended by fencing on each side of the cairn.

At the centre of the cairn and projecting from below the wall a number of large horizontal slabs are just exposed, evidently corbel stones belonging to the upper part of the wall of a chamber which presumably was entered from the SE. They are flat blocks with rounded edges, their upper surfaces at roughly the same height, 2.6 m above ground level on the SE side. The E corbel stone is displaced, and the other four are in an almost straight line. From W to E they are over 0.83, 0.86, 0.56 and 0.7 m long (their NW ends hidden) by 0.44, 0.7, 0.6 and 0.63 m wide, and they vary from 0.3 to 0.16 m thick. These four stones overhang another course, the ends of four or five corbel stones just being visible. At least one of these stones is more massive than those above, being 0.9 m wide by 0.27 m thick. One stone of a lower third course can be glimpsed deep in displaced cairn material. The S ends of the uppermost course extend W to E for 2.3 m, and the course below appears to be somewhat longer. Several large flattish slabs lie on the surface of the cairn, but no more of the chamber structure can be seen.

The horned plan of the cairn was recognised by Stuart in 1866. He described it as 'another ruined cairn with a few large slabs of its central chamber yet in situ'; presumably he was referring to vertical orthostats in the outer part of the chamber which have not been visible since then. When visited by Curle in 1909 the field wall had not been built across the cairn and the corbel stones do not seem to have been exposed (RCAMS). In view of the relatively intact appearance of the cairn his comment that 'it has been much dilapidated, especially on the SE side, from which great quantities of stones have at one time been removed' is perhaps surprising.

56. STRONECHRUBIE

See p. 152.

57. TONGUE HOUSE

Parish Tongue
Location on the E side of the Kyle of Tongue
Map reference NC 592586
NMRS number NC 55 NE 2
References Horsburgh 1868, 277; RCAMS 1911, 188, no. 547; Henshall 1963, 330
Visited 11.7.58, 26.10.92

Description. In a paper recording a range of antiquities in N Sutherland, Horsburgh noted briefly 'the chamber of a cairn of the same description as that near Skelpick, but a little smaller' near Tongue House. His phraseology seems to imply that little of the cairn survived. Horsburgh emptied the inner part of the Skelpick Long chamber (SUT 53) in 1866, but did not realise that the chamber is bipartite with an antechamber. The Tongue House chamber therefore probably appeared to be a single-compartment chamber. Horsburgh cleared it out, presumably in 1866, and 'found that one of the large upright stones has two holes bored artificially a short way into each of its sides, but not quite opposite, the holes were about 3 inches (0.07 m) diameter'.

Horsburgh located the cairn 'a little to the south of Tongue House, and near the fountain head that supplies it with water'. Curle equated the cairn with 'apparently the remains of a cairn' 'in the wood to the E of Tongue House, on the top of a knoll about 70 yards (64 m) E of the gardener's house' (RCAMS). When enquiries were made by Henshall in 1958 she was shown a structure, evidently that referred to by Curle (though SE of Tongue House), which she accepted as the remains of Horsburgh's cairn, and which subsequently was shown titled 'chambered cairn' on the 6-inch OS map surveyed in 1960. Further indication that the identification of the site is correct is provided by the well shown on the 25-inch OS maps published in 1878 and 1908 about 30 m NW of the 'chambered cairn', agreeing with Horsburgh's description. The site is about 220 m from the E shore of the Kyle, on a hillside of untended woodland at about 23 m OD.

A difficulty arose, however, when the site was visited in 1992. The 'chambered cairn' is a circular stone structure overgrown with small trees and covered in leaf litter and moss. A kerb about 15 m in diameter can be traced for much of the circuit. The kerb is of unusually substantial and closely-set boulders which have the appearance of the base of a massive wall such as is appropriate for a dun or a broch rather than a cairn. The interior is filled with loose stones including some quite large boulders, roughly to the level of the top of the kerb. There is no indication that these boulders have formed part of a neolithic chamber or that the structure was a cairn. There seem to be three possibilities: that the structure is not Horsburgh's cairn, that the structure is that which he investigated but that he was mistaken in regarding it as a chambered cairn, that the writers are mistaken in identifying the structure as a ruined broch or dun.

58. TORBOLL (Carn Liath)

Parish Dornoch
Location on the SW side of Strath Fleet, 8.5 km W of Golspie
Map reference NH 741994
NMRS number NH 79 NW 7
References ONB 1873, No. 9, 118; RCAMS 1911, 47-8, no. 134; Henshall 1963, 331, 332
Plan CAG and ASH, amended ASH and JNGR
Visited 5.5.57, 21.5.91

Description. The cairn was formerly in open moorland with wide views in all directions except to the NW, but it is now in a clearing near the W edge of a forestry plantation. The cairn was a conspicuous feature when viewed from the E, at the top of a long steep rise at 168 m OD, but a little below the actual top of

SUT 58

0 10 20 30 Feet
0 1 2 3 4 5 6 7 8 9 Metres

Lintels

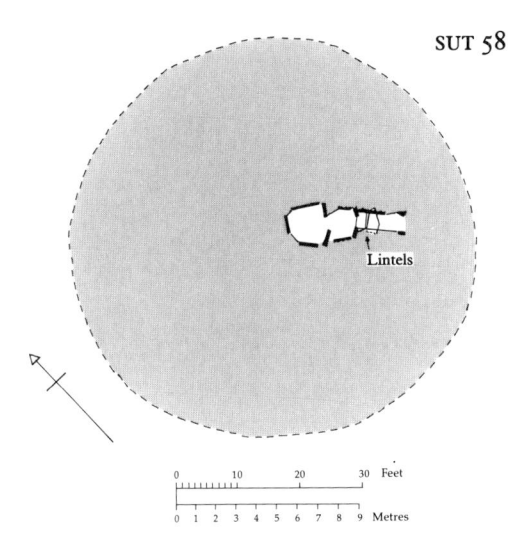

the hill. Craig a' Bhlair (SUT 78) is 500 m to the NW, and between the two cairns and extending over the undulating moorland to the W and S there are traces of prehistoric settlement.

The site of the cairn is fairly level though the ground drops away round the SW side. The steep-sided cairn is bare except for heather growing over the perimeter, and the edge is clear giving diameters of 19 to 20 m. To the NW of the chamber the cairn still stands 3 m high measured from the SE. It has been disturbed in various places, and the passage and chamber have been exposed in a deep hollow. Stones are known to have been removed from the cairn in 1860 (ONB).

When first described in 1909 and when visited in 1957 the passage and chamber contained a relatively small amount of debris, but in 1991 they were found to be largely choked with displaced stones and some details recorded in 1957 could no longer be seen. The passage runs from the SE side of the cairn. At the outer end, about 3 m within the cairn edge, is a pair of portal stones set 0.7 m apart. They measure 0.2 by 0.35 m and 0.3 by 0.3 m, and both are exposed for 0.53 m, almost their full original height. The NE stone is triangular in plan, its S face at an angle to the cairn edge. A hollow through the cairn material gives a misleading impression that the passage continued to the SE edge of the cairn. The passage is 2.3 m long and 0.7 m wide, and still retains two lintels at the inner end. On the SW side for the first 0.5 m the walling is somewhat displaced, but the inner part is well preserved with up to seven courses visible below the lintels. On the NE side the outer 0.55 m of walling has broken away, but a slab 1.4 m long and 0.35 m high forms the base of the inner stretch with four or five courses

above it. The outer lintel has a clearance of 0.65 m below it but is slightly displaced, tilted gently down to the S. It is over 1.1 m long, 0.13 m thick, and 0.57 m from front to back but rather irregular in shape. The inner lintel appears to be rectangular, about 0.9 m long, about 0.15 m thick, and 0.5 m from front to back, set 0.05 m higher than the outer lintel with a clearance of 0.78 m. A pair of portal stones forms the entry to the chamber. They are slightly splayed, 0.44 m apart at ground level but wider apart below the lintel; they are about 0.5 and 0.4 m long, 0.1 and 0.12 m thick, and exposed for 0.68 and 0.7 m. The upper edge of the NE stone slopes steeply down to the NE and bears walling of slanting slabs on its shoulder; the top of the other stone slopes slightly in the opposite direction. Neither stone supports the inner lintel directly, but on each there is a horizontal slab; that on the SW side projects over the passage to steady the end of the lintel which is only just long enough to span the entry.

The chamber is 3.3 m long, with a rather irregular plan. The ante-chamber is 1.4 m long on the NE side by about 1.35 m wide. There is an orthostat on each side, about 0.86 and about 0.63 m long, and both are about the same height as the outer portal stones against which they butt (the NE side slab was not visible in 1991). Three or four courses of vertical walling remain 0.35 m high above the orthostats, and walling fills the gap between the NE orthostat and the adjacent inner portal stone completely masking its SE face. The inner portal stones are 0.63 m apart, slightly splayed and not quite opposite each other. Both are 0.7 m long and 0.2 m thick; and the slightly taller SW stone can be seen in a gap beside it to be over 1 m high; it is 0.55 m higher than the adjacent side-slab.

The main chamber is 1.8 m long by 1.65 m wide. The back-slab has a narrow base but at the maximum is about 0.85 m long, and is 0.11 m thick (only the top edge was visible in 1991). It has a concave vertical face with the top edge slightly curving into the chamber, and this curve was formerly continued by two oversailing courses above (no longer present). The slab on the SW side is about 0.9 m long and 0.13 m thick; that on the NE side is 1.45 m long with the SE end overhanging the adjacent inner portal stone, but it is 1.35 m long lower down, and 0.1 m thick. It is 0.36 m higher than the adjacent inner portal stone and is the tallest orthostat in the chamber, though there is no great difference in the height of the three innermost slabs. The gaps between these three orthostats are filled with walling (hidden by debris in 1991), and in 1957 there were one or two courses remaining above them.

All the orthostats including those at the passage entrance have intact upper surfaces, except for the SW inner portal stone. The orthostats and walling are of flat sandstone slabs, in contrast with the irregular stone used as cairn material.

FINDS
Artefact. In the Dunrobin Castle Museum, Golspie.
A stone lamp (cup) with perforated handle, iron age. Found in 1860 (ONB).
Not illustrated.

59. CAMORE WOOD

See pp. 152–3.

60. CNOC NA MOINE

Parish Durness
Location 2 km SW of Durness
Map reference NC 389660
NMRS number NC 36 NE 13
References Reid, David and Aitken 1967, 37, no. 25; Henshall 1972, 580, 581
Plan ASH and JNGR
Visited 7.10.63, 30.4.92

Description. The cairn is on a shelf at 54 m OD, a little below the summit of a low craggy hill, Cnoc na Moine. The site overlooks the Kyle of Durness and the cultivated land along its E side, and is less than 600 m from the shore. Above the fields the hills are rough pasture and heather moorland. The cairn is in a recently enclosed area of pasture based on a sandy subsoil which is exposed in nearby areas of erosion. The ground level appears to drop gently from S to N below the cairn.

The last remains of the cairn are turf-covered. A low rim of cairn material round the W half indicates that the cairn diameters were roughly 19.5 m N to S by 22 m E to W, but round the E side the cairn merges into the ground and this edge cannot be traced with any confidence. W and N of the chamber the cairn has been totally removed, but elsewhere the surface is uneven with a maximum height of about 1 m inside the chamber. Within the cairn most of the orthostats of the chamber survive, and their heights can be measured from approximately ground level where it is free of cairn material.

A boulder about 3.6 m inside the S edge of the cairn appears to be the W member of a pair of portal stones at the entrance to a short passage. The boulder is 0.85 m long by 0.27 m thick, and is exposed for 0.25 m which is near to its original height as its rounded top is intact. The passage was roughly 1.5 m long.

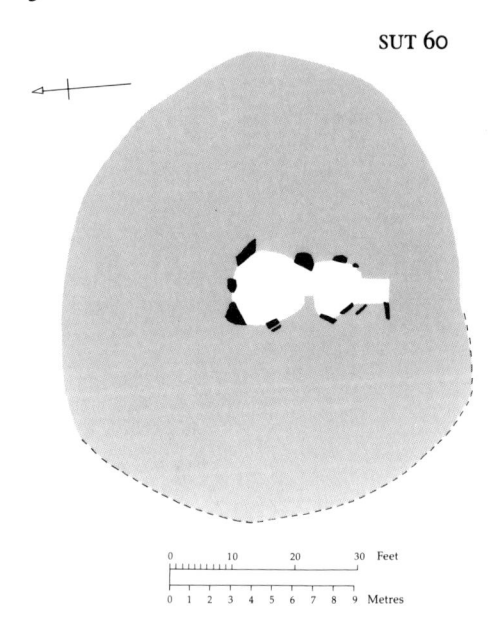

The ante-chamber was about 2.4 m long and about the same width, and its walls were concave and irregular in plan. Two orthostats on the W side, 0.4 m apart, are 0.75 and 0.8 m long, 0.3 and 0.22 m thick, and 0.55 and 0.45 m high. The first is a rounded block with a split flat face towards the chamber, the other is a quarried block. Parallel with the former 0.5 m to the S is a smaller slab, over 0.55 m long, 0.15 m thick and 0.2 m high, its function not evident. The E wall is represented by two boulders. The S one hardly projects; the N one is 0.6 m long by 0.35 m thick, with its intact top projecting for 0.3 m.

Between the ante-chamber and the main chamber is an irregular boulder with a flat face set skew to the chamber axis. The boulder, 0.9 m long by 0.7 m thick and 0.75 m high, has served as the E inner portal stone; its partner is missing. The main chamber, also rather irregular in plan, is about 3.7 m long by about 3.1 m wide. Four orthostats remain round the inner end, and probably one or two more have been removed. Clockwise from the W orthostat, they are 0.62, 1.25, 0.6, and 1.45 long, by over 0.2, 0.7, 0.43, and 0.65 m thick. The first orthostat is a stump which has split in two and hardly projects. The next is a boulder 1.2 m high, with a flat split face towards the chamber. The orthostat on the axis is a relatively small rounded boulder 0.75 m high, which appears to have lost its top long ago. The last orthostat is a more regular boulder 1.15 m high. The orthostats are 0.96, 0.5, and 0.6 m apart.

61. CREAG AN AMALAIDH

Parish Dornoch
Location 1 km W of Loch Fleet, 8.5 km NNW of Dornoch
Map reference NH 756973
NMRS number NH 79 NE 4
References RCAMS 1911, 47, no. 133; Henshall 1972, 581
Plan ASH and ERM
Visited 6.10.67, 15.4.91

Description. The cairn is in an extensive area of heather moorland, at 137 m OD, where the steep S side of Creag an Amalaidh gives way to a gentler slope leading down to the boggy valley floor. There are widespread remains of prehistoric settlement on the lower slopes of the valley. An old road below the cairn made use of the pass between Creag an Amalaidh and Cnoc Odhar; the cairn is sited just W of the watershed.

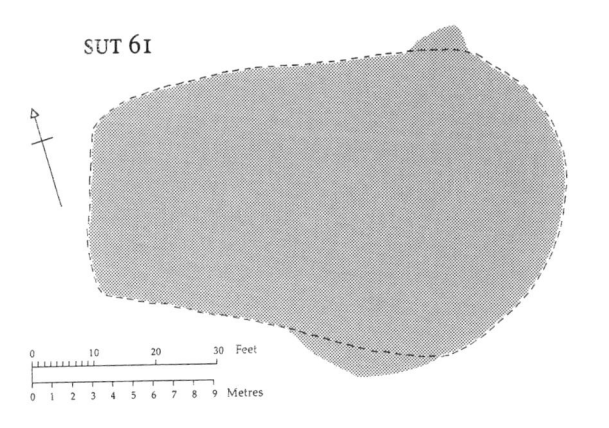

SUT 61

The bare cairn is composed of irregular stones and boulders. The long axis lies ESE to WNW, somewhat skew to the slope with the E end uphill; the ground level is higher along the N than the S side. In spite of considerable disturbance in the centre of the cairn the edges are fairly well defined and the straight N edge is particularly clear. The cairn is about 23 m long, about 13 m wide near the rounded E end, and about 8.5 m wide at the square W end. The cairn rises steeply from the E end to a height of 1.4 m at 4 m from the E edge (measured from the E, but 3.6 m high measured from the S side and 0.76 m high measured from the N side). The long profile is interrupted not only by two contiguous deep hollows, situated on the axis between about 8 m to 13.7 m from the E end, but also by displaced cairn material piled on the W side of the W hollow which increases the former height of the cairn by 0.6 m. At about 8 m from the W end the cairn is 2.7 m high (measured from the S side), diminishing westwards to a negligible height for the last 3.6 m. The W hollow extends to the S edge of the cairn, and displaced cairn material has been spread beyond the cairn edge on both this side and on the N side.

There has been no change in the condition of the cairn since it was visited in 1967, and probably not since Curle's visit in 1909 (RCAMS).

62. DUN RIASKIDH

See p. 153.

63. EMBO

Parish Dornoch
Location on the E coast, 3 km NNE of Dornoch, just S of the village of Embo
Map reference NH 817926
NMRS number NH 89 SW 9
References Henshall and Taylor 1957; Henshall 1960; Henshall and Wallace 1963; *Radiocarbon 13* (1971), 173; Henshall 1972, 582–4
Plan ASH and JCW (see also figure 8)
Excavation Henshall and Wallace 1960
Visited August 1956, July 1960, 16.4.91

Description. The cairn is on the coastal strip of rough ground between flat agricultural land to the W and sand-dunes to the E. It is only 100 m from the shore and less than 10 m above OD. From the site there are wide views to the W across the flat hinterland, to the SE along the coast to Tarbat Ness in Easter Ross, and to the NE as far as the Ord of Caithness. In 1956, when first recorded, the cairn was a small irregular inconspicuous mound in which a burial cist had been exposed by casual digging (Henshall and Taylor). Four years later removal of the mound was proposed in order to build a car park, and a hasty excavation was undertaken in the short time allowed before destruction was to take place. The unexpected discovery that the mound was a chambered cairn led to the replanning of the car park, and the remains of the cairn were retained as a feature within a low wall. After the excavation the adjacent land was developed as a caravan park. Much of the structure exposed during the excavation is still visible though there has been some subsequent deterioration.

The following description is an expanded and revised version of that published by Henshall and Wallace, drawing on the diary and photographs of the excavation (in the possession of Henshall), the original plans and sections (Henshall 1960), and the extant remains.

The cairn covered two back-to-back chambers about 3.25 m apart, entered respectively from the N and the S, the axis of the N chamber being about 1.8 m E of that of the S chamber (plate 17). A cist had been

SUT 63

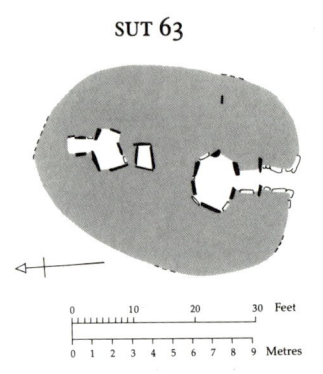

inserted in the space between them; the cist exposed in 1956 was found to have been built inside the S chamber. The cairn was oval, measuring about 13 by 10 m, and appearing at maximum a little over 1 m high, though excavation showed that the maximum height above the old ground surface was nearly 1.5 m. The cairn had been very greatly disturbed, in many areas removed to ground level, and the hollows had been infilled with relatively modern debris, all covered with blown sand and a partial layer of turf (figure 8, *1*).

The N passage and chamber were found to be greatly ruined (figure 8, *8*). About 1.2 m of the passage partly survived. A pair of upright stones, both 0.6 m long, and 0.66 and 0.6 m high, showed that the passage was 0.6 m wide. The E wall was extended northwards by a smaller overlapping stone, and southwards it was linked to the chamber by a course of walling formed by a single flat slab. The entry to the chamber was 0.53 m wide.

Five orthostats, slightly sunk into the gravel subsoil, formed the walls of a single-compartment chamber of irregular plan which measured roughly 1.1 m NNW to SSE by 2 m transversely. The orthostats were 0.45 to 0.97 m long by 0.13 to 0.25 m thick. They were 0.9 to 0.7 m high with rounded tops which seemed to be little damaged, except for the NW slab which had been shattered and was only 0.5 m high. The orthostats were 0.35 to 0.48 m apart, and on the SW side there remained two courses of the walling which had once linked them. Three large displaced slabs were found outside the chamber on the NW.

The only undisturbed deposits in the N chamber were on the E and S sides where a dark earthy layer remained 0.05 to 0.08 m thick. On this, in front of the S and SW orthostats, a few human bones lay in disorder, all from one adult except for one tooth possibly from another individual. Local knowledge that the cairn was a burial place implies that human bones had been found before 1956, and, because the pre-

historic deposits in the S chamber were largely intact until 1956, these bones had probably come from digging in the N chamber. Above the dark layer were rounded cairn stones and sand, and in this material, a little above the bones, there was a cremation. The main cremation deposit was inside the chamber, but bone was scattered round the E end of the S orthostat. The W part of the chamber was filled by modern rubbish reaching to ground level.

The S chamber, which was the better preserved, was entered by a passage 1.6 m long by 0.65 m wide. The passage walls were built of substantial flattish water-worn stones, three courses of which survived on each side to a height of 0.56 m.

The entry into the ante-chamber was between a pair of portal stones set 0.55 m apart. They were over 0.5 and 0.75 m long, 0.18 m thick, and 0.75 and 0.67 m high. The flat top surface of the E stone sloped down to the W, and was lower than the more rounded and weathered W stone. The ante-chamber seemed to have been only slightly wider than the passage. The W side was of walling similar to that of the passage, and stood 0.76 m high in five courses with the two uppermost slightly displaced. The E side of the ante-chamber had been completely removed before the excavation. The inner portal stones were 0.5 m apart at ground level but their inner edges diverged upwards. The stones were not quite opposite each other, but the E stone was found to be loose and leaning to the S and it may have been slightly displaced. The stones were 0.72 and 0.67 m long, both were about 0.25 m thick, and 0.9 and 1.15 m high. The ante-chamber was about 1 m long (figure 8, *1, 2*).

The main chamber was oval, 2.34 by 1.9 m, with the axis transverse to that of the passage. The walls consisted of the inner portal stones and four spaced orthostats with linking walling. Clockwise from the W inner portal stone, the orthostats were 1.22, 0.8, 0.74 and 0.53 m long, and about 0.2 m thick except for the pillar-like E orthostat which was 0.4 m thick; they were 1.1, 1.02, 1.07, and 0.92 m high. The three panels of walling which survived between the orthostats on the SW and NE sides were each of five courses; these reached a height of 0.73 m, and each course generally consisted of one neatly fitting flat stone. Above this level were one or two courses of larger flat corbel-type stones, the largest of which measured about 0.6 by 0.9 m. These stones rested on the walling and on the shoulders of the orthostats, the inner edges of the slabs flush with or slightly overhanging the lower walling, though one or two had slipped or been pulled back from their presumed original positions. The corbel stones were set sloping down from the chamber with their outer ends resting on cairn material. The lower walling which it is assumed had linked the E inner portal stone with the adjacent orthostat was missing at the time of the excavation though a large corbel stone remained spanning most of the gap. There was no walling between the orthostats on the NW side of the chamber; this gap was filled by a small vertical waterworn stone 0.53 m high which had been set on edge to rest against the outer sides of the adjacent orthostats. It seemed to the excavators probable that there never had been walling here. Possibly the gap had been the entry into a cell, though no trace of this was found in the totally disturbed area NW of the chamber. The small upright stone may have been *in situ*, the original closing of the entry. A slab only 0.34 m high leant against the N face of the W inner portal stone; its base was at ground level and its E end projected partly blocking the entrance.

All but one of the chamber orthostats were sandstone slabs, mostly with rounded waterworn edges. All the orthostats retained their original top surfaces, except for the damaged NE stone. Their bases were sunk slightly into the gravel subsoil.

In the areas of the cairn opened during the excavation the undisturbed lower levels were only observed around the NE side of the S chamber and in the cutting running to the E edge of the cairn (figure 8, *1*, *4*); they were also glimpsed but not investigated on the SW side of the chamber, but on the N and W sides they had been removed in antiquity and more recently. Immediately surrounding the chamber, in the NE quadrant, the cairn consisted of a core of flattish slabs laid horizontally and closely packed in up to four layers. Its maximum surviving extent was on the E side where it was about 2.5 m wide. As the core was only 0.6 m high it had the appearance of a platform. At its outer edge on the E side the slabs were laid radially and supported an upright slab 0.76 m high, also set radially with its base slightly penetrating the subsoil. The outer part of the cairn in the E cutting was less carefully constructed, using mainly rounded stones. There did not appear to be a built outer edging, but beyond the edge there was only a thin scatter of smaller stones. The interstices of the cairn stones, from the E edge up to the chamber and including the slabs of its walling, were filled by hard dark gravelly soil which varied in depth from about 0.15 m to about 0.7 m on the N side of the chamber, and roughly coincided with the existing depth of the core. Above this dark layer, in marked contrast, the spaces between the cairn stones were filled with reddish sand, and above the core the cairn material changed to rounded stones. The circumstances of the deposition of the dark soil are unclear (see ¶ 5.8), but the sand was presumably wind-blown into what were originally voids. The outer ends of the lower corbel stones which formed the upper walling of the chamber rested on the stones of the cairn core, but the upper corbel stones were at the level of the rounded stones and sand. Sealed below three of the lower corbel stones on the NE and N sides of the chamber were small deposits of small bones, both human and animal, which seem to have been left as small piles on the stones below and which had certainly been placed whilst the chamber was being built. A few bones found outside the chamber behind the N orthostat and behind the W inner portal stone were not sealed but may belong to the same series of deposits.

The edge of the cairn was also seen on either side of the entrance to the S chamber and in a cutting a little to the W. The edge consisted of flattish rounded stones, presumably the base of a rough wall-face, but remaining only one or two stones high. The cairn backing the walls of the passage and ante-chamber was not examined, and the cairn to the W of this was found to have been greatly disturbed. A cutting on the W side of the cairn revealed rounded cairn material without a built edging. Between the two chambers the original cairn had been removed to build a later cist (see below), and around the N chamber the original cairn had been disturbed to ground level or nearly so.

In 1960 about three-quarters of the lowest layer filling the main chamber and most of that in the antechamber was found undisturbed (figure 8, *1*, *5*). On the gravel floor of the main chamber, and partly pressed into it, and in the lowest part of the filling above, were scattered a few decayed and broken human and animal bones, though in the N half no bones were found (possibly due to total decay). The SE quarter had been dug out in 1956, and a complete cranium, part of another, and other bones in good condition, had been collected from floor level against the N face of the E inner portal stone, and yet more bones had been found in this general area; these bones were mainly well preserved but many were fragmentary. The excavators found charcoal (including pieces up to 25 mm long) on the floor in the SE part of the main chamber, spread over an area of about 0.9 by 1.2 m. On the central and NE part of the floor were a number of quite large thin slabs. On the floor of the ante-chamber were more bones, and beside the W wall an almost complete cranium had been protected by a small upright slab and placed on one of several small slabs which partly covered the floor. The human bones from the lowest levels in the chamber represented parts of at least three adults, a child and an infant. There were a few fragmentary animal bones and mollusc shells. The only artefact was a small piece of pumice.

The floor of the main chamber was covered by a layer of earthy material almost 0.3 m thick, its upper surface uneven. The material was dark and gravelly, mixed with small stones and some larger stones which lay at various angles, and some small pieces of charcoal. This layer was mainly hard but where it had been protected by stones it was quite loose. Over it, around the intrusive cist, the main chamber was filled with rounded stones and sand, but only about half of this deposit remained at the time of the excavation. On the dark layer and amongst the stones and sand above, up to the level of the cist capstone, there were well preserved human and animal bones, broken and in confusion. If they had not already been in this state, they had certainly been completely disturbed and damaged when the cist was inserted, and there was further disturbance during the 1956 operations. The human bones represent partial remains of at least three adults, an adolescent, several children and one or more infants. There were also some beaker sherds. Three deposits of minute fish bones, which the excavators had found puzzling but had assumed to be part of the prehistoric deposits, have now been shown to be otters' droppings. (Details of the filling and burials are given in ¶ 6.4–10 and Appendix 2; the otter droppings were identified by A. Jones, *in litt.*).

The N part of the main chamber was occupied by the cist found in 1956, at which time its S side slab was removed (figure 8, 7). The base of the cist was slightly above the top of the dark filling. Internally the cist measured 0.6 by 0.9 m, and 0.46 m deep. Against the N side slab there was a smaller slab, and 0.3 m to the W there was another vertical slab, possibly intended as additional support for the very large capstone. It is probable that the cist was built of corbel stones from the dismantled upper walling of the chamber. The cist capstone, which measured about 2.36 by 1.47 m and 0.15 m thick and had been somewhat larger before damage to its SW side, had probably been the chamber capstone. The cist was found full of sand, in which were bones of fish, birds, and mammals, and also some miscellaneous human bones, all evidently intrusive. The burial was an adult female, with an intact food vessel in the SE corner, and jet beads about the centre of the cist; fragments of an infant about the newborn stage and a flint knife may have been with her (Henshall and Taylor).

Many bones, human and animal, and mollusc shells, were found immediately below the turf over and around the main chamber. Some of them were probably relatively modern debris, but some, notably the human bones, evidently derived from the prehistoric deposits in the chamber.

The dark layer in the main chamber extended over the ante-chamber floor (interrupted by the recent disturbance in the S part of the main chamber), though here it was about half as thick and not compacted. The passage and ante-chamber had been carefully blocked with substantial slabs placed on the floor of the passage and on the dark layer in the ante-chamber (figure 8 5, 6). At each end of the passage there were two horizontal slabs neatly placed one on the other. Between them, and in the ante-chamber, were more horizontal slabs, and on the E side of the passage there were two upright stones, the outer 0.3 and the inner 0.66 m high. An upper layer of slabs in the ante-chamber slanted up towards the main chamber. The interstices were filled with dark soil which was indistinguishable from the lowest layer in the chamber and which reached to a maximum height of 0.4 m at the inner end of the passage. Outside the entrance to the passage there was more blocking; this consisted of several layers of slabs inclined against the first flat slabs on the passage floor, and around them rounded stones extended for at least 2 m to the S and 2.7 m from E to W.

A second cist had been inserted into the cairn between the two chambers, only about 0.6 m from the N chamber (figure 8, 1, 2). This operation had entailed hollowing out the centre of the cairn and digging a rectangular pit 0.5 m deep into the gravel subsoil. The pit was just large enough to take the cist, and the small space between it and the sides of the pit was filled with gravel. The cist was built of four neatly fitting slabs bearing the thin capstone a little above ground level. The N side slab was lower than the others and had been augmented by several small flat slabs on its upper surface. The cist measured internally about 1 by 0.7 m and 0.66 m deep. It is likely that the cist slabs had come from the N chamber. The cist contained a food vessel, several beaker sherds (presumably intrusive), a speck of corroded bronze, and the decayed bones of two infants. There was a patch of charcoal in the NW corner. Over the cist floor was a layer of silt 0.05 to 0.08 m deep. The hollow above the capstone had been filled firstly with dark soil and small stones, and then by two rows of flat slabs carefully and closely laid in several layers, with the space between them and the edge of the hollow filled by more dark soil and stones.

Besides the cremation found in the N chamber, already noted, two more cremations were found during the excavation. They were in the E cutting, placed amongst the cairn material 2.5 and 1.8 m from the cairn edge and about 0.16 m above the base of the cairn. The first was a young person and probably female, the other was an adult male accompanied by half a burnt bronze razor. After the excavation, when cairn material was being removed from the E side of the cairn, more cremations were found, probably about six, one accompanied by part of a bronze blade. The exact location of only one of these is known, about 0.6 m E of the ante-chamber at nearly ground level. It was placed in a cavity; the long sides were formed by two slabs 0.31 to 0.42 m apart and the taller slab was 0.48 m high, and the short sides were formed by rough walling.

FINDS
Artefacts. In The Royal Museum of Scotland (figure 23).
1. Sherds from the rim and body of a beaker; decorated by fine comb impressions in at least two zones, each zone having two cross-hatched bands edged and divided by horizontal lines, faint transverse impressions across the rim edge; hard gritty grey fabric, breaking along the building rings (EQ 612).
2. Beaker wall sherd with a cordon, presumably from just below the rim; decorated by comb impressions in horizontal rows; gritty grey fabric, pink-buff outer surface (EQ 632).
3. Sherds from the rim, wall and base of a beaker; decorated by horizontal cord impressions; hard heavily gritted grey fabric with brown surfaces, breaking along the building rings, the outer surface abraded (EQ 633).
4. Food vessel, cracked and somewhat distorted; decorated by cord impressions, three zones of horizontal lines edge and divide two zones of chevrons (some rather disorganised), four lines around the rim bevel; coarse grey-brown fabric (EQ 611).
5. Food vessel, buried intact but found collapsed, four rim sherds but otherwise only crumbs surviving; decorated by comb impressions in horizontal lines interrupted by a zone of horizontal rows of triangular impressions from a spatula, nicks across the rim edge, concentric lines and slanting lines of comb impressions on the rim bevel; very friable black fabric, brown surfaces; rim diameter about 200 mm, height about 200 mm (EQ 634).
6. Knife made from a flake of pale grey flint, one edge steeply retouched, the opposite thin edge with very fine retouch (EQ 613).
7. Fusiform bead of jet, perforation diameter 2.2 to 2.8 mm, one end notably diagonal with sharp edges to the end facet probably indicating wear against a disc bead (EQ 614); fusiform bead of cannel coal, perforation diameter 2 to 2.9 mm (EQ 631); fourteen disc beads of cannel coal, regular in shape, 6.7 to 8.1 mm in diameter, perforations (several bevelled around the hole probably due to wear against an adjacent bead) 2.5 to 3.5 mm in diameter, thickness 0.95 to 3.2 mm (EQ 615).
8. Nearly half a bronze bifid razor, corroded, fragmented and distorted, probably about 83 mm long by 38 mm wide originally (EQ 635).
9. Part of a razor, broken at each end and probably from just above the tang, retaining both the original edges and 24 mm wide when found, 2.5 mm thick, one surface flat, the other surface curved in cross-section to form a very slight midrib (EQ 635 A).
10. Flat piece of pumice, one surface grooved by use, 30 by 23 by 8 mm (not registered).
11. Flat sandstone whorl (EQ 636).

1 From the S chamber, between the E wall and the cist, above the dark layer, some sherds and also *2* in material in this area disturbed in 1956; *3* from cist 2, in and below silty soil and presumably redeposited from the cairn; *4, 7* from the cist in the S chamber, found in 1956, though two of *7* were found displaced outside the cist in 1960; *5* from cist 2; *6* from the S chamber, either in the cist or near the cist above the dark layer; *8* from the cremation 1.2 m NE of the S chamber; *9* from one of the cremations found in the cairn SE of the S chamber in 1961; *10* from the floor of the S chamber; *11* unstratified in the cairn.

10, 11, some of *7* not illustrated.

Human remains. Some in The Royal Museum of Scotland.

These are listed in Appendix 2. A full list of the unburnt bones by R. G. Inkster is in Henshall and Wallace, 29–33. Inkster differentiated individuals in the multiple burial phases in the S chamber by letters which are quoted in brackets below, giving the minimum number of individuals present, almost certainly an underestimate (see ¶ 6.18,19). The cremations were examined by F. P. Lisowski, his full report ibid., 33–5.
1. Neolithic burials in the S chamber. First phase: three adults, *(a)* over 30 years old, *(b),* and *(e),* the bones from both the ante-chamber and the main chamber; one child 10–11 years old *(c/f)* and a tooth probably from another child, from the ante-chamber; one infant *(d)* from the ante-chamber. Second phase: three adults *(g) (h) (i)* with fragments *(p)* possibly belonging to one of them (one probably over 30 years old, one about 30 years old, one a large male and one other male judging by parts of two R femora, one female judging by innominate bone); one adolescent between 15 and 20 years old *(j/q);* three children about ten years old *(k) (l) (m),* and *(r)* possibly belonging to one of them; one child about five years old *(n);* an infant about the newborn stage *(o),* possibly another *(s).*
2. In three small deposits outside the S chamber: small bones or pieces of bones from an adult, a child about 10 years old, a child between 3 and 4 years old, an infant a few months old, an infant or foetus.
3. In the N chamber: one adult about 25 years old, one tooth possibly from another individual.
4. In the cist in the S chamber: one adult female, possibly with an infant about the newborn stage.
5. In the cist between the chambers: a child about six months old; an infant about the newborn stage.
6. Three cremations: *(a)* 1.5 m E of the S chamber, ?female, ?15–17 years old; *(b)* 2.2 m E of the S chamber, ?male, 20–26 years old; *(c)* in the N chamber, sex and age

unknown. About six more cremations were found in the E part of the cairn after the excavation, no details available.

Animal remains. In The Royal Museum of Scotland. Identified by A. S. Clarke (his detailed list is in Henshall and Wallace, 35–6).

1. In the S chamber with the first phase burials. In the main chamber: part of bird pelvis, bit of mollusc shell, fish bones. Probably from this phase: dog metapodial, bird bones, limpet. In the ante-chamber: bird vertebra, tooth probably of pole-cat, fish fin ray.

2. In the S chamber with the second phase burials. 3 bones of pig, 2 of adult sheep, 1 of juvenile sheep, 1 of ox, 2 of red squirrel, 1 of dog, 3 of great auk, 1 of guillemot, 1 of capercaillie, 1 of fulmar, 1 of gurnard, other fish bones, amphibian bones.

3. S chamber but phase uncertain. 2 bones of dog, 3 of duck (two species), fish bones probably gurnard and cod, land snail, winkle, dog-whelk.

4. Redeposited material from over the S chamber, some of it possibly modern. Various dog bones and teeth, horse tooth, 2 bones of sheep, ox tooth, 1 bone of otter, one or two bones each of blackbird, starling, gannet, guillemot, razorbill, duck, fish bones, amphibian bones, dog-whelk, cockle, winkle, scallop, Cyprina islandica, mussel, lobster.

5. In small deposits outside the S chamber. 2 or 3 bones of sheep, 1 and tooth of dog, 1 of otter, 2 of shag, 3 of great auk, 6 of guillemot, 2 of duck, 1 of grebe, 2 of gannet, fish bones, amphibian bones.

Radiocarbon dates. See p. 75.

64. KILPHEDIR

See p. 153.

65. KINBRACE FARM

Parish Kildonan
Location in the Strath of Kildonan, 3 km S of Kinbrace
Map reference NC 875287
NMRS number NC 82 NE 7
References Henshall 1972, 585, 587
Plan ASH and MKM, amended ASH and JNGR
Visited 5.10.67, 14.5.93

Description. The cairn is on a terrace on the lower slopes of the E side of the strath at a little over 150 m OD. The level site is at the upper edge of an area of enclosed pasture, 60 m E of a disused steading. Rough grazing formerly surrounded the fields, but to the N and E the hillside was afforested in the 1970s. The outlook from the cairn is to the S, down the strath. The Kinbrace Burn cairn (SUT 33) is visible across the burn 400 m to the S, and Kinbrace Hill Long and Round (SUT 34, 35) are 550 and 900 m to the NW.

The Kinbrace Farm cairn has been almost completely removed, and it is closely surrounded by the foundations of enclosures and rectangular buildings now reduced to confusing turf-covered rickles of stones. The cairn material nowhere remains more than 0.5 m high, and is composed of small rounded stones; the larger stones presumably have been removed for building nearby walls. The turf-covered surface is somewhat uneven with loose stone lying about. The cairn edge cannot be traced with any confidence. Round the N side a slight rim of cairn material indicates approximately the extent of the cairn on this side; on the NW side the cairn edge is overlain by the last vestiges of a wall, and round the S side the outer part of the cairn has been totally removed. On the NE edge of the cairn is a pointed stone, 0.65 by 0.3 m and projecting 0.4 m; its flat face is aligned NE to SW towards the entrance to the passage.

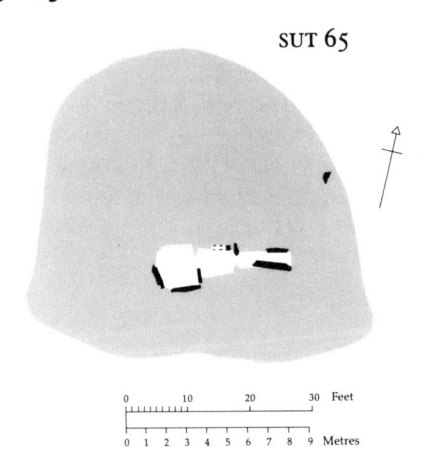

The passage, facing ENE, consists of two slabs laid on edge. They have horizontal and probably intact upper edges flush with the turf, but the space between them has been cleared out and refilled with loose stones. The slabs are 1.85 and 1.1 m long by 0.3 and 0.2 m thick, and measured from nearly ground level they are 0.5 m high. The N slab is aligned parallel to the apparent axis of the chamber and in a satisfactory relationship to the N portal stone at the entry to the chamber. The S slab is slightly skew to the axis and appears almost to block the entry. Though this is a large regular slab which does not appear to be displaced, it seems likely that the W end has been moved inwards, perhaps in an attempt to extract it. The slabs are 0.55 to 0.4 m apart, and the passage is 2.5 m long.

Five surviving orthostats of the chamber have been reduced to shattered stumps projecting 0.3 to 0.6 m above the turf. The N portal stone is 0.6 m long by 0.2 m wide, and 0.75 m high above ground level. The ante-chamber and main chamber are respectively 1.85 and 1.8 m long; the total length of the chamber is 3.9 m. The position of the N wall of the ante-chamber is indicated by a slab of which only the E tip is exposed. The S inner portal stone is 0.72 m long by

0.2 m thick. The main chamber, which was evidently wider than the ante-chamber, is represented by a slab on the S side, and another at the back which is S of and skew to the chamber axis. These slabs are 1.53 and 1.25 m long by 0.25 and 0.3 m thick.

(In Henshall, this cairn was mistakenly equated with the cairn RCAMS 134, no. 384.)

66. LEDBEG

Parish Assynt
Location 16.6 km SE of Lochinver, 8.8 km SSW of Inchnadamph
Map reference NC 234131
NMRS number NC 21 SW 5
References Ordnance Survey 1962, 50; Henshall 1972, 586, 587
Plan ASH and FML, amended ASH and JNGR
Visited 9.10.63, 31.3.93

Description. The cairn is in an area of unenclosed pasture, at 153 m OD on the lower W slopes of the moorland valley of the Ledbeg River. The cairn is in a shallow tributary valley, 50 m W of the fields of Ledbeg croft, and out of sight of the other cairns in the area.

The cairn was built on a small knoll. Except on the SE side the cairn edge is well defined, rising steeply to a rim, slightly hollowed within this, and increasing in height around the chamber. The turf-covered cairn is 1.7 m high measured from the SE side, with diameters of 18.5 to 19.5 m. On each side of the passage entrance the cairn merges into the ground and the edge cannot be traced, and on the SW side the edge has been obscured by old walling.

The entrance to the passage on the SE side of the cairn is marked by two stones set 0.6 m apart. The SW stone has fallen forwards; it is 0.92 m long, and if upright would be 0.35 m thick and 0.4 m high. Its partner leans slightly backwards; it is 0.85 m long by 0.35 m thick and projects 0.35 m. A pair of portal stones 2.3 m to the NW indicates the inner end of the passage. These are substantial blocks set 0.67 m apart; they are 1.1 and 1.14 m long by 0.46 and 0.5 m thick and project 0.46 and 0.55 m. A slightly displaced lintel tilted down to the NW rests on the portal stones. It is 1.86 m long by 1.4 m wide on the chamber axis, and 0.4 m thick.

Two orthostats appear to belong to the walls of the ante-chamber. They are 0.7 and 0.45 m long by 0.55 and 0.2 m thick, set 1.66 m apart. The SW stone has a pointed top projecting 0.45 m, but the top of the NE stone only just shows through the turf. The main chamber is defined by five orthostats. On the S side three contiguous orthostats are 0.7 to 1 m long by 0.31 to 0.35 m thick. The middle one is probably intact, projecting 0.7 m; the others project 0.4 and 0.53 m. The back-slab is the largest but not the tallest orthostat, set SW of the chamber axis and 0.73 and 0.65 m from the adjacent orthostats. It is 1.53 m long increasing to 1.7 m long above ground level, by 0.65 m thick, and projects 0.6 m with an intact upper surface which is broad and nearly horizontal. The orthostat on the N side of the main chamber is 1.16 m long by 0.4 m thick, projecting 0.8 m, but it has been badly damaged. The stone on the NE side does not appear to be an orthostat but may belong to a segment of walling; it is 0.6 m long, over 0.15 m from front to back, and projects for 0.15 m. The five orthostats protrude from a level area, and the highest is 1 m taller than the NE portal stone; this in turn is 0.5 m taller than the NE stone at the passage entrance, so the cairn material in the main chamber is about 1 m deep. The E side of the main chamber, and probably also a pair of inner portal stones between the ante-chamber and the main chamber, have been obscured or removed when the ruined main chamber was adapted as a bothy. This usage involved arranging angular stones across the entry to link with the wall to the NE. The overall length of the chamber is 6.1 m. A large slab, 1.36 by 1.12 m and at least 0.3 m thick, lies 2.9 m from the SW side of the chamber, and several other large slabs lie about the cairn.

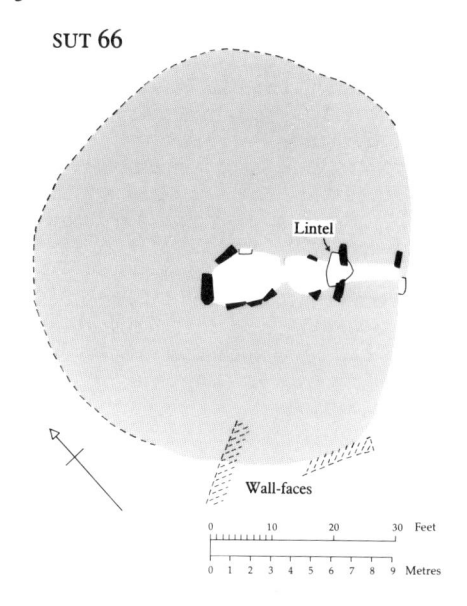

Fifty metres to the SE there is a feature, possibly a small low cairn or perhaps a more recent structure. It has a kerb of very large slabs set on edge which may well have been taken from the chambered cairn.

67. RHICONICH
See p. 153.

68. (ROS 16) CNOC CHAORNAIDH CENTRE
See p. 153.

69. (ROS 15) CNOC CHAORNAIDH NORTH-WEST
Parish Kincardine and Croick
Location 24.5 km SE of Lochinver, 3.5 km SE of Loch Borralan
Map reference NC 299084
NMRS number NC 20 NE 1
References Henshall 1963, 344, 345; Mercer 1980, 71, 152, no. 1, fig. 35
Plan ASH and JNGR
Visited 26.6.54, 12.5.93

Description. The Cnoc Chaornaidh cairns (SUT 68, 69, 70) are in an area which until recently was almost entirely moorland bearing heather and coarse grass, but large tracts of the moor have now been afforested. The cairn SUT 69 is in rough grazing on a spur of Cnoc Chaornaidh, a little below the crest, between 180 and 190 m OD. Cnoc Chaornaidh Centre and South-east (SUT 68, 70) are only 300 and 570 m to the SE, but only the former is visible. There is a long view from the cairn to the SSE down Glen Oykel to mountains in the far distance.

The site of the cairn is level, but the ground drops along the E side immediately in front of the cairn. After having been greatly robbed and disturbed, the cairn has acquired an uneven turf covering with some stones showing through. The highest parts of the cairn on the N and S sides of the chamber are 1.5 m above ground level. A structure has been built in the cairn NW of the chamber, indicated by a rectangular hollow measuring 6.3 by 3.5 m. The approximate edge of the cairn can be traced round the NW side, but the E side has been severely robbed, and on the SW side another rectangular hollow indicates where a small structure has impinged on the edge. The cairn may have been heel-shaped in plan as the E side seems to be straight, but the edge here is very indefinite with the cairn merging imperceptibly into the slope of the ground. Probably the cairn was roughly 21 m wide N to S by about 18 m E to W. On the NNW side an impressive rectangular standing stone is set with its wide face along the edge of the cairn. The stone is 1.65 m long by 0.3 to 0.4 m thick, and 1.6 m high. Two prone blocks previously noted on the edge of the cairn (Henshall) do not seem to be significant. A long narrow slab, probably a displaced lintel, lies on the ENE side of the cairn, sloping down to the SW with its NE end free of the ground. It is over 1.83 m long, 0.3 m wide and 0.45 m thick. About 2 m NE of it is a prone broken slab measuring about 1.2 by 0.7 m, but largely covered by turf.

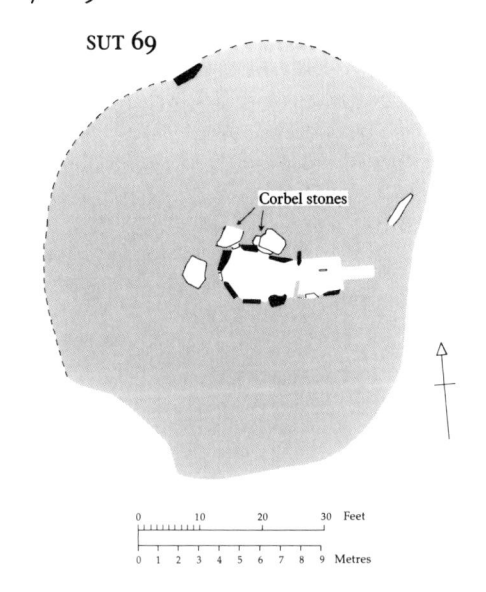

The axis of the chamber is E to W. The S wall of the ante-chamber is indicated by an orthostat, 0.9 m long by 0.18 m thick and protruding 0.2 m, and to the W of it by a horizontal slab only just protruding through the turf. A shattered vertical slab 1.08 m to the N, which is the same height as the orthostat and firmly set, was formerly interpreted as part of the N wall of a passage, implying that the chamber consisted of one compartment. However, when the overall plan is considered it seems probable that the N wall lay farther to the N, and that this part of the structure is an ante-chamber. A pair of portal stones, of which only the N stone survives, formed the entry to the main chamber. The stone is over 0.8 m long by 0.2 m thick, and projects 0.2 m with a horizontal and probably intact upper surface.

Six closely spaced orthostats form the walls of the main chamber, 3.6 m long by 2.4 m wide. The floor is level and may be nearly 1 m above ground level. The orthostats are from 0.75 to 1.25 m long, and from 0.55 to 0.25 m thick. The first orthostat on the S side is an irregular block 0.9 m high; the others are rectangular or nearly rectangular slabs, clockwise 0.65, 0.92, 1.0, 0.8 and 0.55 m high. The second and the fourth orthostats retain their flat but sloping upper surfaces. The innermost orthostat is linked to that on either side by a small horizontal slab just showing above the turf; each slab is a course of the walling which once filled the lower parts of the gaps between the orthostats. Above the northern of these wall slabs, and also between the orthostats on the N side, there are three stacked corbel stones, tilted down to the outside of the chamber. They had each in turn spanned the gap between two orthostats (the gaps increase in width upwards) and had stretched back into the cairn; the upper corbel stones in each stack are displaced outwards. The top stone in the N stack, the largest of these corbel stones, measures 1.35 by 1.07 m by 0.2 thick, and its upper surface is 0.8 m above the chamber floor. A slightly larger slab, 1.4 by 1.05 m and up to 0.4 m thick, lies W of the chamber, and several smaller slabs lie about the cairn. Rough modern walling links the two E orthostats to make the main chamber into a small enclosure.

SUT 70

70. (ROS 17) CNOC CHAORNAIDH SOUTH-EAST

Parish Kincardine and Croick
Location 25.5 km SE of Lochinver, 4.5 km SE of Loch Borralan
Map reference NC 303079
NMRS number NC 30 NW 4
References Curle 1909a, 11th June; 1909b, vol. I, 111–12; Henshall 1963, 345; Mercer 1980, 152, no. 3, fig. 35
Plan ASH and JNGR
Visited 26.6.54, 12.5.93

Description. The cairn occupies an almost level position on a hillside of rough grazing sloping down from NE to SW, at 190 m OD. Cnoc Chaornaidh North-west and Centre (SUT 69, 68) are 570 and 300 m to the NW and WNW.

The last remains of the cairn have been greatly disturbed and left with an uneven turf-covered surface. The cairn is only 0.7 m high at most on the E side and in the NW part of the chamber, and in places the cairn material has been removed to ground level. The edge of the cairn can be traced round the W side with reasonable confidence, but on the NE side the edge is obscured by the growth of peat between the cairn and the hill slope, and round the rest of the circumference the cairn merges imperceptibly into the uneven ground. The drop in ground level on the SW side gives the illusion that a much greater depth of cairn material remains there. The diameter of the cairn seems to have been about 15 m.

The axis of the passage and chamber is SE to NW. A little within the SE edge of the cairn a pair of stones 0.73 m apart marks the outer end of the passage. They are 0.76 and over 0.6 m long by 0.25 and 0.4 m thick. The SW stone is a rather irregular block leaning to the NW and projecting 0.3 m; the NE stone has a horizontal upper edge but is nearly enveloped by the greater depth of cairn material. The passage was about 1.5 m long leading to a pair of portal stones which formed the entry to the ante-chamber. The shattered stump of the SW stone is just visible in the bottom of a hollow, and a neat rectangular hollow shows clearly where its partner formerly stood.

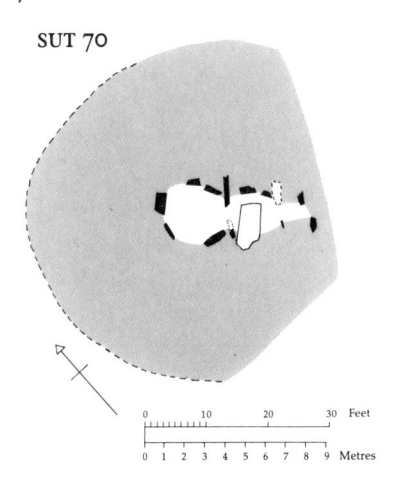

The NE wall of the ante-chamber was concave in plan, with two orthostats 0.6 and 0.82 m long by 0.33 and 0.35 m thick, projecting 0.6 and 0.56 m. Nothing remains of the SW wall where the cairn has been completely dug away. Between the ante-chamber and the main chamber is a pair of inner portal stones. The NE stone leans to the NW; it is 1.52 m long by 0.23 m thick, and in a hollow at its SW end it is exposed for 0.35 m. The shattered stump of the SW stone is flush with the turf, and the NE end is hidden; the stone is over 0.4 m long by 0.2 m thick. This stone (like the SW outer portal stone) was less damaged when seen by Curle in 1909, and he recorded that the gap between the inner portal stones was about 0.6 m wide. The ante-chamber was about 2.3 m long. Much of the interior is occupied by an impressive rectangular slab which was almost certainly the lintel over the inner portal stones. It is 2.25 m long by 1 m wide and 0.53 m thick; it slopes down slightly to the S and its SW end is broken. Curle recorded in 1909 that it was 3.35 m long, and his sketch plan seems to indicate that the slab then rested on its long side just SE of the inner portal stones.

The main chamber is defined by five orthostats, but originally there were probably seven. The orthostats are closely set 0.27 m or less apart, except for gaps of 1.47 and 0.97 m on the SW and the N sides from which presumably orthostats have been removed. The S and NW orthostats are substantial blocks, 1.2 and 1.1 m long by 0.3 and 0.46 m thick. The former is the tallest, exposed for 1.52 m which is probably close to its full original height, and the latter is only slightly lower. The other three orthostats are slighter slabs, 0.7 to 0.85 m long by 0.22 to 0.4 m thick, projecting 0.6 to 0.77 m. These three orthostats, and also those in the ante-chamber and all three portal stones, have shattered tops and obviously have been reduced in height. The main chamber is 3 m long and wide, and the total length of the chamber is 5.63 m.

71. (ROS 28) LOCH AILSH

Parish Kincardine and Croick
Location near the head of Glen Oykel, 13 km SSE of Inchnadamph
Map reference NC 311098
NMRS number NC 30 NW 2
References Henshall 1963, 350; Mercer 1980, 72, 154, no. 21
Visited 27.6.54, 1.4.93

Description. The cairn, at 150 m OD, is close to and a little above the River Oykel near its outflow from Loch Ailsh, though the loch is out of sight. The cairn is in a flat area of deep heather-covered peat which, with the surrounding hills, has recently been planted by the Forestry Commission. Strathseasgaich (SUT 73) is visible on the hillside 1.2 km to the NW. The area immediately around the Loch Ailsh cairn has been left unplanted. The cairn itself is encircled by a curious natural hollow, 2.5 to 4.5 m wide and up to 1 m deep, formed by differential growth of peat.

The cairn is covered by heather growing on a thick layer of peat. Except where there has been deep quarrying on the SE side, the cairn rises in a steep undisturbed profile to a height of 2.5 m. The diameter is 21 m N to S by 17 m transversely. The quarrying has penetrated almost to the centre of the cairn, and in the outer part has reached to nearly ground level. The exposed cairn material is water-worn stones, covered by moss. Seven large flattish slabs lie displaced in the inner part of the disturbed area, the largest about 1.1 by 0.7 by 0.23 m. Near these and close to the centre of the cairn, at a fairly high level, a hole through the peat and heather allows a glimpse into a deep cavity. On its N side it is possible to see three vertical slabs facing S, set close together and at least 0.85 m high. There can be little doubt that the cairn contains a greatly ruined chamber parts of which may survive relatively undisturbed, but the plan is not apparent. There does not appear to have been any interference with the cairn since it was first recorded in 1954.

72. (ROS 43) ALLT EILEAG

Parish Kincardine and Croick
Location in upper Glen Oykel, 14.7 km SSE of Inchnadamph
Map reference NC 313079
NMRS number NC 30 NW 5
References Henshall 1972, 564, 566, 567; Mercer 1980, 71, 152–3, no. 4
Plan ASH and JNGR
Visited 10.10.63, 25.9.93

Description. The upper part of the glen, formerly rough grazing of coarse grass and heather, has been extensively afforested in recent years. The cairn is at 170 m OD, on a hillside sloping gently down from W to E. The cairn has been left free of trees, beside a ride. There are wide views up and down the glen, and Benmore Forest (SUT 75), 700 m to the NNE, was probably in view before the planting, but Cnoc Chaornaidh South-east (SUT 70), 1 km to the W, is not visible.

The cairn is still impressive, 2.7 m high measured from the E and 2 m high measured from the W, with the highest part on either side of the chamber. The cairn is partly bare stone but is mainly covered by grass and moss. It is round with a well defined edge except on the E side. On the NW side the cairn rises steeply in an undisturbed slope, but elsewhere there has been a considerable amount of disturbance. The E side has been affected by investigations of the passage area, and by a wall built within the cairn edge. The E edge of the cairn is distorted and is overgrown and obscured by rushes, which taken together give the impression that the plan is heel-shaped. The cairn is about 18.5 m in diameter, but now measures about 20 m from E to W. A level depression immediately S of the chamber bears traces of a bothy, internally about 4.8 m NE to SW by 1.6 m transversely.

The passage has evidently faced downhill, between NNE and ENE. A hollow filled with many displaced flat slabs and rubble runs from this side of the cairn up to the chamber. Some of the slabs cover cavities, but none of the slabs is certainly *in situ*, and the precise position of the passage is not manifest.

The chamber is not accessible at present, and it may be largely intact. It has lost its capstones, and many of the upper corbel stones are exposed on the top of the cairn. The upper part of the interior of the chamber is choked with large slabs in total disorder. It is possible to peer down into a void below them which is evidently a large oval main chamber, but the side walls are not visible. The corbel stones are substantial horizontal slabs set radially to, and evidently considerably overhanging, the chamber walls. Two courses can be seen, and occasionally a third course

SUT 72

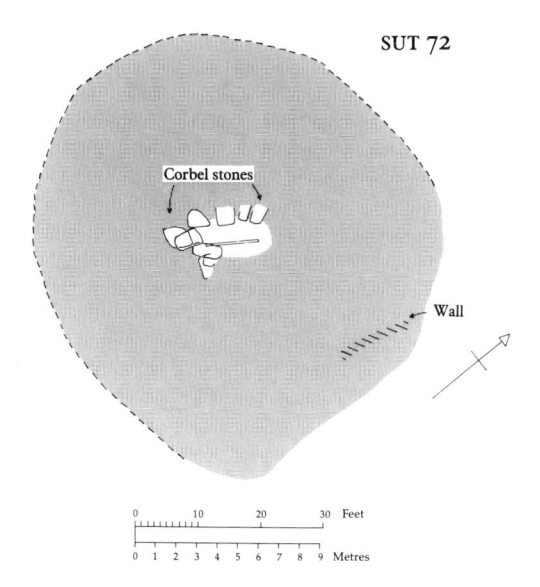

0 10 20 30 Feet
0 1 2 3 4 5 6 7 8 9 Metres

can be glimpsed. In addition, a number of corbel stones lie about on the surface of the cairn. On the NW side of the chamber is a row of four corbel stones, 0.1 to 0.2 m apart, rising from the outer to the inner end; the difference in height is about 0.4 m and the innermost stone is nearly on a level with the highest part of the cairn. A narrow slab lies radially on top of the innermost stone. The outer part of the SE side of the chamber is not visible, but to the S there are two corbel stones, one over the other, more or less *in situ* and sloping down into the chamber. To the SW of them is a more seriously displaced corbel stone, lying at right angles to its neighbours and also sloping into the chamber; the stone is partly supported by a vertical displaced slab within the chamber, described below. A corbel stone has clearly been removed from below the SW end of the displaced corbel stone. This may have happened when the bothy was built against the side of the chamber, and an entry was probably contrived into the chamber; this gap now provides the best view of the interior. At the SW end of the chamber are two corbel stones, one above the other. The lower is probably *in situ*, but the upper seems to have moved to the N and is still partly supported by the displaced corbel stone already mentioned. The corbel stones are generally between 0.9 and 1.3 m long by 0.5 to 0.85 m wide, and 0.2 to 0.3 m thick. The hidden outer part of the chamber has evidently suffered more interference, and a deep hollow has been made at the NE end of the exposed structure.

Deep within the chamber, in the void beneath the tumbled slabs which 'roof' it, there can just be seen a large vertical slab. It is 2.5 m long by 0.1 m thick and about 1 m high. Obviously it is not in its original position, now standing towards the S side of the chamber with its base probably close to floor level. It is likely to have been the capstone of the main chamber, and to have fallen into the virtually empty chamber before the displacement of the corbel stones at the SW end of the chamber.

73. (ROS 50) STRATHSEASGAICH
(Strathsheaskich)

Parish Kincardine and Croick
Location in upper Glen Oykel, 12.3 km SSE of Inchnadamph
Map reference NC 300102
NMRS number NC 31 SW 2
References Henshall 1972, 570, 571; Mercer 1980, 72, 154, no. 22
Plan ASH and FML
Visited 10.10.63, 1.4.93

Description. The cairn is on an east-facing hillside at 200 m OD, in an extensive area of forestry, formerly open moorland. The cairn overlooks the flat land around Loch Ailsh, with the Loch Ailsh cairn (SUT 71) visible 1.2 km to the SE, and a deserted croft 650 m to the ENE. The Strathseasgaich cairn is in a small area of coarse grass and heather which has been left unplanted. The site slopes down slightly from W to E.

The edge of the cairn is fairly clear with a diameter of 14 m. The cairn is an untidy mass of stones amongst which grass and moss are growing, and a number of flat slabs lie about. The central area is fairly level, 1.7 m high when measured from the SE, but due to the rising ground, considerably less in reality.

The entrance has been from the SSE. About 2 m from the edge of the cairn on this side is an upright block, 0.35 by 0.28 m and projecting 0.2 m, which probably marks the E side of the passage entrance. A small slab, 0.4 m long by 0.12 m thick and projecting 0.16 m, belongs to the W side of the inner end of the passage. Between these is a displaced slab, probably

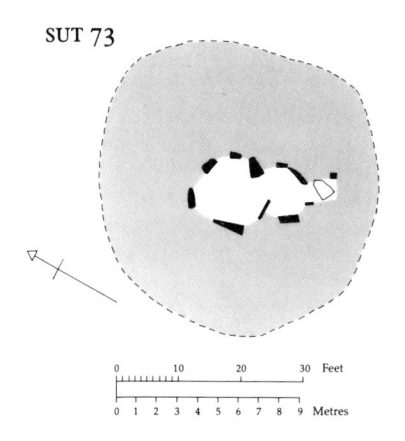

SUT 73

0 10 20 30 Feet
0 1 2 3 4 5 6 7 8 9 Metres

a lintel, which has been reduced in size. The passage was about 1.6 m long and 0.85 m wide at the inner end.

The chamber is 5.6 m long, with an irregular two-compartment plan, built with a mixture of split slabs and rounded boulders. The ante-chamber is 2.5 m wide. On the W side is an orthostat 1 m long by 0.4 m thick; it leans outwards and is broken down the S side, and the pointed top projects 0.9 m. Two contiguous orthostats form most of the E wall. They are 1.2 and 0.5 m long by 0.25 m thick, and project 0.45 m; the N orthostat is an intact boulder leaning slightly outwards. The portal stones between the ante-chamber and the main chamber are a particularly ill-matched pair, set 1.05 m apart. The W stone is a rectangular slab placed at about 45° to the chamber axis; it is 1.1 m long by 0.16 m thick, with a horizontal upper edge projecting 0.45 m. Its partner is a large boulder 1.03 m long by 0.67 m thick, slightly taller than the W stone, with a wide horizontal upper surface. Four more orthostats spaced 0.4 to 1.2 m apart define the main chamber, 3.25 m in width. The W orthostat is a split slab and the others are boulders which are probably intact. The W slab is 1.48 m long by 0.5 to 0.2 m thick, projecting 0.8 m. The end-stone is 0.95 m long by 0.47 m thick, and leans outwards. The NE and E orthostats are 0.87 and 0.46 m long by 0.43 and 0.3 m thick. A flat slab, probably a displaced corbel stone, lies horizontally between these two orthostats but projects into the chamber. Linking walling recorded between orthostats on the SW side of the main chamber (Henshall) appears to be only displaced stones. The orthostat on the W side of the ante-chamber is 0.75 m higher than the adjacent passage orthostat, and 0.4 m higher than the E portal stone and the orthostats on the E side of the ante-chamber; it is about the same height as three orthostats in the main chamber which are exposed for heights of 0.6 to 0.85 m, and only that on the E side is significantly shorter and hardly protruding.

74. ALLT A' CHAORUINN

Parish Durness
Location near the inner end of the Kyle of Durness, 6 km SSW of Durness
Map reference NC 371623
NMRS number NC 36 SE 1
References RCAMS 1911, 55-6, no. 163
Plan ASH and JNGR
Visited 29.4.92

Description. The cairn is on a hillside of rough grazing at nearly 40 m OD, 600 m from the shore (plate 3). The cairn has wide views to the W and N over the Kyle. The site is a small shelf on the hillside, but a more commanding position is available uphill immediately to the W. There are remains of prehistoric and more recent occupation extending along the hillside to SW and NE of the cairn at roughly the same elevation. Nearby there are several outcrops of distinctive black stone, clearly the source of the few black structural stones in the cairn.

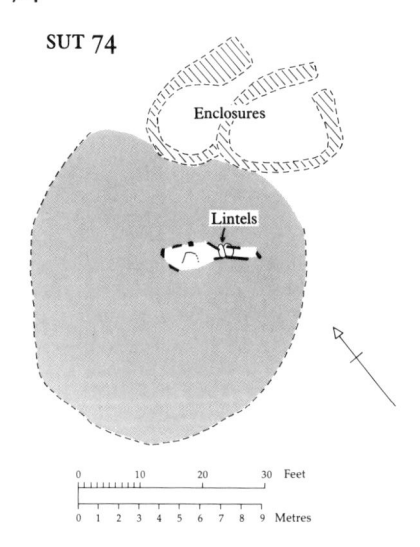

The cairn of bare rounded stones and boulders has diameters of 13.5 to 15 m. The edge is well defined except on the E side where relatively modern small enclosures impinge upon it. The cairn rises steeply to a height of 2.25 m measured from the N side, though on the SW side it is 0.5 m higher due to the addition of cairn material from the investigation of the interior. When visited in 1909 no internal structure was visible. Since then, though not recently, the passage and chamber have been cleared out virtually to ground level and refilled with flat slabs and cairn material. Ten orthostats can be seen amongst the chaos, and all but one (noted below) are quarried slabs.

The passage is 1.77 m long. At the outer end, 2.3 m from the SE edge of the cairn and set skew to the chamber axis, there is a black portal stone 0.3 m long by 0.13 m thick, which projects 0.7 m for almost its full height. To the NW a pair of slabs forms the sides of the passage. They are over 1.27 and 0.73 m long, 0.15 and 0.13 m thick, and 0.6 and 0.73 m high. The slabs are 0.45 m apart and both lean to the NE. They bear a lintel, 0.6 by 0.5 m and 0.1 m thick, though the highest part of the NE orthostat rises above the level of the lintel.

The chamber is of unusually narrow proportions, 2.74 m long by probably about 1.6 m wide. A pair of slabs just NW of the passage orthostats is set splayed to form the entrance. They are 0.43 and 0.64 m long, both are 0.1 m thick, and their true heights are about 0.9 and 0.7 m. A second lintel, 0.7 by 0.23 m and 0.2 m thick, rests on their SE ends and just overlaps the upper surface of the first lintel. On the SW side of the chamber there are two more orthostats. The first, over 0.7 m long, 0.2 m thick and over 0.75 m high when vertical, leans acutely across the chamber; the second, 0.6 m long, barely protrudes. On the NE side of the chamber two orthostats are 0.23 and 0.5 m long by 0.23 and 0.1 m thick, but only their upper parts are visible. The first is a round-topped boulder which appears to be intact and is the same height as the adjacent orthostat to the SE, i.e. 0.7 m; the other orthostat is about 0.85 m high with a narrow pointed top on which rests a corbel stone. The orthostat at the rear of the chamber is black and much weathered, 0.33 m long by 0.14 m thick; it can be estimated as about 1.6 m high, and is the highest in the chamber though protruding only 0.94 m. The chamber orthostats are 0.3 to 0.7 m apart.

75. BENMORE FOREST

Parish Kincardine and Croick
Location in upper Glen Oykel, 14.5 km SSE of Inchnadamph
Map reference NC 317085
NMRS number NC 30 NW 6
References Howell 1976; Mercer 1980, 71, 153, no. 5
Plan ASH and JNGR
Visited 13.5.93

Description. The cairn is in a small level unplanted area in the extensive conifer forest which has been established over both sides of this part of Glen Oykel; formerly the area was all rough grazing. The cairn is 40 m from the River Oykel, and a little above it at 130 m OD.

The heel-shaped cairn faces ESE (for convenience described here as E). It has been greatly reduced and disturbed, at maximum remaining 1.3 m high measured from the E side, and it is covered with grass, bracken and rushes. The edge along the E side and round the NE and SE corners is fairly clear, but on the SW side the cairn has been robbed to ground level, and round the rest of the perimeter the edge is indistinct. Across the E side the cairn is about 16 m wide, and from front to back it is roughly 17 m long. In the centre of the E side, a little within the edge of the cairn, the E side of a boulder is exposed in the slope of the cairn material. The boulder is 0.92 m long, over 0.35 m thick, and it projects 0.3 m. It is likely to be the S portal stone at the entrance to a passage which is completely hidden.

An orthostat, 3.8 m to the W, belongs to the S side of an ante-chamber. The orthostat is an intact rectangular slab 0.64 m long by 0.24 m thick, with its horizontal upper edge just visible. At about the same level as the orthostat, 1.45 m to the N, the exposed smooth S edge of a substantial horizontal slab, 0.7 m long by 0.18 m thick, appears to be part of the N wall of the ante-chamber. NW of the slab the SE part of a corbel stone is exposed. Between the ante-chamber and the main chamber is a lintel, an impressive regular block 2.8 m long by 0.87 m wide and up to 0.4 m thick. It is tilted down to the E; its upper edge is 1.65 m above the ground level to the E of the cairn and about 0.6 m above the ante-chamber orthostat. The portal stones which presumably exist below the lintel are hidden, and its S end rests on a corbel stone.

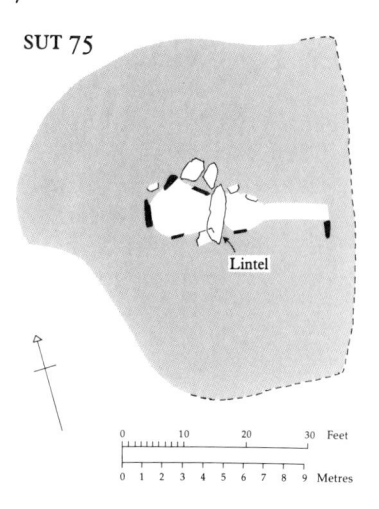

Four orthostats set 1.12 to 0.83 m apart define a main chamber of rather irregular plan, 2.9 m long from the lintel and about 2.15 m wide. Clockwise from the S, the orthostats are over 0.5, 1.24, 0.9 and 0.9 m long by 0.18, 0.3, 0.35 and 0.17 m thick. The E orthostat projects 0.5 m and its top is level with the top of the lintel, and the other orthostats are only a little lower. Besides the corbel stone already mentioned, the inner end of another can be seen on the NW side of the main chamber, and two more are fully exposed on the NE side; the corbel stone beside the lintel is 1.27 m long by 0.8 m wide and up to 0.15 m thick. All three have been displaced outwards.

76. BLANDY

Parish Tongue
Location on the E side of the Kyle of Tongue, 3.3 km NE of Tongue
Map reference NC 622601
NMRS number NC 66 SW 6
References Ordnance Survey Record Card
Plan ASH and JNGR
Visited 26.10.92

SUT 76

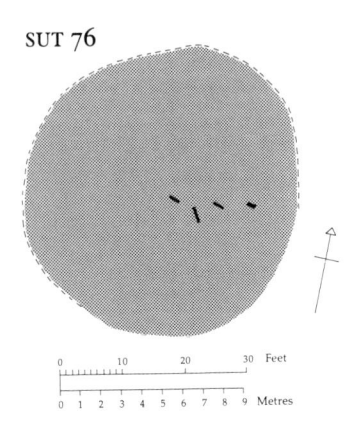

Description. The cairn is in heather moorland, on a narrow shelf between enclosed land sloping down to the valley on the W and a steep rise on the E, at about 110 m OD.

The heather-covered cairn has a diameter of 13.5 m. The cairn material is irregular angular stones. The cairn is steep-sided, 1.7 m high, with the top slightly hollowed. In this central area three slabs project, and a fourth slab is exposed in a hollow made long ago into the E side of the cairn. From E to W the slabs are 0.42, 0.6, 0.85, and 0.65 m long by 0.26 to 0.12 m thick. They project 0.3 to 0.35 m, though the true height of the first slab is considerably less than that of the others. The arrangement of the slabs does not suggest the plan of a chamber, but the existence of a small chamber within the cairn cannot be entirely ruled out.

77. COILLELYAL

Parish Farr
Location in Strathnaver, 2.2 km SSE of Bettyhill
Map reference NC 717598
NMRS number NC 75 NW 49
References Ordnance Survey Record Card
Plan ASH and JNGR
Visited 27.10.92

SUT 77

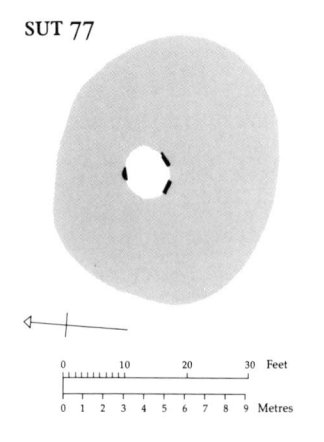

Description. The cairn is on the W edge of the plateau of undulating moorland which stretches eastwards from the Naver valley. The actual site is at about 85 m OD, on the edge of a small shelf facing W. The cairn is the northernmost of three closely-spaced cairns built in line along the shelf; the other two are larger but with no features exposed. The ground drops away gently on the W side of the chambered cairn, and more steeply just to the N where the shelf ends. The cairns are surrounded by an extensive prehistoric field system.

The cairn is made of irregular field stones. The edge of the cairn is overgrown with peat and heather, and as it merges into the ground it is difficult to define precisely. The diameter N to S is about 11 m and E to W is about 13 m. The cairn has been reduced in height, remaining 1.1 m high measured from the E side, and, due to the slope of the ground below the cairn, 1.7 m high measured from the W side. In the centre bare stones are exposed in an area about 7.5 m in diameter, though within the chamber the surface is lower and covered with heather.

Three orthostats project at the centre of the cairn and appear to be part of a small chamber, the plan of which is not evident. The two orthostats on the S side are rectangular in section, set obliquely to each other 0.65 m apart. They are 0.65 and 0.75 m long by 0.23 m thick; the SW orthostat is splitting into vertical slivers. The third orthostat is 1.93 and 1.85 m from the other two. It is an irregular block with a flat face set towards the chamber, 0.65 m long by 0.25 m thick in the centre. All three orthostats are pointed and are about the same height; they project 0.4 m, though in hollows made beside the S orthostats it can be seen that their true height is hardly more than 0.7 m.

78. CRAIG A' BHLAIR

Parish Dornoch
Location above the SW side of Strath Fleet, 8.7 km W of Golspie
Map reference NH 737998
NMRS number NH 79 NW 1
References RCAMS 1911, 48, no. 135
Plan ASH and JNGR
Visited 21.5.91

Description. The cairn is in a extensive area of upland moor, at 167 m OD. The actual site is relatively level, sloping down slightly from N to S across the chamber, but Craig a' Bhlair rises steeply immediately to the N. The ground drops away to a shallow valley on the S, and there are widespread remains of prehistoric settlement in this area. Southwards from the cairn there is a wide view over undulating moor

SUT 78

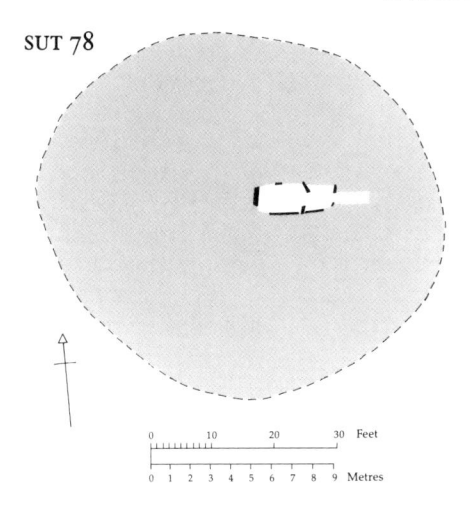

and across Strath Carnaig, a tributary of the River Fleet; to the E there is a view down a minor valley and across the mouth of Strath Fleet. Torboll (SUT 58) is 500 m to the SE and was visible from the cairn before afforestation.

The cairn is of irregular bare stones. The edge is fairly clear though overgrown with heather, and gives diameters of 19.5 m E to W by 17.5 m N to S. The greatest height is 2.3 m at the back of the chamber, measured from the E.

The tops of eight orthostats which define the chamber are just visible amongst the loose cairn material, and cavities beside them sometimes allow a little more of these vertical slabs to be seen. They are substantial roughly rectangular blocks, mostly with fairly level upper edges; it is difficult to estimate their height due to the uneven ground level around the cairn. The chamber, aligned E to W, is 3.6 m long. A pair of outer portal stones, set 0.6 m apart and somewhat skew to each other, forms the entry into the ante-chamber. The stones are 0.24 and 0.44 m long by 0.06 and 0.13 m thick, and the S stone, which is only slightly higher than its partner, can be seen for a depth of 0.4 m. On the S side of the ante-chamber is a slab the same height as the adjacent outer portal stone; the slab is over 0.8 m long by 0.06 m thick with an intact upper edge. It butts against the S inner portal stone, and probably against the S outer portal stone though the actual junction is obscured. The inner portal stones are skew to each other and staggered, set 0.7 m apart. They are over 0.42 and 0.6 m long, by 0.14 and 0.2 to 0.13 m thick. They are the same height, and the N stone has an intact upper surface. The main chamber is about 2.25 m long by 1.25 m wide. The back-slab is over 0.9 m long by 0.27 m thick; it is the tallest orthostat, projecting 0.5 m above the cairn material and 0.4 m higher than the adjacent S side-slab. This stone is over 1.44 m long (its W end not visible) by 0.08 m thick, and it probably butts against the S inner portal stone. Only the jagged shattered tip of the N side-slab can be seen, 0.35 m long, 0.1 m thick, obviously part of a much longer slab.

79. KNOCKAN EAST

Parish Assynt
Location 16 km SE of Lochinver, 1.5 km SW of Elphin
Map reference NC 205104
NMRS number NC 21 SW 13
References Ordnance Survey 1974, 75
Plan ASH and JNGR
Visited 30.3.93

Description. The cairn, with Knockan West (SUT 80), appears to relate to the area of cultivatable ground belonging to the crofts of Knockan and Elphin, two small isolated communities in a mountainous and largely uninhabited region. Knockan West is visible at a slightly higher level only 100 m to the WSW. Knockan East is at 150 m OD, in a level position at the foot of a steep hillside and a little above the boggy valley floor. The land around the cairn was once cultivated, and the present enclosed pasture is only a short distance away. A more commanding position for the cairn was available on a rise just to the NE.

The original size and plan of the cairn are uncertain as the present edge is the result of encroachment by agriculture, and a projection to the NE appears to be mainly field-gathered stones. On the NW side the cairn has been quarried away to ground level, and from here the remaining turf-covered cairn material misleadingly appears to be 1.7 m high.

A group of five rectangular quarried orthostats, rather irregularly placed, indicate the presence of a

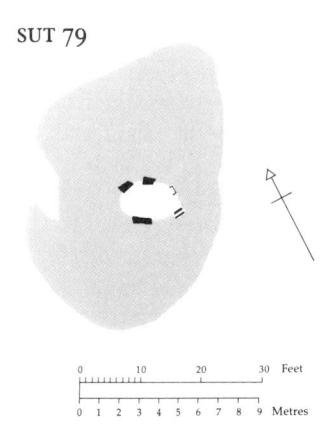

SUT 79

chamber. On the W side the three largest protrude from the level top of the cairn. From SW to NE these orthostats are 0.9, 0.62 and 0.55 m long by 0.33, 0.28 and 0.38 m thick. Their overall heights are difficult to estimate. They are exposed for 0.48, 0.6 and 0.35 m; the first two are about the same height, but the third orthostat has apparently been damaged and reduced. On the E side of the group a fourth orthostat leans to the E. It is 0.5 long by 0.2 m thick; its top is just visible, but if upright it would probably be about the same height as the other orthostats and would stand W of its recorded position. On the SE side of the group the damaged fifth orthostat projects 0.33 m where the cairn surface is lower; the stone is 0.45 m long and was about 0.22 m thick before splitting vertically.

80. KNOCKAN WEST
Parish Assynt
Location 16 km SE of Lochinver, 1.5 km SW of Elphin
Map reference NC 204104
NMRS number NC 21 SW 12
References Ordnance Survey 1974, 75
Plan ASH and JNGR
Visited 30.3.93

Description. The cairn is unusually sited on a very steep north-facing hillside of rough pasture, at 160 m OD. Knockan East (SUT 79) is visible only 100 m to the ENE.

The cairn was built on a small platform which slopes gently down from S to N. The cairn has been greatly disturbed and quarried, though to the N of the centre it is still 2 m high measured from the W side. It has a thin turf cover with many stones showing through. The edge round the NW side is fairly clear and indicates that the original diameter was about 17 m, though displaced stone has tumbled down the slope to the W. On the N side the edge has been disturbed by the insertion of an electricity pole. Round the SE side the cairn merges into the ground and the edge has been covered by hill-wash lodged against the cairn. A hollow has been made into the cairn near the centre, in the E side of which two orthostats are exposed above cairn material which is likely to be 1 m or so deep. They are rectangular slabs, set nearly parallel 1.48 m apart. The S slab is 0.8 m long by 0.35 m thick, and projects 0.35 m, with a probably intact horizontal upper surface. The N slab is 0.3 higher with a pointed top; it is 0.9 m long by 0.35 m thick and projects 1 m. To the SE of this stone is a horizontal slab 0.8 m long, over 0.5 m from front to back, and 0.2 m thick. These slabs appear to be part of a ruined chamber. A second smaller hollow to the E of them is filled with loose stones.

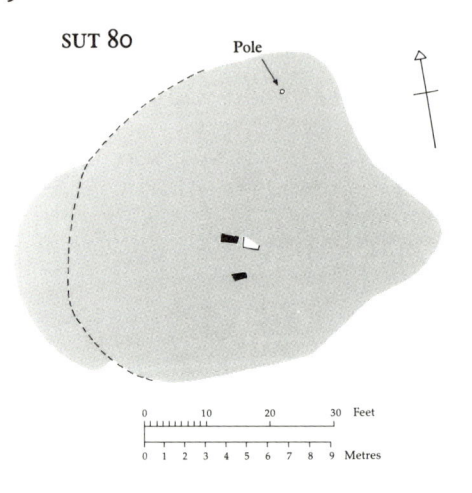

81. LOCH BORRALAN SOUTH
Parish Assynt
Location 20 km SE of Lochinver, 200 m above the E shore of Loch Borralan
Map reference NC 265110
NMRS number NC 21 SE 3
References RCAMS 1911, 5, no. 15; Mercer 1980, 43, 128, no. 38
Visited 28.3.93

Description. The cairn is on a moorland hillside overlooking the loch, at 160 m OD. Loch Borralan East (SUT 43) is visible on the same hillside 0.3 km to the NW. The cairn is 2 m high, but due to the gentle slope of the site, it is about 1 m higher measured from the S side. The cairn, rising steeply from a well defined edge, has a diameter of 15 m, and is covered with heather except where disturbance on the E side and the top has exposed cairn material of rounded and angular stones. Lying on and in the cairn material, and mainly at a relatively high level, are a number of flat slabs, and there can be little doubt that they belong to the upper part of a hidden roofless chamber and a passage running to the NNE.

A line of five irregularly shaped flattish slabs extends from 3 m within the NNE edge towards the centre of the cairn for a distance of 3.1 m. They appear to have been lintels of a passage, now mostly somewhat displaced. The largest, innermost, slab measures 1 by 0.4 m and 0.4 m thick, with a void below and extending to the N, but nothing can be seen of the walls of the putative passage. To the SE of this lintel there is a flat horizontal slab 1.1 m long which is probably a corbel stone, set radially to the assumed position of the chamber in the centre of the cairn. On the SW side of the central disturbed area, partly exposed in a hollow, is a stack of three slabs which is likely to be part of the wall on this side of the chamber.

A number of large flat slabs which lie near the SE side of the supposed passage and around the area of the chamber are probably displaced corbel stones.

The cairn was in much the same condition when visited in 1909 (RCAMS), and there has been only slight superficial recent disturbance.

82. TRALIGILL
Parish Assynt
Location 17 km E of Lochinver, 1 km E of Inchnadamph
Map reference NC 261217
NMRS number NC 22 SE 1
References RCAMS 1911, 4, no. 9
Visited 30.3.93

Description. The cairn is in Gleann Dubh, a short valley drained by the River Traligill. The river issues from the impressive Ben More Assynt range of mountains which dominate the valley, and flows into Loch Assynt at the foot of the valley. The valley floor is rough grazing of coarse grass and heather. The cairn is sited on a small limestone outcrop at 114 m OD, in a relatively flat area above a steep drop to the river (plate: frontispiece).

The large cairn of bare irregular rounded stones has suffered considerable interference in the past, including robbing around the edges which are covered by turf. On the E side robbing has left the appearance of a platform, and the W side has been hollowed near where an old wall clips the edge. The cairn is 20 m in diameter, and 2.5 m high. A large stone exposed 4.3 m from the S edge of the cairn is almost certainly a lintel, probably *in situ*. It is a rounded rectangular block set on edge, aligned almost E to W, 1.6 m long, 0.5 m wide, and over 0.6 m deep; the lower edge is not visible. On the S side of the cairn, 1.8 m within the edge, two upright slabs are partly exposed 0.8 m apart. They are 0.55 and 0.75 m long by 0.2 and over 0.4 m thick, and project for 0.2 and 0.5 m. Their position, slightly to the E of the expected axis of the passage, indicates that they are unlikely to be portal stones at its outer end. On top of the cairn are several flattish slabs which contrast in character with the cairn material and which are likely to be displaced corbel stones from the vault of the chamber. It is probable that a passage and chamber remain substantially intact within this cairn.

Postscript

In 1995 staff of the Afforestable Land Survey of the RCAHMS discovered two greatly denuded chambered cairns (visited by us 4.7.95). They are in the parish of Rogart, in tributary valleys of Strath Rogart, only 1.5 km NNW and 0.7 km NE of Pittentrail (SUT 50).

SUT 83. CREAG A'BHATA
Map reference NC 719035. *NMRS number* NC 70 SW 52.
The cairn, 14.5 to 13 m in diameter and up to 1.5 m high, is edged by kerb-stones. The entrance on the SSE is indicated by a lintel. On the E and W sides of the hollowed centre of the cairn two orthostats 1.85 m apart project 0.55 and 0.4 m.

SUT 84. MILLNAFUA BRIDGE
Map reference NC 731026. *NMRS number* NC 70 SW 51.
The cairn, 16.5 m in diameter and up to 1.6 m high, is partly edged by substantial kerb-stones, but the E side has been totally removed. On the SE side a pair of low portal stones with a displaced lintel in front of them mark the passage entrance. A second pair of portal stones about 1 m NW mark the inner end of the passage. Walling and a fifth portal stone belong to the NE side of the ante-chamber, about 1 m long. The position of the main chamber is only indicated by a hollow in the cairn.

Appendix 1

Structures previously published as chambered cairns or long cairns, but not included in the Inventory

SUT 1 ABERSCROSS, *Strathfleet*
Map reference NH 765997. *NMRS number* NH 79 NE 2.
References RCAMS 1911, 98, no. 286; Henshall 1963, 304.
A greatly-robbed cairn which retains a few kerbstones. The one 'horn' (which suggested the possibility that the cairn might be neolithic) appears to consist of field clearance stones. Visited 20.5.91.

SUT 30 GRUMBEG, *Loch Naver*
Map reference NC 634384. *NMRS number* NC 63 NW 10.
References Horsburgh 1867; Henshall 1963, 319; 1972, 576, 577.
The structure was listed as possibly the remains of a chamber on the basis of Horsburgh's description and illustration (see Henshall 1963, plate 8A). Subsequently the structure was identified at a point some 50 m NW of an old burial ground, but its interpretation as a ruined chamber was not convincing (Henshall 1972). Reconsideration of the remains suggests that the upright stones were probably part of the foundation of a wall (similar wall foundations may be seen here and there amongst the buildings and field walls of the extensive settlement in which the 'chamber' lies), and the cairn-like material around the structure is probably field-gathered stone. The 'covering stone' recorded by Horsburgh, no longer in place, was only about 1.8 m long and thus did not cover the whole 'chamber'; it is likely to have been a relatively modern makeshift arrangement, and the stone may well have been brought from the burial ground where many grave stones lie about, and indeed it may have been returned there. Visited 23.5.92.

SUT 38 LAIRG MOOR NORTH, *near Lairg*
Map reference NC 593074. *NMRS number* NC 50 NE 26.
References RCAMS 1911, 156–7, no. 454; Henshall 1963, 322.
The turf-covered remains of a cairn 21 m in diameter. The edge is fairly clearly defined and the one 'horn' (which suggested the possibility that the cairn might be neolithic) is likely to be the result of the former agricultural activity which is evident all around. Visited 24.5.91.

SUT 39 LAIRG MOOR SOUTH, *near Lairg*
Map reference NC 590073. *NMRS number* NC 50 NE 37.
References RCAMS 1911, 156, no. 453; Henshall 1963, 322.
A much-robbed turf-covered cairn, 16 m in diameter, from which some earthfast blocks of stone protrude, but as they are not central and make no obvious pattern they are unlikely to be remains of a chamber. Visited 24.5.91.

SUT 47 MELVICH, *on the N coast*
Map reference NC 882644. *NMRS number* NC 86 SE 1.
References ONB 1873, No. 20, 99; RCAMS 1911, 85, no. 246; Henshall 1963, 326; Mercer 1981, 9, 10, 131, no. 247b.
The cairn, 24.5 m in diameter and up to 1.6 m high, has been reduced to a substantial mass of loose stone, the centre covered by a tangle of gorse. An upright stone, 9.4 m from the N edge, faces NE and SW; it is 0.9 m long, 0.3 m thick, and projects 0.4 m though its true height is probably over 1 m. Its off-centre position, taken with its alignment, indicate that it is unlikely to be part of a chamber. A cremation in a small cist seems to have been found in the cairn some years before 1873 (ONB). Visited 29.9.93.

SUT 56 STRONECHRUBIE, *near Inchnadamph*
Map reference NC 248192. *NMRS number* NC 21 NW 1.
References Henshall 1963, 330; 1972, 580.
This enigmatic structure was removed in 1962 during road widening. The interpretation of a small arc of stones as the ruined façade of a cairn is very dubious; it is likely that the remains were no more than the base of an old curved wall with field-gathered stones behind it.

SUT 59 CAMORE WOOD, *near Dornoch*
Map reference NH 771897. *NMRS number* NH 78 NE 1.
References RCAMS 1911, 49, no. 141; Henshall 1972, 580.
The cairn, in a mature Forestry Commission plantation, had been severely robbed before 1909. The diameters are roughly 17 to 22 m. Near the centre is a stone projecting for 0.55 m and leaning to the E; it is square in cross section measuring 0.35 by 0.35 m. The true vertical height of the stone above ground level would probably be over 1 m. A second slab is ex-

posed in a small hollow 4.4 m to the SSW. It is a regular block of quartzite, facing E and W, over 1.1 m long by 0.22 m thick, and projects 0.4 m. The true height is probably 1 m, but it was once higher as the broken top lies close by. The relationship of the stones does not suggest that they are part of a chamber, and they are unlikely to be parts of cists, so the character of the cairn is unclear. Visited 18.4.91.

SUT 62 DUN RIASKIDH, *on the N coast*
Map reference NC 687614. *NMRS number* NC 66 SE 1.
References RCAMS 1911, 184, no. 529; Henshall 1972, 582; Mercer 1981, 6, 107, no. 5.
The cairn-like structure, on the top of an isolated rocky knoll, has an overall spread of about 17 m including stone displaced downhill, and a height of 1.6 m on the S side. On the summit a group of upright slabs protrudes up to 0.35 m, and forms a rough oval 5.5 m E to W by 4.5 m N to S. They seem to be on the inner side of a ring of stony material about 2.5 m thick. In the interior is a disorganised mass of lintel slabs and three earthfast upright slabs. The structure appears to be a house with spaced uprights in the inner face of the wall, and with a series of uprights which helped to support a partly lintelled roof. A hollow on the N or seaward side probably indicates the position of the entrance. Visited 29.9.93.

SUT 64 KILPHEDIR, *Strath of Kildonan*
Map reference NC 995186. *NMRS number* NC 91 NE 32.
References Ordnance Survey 1960, 44; Henshall 1972, 585.
The cairn, 15 to 16 m in diameter and 1.5 m high, has been greatly disturbed. Near the centre an upright stone facing NW and SE is exposed in a deep hollow. The stone is 1.2 m long, 0.3 m thick, and 0.6 m high, its base at about ground level, its NE end about 6 m from the N edge of the cairn. The off-centre position and the orientation of this stone make it unlikely that it is the back-slab of a chamber, as formerly suggested. The two other stones recorded in 1972 are respectively a loose boulder and a probable kerb-stone. There is no evidence that the cairn contained a chamber. Visited 30.9.93.

SUT 67 RHICONICH, *on the NW coast*
Map reference NC 253517. *NMRS number* NC 25 SE 1.
References Welsh 1969, 51; Henshall 1972, 586.
The round cairn, about 10.5 m in diameter, incorporates a large boulder. The cairn has been drastically modified to form an internally rectangular shelter, itself now greatly ruined. In a hollow on the NW side of the boulder there were formerly three upright slabs but only that on the NW side may be *in situ*. There is no evidence that the cairn contained a chamber. Visited 1.5.92.

SUT 68 (ROS 16) CNOC CHAORNAIDH CENTRE, *Glen Oykel*
Map reference NC 301081. *NMRS number* NC 30 NW 3.
References Henshall 1963, 344; Mercer 1980, 152, no. 2.
The cairn, consisting of an untidy mass of loose stones, is rectilinear in plan though presumably it was originally round. The diameter is about 15 m and the height on the SW side is about 3 m. The cairn appears to have been built beside, and partly over, a natural feature comprising a group of large irregular slabs and several very large boulders. These are heaped on the S side of the cairn, the largest boulder being 2.2 m long. On the SSW edge of the cairn two elongated boulders lie parallel 1.4 m apart, aligned SSW to NNE. About 3 m within the SSW edge, and below a tilted slab which resembles a lintel, there can be glimpsed a rectangular vertical slab aligned N to S with a void on its W side. The slab looks like part of some structure, but it does not lead into the centre of the cairn. It is difficult to interpret the puzzling remains as a chambered cairn. Visited 28.3.93.

The following structures were not included in Henshall 1963 or 1972, and therefore do not have code numbers, but they have been published either on recent editions of the 1:10,000 OS maps or elsewhere, as chambered cairns, possible chambered cairns, or possible long cairns. An asterisk * indicates that the writers are in agreement with the reports (held in the NMRS) made in the 1970s by the officers of the former Archaeology Division of the Ordnance Survey.

ACHAMORE, *near Bettyhill*
Map reference NC 741577. *NMRS number* NC 75 NW 58.
Probably a very ruined dun on which are the foundations of two rectangular structures; unlikely to have been a chambered cairn. Visited 23.5.92.

LOCH HOPE
Map reference NC 468589. *NMRS number* NC 45 NE 2.
A hut circle, subdivided by walls in antiquity. Visited 30.4.92.

KYLE OF DURNESS
Map reference NC 373631. *NMRS number* NC 36 SE 2.
Reference RCAMS 1911, 56, no. 164.
A round cairn with a central cist. Visited 29.4.92.

KYLE OF DURNESS
Map reference NC 388655. *NMRS number* NC 36 NE 47.
Reference Reid, David and Aitken 1967, 37, no. 14.
* A small structure, the date and purpose of which are unknown. Visited 29.4.92.

LAIRG MUIR, *near Lairg*
Map reference NC 587071. *NMRS number* NC 50 NE 2.
References Welsh 1973, 55; Kinnes 1992b, 83.
A natural feature. Visited 27.4.92.

LOUBCROY 6, *Glen Oykel*
Map reference NC 315088. *NMRS number* NC 30 NW 7.
Reference Howell in Mercer 1980, 153.
* Possibly a small cairn at the higher end of a slight ridge, the orthostats at the lower end of the ridge partly or entirely a natural feature (there are many outcrops in this area which tend to break up into slabs). Visited 1.4.93.

LOUBCROY 7, *Glen Oykel*
Map reference NC 315090. *NMRS number* NC 30 NW 8.
Reference Howell in Mercer 1980, 153, figure 35.
* A fortuitous arrangement of boulders and slabs, though two large parallel slabs appear to have been deliberately set. Visited 1.4.93.

LOUBCROY 8, *Glen Oykel*
Map reference NC 314090. *NMRS number* NC 30 NW 9.
Reference Howell in Mercer 1980, 153, figure 35.
* A natural deposit of boulders with exposed slabby rock. Visited 1.4.93.

LOUBCROY 9, *Glen Oykel*
Map reference NC 315088. *NMRS number* NC 30 NW 10.
Reference Howell in Mercer 1980, 71, 153, figure 35.
* A natural feature. Visited 1.4.93.

SKELPICK, *Strathnaver*
Map reference NC 724568. *NMRS number* NC 75 NW 11.
Reference Stuart 1868, 296.
Stuart recorded 'an extensive group of small cairns, with a large central one yet undisturbed. Its chamber can be detected from the top'. The large round cairn is 3 m high with a large flat slab exposed at a high level, but there is no evidence at present of a chamber.

Appendix 2

Human bone recovered from the excavations at Embo (SUT 63)

Condensed from the list by R. G. Inkster in Henshall and Wallace, 29–33.

1. S chamber, first phase, on the floor of the main chamber.
Adult(s): reconstructed skull of an individual over 30 years old *(a)*, fragments of a skull including pieces of mandible and maxilla in which there had been an abscess and consequent loss of the L lateral incisor during life *(b)*, pieces of ulna, 1 metacarpal, 3 phalanges, cuboid, pieces of tibia, patella, 2 whole and pieces of other vertebrae, R scapula, L clavicle, ankle bone. (See also the jaw and teeth listed under 5.)

2. S chamber, first phase, on the floor of the antechamber.
Adult(s): R maxilla, fragment of skull vault, fragments of ribs and long bones, 3 teeth from an individual over 20 years old. Children 10–11 years old: most of the vault of a skull *(c)*, 10 loose teeth probably mostly from this skull but at least one probably from another individual, fragment of scapula, piece of rib. Infant about the newborn stage: fragments of skull and long bones *(d)*.

3. S chamber, taken out in 1956 and considered to be from the first phase.
Adult(s): incomplete skull of an individual between 25 and 40 years old *(e)*, 5 vertebrae, a few small pieces of long bones, metacarpal, 3 phalanges, calcaneum, 2 metatarsals, part of scapula. Child or children 10–13 years old: lower jaw *(f)* probably belonging to the skull *(c)*, incomplete L and R femora, part of humerus, pieces of tibia, pieces of R pelvis.

4. S chamber, second phase in the main chamber.
Adults: fragments of unusually thick skull vault *(g)*, incomplete skull vault of an individual about 30 years old *(h)*, fragments of a skull *(i)* which may be part of *(e)* above [*(i)* was found in disturbed material but was thought at the time of excavation to have come from the second phase], part of a mandible, part of a large male femur and tibia, female innominate bone, L radius and piece of L radius, ulna, piece of fibula, fragments of R and L scapulae, L calcaneum, 2 phalanges, 3 whole and three incomplete metacarpals, 2 phalanges, 2 vertebrae, humerus, 4 teeth. (See also fragments of femur listed under 8.) Adolescent between 15 and 20 years old: tooth, most of L ulna, part of radius *(j)*. Three children all about 10 years old: piece of tibia *(k)*, piece of tibia and shaft of L femur *(l)*, part of L femur *(m)*, a few ribs, R and L parts of pelvis, piece of scapula, tooth. Child about 5 years old: part of mandible, part of humerus *(n)*. Infant about the newborn stage: pieces of skull, pieces of long bones, clavicle, part of tibia *(o)*. (See also bones listed under 8.)

5. Disturbed material from above the S chamber, mostly from the second phase.
Adult: Fragments of skull *(p)*, fragments of mandible (a tooth from the first phase in the main chamber and another tooth thought to be from this phase fit two of the sockets, so presumably the jaw came from the first phase burials), 2 metacarpal, 2 phalanges, L scaphoid, piece of ulna, fragments of long bones, 2 teeth, vertebrae, rib fragments, fragments of L innominate bone, parts of male R femur, shaft of L femur, L and 2 R tibiae, R heel bone, part of L and R humerus, many fragments of long bones. Adolescent about 15 years old: pieces of mandible *(q)*, probably belonging to *(j)*. Child about 10 years old: parts of scapula and radius and humerus, ankle bone, heel bone *(r)*, probably belonging to *(k)*, *(l)* or *(m)*. Infants, foetal or newborn: pieces of skull, humerus, 3 femora *(s)*, some probably belonging to *(o)*.

6. Deposits outside the S chamber.
i) Behind the NE orthostat. Adult: 3 metacarpals, 6 phalanges, 1 tooth. Child about 10 years old: part of humerus. Infant or foetus: pieces of skull vault.
ii) Behind the N orthostat. Adult: 3 phalanges, spine of a vertebra. Child between 3 and 4 years old: fragment of mandible. Infant a few months old: piece of skull vault.
iii) Behind the W inner portal stone. Adult: 2 teeth. Child about 4 years old: R maxilla, matching fragment of mandible listed under ii.

7. N chamber.
Adult about 25 years old: fragments of skull including part of mandible, most of L clavicle, pieces of

radius and ulna, 4 carpal bones, pieces of metacarpals and phalanges, teeth including one possibly from another individual.

8. From the cist in the S chamber.
Adult female: 2 pieces of L and R mandible, L and fragment of R female innominate bone, piece of sacrum, fragments of vertebrae and ribs and tibia, pieces of L and R humerus, parts of L ulna, shaft of radius, part of L fibula and another fragment, cuboid, patella, pieces of L and R femora. (Also fragments of a second R femur, evidently one of these being intrusive from the second phase burials. Also fragments of skull vault and piece of humerus from an infant about the newborn stage, possibly with the female burial but as likely to be intrusive.)

9. From the cist between the chambers.
At W end, child about six months old: part of R maxilla, teeth, upper half of L femur. At E end, infant about the newborn stage: pieces of skull vault, part of humerus.

Appendix 3

Note on the location of the finds at The Ord North, SUT 48.

The findspots were recorded in the excavator's Finds Register and Notebook, and on annotated plans and sections (Corcoran 1967a).

In the main chamber the horizontal locations were recorded in the Finds Register by co-ordinates related to a grid of 1 ft (0.3 m) squares aligned N to S and E to W (their position shown on a large scale pencil plan). The sections through the main chamber (figure 20) were taken on the same grid, intersecting at 75′ W and 72′ N. The quadrants were noted in the Finds Register as NEQ, NWQ, SEQ, SWQ. The vertical positions of artefacts were recorded in relation to a datum line 'TBM B' or 'horizontal', almost 7 ft (2.08 m) above the old ground surface, as shown on the only completed section; the height of the datum can be checked by the depth recorded for two soil samples known to come from the clay floor. The floor was uneven, and in the following list it has been taken as 6 ft 10 ins below datum as a fair average. The levels of three other datum lines have not been ascertained.

In the ante-chamber (with two exceptions) the horizontal positions of finds were recorded only in general terms or not at all. Several datum lines were used to record the vertical position of artefacts, but the level of none of these lines is known with certainty, e.g. TBM B seems to be higher than TBM B used for the main chamber. Fortunately most artefacts were recorded in relation to the base or the top of the pile of stones in the ante-chamber, and this is shown on a section drawing.

Outside the cairn the co-ordinates giving the horizontal positions of finds can be reconstructed from the pencil plan of the blocking outside the passage entrance, and from the inked general plan of the cairn. Because the levels of neither the ground nor the top of the platform surrounding the cairn were recorded, the stratigraphic positions of the artefacts are uncertain, except that the two deposits outside the entrance were described as below the blocking.

Only items with reliable locations are included in the following list. The excavator's finds numbers are prefixed by ON, and some numbers refer to a group of sherds and/or flints. The numbers in the left column refer to the catalogue of artefacts on pp. 123–4.

Main chamber

1a (2 joining decorated sherds). ON 56: 0.13 m above floor, SEQ. 0.46 m from S wall. ON 94: in the floor, in the entry from the ante-chamber.

4 (many sherds of an undecorated pot). ON 16 (joins ON 62 in ante-chamber): NWQ above W part of slab structure. ON 31: 0.38 m above floor, NEQ. ON 36: 0.36 m above floor, NWQ. ON 38: 0.18–0.25 m above floor, NWQ. ON 43: from floor level to 0.33 m above floor, SWQ. ON 46: about 0.3 m above floor, beside S inner portal stone. ON 52: about 0.25 m above floor, scattered between SEQ and NEQ. ON 57: 0.18 m above floor, SEQ. ON 70: 0.2 m above floor, SEQ. ON 84: near floor level, in front of the tall orthostat. ON 86: about 0.3 m above floor level, in top of the filling of the 'box' in slab structure. ON 93: 0.05 m above floor, in entry from ante-chamber. ON 98: on or just above floor level, in entry from ante-chamber.

5 (undecorated sherd). ON 84: level not known, but found with a small sherd of pot *4*.

8 (sherds of beaker). ON 33: about 0.48 m above floor, SWQ about 0.2 m from wall on SW side.

9 (food vessel). ON 30: 0.56–0.76 m above floor, SWQ spread near SW side of chamber above fallen corbel stone.

10–13, 15 (flints). ON 51, 71: 0.25 m above floor, SWQ and SEQ near centre of chamber, in a patch of grey clay.

16, 28 (flint and quartz). ON 69: 0.25 m above floor, on N–S section 0.71 m from S wall.

17 (flint). ON 60: 0.10 m above floor, by S tip of N inner portal stone.

18 (flint). ON 45: 0.33 m above floor, against W side of N inner portal stone.

19, 24 (flint and quartz). ON 22, 23: level uncertain but 0.13 and 0.20 m above ON 16 (pot *4*), among or above collapsed corbel stones, NWQ and on N–S section 0.94 m N of intersection.

32 (bone mount). ON 27: 0.91 m above floor, close to W end of chamber, with a deposit of cremated bone.

Ante-chamber

1b (sherd probably from the same pot as *1a* in the main chamber). ON 92: 0.15 m or less above floor, sealed beneath the pile of stones.

2 (two decorated sherds). ON 65, 91: about 0.15 m above floor, NE side of ante-chamber, and beneath the pile of stones, same level as pot *3*.

3 (Unstan pot). ON 35, 63, 64, 66, 68, 82, 88, 89, 90: about 0.15 above the floor, widely scattered but mainly on the NE and N sides of the ante-chamber, a few beneath the pile of stones.

4 (undecorated pot). ON 61: about 0.38 m above floor, about 0.25 m higher than pot *3*. ON 62 (joins ON 16 in main chamber): about 0.33 m above floor, just E of N end of inner S portal stone. ON 64: about 0.15 m above floor, with sherds of pot *3*. ON 67: about 0.3 m above floor,

0.15 m above pot *3*. ON 76: with sherds of pot *3*. ON 80: about 0.46 m above floor, above the pile of stones. ON 96: near floor level.

25, 26, 30 (quartz). ON 58: about 0.38 m above floor.

22 (quartz). ON 74: about 0.15 m above floor, SE side.

31 (pumice). ON 72: on or just above floor, in entry from the passage.

Outside the chamber

29 (quartz). ON 54: over 1.22 m above chamber floor, above N inner portal stone.

6 (sherds of decorated pot). ON 102, 103: below the blocking and immediately above bedrock, close to the cairn kerb just S of the entrance to the passage, and 0.91 m further to the E.

7 (sherds of decorated pot). ON 102: as above.

23, 27 (quartz). ON 102: as above.

4a (sherd). ON 101: in or below the platform, about 5.94 m S of the passage entrance, 0.84 m from the cairn kerb.

14 (flint). ON 100: in or below the platform, about 6.4 m S of the passage entrance, 1.83 m from the cairn kerb.

20 (flint). ON 40: in or below the platform, about 5.18 m SSE of the passage entrance, 2.43 m from the cairn kerb.

21 (pitchstone). ON 41: 3.43 m NNE of the passage entrance, just outside the cairn kerb.

The cremation *I* (ON 29) was at the E end of the lintel displaced from over the transverse stones in the passage, at the level of the top of the blocking. The cremation was found on 10th August, and the blocking was not removed until 10th September, thus the cremation must have been above the blocking.

References

Aitken, D. (1788) Volume of 27 coloured plans of farms in Skelbo, surveyed by David Aitken, housed in the Map Room of The National Library of Scotland, Dep 313/3587 1c.

Anderson, J. (1868) On the horned cairns of Caithness: their structural arrangement, contents of chambers, etc. *Proc. Soc. Antiq. Scot. 7*, 480–512.

Anderson, J. (1880) Notice of the excavation of the brochs of Yarhouse, Brounaben, Bowermadden, Old Stirkoke, and Dunbeath, in Caithness, with remarks on the period of the brochs. *Archaeologia Scotica 5 part 2*, 131–98.

Anderson, J. (1886) *Scotland in Pagan Times, the Bronze and Stone Ages*. Edinburgh.

Ashmore, P. J. (1989) Excavation of a beaker cist at Dornoch Nursery, Sutherland. *Proc. Soc. Antiq. Scot. 119*, 63–71.

Barber, J. (1988) Isbister, Quanterness and the Point of Cott: the formulation and testing of some middle range theories, in Barrett and Kinnes eds. (1988) 57–62.

Barber, J. (1992) Megalithic architecture, in Sharples and Sheridan eds. (1992) 13–32.

Barrett, J. C. and Kinnes, I. A. eds. (1988) *The Archaeology of Context in the Neolithic and Bronze Age: Recent Trends*. Sheffield.

Boon, G. C. and Lewis, J. M. eds. (1976) *Welsh Antiquity, essays mainly on prehistoric topics presented to H. N. Savory*. Cardiff.

Boyd, A. J. (1952) Some observations on the Badnabay corridor-tomb, near Laxford Bridge, Sutherland. *Proc. Soc. Antiq. Scot. 86*, 206–8.

Burgess, C. (1974) The bronze age, in Renfrew ed. (1974) 165–232.

Burgess, C. (1976) Burials with metalwork of the later bronze age in Wales and beyond, in Boon and Lewis eds. (1976) 81–104.

Burl, H. A. W. (1982) Pi in the sky, in Heggie ed. (1982) 141–69.

Burl, H. A. W. (1984) Report on the excavation of a neolithic mound at Boghead, Speymouth Forest, Fochabers, Moray, 1972 and 1974. *Proc. Soc. Antiq. Scot. 114*, 35–73.

Calder, C. S. T. (1951) Note on long cairns near Rhinavie, Strathnaver, Sutherland. *Proc. Soc. Antiq. Scot. 85*, 157–8.

Callander, J. G. and Cree, J. E. (n.d.) Draft report on the excavation of a cairn near Ardvreck Castle by Callander, and a plan of the cairn by Cree, Ms 501 (vii) housed in the library of the National Museums of Scotland.

Callander, J. G., Cree, J. E. and Ritchie, J. (1927) Preliminary report on caves containing palaeolithic relics, near Inchnadamph, Sutherland. *Proc. Soc. Antiq. Scot. 61*, 169–72.

Cardonnel, A. M. L. de (1788) *Picturesque Antiquities of Scotland*. London.

Cardonnel, A. M. L. de (1800) *Relicta Antiqua*, 2 vols, Ms housed in the library of the National Museums of Scotland.

Childe, V. G. (1935) *The Prehistory of Scotland*. London.

Clarke, D. L. (1970) *Beaker Pottery of Great Britain and Ireland*. Cambridge.

Clarke, D. V., Cowie, T. G. and Foxon, A. (1985) *Symbols of Power at the Time of Stonehenge*. Edinburgh.

Close-Brooks, J. (1983) Some early querns. *Proc. Soc. Antiq. Scot. 113*, 282–9.

Coles, J. M. (1964) Scottish middle bronze age metalwork. *Proc. Soc. Antiq. Scot. 97*, 82–156.

Coles, J. M. and Simpson, D. D. A. eds. (1968) *Studies in Ancient Europe*. Leicester.

Collcutt, S. N. ed. (1986) *The Palaeolithic of Britain and its Nearest Neighbours: Recent Trends*. Sheffield.

Corcoran, J. X. W. P. (1966) Excavation of three chambered cairns at Loch Calder, Caithness. *Proc. Soc. Antiq. Scot. 98*, 1–75.

Corcoran, J. X. W. P. (1967a) Notebook, plans and drawings made during the excavation of The Ord North, Ms/270, SUD/115/1–30 housed in the National Monuments Record of Scotland.

Corcoran, J. X. W. P. (1967b) The Ord North, Lairg. *Discovery and Excavation in Scotland 1967*, 53.

Corcoran, J. X. W. P. (1969a) Excavation of two chambered cairns at Mid Gleniron Farm, Glenluce, Wigtownshire. *Trans. Dumfriesshire and Galloway Nat. Hist. and Antiq. Soc., 3rd series, 46*, 29–90.

Corcoran, J. X. W. P. (1969b) The Cotswold-Severn group, 2, discussion, in Powell, T.G.E. et. al. (1969) 73–104.

Corcoran, J. X. W. P. (1972) Multiperiod construction and the origins of the chambered long cairn in western Britain and Ireland, in Lynch and Burgess eds. (1972) 31–63.

Cowie, T. G. and Ritchie, J. N. G. (1991) Bronze age burials at Gairneybank, Kinross-shire. *Proc. Soc. Antiq. Scot. 121*, 95–109.

Cree, J. E. (1928) Three notebooks relating to excavations of cairns and fieldwork, Ms/28/632 housed in the National Monuments Record of Scotland.

Crone, A. (1993) Excavation and survey of sub-peat features of neolithic, bronze and iron age date at Bharpa Carinish, North Uist, Scotland. *Proc. Prehist. Soc. 59*, 361–82.

Curle, A. O. (1909a) Five field notebooks, Ms/36/4–8, unpaginated, housed in the National Monuments Record of Scotland.

Curle, A. O. (1909b) Diary of field work in Sutherland, 2 vols, Ms/36/9–10 housed in the National Monuments Record of Scotland.

Curle, A. O. (1910) Exploration of a chambered cairn at Achaidh, Spinningdale, in the Parish of Creich, Sutherland. *Proc. Soc. Antiq. Scot. 44*, 104–11.

Daniel, G. E. (1962) The megalith builders, in Piggott ed. (1962) 39–72.

Davidson, J. L. and Henshall, A. S. (1989) *The Chambered Cairns of Orkney*. Edinburgh.

Davidson, J. L. and Henshall, A. S. (1991) *The Chambered Cairns of Caithness*. Edinburgh.

Davidson, J. M. (1946) A miscellany of antiquities in Easter

Ross and Sutherland. *Proc. Soc. Antiq. Scot. 80*, 25–33.
Dennison, S. (1994) The hunt for palaeolithic Scotland. *British Archaeological News* 13, 6–7.
Fraser, D. (1983) *Land and Society in Neolithic Orkney* (= British Archaeol. Reports, British Series, no. 117). Oxford.
Gourlay, R. B. (1984) A short cist beaker inhumation from Chealamy, Strathnaver, Sutherland. *Proc. Soc. Antiq. Scot. 114*, 567–71.
Graham, A. (1956) A memorial of Alexander Ormiston Curle. *Proc. Soc. Antiq. Scot. 88*, 234–6.
Halliday, S. P., Hill, P. J. and Stevenson, J. B. (1981) Early agriculture in Scotland, in Mercer ed. (1981) 55–65.
Hedges, J. W. (1983) *Isbister, a Chambered Cairn in Orkney* (= British Archaeol. Reports, British Series, no. 115). Oxford.
Hedges, J. W. (1984) *Tomb of the Eagles*. London.
Heggie, D. C. ed. (1982) *Archaeoastronomy in the Old World*. Cambridge.
Henshall, A. S. (1960) Plans made during the excavation of the chambered cairn at Embo, SUD/108/1–6 housed in the National Monuments Record of Scotland.
Henshall, A. S. (1963, 1972) *The Chambered Tombs of Scotland*, 2 vols. Edinburgh.
Henshall, A. S. (1982) The distant past, in Omand ed. (1982) 135–45.
Henshall, A. S. (1983) The neolithic pottery from Easterton of Roseisle, Moray, in O'Connor and Clarke eds. (1983) 19–44.
Henshall, A. S. and Taylor, H. W. Y (1957) A bronze age burial at Embo, Sutherland. *Proc. Soc. Antiq. Scot. 90*, 225–7.
Henshall, A. S. and Wallace, J. C. (1963) The excavation of a chambered cairn at Embo, Sutherland. *Proc. Soc. Antiq. Scot. 96*, 9–36.
Horsburgh, J. (1867) Manuscript of Horsburgh 1868, Ms/28 housed in the National Monuments Record of Scotland (formerly Soc. Antiq. Scot. Ms 364).
Horsburgh, J. (1868) Notes of cromlechs, duns, hut-circles, chambered cairns, and other remains, in the county of Sutherland. *Proc. Soc. Antiq. Scot. 7*, 271–9.
Howell, J. M. (1976) Plan of Benmore Forest, SUT 75, RCD/115/4 housed in the National Monuments Record of Scotland.
Joass, J. M. (1864a) Manuscript of Joass 1864b, Ms 501 (xx) housed in the library of the National Museums of Scotland.
Joass, J. M. (1864b) Notes of various objects of antiquity in Strathnaver. *Proc. Soc. Antiq. Scot. 5*, 357–60.
Jöckenhovel, A. (1980) *Die Rasiermesser in Westeuropa*. Prähistoriche Bronzefunde, Abteilung 8, Band 3. Munich.
Kerr, C. (1891) Draft of Kerr 1892, with drawings, Ms SAS 317 housed in the National Monuments Record of Scotland.
Kerr, C. (1892) Notice of the excavation of a chambered cairn in the parish of Farr, Sutherlandshire. *Proc. Soc. Antiq. Scot. 26*, 65–7.
Kinnes, I. (1985) Circumstance not context: the neolithic of Scotland as seen from outside. *Proc. Soc. Antiq. Scot. 115*, 15–57.
Kinnes, I. (1992a) *Non-Megalithic Long Barrows and Allied Structures in the British Neolithic* (= British Museum Occasional Paper 52). London.
Kinnes, I. (1992b) Balnagowan and after: the context of non-megalithic mortuary sites in Scotland, in Sharples and Sheridan eds. (1992) 83–103.
Kirk, J. (1772) A Book of Plans of the Parish of Loth, Sutherland Papers, Dep 313/3583, on loan to the National Library of Scotland Map Room.
Lawson, T. J. and Bonsall, C. (1986a) Early settlement in Scotland: the evidence from Reindeer Cave, Assynt. *Quaternary Newsletter* 49, 1–7.
Lawson, T. J. and Bonsall, C. (1986b) The palaeolithic in Scotland: a reconsideration of evidence from Reindeer Cave, Assynt, in Collcutt ed. (1986) 85–9.
Lynch, F. and Burgess, C. eds. (1972) *Prehistoric Man in Wales and the West*. Bath.
McCullagh, R. (1991) Achinduich (Creich Parish) prehistoric kerbed burial mound. *Discovery and Excavation in Scotland 1991*, 46.
McCullagh, R. (1992) *Lairg: the Archaeology of a Changing Landscape*. Edinburgh.
McKay, W. (1867) Letter and plans of chambered cairns in Strathnaver, Ms/28 housed in the National Monuments Record of Scotland (formerly Soc. Antiq. Scot. Ms 331).
Masters, L. J. (1981) Chambered tombs and non-megalithic barrows in Britain, in Renfrew ed. (1981) 97–112.
Mercer, R. J. (1980) *Archaeological Field Survey in Northern Scotland 1976–1979* (= University of Edinburgh Department of Archaeology Occasional Paper 4). Edinburgh.
Mercer, R. J. (1981) *Archaeological Field Survey in Northern Scotland, vol 2, 1980–1981* (= University of Edinburgh Department of Archaeology Occasional Paper 7). Edinburgh.
Mercer, R. J. ed. (1981) *Farming Practice in British Prehistory*. Edinburgh.
Mercer, R. J. (1985) *Archaeological Field Survey in Northern Scotland, vol 3, 1982–1983* (= University of Edinburgh Department of Archaeology Occasional Paper 11). Edinburgh.
Mercer, R. J. (1992) Cumulative cairn construction and cultural continuity in Caithness and Orkney, in Sharples and Sheridan eds. (1992) 49–61.
Mitchell, M. E. C. (1934) A new analysis of the early bronze age beaker pottery of Scotland. *Proc. Soc. Antiq. Scot. 68*, 132–89.
Munro, R. (1884) Notice of long cairns near Rhinavie, Strathnaver, Sutherlandshire. *Proc. Soc. Antiq. Scot. 18*, 228–33.
NMRS. Records housed in the National Monuments Record of Scotland, Edinburgh.
NMRS Ms SUD/21/3 (Copy of) Cairns of Shenachu in Kinbrace [mid-18th-century plan of a battle, probably by Mr Pope, minister of Reay], the original in private hands.
NSA (1845) *New Statistical Account of Scotland 15*. Edinburgh.
O'Connor, A. and Clarke, D. V. eds. (1983) *From the Stone Age to the 'Forty-five, Studies presented to R. B. K. Stevenson*. Edinburgh.
Omand, D. ed. (1982) *The Sutherland Book*. Golspie.
ONB (1871–4) Object Name Books of the Ordnance Survey of Sutherland, housed in the Scottish Record Office, Edinburgh.

Ordnance Survey (1960) (Report from the) Archaeology Division, Ordnance Survey. *Discovery and Excavation in Scotland 1960*, 42–4.

Ordnance Survey (1962) (Report from the) Archaeology Division, Ordnance Survey. *Discovery and Excavation in Scotland 1962*, 50–1.

Ordnance Survey (1974) (Report from the) Archaeology Division, Ordnance Survey. *Discovery and Excavation in Scotland 1974*, 70–5.

Ordnance Survey Record Card. Records now part of the NMRS database.

Piggott, S. (1954) *The Neolithic Cultures of the British Isles*. Cambridge.

Piggott, S. ed. (1962) *The Prehistoric Peoples of Scotland*. London.

Pococke, R. (1887) *Tours in Scotland 1747, 1750, 1760*, ed. D. W .Kemp. (= Scot. Hist. Soc. 1). Edinburgh.

Powell, T. G. E. (1963) The chambered cairn at Dyffryn Ardudwy. *Antiquity 37*, 19–24.

Powell, T. G. E. et al. (1969) *Megalithic Enquiries in the West of Britain*. Liverpool.

RCAHMS (1993) *Strath of Kildonan: an Archaeological Survey*. Edinburgh.

RCAMS (1911) Royal Commission on the Ancient and Historical Monuments and Constructions of Scotland, *Second Report and Inventory of Monuments and Constructions in the County of Sutherland*. Edinburgh.

Reid, A. G., Shepherd, I. A. G., and Lunt, D. A. (1986) A beaker cist at Upper Muirhall, Perth. *Proc. Soc. Antiq. Scot. 116*, 63–7.

Reid, R. W. K., David, G., and Aitken, A. (1967) Prehistoric settlement in Durness. *Proc. Soc. Antiq. Scot. 99*, 21–53.

Renfrew, C. ed. (1974) *British Prehistory, a New Outline*. London.

Renfrew, C. (1979) *Investigations in Orkney* (= Rep. Research Comm. Soc. Antiq. London 38). London.

Renfrew, C. ed. (1981) *The Megalithic Monuments of Western Europe*. London.

Richards, C. (1992) Doorways into another world: the Orkney-Cromarty chambered tombs, in Sharples and Sheridan eds. (1992), 62–76.

Ritchie, A. (1983) Excavation of a neolithic farmstead at Knap of Howar, Papa Westray, Orkney. *Proc. Soc. Antiq. Scot. 113*, 40–121.

Ritchie, J. N. G. (1970) Excavation of the chambered cairn at Achnacreebeag. *Proc. Soc. Antiq. Scot. 102*, 31–55.

Ritchie, J. N. G. (1972) Excavation of a chambered cairn at Dalineun, Lorn, Argyll. *Proc. Soc. Antiq. Scot. 104*, 48–62.

Ritchie, J. N. G. and Shepherd, I. A. G. (1973) Beaker pottery and associated artefacts in south-west Scotland. *Trans. Dumfries and Galloway Nat. Hist. and Antiq. Soc. 50*, 18–36.

Scott, J. G. (1969) The Clyde cairns of Scotland, in Powell et al. (1969) 175–222.

Sharples, N. M. (1981) The excavation of a chambered cairn, The Ord North, at Lairg, Sutherland by J. X. W. P. Corcoran. *Proc. Soc. Antiq. Scot. 111*, 21–62.

Sharples, N. M. (1985) Individual and community: the changing role of megaliths in the Orcadian neolithic. *Proc. Prehist. Soc. 51*, 59–74.

Sharples, N. M. (1986) Radiocarbon dates from three chambered tombs at Loch Calder, Caithness. *Scot. Archaeol. Rev. 4, pt. 1*, 2–10.

Sharples, N. M. and Sheridan, A. eds. (1992) *Vessels for the Ancestors*. Edinburgh.

Sheridan, J. A. and Davis, M. (forthcoming) Scottish prehistoric 'jet' jewellery; new research. *Antiquity*.

Simpson, D. D. A. (1968) Food vessels: associations and chronology, in Coles and Simpson eds. (1968) 197–211.

Simpson, W. D. (1928) A chambered cairn at Allt-nam-Ban, Strathbrora, Sutherland. *Antiq. J. 8*, 485–8.

Simpson, W. D. (1936) A chambered cairn at Allt-nam-Ban, Strathbrora, Sutherland (reprint of Simpson 1928). *Scottish Archaeological Studies, 2nd Series*, 171–6. (= Aberdeen University Studies 106). Aberdeen.

Stuart, J. (1868) Report to the Committee of the Society of Antiquaries of Scotland, appointed to arrange for the application of a fund left by the late Mr. A. Henry Rhind, for excavating early remains. *Proc. Soc. Antiq. Scot. 7*, 289–307.

Stuiver, M. and Reimer, P. J. (1993) Extended 14C database and revised CALIB3.0 14C age calibration programme. *Radiocarbon, 35, no. 1*, 215–30.

Tait, L. (1868) Note on the shell-mounds, hut-circles, and kist-vaens of Sutherland. *Proc. Soc. Antiq. Scot. 7*, 525–32.

Watkins, T. (1982) The excavation of an early bronze age cemetery at Barns Farm, Dalgety, Fife. *Proc. Soc. Antiq. Scot. 112*, 48–141.

Welsh, T. C. (1969) (Report on archaeological sites in Sutherland) *Discovery and Excavation in Scotland 1969*, 48–51.

Welsh, T. C. (1973) (Report on archaeological sites in Sutherland). *Discovery and Excavation 1973*, 55–8.

Wickham-Jones, C. R. (1994) *Scotland's First Settlers*. London.

Wilson, D. (1851) *The Archaeology and Prehistoric Annals of Scotland*. Edinburgh.

Woodman, P. C. (1989) A review of the Scottish mesolithic: a plea for normality! *Proc. Soc. Antiq. Scot. 119*, 1–32.

Wordsworth, J. (1985) The excavation of a mesolithic horizon at 13–24 Castle Street, Inverness. *Proc. Soc. Antiq. Scot. 115*, 89–103.

Index

References to Inventory entries are printed in **bold** type, and to illustrations in *italics*.

Aberscross (SUT 1), not now considered a chambered cairn, **79**, 152
Ach Cill na Borgan, Rhinavie, *see* Coille na Borgie South (SUT 23)
Achaidh (SUT 2), 9, 74, **79–80**
  animal bones, 80
  burial deposits, 50, 55, 57, 80
  cairn structure, 41, 49, 61, 79–80
  chamber and roof, 23, *23–24*, *25*, 27, 49, 69, 80
  corbel stones, 22, *23*, 23–4
  entry and height, 24, 79–80
  floor, 80
  horns, 79
  lintel, *27*, 79
  passage, 21, 79
  portal stones, 79
  pottery, medieval, 55, 80
  roof, *23*, 23–24, *25*, 27, 69, 80
  scraper, 57, 63, 66
  skeletal material, 80
Achamore, not now considered a chambered cairn, 153
Achany (SUT 3), 6, 9, **80–2**
  cairn structure, 37, 38–9, *40*, 49, 71, 80–2
  chamber, 32, *32*, 81–2
  façade, 38, 49, 71, 74, 81
  forecourt, 59, 71, 74, 81
  orthostats, 49, 81
  passage, 21, 49, 81
  portal stones, 49, 81
Achcheargary (SUT 4), 9, **82**
  cairn structure, 37, 82
  chamber, 82
  orthostats, 82
afforestation, and cairns, 62, 151
Allt a' Chaoruinn (SUT 74), 17, *19*, **146–7**
  cairn structure, 62, 146
  chamber, *25*, 25, 27, 62, 69, 146–7
  orthostats, 146–7
  passage, 21, 146
Allt a' Mhuilinn (SUT 5), **82–3**
  cairn structure, 62, 82–3
  chamber, *32*, 33, 34, 69, 70, 83
  damage to, 62
  entrance and portal stones, 21, 83
  orthostats, 83
  portal stones, 83
Allt Eileag (SUT 72) (ROS 43), **144–5**
  cairn structure, 35, 41, 144
    interference to, 61
  chamber, 24, 35, 58, 144–5
  corbel stones, 144–5
Allt nam Ban (SUT 6), 9, **83–4**
  cairn structure, 38, 62, 83–4
  chamber, *32*, 33–4, 69, 84
  damage to, 62
  entry height, 24
  orientation of, 68
  passage and lintels, 21, 22, 24, 84
  portal stones, 24, 84
Allt nan Eun (SUT 7), **85**
  blocking, 85
  cairn structure, 38, 61, 85–6
  entrance, 21, 85
  portal stones, 85
Allt Sgiathaig (SUT 8), **85–6**
  cairn structure, 37, 85–6
  chamber, 29, 37, 86
  orthostats, 86
'amulet', 109
Anderson, J., Rhind Lectures, 8
  on Benbhraggie Wood, 89, 90
  on chambered cairns, 6, 7, 8, 129
animal bones, *see also below* for species, 3, 10, 17, 50, 52, 55, 56–7, 80, 101, 137–8, 140
  amphibian, 50, 57, 140
  birds:
    blackbird, 140; capercaille, 57, 140; cormorant, 50; duck, 50, 57; fulmar, 57, 140; gannet, 50, 57, 140; great auk, 50, 57, 140; grebe, 50, 57, 140; guillemot, 50, 57, 140; razorbill, 140; shag, 50, 140; starling, 140
  deer, 17
    antlers, pre-glacial, 15–16
  dog, 17, 50, 57, 140
  fish, 50, 57, 138, 140
  otter, 50, 57, 138, 140
  ox, 17, 57, 140
  pig, 57, 140
  pole-cat, 57, 140
  sheep, 17, 50, 57, 140
  squirrel, 57, 140
animal disturbance, otters, 51, 57, 138
antlers, pre-glacial, 15–16
Ardvreck (SUT 9), 9, 20, 63, 74, **86–7**
  cairn structure, 35, 74, 86
  chamber, 35–6, *36*, 55, 74, 86–7
  corbels, 35–6, *36*
  damage to, 62
  lintels, 35–6, *36*
  'passage', 87
  skeletal material from, *36*, 87
axehead, stone, Lothbeg, 57, 118

Badnabay (SUT 10), 9, 17, **87–8**
  cairn structure, 87, 88
  chamber, *25*, 28, 31, 69, 87–8
  entry height, 24
  orthostats, 88
  passage and entrance, 21, 87–8
  portal stones, 87–8
Balblair, Bonar Bridge, razor from, 67
Balcharn (SUT 11), **88–9**
  cairn structure, 38, 61, 88, 89
  orthostats, 88
  intervisibility with Ord cairns, 88
Barber, J., on chambered tombs, 22, 37, 55, 74, 76
Beacharra, Argyll, 65
beads, cannel coal, 66, 67
  jet, 60, 66, 67, 138, 139
  shale, 66
beakers, 59–60, 65–6, *66*, 139, 157
  and bronze age burials, 59–60
Benbhraggie Wood (SUT 12), 6, 8, 9, **89–90**
  cairn structure, 8, 38, 89
  chamber, 32, *32*, 89–90
  orthostats, 89, 90
  portal stones, 89
benches, in Orkney and Caithness, 56
  possible, at The Ord North, 52, *53*, 56
Benmore Forest (SUT 75), **147**
  cairn structure, 41, 71, 147
  chamber, 29, 30, 49, 147
  corbel stones, 147
  orthostats, 147
  passage, 21
  portal stones, 147
bipartite chambers, *see also* chamber types and **Inventory entries,** 8, 9, 10, 20, *25*, 27–30, 31, 32, *32*, 38, 49, 69
  Caithness-type, *25*, 27–9, 32, 69
  Skelpick-type, *25*, 28, *29*, 29–30, *31*, 38, 49, 69
  unclassified, 31–2, *32*
Blackhammer, Orkney, 65
Blandy (SUT 76), **147–8**
  cairn structure, 148
  possible chamber, 148
blocking, 36, 58–9, *59*, 63, 123, 129, 158
  of entrances, 39
  of forecourts and passages, 58–9, *59*
Boghead, Moray, 60
bone artefacts, mount, 60, *64*, 67, 122, 157

INDEX

bones:
  animal, *see under* animal bones
  human, *see under* skeletal material
Boyd, A. J., work at Badnabay, 9
bronze age:
  burials, and beakers, 59–60, 66
  re-use of cairns, 10, 11, 55
bronze artefacts:
  fragment, 60, 138
  razors, 60, 66, 67, 139
burial deposits, 3, 50–8, 59–60
  interpretation of, 55–8
burial rites, *see also* burial deposits and skeletal material
  cremations, 27, 56, 60, 122–3, 124, 136, 138–9, 140, 158
  disposition of skeletal material, 51–2, 55, 56–8, 136, 137, 138, 139–40, 155–6
  excarnation, 56

Caen Burn East (SUT 13), 18, **90**
  cairn structure, 20, 43–4, 72–3, 90
  chamber, absence of, 20, 73
  prehistoric settlement, 90
Caen Burn North (SUT 14), 18, **90–1**
  cairn structure, 20, 43–5, 72–3, 90–1
Caen Burn South (SUT 15), 8, *42*, *43*, *44*, **91–2**
  cairn structure, *42*, *43*, 43–4, 61, 72–3, 91–2
Caen Burn West (SUT 16), 8, 18, 20, **92–3**
  cairn structure, 20, 43–5, 72–3, 92–3
  condition of cairn, 61, 93
  chamber, absence of, 20
Cairnlea, *see* Lothbeg (SUT 45)
cairns: *see also* site names and **Inventory entries**, 37–49
  architecture of, 3, 20, 76
  buried soils under, 4
  chambers, *see under* chambers
  chronology and dating, 74–6
  conventions used in depictions of, 4–5
  destruction of, 61–2
  development of study of, 3–12
  distribution and typology of, 71–4
  distribution maps of, *70*, *72*
  and environment, 16–19
  and geology and topography, 13–15
  heel-shaped, *see under* cairn types
  and hut circles, 9
  kerbs and kerb-stones, 39, 97, 100, 116, 121, 124–5, 151
    possible, 141
  long, *see under* cairn types
  orientation of, 68
  possibly non-megalithic, 73

retaining walls, 37, 38
round, *see under* cairn types
short horned, *see under* cairn types
siting of, 17–19
social significance of, 3, 76
and society, 76
structure, and plans of, 37–49, 71–4
cairn types: distribution maps of, *70*, *72*
  heel-shaped, 37, *40*, 40–1, 46, 47, 49, 71, 72
    Benmore Forest (SUT 75), *see also* main site entry, **147**
    Coille na Borgie North (SUT 22), *see also* main site entry, **97–9**
    Kinbrace Hill Long (SUT 34), *see also* main site entry, **109–10**
    Kyleoag (SUT 37), *see also* main site entry, **111–12**
  heel-shaped, possible:
    Cnoc Chaornaidh North-West (SUT 69), *see also* main site entry, **142–3**
  long cairns, 20, 37, 41–9, 71–4
    Caen Burn East (SUT 13), *see also* main site entry, **90**
    Caen Burn North (SUT 14), *see also* main site entry, **90–1**
    Caen Burn South (SUT 91), *see also* main site entry, **91–2**
    Caen Burn West (SUT 16), *see also* main site entry, **92–3**
    Carn Laggie (SUT 17), *see also* main site entry, **93–4**
    Coille na Borgie South (SUT 23), *see also* main site entry, **99–101**
    Kilournan (SUT 32), *see also* main site entry, **107–8**
    Salscraggie (SUT 51), *see also* main site entry, **125–7**
    Skelpick Long (SUT 53), *see also* main site entry, **128–30**
  long cairns, composite:
    Coille na Borgie North (SUT 22), *see also* main site entry, **97–9**
    Kinbrace Hill Long (SUT 34), *see also* main site entry, **109–10**
  round cairns, 9, 37–40, *40*, 49
    Achany (SUT 3), *see also* main site entry, **80–2**
    Allt a' Mhuillin (SUT 5), *see also* main site entry, **82–3**
    Allt Eileag (SUT 72) (ROS 43), *see also* main site entry, **72–3**
    Allt nam Ban (SUT 6), *see also* main site entry, **83–4**
    Allt nan Eun (SUT 7), *see also* main site entry, **85**

Allt Sgiathaig (SUT 8), *see also* main site entry, **85–6**
Ardvreck (SUT 9), *see also* main site entry, **87**
Balcharn (SUT 11), *see also* main site entry, **88–9**
Benbhraggie Wood (SUT 12), *see also* main site entry, **89–90**
Blandy (SUT 76), *see also* main site entry, **147–8**
Clashmore (SUT 19), *see also* main site entry, **95**
Cnoc na Moine (SUT 60), *see also* main site entry, **135**
Coillelyal (SUT 77), *see also* main site entry, **148**
Creag nan Caorach East (SUT 24), *see also* main site entry, **101–2**
Craig a' Bhlair (SUT 78), *see also* main site entry, **148–9**
Druim Liath (SUT 26), *see also* main site entry, **103**
Embo (SUT 63), *see also* main site entry, **135–40**
Evelix (SUT 28), *see also* main site entry, **104**
Fiscary (SUT 29), *see also* main site entry, **105–7**
Kinbrace Hill Round (SUT 35), *see also* main site entry, **110**
Kinloch (SUT 36), *see also* main site entry, **110–11**
Ledmore (SUT 40), *see also* main site entry, **112–13**
Ledmore Wood (SUT 41), *see also* main site entry, **113–14**
Loch Awe (SUT 42), *see also* main site entry, **114–15**
Loch Borralan East (SUT 43), *see also* main site entry, **115–16**
Loch Borralan West (SUT 44), *see also* main site entry, **116–17**
Lyne (SUT 46), *see also* main site entry, **118–19**
The Ord North (SUT 48), *see also* main site entry, **119–24**
The Ord South (SUT 49), *see also* main site entry, **124–5**
Skail (SUT 52), *see also* main site entry, **127**
Skelpick Round (SUT 54), *see also* main site entry, **130–1**
Strathseasgaich (SUT 73) (ROS 50), *see also* main site entry, **145–6**
Torboll (SUT 58), *see also* main site entry, **132–4**
short horned, 8, 37, *40*, 41, 49, 74
  Achaidh (SUT 2), *see also* main site entry, **79–80**

INDEX

Creag nan Caorach West (SUT 25), *see also* main site entry, **102–3**
Kinbrace Burn (SUT 33), *see also* main site entry, **108–9**
Skelpick South (SUT 55), *see also* main site entry, **131–2**
formerly considered short horned
Carn Richard (SUT 18), *see also* main site entry, **94**
Caithness, 12, 37, 40, 43, 69
  beakers from, 67
  long cairns, cairn structure, 8, 37, 43, 45, *46*, 47, 69, 70–2
  -type chambers, bipartite *25*, 27–9, 32, 69
  chambers, details, 22, 34–5
  Loch Calder cairns, 10
Calder, C. S. T., work at Coille na Borgie, 9
Callander, J. G., plan of Ardvreck, 36
Camore Wood (SUT 59), not now considered a chambered cairn, **134**, 152–3
Camster Long, Caithness, 11
  excavation of, 23, 59
Camster Round, Caithness, 40
Carn Chaoile, *see* Fiscary (SUT 29)
Carn Glas, Ross and Cromarty, 66
Carn Laggie (SUT 17), 18, **93–4**
  cairn structure, 44, *46*, 72–3, 93–4
  chamber, possible, 44, 94
  forecourt, 94
  horns, 46, 94
  'passages', 44, 94
Carn Liath, *see* Druim Liath (SUT 26), **103** and Torboll (SUT 58), **132–4**
Carn Richard (SUT 18), *17*, 18, **94–5**
  cairn structure, 41, 94–5
  orthostats, 94–5
Carn Tigh nan Coileach, *see* Carn Richard
cereal production, 17
chambers, *see also* individual sites and **Inventory entries**,
  8, 20, 49, 50, *70*
  bipartite, 8, 9, 10, 20, *25*, 27–30, *31*, 32, 38, 49, 69
    Caithness-type, *25*, 27–9, 32, 69
    Skelpick-type, 25, 28, *29*, 29–30, *31*, 38, 49, 69
    unclassified, 31–2, *32*
  blocking, 58–9
  burial deposits, 50–8
  Clyde group, 35
  construction, 22–36
  deposits, ritual during building, 50
  distribution and typology of, 68–70, *70*, 71
  flooring, 55, 80
  Orkney-Cromarty-type, 4, 10, 20, 35, 68–9
  roof structure *see also* under corbel stones, 7, 8, 22–4, 25
  single-compartment, 9, 20, *25*, 25–8
  possible, 31
  Skelpick-type, 20, *29*, 29–30, 31, *31*, 38, 49, 69
  terminology and morphology, 20
  tripartite, 8, 9, 20, *32*, *33*, 32–5, 69–71
  charcoal, and wood, 52–3, 101, 106, 122, 137
Childe, V. G., work on chambered cairns, 10
chronology and dating, 74–6
cists, 26–7, 55, 57, 60, 63, 66–7, 136, 138
  Ardvreck (SUT 9), 35–6, 55, 63
  Embo (SUT 63), *26*–7, 57, 60, 65–7, 136, 138
Clarke, A. S., work on animal bones from Embo, 52
Clashmore (SUT 19), **95**
  cairn structure, 39, 95
  chamber, 35, 95
  orthostats, 35, 95
Clyde cairns, 35, 73–4
Cnoc an Daimh (SUT 20), **95–6**
  cairn structure, 37, 95–6
  chamber, *25*, 28, 29, 37, 69, 96
  orthostats, 96
  portal stones, 96
Cnoc Chaornaidh (SUT 68) (ROS 16), not now considered a chambered cairn, **142**, 153
Cnoc Chaornaidh North-West (SUT 69) (ROS 15), **142–3**
  cairn structure, 41, 71, 142
  chamber, 29, 30, 31, 49, 142–3
  corbel stones, 143
  orthostats, 142–3
  portal stones, 142
Cnoc Chaornaidh South-East (SUT 70) (ROS 17), **143–4**
  cairn structure, 38, 41, 143–4
  chamber, 29, 30, 143–4
  lintel, 24, 143
  orthostats, 143–4
  passage, 21, 143
  portal stones, 24, 143
Cnoc Dair-chair, Sutherland, cairn, unchambered, 49
Cnoc na Moine (SUT 60), **134**
  cairn structure, 39, 134
  chamber, 29, 30, 69, 134
  orthostats, 134
  passage, 21, 134
  portal stones, 134
Cnoc Odhar (SUT 21), 8, **96–7**, 135

cairn structure, 96–7
  chamber, 35, 96
  orthostats, 96
Coille na Borgie North (SUT 22), 7, 8, 9, 18, **97–9**
  blocking of forecourts, 59, 97–8
  cairn structure, 37, 41, 44–5, *46*, 46–7, 49, 71, 73, 74, 97–9
  chamber, 34, 35, 49, 98
  façade, 47, 49, 73, 97–8
  forecourt, 45, 46, 59, 97, 99
  horns, 45, 46, 98
  kerb-stones, 97
  orientation of, 68
  orthostats, 44–5, 47, 73, 97–8
  passage, 8
  wall-face, 37, 44–5, *46*
Coille na Borgie South (SUT 23), 7, 8, 9, 18, 70, **99–101**
  animal bones from, 55, 101
  blocking of forecourts, 59
  cairn structure, 37, 44–5, *46*, 46–7, *48*, 49, 73, 74, 99–100
  chambers, *32*, 34, 35, *48*, 48–9, 70, 100–1
  corbels, 35
  façade, 47, 48–9, 73, 99
  forecourt, 45, 46–7, 48–9, 59, 99–100
  horns, 45, 99
  kerb-stones, 100
  lintels, 35
  orientation of, 68
  orthostats, 35, 48–9, 73, 99, 100
  passage, 21, 22, *48*, 48–9, 100
  portal stones, 100–1
  wall-face, 37, *46*
  wood, 101
Coillelyal (SUT 77), **148**
  cairn structure, 148
  orthostats, 148
corbels and corbel stones, 22, 23, 23–4, 35
  and chamber construction, 22–4, 30, 35
Corcoran, J. X. W. P.,
  excavation of Camster Long, 11
  excavations at The Ord North (SUT 48), 10–11, 29–30, 38, 50, 119–20, 157–8
  excavations at Tulach an t'Sionnaich, Caithness, 11, 56
  excavations at Tulloch of Assery, Caithness, 56
Corrie, *see* Pittentrail (SUT 50)
Craig a' Bhlair (SUT 78), **148–9**
  cairn structure, 148–9
  chamber, 32, *32*, 149
  interference to, 61
  orthostats, 149
  portal stones, 149

INDEX

Creag a' Bhata (SUT 83), **151**
  kerb-stones, 151
  orthostats, 151
Creag an Amlaidh (SUT 61), 19, **135**
  cairn structure, 41, 43, 72, 73, 135
  chamber, lack of, 20
Creag nan Caorach East (SUT 24), 18, **101-2**
  cairn structure, 101
  chamber, 101-2
  corbels, 102
  orthostats, 101
  prehistoric settlement, 101
Creag nan Caorach West (SUT 25), 18, **102-3**
  cairn structure, *38*, 41, 62, 74, 102-3
  chamber, *32*, *33*, 62, 49, 69, 102-3
  corbel stones, 102-3
  lintels, 25, 102-3
  orthostats, 102-3
  passage, 102
  portal stones, 102-3
Cree, J. E., work at Ardvreck, 9, 36, 86-7
cremations, 27, 56, 60, 122-3, 124, 136, 138-9, 140, 158
Curle, A. O., work on Sutherland cairns, 9, 11, 61-2, 81, 85, 126, 127, 131, 143
  excavation of Achaidh, 23, 41, 61-2, 79
  sketch of Lyne chamber, *34*

dating and chronology of chambered cairns, *see also* radiocarbon dates, 4, 10, 11, 69, 74-6
Davidson, J. L. & Henshall, A. S., work on Caithness cairns, 28, 40, 43, 52, 56
de Cardonnel, A., 6
deposits, ritual during cairn building, 39, 50
disturbance to chamber contents by animals, 57
Dornoch Nursery, beaker cist, 66
Druim Liath (SUT 26), **103**
  cairn structure, 39, 103
  chamber, *29*, 30, 69, 103
  orthostats, 103
  passage, 103
Dun Riaskidh (SUT 62), not now considered a chambered cairn, **135**, 153
Dun Viden (SUT 27), 6, 7, **104**
  cairn structure, 38, 104
  chamber, 35, 38, 104
  orthostats, 35, 104
  passage, 21, 104
  portal stones, 104

Dunrobin Castle Museum, 7, 63, 109, 116, 127, 134
Dunrobin Park, cist, 66, 67

eke-stones, 20, 24
Embo (SUT 63), 4, 10, 17, 39, **135-40**
  animal bones, *see under* main heading, animal bones, for species; 17, 50, 52, 57, 137-8, 140
  beads, cannel coal, 66, 67
    jet, 60, 66, 67, 138, 139
  beaker, 57, 59-60, 65-6, 66, 138, 139
  bronze artefacts: fragment, 138
    razor, 60, 66, 67, 139
  burial deposits and skeletal remains, 50-2, 56, 57, 136, 137, 138, 139-40
  cairn structure, 37, 39, 135-6, 137
  chamber, 22, *25-7*, 28, 39, 69, *71*, 71, 136, 137, 138
  charcoal, 137
  cists, *26*, *27*, 57, 60, 66-7, 136, 138
  cremations, 136, 138-9, 140
  fish bones, 138
  flint artefacts, knife, 57, 60, 65, 66, 138, 139
  food vessel, 60, 66, 67, 138, 139
  infant and child burials, 51, 60, 67, 138, 139
  molluscan remains, 138, 140
  orthostats, 136, 137
  passage, 21, 58, 136
  pottery, 59-60, 65-66, 66, 139
    beaker, 57, 59-60, 65-6, 66, 138, 139
    food vessel, 60, 66, 67, 138, 139
  portal stones, 21, 136, 137
  pumice, 57, 63, 139
  radiocarbon dates, 10, 75-6
  ritual deposits during building, 39, 50
  skeletal material, 50-2, 56, 57, 136, 137, 138, 139-40, 155-6
  spindle whorl, 139
  wall-face, 37
environment, and neolithic settlement, 16-19
Evelix (SUT 28), 9, **104-5**
  cairn structure, 38, 104
  chamber, *25*, 28, 69, 104-5
  orthostats, 104
  passage, 21, 104
  portal stones, 104-5
excarnation, 56

façades, *see also* individual site and **Inventory entries**,
  7, 8, 21, 38-9, 40, 41, 44-5, 47-9, 71, 73, 74

Fiscary (SUT 29), 7, 8, 17, *34*, 70, **105-7**
  cairn structure, 39-40, 105-7
  chamber, *32*, *33*, *34*, 39, 69, 70, 105-6
    contents, 55
  kerb, 106-7
  lintel, 105
  orientation of, 68
  orthostat, 106
  platform, 39, 105, 107
  passage, 105
  portal stones, 105, 106
fish bones, 50, 57, 138, 140
flint artefacts:
  arrowheads, 66
  blades/flakes, 57, 63, *64*, 65, 124, 157
  knife, 57, 65, 66, 138, 139
  mesolithic, 16
  scrapers, 57, 63, *64*, 65
  strike-a-light, 66
  unspecified, 10
flooring, of chambers, 55, 80
food vessels, 60, 66, 67, 124, 139
forecourts (*see also* individual sites and **Inventory entries**),
  8, 38, 41, 44-5, 46, 47-9, 58-9, *59*, 71, 74
  and heel-shaped cairns, 41, 49, 71
  and long cairns, 45, 46-7, 58-9, 71, 74
  and short horned cairns, 41, 58, 74

geology, topography and cairns, 13-15
Grumbeg (SUT 30), not now considered a chambered cairn, 7, **107**, 152

Hedges, J., work at Isbister, Orkney, 50, 56
heel-shaped cairns, *see* cairn types, heel-shaped cairns and possible heel-shaped cairns
Henshall, A. S.:
  1950's chambered cairn survey, 10-11
  & Davidson, J. L., work on Caithness cairns, 28, 40, 43, 52, 56, 58
  & Wallace, J. C., excavations at Embo, 10, 50, 135-9
horns, *see also* individual **Inventory entries**,
  9, 41, 43-6, 49, 79, 94, 99, 108, 126, 129, 131
Horsburgh, J., 7, 130, 132
Howell, J. M., work on Ledmore/Loubcroy, pre-afforestation survey, 12
human bones, *see under* skeletal material

INDEX

hut circles and cairns, 9

Inchnadamph cairns, 69, 71
   caves, 15–16
infant and child burials, *see also* skeletal material, 60, 67, 138, 139
Invershin (SUT 31), **107**
   cairn structure, 107
   chamber, *29*, 31, 34, 107
   orthostats, 107
   portal stones, 107
iron ore nodule, 66
Isbister, Orkney, 50, 65, 75

jet beads, 60, *66*, 67, 138, 139
Joass, Rev. J. M., work on Sutherland cairns, 6–7, 130
   Benbhraggie Wood, 89, 90
   Kinbrace Burn, 108
Johnson, A. H., work on soils from Embo, 39

Kenny's Cairn, Caithness, 69
kerbs and kerb-stones, 39, 97, 100, 106–7, 116, 124–5, 151
   possible, 81, 141
Kerr, C., work at Fiscary, 8, *34*, 81, 105–6
Kilcoy South, Ross and Cromarty, 66
Kilearnan, *see* Kilournan (SUT 32)
Kilournan (SUT 32), 8, **107–8**
   cairn structure, 41, *42*, 43, 46, 61, 72–3, 107–8
   lack of chamber, 20, 73, 108
Kilphedir (SUT 64) not now considered a chambered cairn, **140**, 153
Kinbrace Burn (SUT 33), 6, 7, 9, 20, **108–9**
   'amulet', 109
   cairn structure, 41, 49, 74, 108
   chamber, 24, 28, 32, *32*, *33*, 35, 49, 69, 108–9
   corbel stones, 108
   forecourt, 49, 59
   horns, 41, 108
   lintels, 108
   passage and portal stones, 20, 21, 22, 108–9
   roofing of, 20–1, 24
Kinbrace Farm (SUT 65), **140–1**
   cairn structure and condition, 61, 140
   chamber, *25*, 28, 69, 140–1
   intervisibility with Kinbrace Burn (SUT 33), 140
   passage, 21, 140
   portal stones, 140
Kinbrace Hill Long (SUT 34), 6, 9, 18, 20, **109–10**

cairn structure, 41, *42*, *45*, 46, 47, 49, 61, 71, 72–3, 109–10
chamber, lack of, 20
forecourt, 49
horn, 110
Kinbrace Hill Round (SUT 35), 6, 9, 20, **110**
   cairn structure, 38, 61, 110
   chamber, presumed, 20
   orthostats, 110
Kinloch (SUT 36), **110–11**
   cairn structure, 110, 111
   chamber, 31, *32*, 111
   orthostats, 111
   portal stones, 24, 111
   passage entrance, 21, 110–11
Kinnes, I., work on long barrows, 73
Knap of Howar, Orkney, 17, 63
Knockan East (SUT 79), **149–50**
   cairn structure, 149
   orthostats, 149–50
Knockan West (SUT 80), **150**
   chamber, 150
   orthostats, 150
Kyle of Durness, sites not now considered as chambered cairns, 153–4
Kyleoag (SUT 37), **111–12**
   cairn structure, *40*, 40–1, 49, 61, 71, 112
   chamber, *25*, 27, 33, 49, 61–2, 69, 111–12
   corbels, 112
   entrance, 21, 111
   entry height, 24
   lintels, 112
   orthostats, 112
   passage, 111
   portal stones, 24, 111
   roof slab, 112

Lairg Moor North (SUT 38), not now considered a chambered cairn, **112**, 152
Lairg Moor South (SUT 39), not now considered a chambered cairn, **112**, 152
Lairg Muir, not now considered a chambered cairn, 154
lamp, stone, iron age, 134
Langwell, Caithness, 71
Learable, Strath of Kildonan, razor from, 67
Ledbeg (SUT 66), **141**
   cairn structure, 141
   chamber, *29*, 30, 141
   orthostats, 141
   passage, 21, 141
Ledmore (SUT 40), **112–13**
   cairn structure, 112–13
   chamber, 113

corbel stones, 113
orthostats, 113
Ledmore Wood (SUT 41), **113–14**
   orthostats, 113, 114
Ledmore/Loubcroy, pre-afforestation survey, 12
lintels, 21, 22, 24–5, 35–6, 79, 84, 102–3, 105, 108, 112, 114, 115, 118, 119–20, 121, 129, 133, 143, 146, 150, 151
   and chamber and passage construction, 21, 24–5, 35
Little Ferry, 63
Loch Ailsh (SUT 71) (ROS 28), **144**
   cairn, condition of and structure, 61, 144
   chamber, 144
Loch Awe (SUT 42), *18*, 18, **114–15**
   cairn structure, 24, 37, 38, 61
   chamber, 24, 30, 114
   corbel stones, 24, 114–15
   lintels, 24–5, 114
   orthostats, 114, 115
   roof, 115
Loch Borralan East (SUT 43), **115–16**
   cairn structure, 115
   chamber, 24, *25*, 27–8, 34, 49, 69, 115–16
   lintels, 115
   passage, 21, 115–16
   orthostats, 115
   portal stones, 115
   pottery from, 57, 63, 116
   roof, 24
Loch Borralan South (SUT 81), **150–1**
   cairn structure, 150, 151
   chamber, 24, 35, 150–1
   corbel stones, 150–1
   lintels, 150
Loch Borralan West (SUT 44), **116–17**
   cairn structure, 61, 116–17
   chamber, *25*, 28, 69
   corbel stones, 117
   entry height, 24
   kerb, 116–17
   orthostats, 117
   passage, 117
   platform, 39, 116–17
   portal stones, 24, 117
Loch Calder, Caithness, cairns, 10
Loch Hope, not now considered a chambered cairn, 153
long cairns, *see* cairn types, long cairns and composite long cairns
Lothbeg (SUT 45), 6, 18, **117–18**
   axehead, 57, 118
   cairn structure, 40, 41, 61, 117–18
   chamber, 24, 32, 118
   lintels, 24–5, 118
   passage, 21, 117–18

portal stone, 118
roof, 24
Loubcroy, sites not now considered
    to be chambered cairns, 154
Lower Dounreay, Caithness, 66
Lyne (SUT 46), *34*, **118–19**
    chamber, *34, 35*, 119
    orthostats, *34*, 119

Maes Howe, Orkney, 10, 68
Maes Howe-type cairns, 10
Masters, L. J., excavation of Camster
    Long, Caithness, 11
McKay, W., work at Coille na Borgie,
    7–8, 35, *48*, 99
Melvich (SUT 47) not now considered
    a chambered cairn, **119**, 152
Mercer, R. J., work in Sutherland, 4,
    11–12
mesolithic activity in Sutherland, 16
    Rhum, 16
Midhowe, Orkney, 56
Millnafua Bridge (SUT 84), **151**
    cairn structure, 151
    chamber, 151
    kerb-stones, 151
    portal stones, 151
molluscan remains, 57, 138, 140
Munro, Rev. R., and Coille na Borgie
    cairns, 8, 35, 48, 101

National Monuments Record of
    Scotland, 4, 5

The Ord North (SUT 48), 4, 10–11,
    18, 76, **119–24**
    beaker, 59–60, *64*, 65, 123–4, 157
    bench, possible, 52, *53*, 56
    blocking, 58, *59*, 63, 123, 158
    bone mount, 60, *64*, 67, 122, 124,
        157
    burial deposits, 50, 52–5, 57, 58
    cairn structure, 37, 38–9, *39*, 40,
        40, 119–21
    chamber, 22, *23*, 24, *29*, 29–30, *30*,
        35, 52, *53*–4, 55, 58, *61*, 69, 71,
        121–3
    charcoal, 122
    corbel stones, 22, 24, 121, 122
    cremations, 122–3, 124, 158
    eke-stones, 24
    entry height, 24
    finds from, 53, 55, 57, *64*, 123–4,
        157–8
    flint blades/flakes, 57, *64*, 65, 124,
        157
    forecourt, 71, 120
    kerb, *39*, 121
    lintels, 121
    orthostats, 35, 121
    passage, 21–2, 58–9, *59*, 119, 121

platform, *39*, 120–1
pitchstone, blade/flake, 65, 124, 128
portal stones, 21, 121
pottery, 55, 57, 63, *64*, 64–5, 67,
    123–4, 157, 158
    beaker, 59–60, *64*, 65, 123–4,
        157
    food vessel, *64*, 67, 124, 157
    Unstan Ware, 55, *64*, 64–5, 123
pumice, 57, 63, 124, 158
quartz artefacts, 57, 58, *64*, 65,
    122, 124, 157, 158
radiocarbon dates, 11, 74–6
skeletal material, 122, 123, 124
wall-face, 37, *39*, 120
The Ord South (SUT 49), 18, 21,
    124–5
    cairn structure, 124, 125
    chamber, *25*, 28–9, *61*, 69, 124–5
    corbel stones, 125
    entry height, 24
    kerb-stones, 124
    orthostats, 124–5
    passage, 21, 38, 124–5
    portal stones, 24, 124–5
Ordnance Survey, work in
    Sutherland, 4, 8, 10, 132
orientation of cairns and passages, 68
Orkney, chambered cairns, see also
    site names, 6, 8, 12, 55–6, 69, 76
    beakers from cairns, 60
Orkney-Cromarty-type chambers, see
    also passage-graves, 4, 10, 20, 35,
    68–9
orthostats, see under site names
otters, 50, 57, 138, 140
    activity, 51, 57, 138

passages, see also site names and
    Inventory entries,
        20–2, 38
    and cairns, orientation of, 68
    sealing and blocking, 58–9
passage-graves, 55, 71, 73, 74
    Orkney-Cromarty group,
        distribution of, 4, 10, 55
Petrie, G., work on Sutherland
    cairns, 7
Piggott, S., work on British neolithic,
    10
pitchstone, blade/flakes, 65, 124
Pittentrail (SUT 50), 6, 8, **125**
    cairn structure, *61*, 125
    chamber, 35, 125
    condition of, 61
    misidentification as stone circle,
        125
platforms, 11, 39, 105, 107, 116–17,
    120–1
Pococke, Bishop R., 6
    on Lothbeg, 117, 118

Point of Cott, Orkney, 55, 74
portal stones, see individual site
    entries
pottery, 59–60, 65–6, *66*, 80, 116,
    123–4, 139, 157, 158
    and blocking, 58
    and burial ritual, 55, 57
    beakers, 57, 59–60, *64*, 65–6, *66*,
        123–4, 157
    deposition of, 55, 57, 63–5
    food vessels, 60, *64*, *66*, 67, 124,
        139
    medieval, 55, 80
    neolithic, 10–11, 55, 57, 63–5, *64*
    Unstan Ware, 55, 63, *64*, 64–5,
        124–5
pumice, 57, 63, 124, 139, 158

Quanterness, Orkney, 56, 75
quartz artefacts:
    blades/flakes/pebbles, 57, 58, *64*,
        65, 122, 124, 157, 158

radiocarbon dates, 74–6
    and chronology of chambered
        cairns, 4, 10
    Embo (SUT 63), 10, 75–6
    Inchnadamph caves, 15–16
    The Ord North (SUT 48), 11, 74–6
razors, bronze, 60, 66, 67, 139
Rhiconich (SUT 67), not now
    considered a chambered cairn,
    142, 153
Rhinavie, see Coille na Borgie South
    (SUT 23)
Rhind, A. H., bequest, 7–8
    work on Caithness cairns, 6
Rhind Lectures, Anderson 1882, 8
Rhives, see Benbhraggie Wood (SUT
    12)
Rhum, mesolithic settlement, 16
ritual deposits, made during building,
    50
roofing methods, 22–5, 27–9, 32–3,
    35, 69
round cairns, see cairn types, round
    cairns
Royal Commission on the Ancient
    and Historical Monuments and
    Constructions of Scotland,
    Curle's survey, 9
Royal Commission on the Ancient
    and Historical Monuments of
    Scotland, Afforestable Land
    Survey, 151

Salscraggie (SUT 51), 7, 8, 18, **125–7**
    cairn structure, 44, 49, 72–3,
        126–7
    chamber, 44, 126, 127
    façade, 44, 126

forecourt, 44, 49, 126
horns, 44, 126
secondary burials, *see also* cists, 60, 67
settlement, prehistoric and cairns, 16–19, 90, 101, 135
Sharples, N. M., publication of Corcoran's work at The Ord North, 11, 65, 75
Shearer, R. I., 6, 7
shellfish and molluscs, 138, 140
short horned cairns, *see* cairn types, short horned cairns
Simpson, W. D., work at Allt nam Ban, 9, 84
single-compartment chambers, 8, 9, 20, *25*, 25–8, 49, 69
Skail (SUT 52), 6, 7, 61, **127**
    cairn structure, 127
    chamber, *32*, 127
    orthostats, 127
    portal stones, 127
    steatite cup, 127
Skail, Strathnaver, cists, 66
skeletal material, *see also* site names and **Inventory entries**, 50–2, 56, 57, 80, 122–3, 124, 136, 137, 138, 139–40
    Achaidh, 80
    Ardvreck, 87
    age at death, 51–2, 56
    cremations, 27, 56, 60, 122–3, 124, 136, 138–9, 140, 155–6, 158
    deposition of, 50, 55, 56–8
    disposition of, 51–2, *55*, 56–8
    Embo, 50–2, 56, 57, 136, 137, 138, 139–40, 155–6
    excarnation, 56
    infant and child burials, 60, 67, 138, 139
    interpretation of deposits, 55–8
    The Ord North, 122, 123, 124
    pathology, 51
    preservation, 51–2
    skulls, 51, 56
Skelpick, cairn, not now considered a chambered cairn, 154
Skelpick Long (SUT 53), 6, 7, 7, 8, 18, **128–30**
    blocking, 58–9, 128, 129
    cairn structure, *42*, *44*, 45, 46, 49, 73, 128–9
    chamber, 24, 28, 29, *29*, 32, 49, 69, 129–30
    corbel stones, 129, 130
    entries, height, 24

forecourt, 45, 49, 128–9
horns, 45, 129
lintels, 24, 129
orientation of, 68
orthostats, 129–30
passage, 20–1, 22, 58–9, 129
portal stones, 20–1, 22, 24, 129
roofing, 20–1
Skelpick Round (SUT 54), 6, 7, 8, **130–1**
    cairn structure, 38, 61, 130
    chamber, 30, 69, 130–1
    orthostats, 131
    passage, 21, 131
    portal stones, 131
Skelpick South (SUT 55), 7, 8, 9, 18, **131–2**
    blocking of forecourt, 59
    cairn structure, 37, *40*, 41, 49, 61, 74, 131–2
    chamber, 24, 35, 131–2
    corbel stones, 24, 131–2
    forecourt, 49, 59
    horns, 41, 131
    roof, 24
Skelpick-type chambers, 25, *29*, 29–30, *31*, 38, 49, 69, 131–2
Society of Antiquaries of Scotland, investigations in Sutherland, 6–8
soils, buried beneath cairns, 4
and neolithic settlement, 16–17
South Yarrows, Caithness, *46*, 47, 49
spindle whorl, 139
steatite cup, 127
stone artefacts, *see also* flint, quartz, pitchstone
    'amulet', 109
    axehead, Lothbeg, 57
    beads, cannel coal, 66, 67
    jet 60, *66*, 67, 138, 139
    bracer, 66
    cup, 127
    discs, 66
    lamp, iron age, 134
    pumice, 63, 124, 139, 158
    sandstone whorl, 139
Strath of Kildonan, *see also* individual site names, 7, 9, 14, 17, 18, 49, 70–3
Strathnaver, *see also* individual site names, 6, 7, 9, 19, 72–3
Strathseagaich (SUT 73) (ROS 50), **145–6**
    cairn structure, 38, 145–6
    chamber, *29*, 30, 34, 146
    lintels, 146

orthostats, 146
passage, 21, 146
portal stones, 24
Stronechrubie (SUT 56) not now considered a chambered cairn, **132**, 152
Stuart, J., work on Sutherland cairns, 7, 8, 126, 130, 132
Sutherland Estates records, 6, 7

Tait, G. L., work on Sutherland cairns, 8
Taversoe Tuick, Orkney, 65
Tongue House (SUT 57), 7, 20, **132**
    cairn structure, 132
    chamber, 132
Torboll (SUT 58), 8, 9, **132–4**, 149
    cairn structure, 38, 132–3
    chamber, *25*, 28, 33, 69, 133
    damage to, 62
    eke-stones, 24
    entry height, 24
    lamp, iron age, 134
    lintels, 24, 133
    orthostats, 133–4
    passage, 21, 133
    portal stones, 24, 133
Traligill (SUT 82), *frontispiece*, **151**
    cairn structure, 151
    chamber, 24, 35, 151
    condition of, 61
    corbel stones, 151
    lintels, 25, 151
    passage, 151
    portal stones, 151
tripartite chambers, 8, 9, 20, *32*, *33*, 32–5, 49, 69–71
Tulach an t-Sionnaich, Caithness, 10, 11, 40, 43, 44, 56, 66
Tulloch of Assery A, Caithness, 41, 52, 56, 59, 74
Tulloch of Assery B, Caithness, 50, 56, 75

Unival, North Uist, 65
Unstan Ware, 55, 63, *64*, 64–5, 123
Upper Muirhall, Perthshire, cist, 66

wall-faces, *see also* individual site and **Inventory entries**, 37, 38, 44–5
Wallace, J. C. & Henshall, A. S., excavations at Embo, 10, 135–9
Wilson, D., 6
wood and charcoal, 53, 74–5, 101, 106, 122, 137